SERBO-CROATIAN
IN
TWO VOLUMES

A1-C1

BOOK
1

JACOB ELI GOODSON

INTRODUCTION

The present volume has been four years in the making. During this time it has been tested and revised. In the meantime theories of language learning have been proliferated. Were this course to be re-written, it would undoubtedly look quite different. Nevertheless, the basic outlook would of necessity remain - familiarization with the structure of the language by constant use. It is felt that sufficient material has been given in the course that it may be used effectively either as it is or more imaginatively.

The drills are extensive and are intended for use in full. If there is not class time to do this, the student is to perform all drills outside of class which are not taken up in class. At the same time it is not felt that they exhaust either the possibilities for drill or the student's need for it. They stress the type of exercise in which the response is completely predictable. The less predictable - 'free' conversation type of drill - is to be encouraged at later stages of the course. The conversations given at the end of each unit may be used as a bridge to free, or at least freer, conversation. The question and answer drills also serve as models of what may be used in less formal give and take conversation.

The Question and Answer Drill with Prompt is a type which may be used to drill Basic Sentences and which may lead to freer discussion. In this exercise the first sentence is the data sentence, which gives the information on which the student is to base his answer. While the early examples are very simple, it is clear that once the student has gone through a number of units, the data sentence - and the answer - may be quite complex. It is not felt necessary to spell out drills of this sort but the relative complexity of the answer expected should be controlled. The question may imply 1) a yes or no answer, 2) information based on the data sentence, 3) a conclusion drawn on the basis of the data given, 4) an opinion expressed on the basis of the data given.

Recently an approach to language learning has been suggested which would encourage the introduction of new vocabulary as the need arose for the latter in the student's efforts to express himself. The present course has very deliberately controlled the vocabulary, restricting new words to the Basic Sentences until the later lessons. There is no question but what the introduction of words relevant to the student makes drill and freer conversation much more interesting. However, no matter what supplementary vocabulary lists might be given, they would never satisfy all students. The person primarily concerned with mastering the structure may proceed through the course just as it is. Where much greater involvement of the student would result, new vocabulary may be introduced. The goal of the course remains mastery of the structure, with a limited but active vocabulary. Audio for the text can be obtained for free from WWW.A1-C1.com.

SERBO-CROATIAN

TABLE OF CONTENTS

Classroom Expressions

Serbo-Croatian	English
Ponóvite zà mnõm.	Repeat after me.
Svȉ zàjedno.	All together.
Pojedínačno.	Individually.
Jòš jȅdanput.	Once again.
Prodúžite.	Continue.
/ Nástavite.	
/ Dàlje.	/ Next. Go on.
Pòčnite.	Begin.
Vàš je rȅd, gospódine N.	It's your turn, Mr. N.
Dòvõljno, hvála.	That's enough, thanks.
/ Dòsta, hvála.	
Čekājte màlo.	Wait a minute.
Gdè smo stȁli?	Where did we stop?
Ódmor. / Prékid.	Break
Strána dvȁdeset pȑva, drùgã, òsmã ...	Page twenty one, two, eight ...
Okrénite stránu dvȁdeset òsmū.	Turn to page 28.
Da prȅđemo na stránu ...	Let's turn to page ...
Prevédite.	Translate.
Ȉmam jȅdno pȋtanje.	I have a question.
Stà znȁči rȅč 'đȁk'?	What does the word 'đak' mean?
Rȅč 'đȁk' znȁči 'stùdent'.	The word 'đak' means 'student'.
Kàko se kȁže 'màtch' na srpskohŕvātskõm?	How do you say 'match' in Serbo-Croatian?
Kȁže se 'šȉbica'.	(It is / you say) šibica.
/ Kȁže se 'žȉgica'.	

UNIT 1

Basic Sentences - Osnovne rečenice - Основе реченице

Greetings	Pózdravljānje	Поздрављање
	2ı 3ˎ1	2ı 3ˎ1
Good morning. (up to about 9:00)	Dobro jutro.	Добро јутро.
	2ı 3ˎ1	2ı 3ˉ
Hello. or Good afternoon. ('Good day', used from about 9 AM until dusk)	Dobar dan.	Добар дан.
	2ı 3ˎ1_	2ı 3ˎ1-
Good evening.	Dobra večer.	Добро вече.
	2ı 3ˎ 1	2ı 3ˉ 1
Good-bye. or I'll be seeing you. (to someone you expect to see again soon - 'to seeing')	Do viđenja.	До виђена.
	3 ˎ1	3 ˎ1
Good-bye. (a farewell, said on parting for a longer period of time)	Zbogom.	Збогом.
	2ı 3ˎ1	3ˎ2 ı2ˎ1
Good night ('light night').	Dobra noć.	Лаку ноћ.
	23ˎ 1	3 ˎ1
Hi!	Živjeli.	Здраво
how	3ˎ1 kako	3ˎ1 како
How are you?	3ˎ1 # Kako ste?	3ˎ1 # Како сте?
thanks	23ˎ1 hvala	23ˎ1 хвāла
I'm well	3ˎ 1 dobro sam	3ˎ 1 добро сам
you	3ˎ1 vi	3ˉ1 ви
I'm fine, thanks, how are you?	23ˎ ı 2ˎ 1 # Hvala, dobro sam, 3ˎ2 ı2ˎ1# kako ste ı vi?	23ˉ ı 2ˎ 1 # Хвала, добро сам, 3ˎ2 ı2ˉ1# како сте ı ви?
Please. or You're welcome.	3 ˎ1_ Prosim.	3ˎ1- Молим.
Excuse me.	2 3ˎ 1 Izvinite.	2 3ˉ 1 Извините.
Pardon me.	2 3ˎ 1 Oprostite.	2 3ˎ 1 Опростите.
Yes.	3ˎ1 Jest.	3ˎ1 Јесте.

or	3ˎ1 Da.	3ˎ1 Да.
No.	3ˎ1 Ne.	3ˎ1 Не.
Please, sit down.	2 3ˏ 2 | 2 ˎ1 Izvolite sjesti.	2 3ˏ 2 | 2ˎ1 Изволите сести.
or	2 3ˏ 2 # 2 ˎ1 Izvolite sjedite.	2 3ˎ1 #2ˎ1 Изволите седите.

How is Mr. Jović?	3ˎ2 |2 ˎ |
	Kako je gospodin
	  ˏ 1#
	Jović?
		3ˎ2 |2 ˎ
		Како је господин
		  ː 1#
		Јовић?

How is Mrs. Jović?	3ˎ2 |2ˎ
	Kako je gospođa
	  ˏ 1#
	Jović?
		3ˎ2 je |2ˎ
		Како је госпођа
		  ˏ 1#
		Јовић?

How is Miss Jović?	3ˎ2 |2ˎ
	Kako je gospođica
	  ˏ 1#
	Jović?
		3ˎ2 je |2ˎ
		Како је госпођица
		  ː 1#
		Јовић?

Fine, thanks.	3ˏ |2 ˏ 1 Dobro, hvala.	3ˏ |2 ː 1 Добро, хвала.

The Serbo-Croatian Language

Serbo-Croatian is a Slavic language and as such belongs to the Indo-European (or Indo-Hittite) family of languages. This family includes languages from East Pakistan to Great Britain and the New World. Slavic is one of the branches of this family and includes Russian, Ukrainian, Polish, Czech, Slovak, Slovenian, Serbo-Croatian, Macedonian and Bulgarian. Other branches are: Germanic (English, German, Dutch, Norwegian, Danish, Swedish, etc.), Italic (Latin, from which we get the Romance languages such as Rumanian, Italian, Spanish, French, and Portuguese), Celtic (Welsh, Irish, etc.), Hellenic (Greek), Armenian, Albanian, Baltic (Lithuanian, Latvian), Indic (Sanskrit, Hindi-Urdu, Bengali, Gujerati, etc.), Iranian (Persian, Pashto, Kurdish, etc.).

Serbo-Croatian is one of three official languages in Yugoslavia, the other two being Slovenian and Macedonian. Slovenia is one of six people's republics of Yugoslavia. It is situated in the extreme northwest, bordering on Italy, Austria and Trieste, as well as the people's republic of Croatia in Yugoslavia itself; the capital is Ljubljana. Macedonia is the most southern people's republic of Yugoslavia, being wedged between Albania and Bulgaria, with Greece on the south. On the north it is bounded by the people's republic of Serbia and by the autonomous region of Kosovo-Metohija (Kosmet). The capital of Macedonia is Skopje. In the rest of Yugoslavia (the republics of Serbia, Croatia, Bosnia-Hercegovina, Montenegro [Crna Gora], the autonomous province of Vojvodina and the autonomous region of Kosovo-Metohija) the official language is Serbo-Croatian. (One may, however, use standard Serbo-Croatian everywhere in the country.) These three languages are closely related and have a great deal in common both in vocabulary and construction. In all three of these official languages there is considerable dialect variation. The whole of Yugoslavia is part of the larger South Slavic speech area, which includes Bulgaria. Although official languages change at the frontier, the local dialects shade off into each other from the Adriatic to the Black Sea. This area is surrounded by peoples speaking non-Slavic languages (Italian, German, Hungarian, Rumanian, Turkish, Greek, Albanian).

As mentioned above, there are local variations throughout Yugoslavia. Even within the standard language there are accepted variations, which set off an eastern variety of dialect from a central one. Although they are the same language and mutually intelligible, there are enough differences between the two to make it more advisable for a beginner to learn one or the other, rather than mix the two. The eastern dialect is spoken in Serbia, the central in Croatia, Bosnia and Hercegovina, Montenegro and parts of western Serbia. The eastern type is standard for Belgrade and the central is the accepted standard in Zagreb, though the local dialect of the latter is somewhat different.

The eastern dialect is normally written in cyrillic letters and the central uses latin letters in Croatia, but cyrillic in Montenegro, and both cyrillic and latin in Bosnia and Hercegovina. In these units the Basic Sentences and Conversation drills are given in both latin and cyrillic, the version in latin letters being representative of central speech and that in cyrillic representing an eastern variety. Elsewhere latin letters are used but eastern speech.

A quite regular difference between standard eastern and central Serbo-Croatian may be mentioned. A very large number of words which have /e/ in eastern speech have /je/ (or a change in the preceding consonant called palatalization) in central Serbo-Croatian. Likewise many eastern words with long /e/ (written here /ē/) have /ije/ in central Serbo-Croatian. For example:

Eastern	Central	
gdè	gdjè	where
médved	médvjed	bear
razúmēm	razúmijem	I understand
lèvo	lìjevo	left

This difference is part of a wider pattern which has its reflexes all over the South Slavic speech area. Compare:

Slovenian	Coastal S-C	Central S-C	East. S-C	W. Bulg.	E. Bulg.	
mlẽko	mlīkò	mlijéko	mlẽko	mléku/mlīkó	mlyáku	milk

Besides these differences, there are also vocabulary variations and different sentence constructions. For example, the central form of /hlèb/ 'bread' is /hljèb/, but in Zagreb they use an entirely different word: /krùh/. In the Basic Sentences /pròsīm/ is given in latin letters, /mòlīm/ in cyrillic. Actually the distribution of these forms is not so simple. /mòlīm/ is the more widespread, being used, for example, in Serbia, Bosnia, Hercegovina and Dalmatia, while /pròsīm/ is more local to Zagreb and nearby. Central Serbo-Croatian often uses an impersonal /-ti/ form, where eastern Serbo-Croatian has a personal verb form. For example, an eastern speaker says /žèlīm da jèdēm/ 'I want that I eat'. The central expression would be /žèlīm jèsti/ 'I want to eat'. Both the eastern and central dialects have /da jèdēm/ and /jèsti/, but they use them in slightly different ways. The differences between eastern and central Serbo-Croatian are quite comparable to the differences between dialects of American English. Compare Bostonian, Middle Western and Southern pronunciations of such words as 'car, out, many' and vocabulary differences such as 'faucet' vs. 'spigot'. Variations in language are perfectly natural. They are to be expected. Any language which does not change or which has no variation is a dead language.

This Course

These lessons are intended to give the beginner a useful oral command of the language and a reading knowledge somewhat broader than his speaking ability. It is designed to be used with a native speaker of the language as instructor, the tapes being supplementary.

Given the dialect situation mentioned above, it is obvious that all speakers of Serbo-Croatian do not speak in exactly the same manner. The model for imitation should be one whose language is standard but not bookish. It is also important to note that the same speaker will not always say the same sentence in the same way. This is perfectly natural and the same situation exists in English. In both Serbo-Croatian and English (and all other languages as well) such variations are limited in scope and always follow the general pattern of the language. (For example, there may be variation as to which sound is used in a given word, but both sounds must be Serbo-Croatian sounds.) If one is listening to the recordings, he will find that they follow the printed material pretty closely. However, the speakers who made the recordings would not always say these things in exactly the same way. The differences might not be very great, but there would be frequent differences. Variations in intonation and in which word has the primary stress in a phrase or clause are to be expected. If one is working with a Serbo-Croatian speaker, he or she will undoubtedly say some things in a slightly different way than is found in these units. In every such case, his or her pronunciation is to be followed. One should, however, remember that there is no one single right way of speaking Serbo-Croatian or any other language. In this course an acceptable 'standard' form of spoken Serbo-Croatian is presented, but it is not the only such acceptable form.

Whether one is working with a native speaker or with recordings, each Serbo-Croatian word, phrase or sentence must be repeated in a loud, clear voice, the attempt being to imitate the pronunciation as closely as one can. While it is desirable to drill with books closed as much as possible, one may keep the book open and only use it when absolutely necessary. It is important to imitate the speaker and not read the Serbo-Croatian. The meaning of the Serbo-Croatian is to be kept constantly in mind, and it may be necessary to glance at the English equivalent occasionally. It is a waste of time to fumble for the meaning of a sentence and far preferable to look and see what it is.

In the first few units the student should not under any circumstances attempt to pronounce the Serbo-Croatian before he has heard it.

Students should also be reminded that language is arbitrary. Time should not be wasted in discussions of why Serbo-Croatian expresses something in the way it does. The student is to learn how something is said, not why. There is no answer to the question 'why' something is said the way it is.

Symbols used in the Basic Sentences

On the English side, parentheses and quotation marks are used together ('...') when a more literal translation is given in addition to the ordinary English equivalent. Brackets [ ] are used to indicate words in the English equivalent which do not have an equivalent in the Serbo-Croatian. Parentheses indicate words which translate something in the Serbo-Croatian but would not be used in a normal English equivalent. Note that on the English side we have what is ordinarily said in English in this situation, not necessarily a literal translation. The use of the parentheses and brackets as explained above should make the situation clear in each case.

Notes

Note 1.1   The Sounds of Serbo-Croatian

The following outline gives a survey of Serbo-Croatian sounds. Although long, it is not exhaustive, and technical details are left to technical books. In conjunction with this outline there is a set of pronunciation drills. Their purpose is to help the student hear and produce the Serbo-Croatian sounds, especially those sounds and combinations of sounds which are very different from those in English. These drills concentrate attention on particular pronunciation points and will, if properly drilled, aid one to say Basic Sentences naturally. The meanings of the words are given, but the student is not expected to learn these meanings or even pay any particular attention to them at this time.

Although most of the latin letters used in writing Serbo-Croatian are the same as those we use in English, they represent a very different set of speech habits. Even letters which seem to represent the same sound may actually be quite different. /t/ for example, represents an English sound made by touching the tongue to the ridge back of the upper teeth, but in Serbo-Croatian it represents a sound made by touching the tongue to the upper front teeth. It is important to know these differences and make a determined effort to form new speech habits.

Note 1.1.1   Survey of Symbols

Following is the latin alphabet as used for Serbo-Croatian, with the cyrillic equivalents. The description of the sounds is only approximate. For details see other notes.

Latin		Cyrillic		Hints on Pronunciation
A	a	А	а	a as in father
B	b	Б	б	b as in book but fully voiced
C	c	Ц	ц	ts as in cats
Č	č	Ч	ч	a ch sound made with tongue curled back. Compare ch of arch.
Ć	ć	Ћ	ћ	a ch sound made with the tip of the tongue against the upper teeth. Compare ch in cheap.
D	d	Д	д	like d of done but fully voiced and with tip of tongue against upper teeth
Đ	đ	Ђ	ђ	something like j of jeep (j with tongue forward); the voiced counterpart of /ć/. Also written /dj/.
DŽ	dž	Џ	џ	something like g of large (j with tongue back); the voiced counterpart of /č/
E	e	Е	е	e of bet, but higher when long
F	f	Ф	ф	f of foot
G	g	Г	г	g of gone but fully voiced
H	h	Х	х	not in English. A sound made in the same place as /k/ but letting the air slide through instead of stopping it
I	i	И	и	a high i sound something like ee of beet but without the y-glide of English ee
J	j	Ј	ј	like y of yet but higher than English y in combinations such as /aj/ (ah-ee)
K	k	К	к	like c of cat but without the strong puff of breath
L	l	Л	л	much like English l but not as deep. Compare l of million.

Lj	lj	Љ	љ	an l made with the tongue in position to say y. Not in English.
M	m	M	м	m as in man but fully voiced
N	n	H	н	n as in noon but fully voiced and with the tip of the tongue against the upper teeth
Nj	nj	Њ	њ	an n made with the tongue in position to say y. Not in English.
O	o	O	о	something like o of horse, ough of ought or of law
P	p	П	п	p of pat but without the strong puff of breath following it
R	r	P	p	a couple of flaps of the tip of the tongue against the ridge back of the upper teeth. Not in English. Before pause it is usually voiceless.
S	s	C	c	like s of sing
Š	š	Ш	ш	a sh sound made with the tongue back. Compare sh of harsh.
T	t	T	т	like t of top but made with the tip of the tongue against the upper teeth
U	u	У	у	a high u something like the oo of boot but without the w glide of English oo.
V	v	В	в	a light v sound, like v of veal. May be w in the combination /hv-/.
Z	z	З	з	like z of zeal but fully voiced
Ž	ž	Ж	ж	a zh sound (compare s of pleasure) made with the tongue back. Voiced counterpart of /š/.

    The ordinary spelling (both latin and cyrillic) does not indicate certain features, such as the stress, vowel length or pitch. Junctures (see below) are partly represented by word division and punctuation. To represent the language more accurately, additional symbols are therefore necessary. Following is a rearrangement of the latin letters listed above, followed by the other symbols used in this course:

Vowels: i   e   a   u   o   r

Voiceless Consonants: A.   p   t   k   s   š   c   ć   č   f   h

Voiced Consonants: B.   b   d   g   z   ž   dz   đ   dž   v

                         C.   r   l   lj   m   n   nj   j

Stress: Primary ´ or ` Secondary ˈ Weak (unmarked)

Vowel length: ¯

Pitch: Low   1   Mid   2   High   3   Extra high   4

Junctures: | ‖   #   (also, in part, space between words)

(See page 35 for the traditional symbols for primary stress.)

[G.D. 1.1.1] Pronunciation Drill

      The letters of the alphabet will serve as simple pronunciation drill.
Each letter is pronounced as a syllable. The vowel sound (as /a/) is the
name of the vowel. The name of a consonant is that sound plus /ə/ (a of sofa)
for cyrillic letters, or that sound plus /e/ for latin letters. /b/ therefore
has two names: /bə/ for б and /be/ for b. Repeat each alphabet after the
instructor or tape, being very careful to imitate exactly.

Cyrillic

а	б	в	г	д	ђ	е	ж	з	и	ј	к	л	љ	м	н
a	bə	və	gə	də	đe	e	žə	zə	i	jə	kə	lə	ljə	mə	nə

њ	о	п	р	с	т	ћ	у	ф	х	ц	ч	џ	ш
njə	o	pə	rə	sə	tə	će	u	fə	hə	cə	čə	džə	šə

Latin

a	b	c	č	ć	d	dž	đ	e	f	g	h	i	j	k	l	lj	m	n
a	be	ce	če	će	de	dže	đe	e	fe	ge	he	i	je	ke	le	lje	me	ne

nj	o	p	r	s	š	t	u	v	z	ž
nje	o	pe	re	se	še	te	u	ve	ze	že

      The above alphabets also illustrate the difference in the order of the
letters between cyrillic and latin. The latin order is that of English, with
added letters in appropriate places. The cyrillic order must be learned.

Note 1.2 Vowels

Examples of the six vowels found in Serbo-Croation are:

[G.D. 1.1.2]

Vowel	Short	Long	Short unstressed	Long unstressed
/i/	ìdite	mȉr	stànica	gòvorȉte
	go!	peace	station	you are speaking
/e/	žèlīm	mȅso	vòlīte	ìdēm
	I wish	meat	you like	I'm going
/u/	razúmēm	pȕt	nèkud	gòlūb
	I understand	road	somewhere	dove
/o/	dòbro	vȍz	kàko	pèrōn
	well	train	how	platform
/a/	nàprēd	dȁn	sȉla	ìmām
	forward	day	power	I have
/r/	vȑt	bȓz	prȅtrpān	nèkȓst
	garden	fast	crowded	unbeliever

Note that the quality of these vowels, while there is some variation, is quite clear whether they are short, long, stressed or unstressed. This is quite different from English where a clear _a_ (as in _father)_ does not usually occur unstressed. The _a_'s of _sofa, woman, seaman, alike, afloat_ are all _uh_'s. (phonetically [ə]). Most unstressed simple vowels in English are this [ə]. This means that one must be careful to pronounce unstressed vowels in Serbo-Croatian as clearly /i/, /e/, /u/, /o/ or /a/, not as English _uh_ [ə].

Another very important factor is vowel length. In English the length of vowels varies from dialect to dialect, but there is often a correlation of length and the nature of the following consonant. For example, the vowel in _had_ is longer than in _hat._ Compare _bad_ and _bat_, _sad_ and _sat_, _cad_ and _cat._ Before the voiced _d_ the vowel is longer. In Serbo-Croatian the vowels may be long or short regardless of what follows. In fact, differences of meaning may depend on vowel length. For example, /grȁd/ is 'city', but /grȁd/ 'hail', /sùpruga/ is 'of a husband' or 'wife' but /sùprūgā/ 'of husbands'.

In the last example, as well as in the above list, there are examples of unstressed long vowels. This occurrence of long vowels in unstressed syllables sometimes confuses the English learner, who either does not hear the length or thinks that the long vowel is stressed. The student should listen very carefully for the length of vowels in Serbo-Croatian, especially in unstressed syllables.

Speech sounds are most easily described in terms of how they are made. The lips, teeth, tongue, uvula, larynx, etc., all enter into the production of speech. For our purpose here (as speakers of English learning to speak Serbo-Croatian) the position of the tongue and the manner in which it is used are the most important factors.

If the vowels are plotted with regard to tongue height and relative position front to back, we have the following pattern:

	Front	Central	Back
High	i		u
Mid	e	r	o
Low		a	

There is some variation in vowel quality between short and long, and between those in closed vs. open syllables. This is particularly noticeable with /i/, /e/ and /u/. /dȉm/ 'smoke' has a vowel higher than English dim but not as high as /dívan/ 'wonderful'. /mèk/ 'soft' has a vowel close to the e of bet but /némati/ 'not to have' has a higher e sound quite unlike any English sound. /r/ is listed here as a vowel. This is the symbol for a kind of uh [ə] vowel, interrupted by a few taps of the tip of the tongue. It is, then, a combination of a vowel sound, [ə], and a consonant (the taps or flaps). /r/ also occurs as a plain consonant, before and after the other vowels.

We may make a similar pattern of English vowels:

	Front	Central	Back	Examples		
High	i	ɨ	u	bit	'jist'	put
Mid	e	ə	o	bet	but	horse
Low	æ	a	ɔ	bat	hot	ought

11

English has nine vowels (fewer in some dialects), so has more than Serbo-Croatian. The student should not be misled by the use of the same symbols for English 'i, e, a, u, o' and for Serbo-Croatian sounds. Serbo-Croatian /i/, /e/ and /u/ are higher in tongue position. /o/ and /a/ are about the same, but a plain 'o' is rather rare in English. The diphthong 'ow' (as in low) occurs so much more frequently that we always think of 'ow' when we think of the English sound 'o'. The confusion between English diphthongs and Serbo-Croatian vowel quality and length presents the greatest difficulty to the learner. A Serbo-Croatian /i/ sounds like the English ee of beet to an untrained ear. This is due to the nature of the English diphthongs. Frequent English diphthongs are:

iy	beet		uw	boot
ey	bait		ow	boat
			ɔy	boy

		ay	bite
		aw	bout

Each of these diphthongs starts with a lower position and glides to a higher one. 'iy' begins like i of bit and ends like the y of yet. The y of yet is about the tongue position of Serbo-Croatian /i/ so this /i/ and English 'iy' are confused. The glides of the above English diphthongs are:

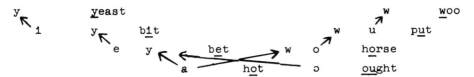

'iy' (beet) begins with the i of bit and ends with the y of yeast. 'ey' (bait) begins with the e of bet and ends with a y the height of i in bit, etc. What we have in English been taught to consider vowels are really diphthongs (the names of the letters a [ey], e [iy], i [ay], o [ow], u [yuw]). Serbo-Croatian also has diphthongs, which are written as such: /ij/, /aj/, /ej/, etc. The Serbo-Croatian simple vowels must not be confused with these or with the English diphthongs. The simple vowels may be long or short and may have different kinds and degrees of stress (accent), but they remain more constant in quality than the English sounds most like them.

Note 1.3 Serbo-Croatian Stress and Intonation

In both Serbo-Croatian and English there are regular differences made in
the degrees of stress of given sounds. For example, we distinguish the nouns
'ímpact, íncrease, ínsult' from the verbs 'impáct, incréase, insúlt' only by
the different position of the stress. In the nouns the first syllable is
stressed; in the verbs the second syllable is stressed.

There are also regular differences in the relative height of tone or
pitch. For example, the sentence 'John! come home!' is composed of two phrases
with two high pitches. 'John came home.' is only one phrase and has only one
high pitch (usually on 'home'). Note that the high pitches in these sentences
are on the vowels which have the strongest stress.

Any given syllable in English has both stress and pitch. The vowels are
the centers of stress and pitch. As noted at the end of the last paragraph,
there is often close correlation between high pitch and strong stress. This is
not always the case, though. Compare 'John!' (calling him) and 'Oh, John!'
(said to the naughty boy who has drawn pictures all over the bedroom wall). The
second is on low pitch, the first starts high and goes low. You cannot predict
what stress a word will have from its pitch or vice versa. It is therefore
necessary to have separate symbols for both.

There are four distinctive stresses and four pitches in English. The
stresses are all seen in a sentence like:

Lòng Íslănd Ĭs ă lône Íslănd.

Here the primary (strongest) stress is shown by ´, secondary by ˇ, tertiary
by ` , and the weak syllables are marked ˘.

We may show pitch with a curve as:

John came home.

Where did he go?

13

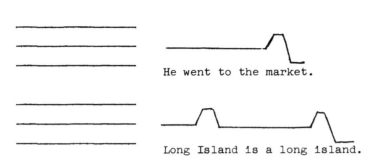

He went to the market.

Long Island is a long island.

The three lines on the left show the levels of pitch. You may have a
fourth, when you hit something extra high. Since there are only four basic
pitch levels, they may be indicated very conveniently by numbers (1 for low,
2 mid, 3 high, 4 extra high). An example of 4 is:

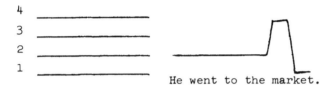

He went to the market.

Here 'market' is stronger (louder and going higher on mar-). The pitches
and stresses of these sentences may be shown thus:

```
2∧        ∧     3ʌ1
John     came   home.

2 ∧       `     `     3ʌ1
'Where   did   he    go?

2`       ∧      ˘     ˘   3ʌ  1˘
He       went   to   the  market.

2`       ∧      ˘     ˘   4`  1˘
He       went   to   the  market.

2`  3ʌ 2˘  |2`   ˘    ∧   3ʌ 1˘
Long Island  is  a   long  island.
```

Note that the 'question' (Where did he go?) has the same pitch pattern
as the statements. A question may have a different pitch pattern but frequently
there is no difference. The word 'question' does not mean either in English or
in Serbo-Croatian that the voice always rises at the end. It refers merely to
the situation of asking for information.

Note also that the sentence with two phrases has the boundary between the
two marked with a single line | . This is one type of phrase (or clause)

14

boundary. Each phrase has only one loud stress /´/. We find this kind of
pattern in Serbo-Croatian, too, and use the same symbol /|/. We could also
add the symbol /#/ at the end of each of the above sentences, showing that they
all end in the fading out type of sentence final.

Coming now to Serbo-Croatian we find that we have a situation which is
similar to English in many ways but with some striking differences:

[G.D. 1.1.3] Some examples are:

```
       3      ` 1   #
1.   Z  d  r  a  v  o.                        Hello.

       3    `1#
2.   D  v  a.                                 Two.

       2           3  `      1   #
3.   R  a  z  u  m  e  t  e  1  i?            Do you understand?

      23`  |  2`     1   #  2`        3`1#
4.   Hvala,  dobro  sam,  kako  ste  vi?      Thank you, I'm fine.  How are you?

      2`     3 `2  | 3`2 ‖ 2    `  1_ #
5.   Želim  hleb,   meso  i  krompir.         I want bread, meat and potatoes.

      2 3`   2 | 2 `      `  1 #
6.   Koliko  su   tri  i  četiri?             How much are three and four?
```

Here are three pitch symbols (/1/, /2/, /3/ - with the possibility of /4/
also, as in English). There are several important differences. One is in the
pattern with several phrases. English goes up to /3/ in each phrase of most
sentences (pattern /231/ or /31/). This is not a 'rule'; it is just an obser-
vation of the most frequent pattern. In Serbo-Croatian a sentence which consists
of only one phrase usually has pitch pattern /231#/, the /3/ occuring together
with the primary stress of the phrase (for example, sentence 3 and the second
part, after #, of 4). If the primary stress begins the phrase, there is no
/2/ (sentences 1, 2). There is a very frequent sequence of the phrases, the
first /232|/, the second /21#/ (sentences 4 and 6). Or you may have a series
of phrases, the earlier ones /232|/, the last /21#/ (compare 5). Listen
carefully for the difference between Serbo-Croatian final phrase /21/ and the
English /231/.

The symbol /|/ indicates a phrase which ends continuing the last pitch
given. The symbol /‖/ indicates a rising intonation - not to the next pitch
but very noticeable. At the end of a sentence (where there is ? or .) the

voice usually dies out as in English, though a sentence may end in /‖/ or, more rarely, /|/. The final sounds of a sentence are often whispered in Serbo-Croatian.

The symbol /#/ is used to indicate the dying out of the voice, as opposed to the sustaining phrase final /|/ or the rising /‖/. Since a period normally shows this, /#/ is only used where the punctuation is not helpful. For example, it is used over a comma (,), where the pronunciation is really like that of the end of a sentence or over a question mark (?), where there is no rise in pitch. (Both of these are illustrated in sentence 4 above.)

The stress system is more complex and is closely related to pitch. There are three degrees of stress - primary (/ ´ or `/), secondary (/'/) and weak (unmarked). Vowels with stresses /ˆ`'/ may be short (unmarked) or long (with /¯/), and unstressed vowels in words with primary stress may be short or long. In a word with secondary stress /'/, only the stressed syllable may be long (indicated by /¹/). As in English, each phrase has one primary stress (/´/ or /`/) and an undetermined number of secondary and weak stresses. Use the Basic Sentences for examples of primary and secondary stresses. The two symbols for primary stress basically indicate either a carryover of the stress into the following syllable, indicated by /´/, or a non-carryover of the stress, indicated by /`/. This has no parallel in English. For convenience we will use an 'explanatory spelling' here alongside the one used in the course. This spelling uses /°/ for the primary stress, doubles the vowels to show length, and shows the pitch contour with a line, as we did above for English.

	Unit Spelling	Explanatory Spelling

Pitch   3   1

Stress   `

      z   d   r   a   v   o   z   d   r   a   v   o   'hi!'

Pitch   3   1

Stress   ˎ

      d   v   a   d   v   a   a   'two'

The two words illustrate what is traditionally known as 'falling accent', short and long. The pitch falls immediately after the stress. When the vowel is long the pitch falls during the vowel as only the first part of the vowel (the first of the double vowels in the explanatory spelling) has primary stress. The accents /ˋ/ and /ˊ/ both correspond to only one / ° / of the explanatory spelling.

[G.D. 1.1.4]

```
Pitch     2   3       1           ─────
Stress            ′                ─────                                    'How much are
                                   ─────                                       they?'
          k o l i k o   s u        ─────    k o l i k o s u
      ʃ
```

```
Pitch     2   3     1             ─────
Stress          ′   -              ─────                                    'I understand.'
                                   ─────
          r a z u m e m            r a z u m e e m
```

```
Pitch     2         3   1         ─────
Stress            ⌐                ─────                                    'do you under-
                                   ─────                                       stand?'
          r a z u m e t e   l i    ─────   r a z u m e e t e   l i
```

```
Pitch     2   3   1   2   3 1      ─────
Stress      ⌐          ⌐           ─────              or                    'thanks'
                or                 ─────
          h v a l a   h v a l a    ─────   h v a a l a   h v a a l a
```

/ˊ/ and /ˊ/ are traditionally known as 'rising accents' (note pitch patterns). The stress continues from one syllable into the next and the pitch (if /3/ or /4/) rises slightly in the second syllable (if this is not the last syllable). This type of stress is quite distinctive. We have nothing like it in English. While the /ˊ/ of /dȁn/ sounds very much to us like a slightly drawn out 'Don', the /ˊ/ or /ˊ/ is quite a different matter. It must be listened to very carefully. Note that in /razúmēm/, the carryover is only on the first part of the long vowel. /ˊ/ and /ˊ/ correspond to two stresses / ° ° / of the explanatory spelling, except in the second pronunciation of /hvála/.

17

The last example, /hvála/, shows the possibility of /ᷓ/ representing either the double stress or only the stress on the second part of a long vowel. The first version shows the double stress /••/ in the explanatory spelling. The second shows only the one. When, as here, the syllable on which the stress begins is followed by only one other syllable, and the word ends in a period juncture /#/, the final syllable may lose its stress. Before the juncture /|/ or /‖/ the stress is not lost. In the Basic Sentences the /1/ of a final pitch will be placed on or after the last vowel to indicate the possibility of stress carryover even in this position (see the first spelling of /hvála/ above). Examples showing carryover and non-carryover, according to whether the syllable is final, are:

<u>Explanatory Spelling</u>

```
        2   3 ´     1 #          2  3 •   o  1  #
        k o l i k o  s u .        k o l i k o   s u .
                                                        'how much are
but     2   3 ` 1 #                2   3 • 1  #              they?'
        k o l i k o .               k o l i k o .


        23  ᷓ     | 2 ´      1    # 2  3 o   • | 2 •    o   1    #
        h v a l a  d o b r o  s a m . h v a a l a  d o b r o  s a m .

        23 ᷓ 1 #                    2   3 o 1 #
but     h v a l a .                 h v a a l a .        'thanks, I'm
                                                             fine.'
        3 ` 1    #                   3 o 1   #
        d o b r o .                  d o b r o .
```

Note that when a short rising primary stress /´/ (as in /kolíko/) loses the stress on the syllable following, it is replaces by /`/ (/kolìko/). The explanatory spelling shows how two stresses /oo/ are replaced by one /o/ for both /kolíko/ and /hvála/ in this situation. This is not true of all speakers. Some do not drop the second of the two accents /oo/ before a period juncture /#/. They would say /kolíko/, /dóbro/, as well as /hvála/ (h v a a l a). The units mark the words in their most distinctive form (only /kolíko/) when under primary stress, as the difference is automatic.

A word given in isolation, as in the build-ups to the sentences, will naturally have primary stress. This is because a single word said by itself is given the intonation of a whole phrase and must have, as a phrase, a primary stress. This means that the word is very likely to change in the sentence to secondary stress where it is part of a longer phrase.

Secondary stress is less loud than primary and does not carry over into the following syllable. A short secondary stress (/'/) will correspond to both /´/ and /ˆ/, a long secondary stress (/ᴸ/) is a long stressed vowel corresponding to both /⁴/ and /ˣ/. Long unstressed vowels, as /ā/, occur only in words with primary stress (/´/ or /ˆ/).

[G.D. 1.1.5]

3ˎ 1# ja.		but	2ᴸ ja	3ˏ _1# vas razumem.		'I understand you'
3ˏ _1# želim.		but	2ˋ želim	3ˏ1_ # da jedem.		'I want to eat'
3ˎ1 # kako.	3ˎ1# to.	3ˏ _1# zove.	but	2ˏ kako se to zove	ᴸ ˏ na	3ˏ 1 # srpskom.	'how is that said in Serbian?'

Both /´/ and /ˆ/ change to /'/, /⁴/ and /ˣ/ to /'/. Unstressed length /¯/ is lost if not in a word with / ˆˋ/, as in /želīm/ but /želim/.

As mentioned above, /ˆ/ and /ˣ/ have been known as 'falling accents' and /´/ and /⁴/ as 'rising accents'. This is phonetically true when they occur with pitch /3/ and carry over into the following syllable (see line drawings of the pitch above.) When they are on pitch, they indicate a carryover of stress into the following syllable but not necessarily a rise in pitch:

[G.D. 1.1.6]

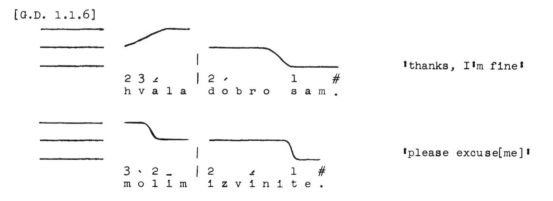

2 3 ᴢ | 2 ˏ   1   #   'thanks, I'm fine'
h v a l a   d o b r o   s a m .

3 ˎ 2 _ | 2   ᴢ   1   #   'please excuse[me]'
m o l i m   i z v i n i t e .

The terms 'rising' and 'falling' are used for convenience, but they are not quite accurate.

Grammatical Drill

GD 1.2 Vowels

These drills are practices on the vowels, arranged according to stress. Particular attention is to be paid to both pitch and stress in imitating. Care should also be taken not to add an English y off-glide to Serbo-Croatian /ē/, /i/, /ĭ/ or to final short /e/. /o/, /u/, /ŏ/ and /ŭ/ should be rounded with no w glide.

GD 1.2.1 /a/

/à/ short 'falling' stress

bàš	kàd	àko	àli	pàs
just	when	if	but	dog

These are shorter than ordinary a in English. Keep them clear 'a' in quality and clip them short. Don't drawl.

/ā̀/ long 'falling' stress

pā̀d	bā̀nda	mrā̀k	prā̀vda	jā̀k
fall	band	darkness	justice	strong

These are very much like the a sound in English pond, pod, etc. We can also symbolize them by such a spelling as /pȧad/, /bȧanda/, where the stress is on the first part of the long vowel.

/á/ short 'rising' stress before a short vowel

botánika	kášika	dánas	sástanak	nápredak
botany	spoon	today	meeting	progress

/á/ short 'rising' stress before a long vowel

mládī́ć	kápūt	izlágāč	Slávēn	pásūlj
young man	coat	exhibitor	Slav	beans

/a/ after /ˊ/

sázvati	sádašnjī	sáznati	mágla	
convoke	present	find out	fog	

krétati	snága	hrána	klíma	
be moving	strength	food	climate	

/ǎ/ long 'rising' stress

ambasáda	dátum	národnȋ	rázlog	náročito
embassy	date	national	reason	especially

/ā/ after /´/

óvāmo	óstālȋ	péšāk	séljāk	rezúltāt
hither	remaining	pedestrian	peasant	result

/a/ short unstressed

glédati	ȉznad	ȉzrada	sòbarica	sažaljénje
look	above	manufacture	chambermaid	compassion

/ā/ long unstressed

òblāk	ȉznenāda	ráspadānje	knjȉžār	ópadānje
cloud	suddenly	dissolution	bookseller	decreasing

GD 1.2.2 /e/

/è/ short 'falling' stress

mèk	vèza	bèz	èto	jèlo
soft	connection	without	there!	food

/ȇ/ long 'falling' stress (often - /ije/)

bȇlȋ	lȇp	lȇvo	mȇso	mȇtar
the white	beautiful	(on the) left	meat	'meat'

/é/ short 'rising' stress before a short vowel

sélo	péći	téle	péro	délimično
village	to roast	calf	pen	partly

/é/ short 'rising' stress before a long vowel

bénzȋn	bulévār	déčāk	jélōvnȋk	métōd
gasoline	boulevard	boy	menu	method

/e/ after /ˊ/

nédelja	préterati	kóverat	železnica	pónešto
Sunday	exaggerate	envelope	railroad	somewhat

/ế/ long 'rising' stress (often - /ijé/)

pḗtak	tḗško	šḗtnja	lḗđa	prḗpis
Friday	difficult	walk	back	copy
dḗte	mlḗko	vḗnac	blḗdo	
child	milk	wreath	pale	

/ḕ/ long after /ˊ/ (often - /ije/)

íznēti	pódēljen	péčēm	kvalítēt	névēram
to take out	divided	I'm roasting	quality	unfaithful

/e/ short unstressed

Beógrad	mešóvit	ràzmena	lepóta	meteorológija
Belgrade	mixed	exchange	beauty	meteorology

/ē/ long unstressed

slàbljēnje	rùšēnje	ùglēdan	jèdēm	pùšēnje
weakening	destruction	prominent	I'm eating	smoking

GD 1.2.3 /i/

/ì/ short 'falling' stress'

bìoskop	bìtan	bìti	dìm	ìme
movie theater	essential	to be	smoke	name

/ȋ/ long 'falling' stress

dȋvan	fȋnȋ	mȋ	vȋ	sȋn
wonderful	fine	we	you	son

/í/ short 'rising' stress before a short vowel

blizína	ímati	klízav	proízvod	žívot
nearness	to have	slippery	product	life

/í/ short 'rising' stress before a long vowel

bríjānje	ínače	príznāt	mínūt	ínvāzija
shaving	otherwise	recognized	minute	invasion

/i/ after /´/

gránica	iséliti	málina	stólica	óni
border	to move away	raspberry	chair	they

/í/ long 'rising' stress

blízu	prílike	gubítak	líce	víza
near	occasion	loss	face	visa

/ī/ after /´/

kóstīm	krómpīr	magázīn	bolésnīk	useljénīk
costume	potatoes	department store	sick man	immigrant

/i/ short unstressed

jèftin	stànica	gràđanin	divóta	sitnína
cheap	station	citizen	beauty	change

/ī/ long unstressed

vòlīm	màlī	sèdīšte	sáveznī	únutrašnjī
I like	small	seat	federal	internal

GD 1.2.4 /u/

/ù/ short 'falling' stress

drùgī	dùg	jùg	kùvati	mùka
second	long	south	cook	trouble

/ȕ/ long 'falling' stress

dȕž	glȕp	krȕg	mȕž	zȕb
along	stupid	circle	husband	tooth

kȕjna

  kitchen

/ú/   short 'rising' stress before a short vowel

gúbiti	kúpina	múzika	dúbok	pústiti
to lose	blackberry	music	deep	to let

/ú/   short 'rising' stress before a long vowel

gúbīm	múnīcija	izúzēv	júnāk	konzúlāt
I'm losing	ammunition	except	hero	consulate

/u/   after /´/

víljuška	sánduk	póstupak	póstupno	ústupak
fork	chest	procedure	gradually	concession

krénuti	uzálud			
move	in vain			

/ū̃/   long 'rising' stress

kúpiti	čúvati	dúvati	prúga	blúza
buy	to keep, guard	blow	track	blouse

/ū/   after /´/

sápūn	pródužīm	ráčūn	óružje	úgūšen
soap	I continue	bill	weapon	suffocated

/u/   short unstressed

jàbuka	urádíti	kukúruz	budúćnost	ustanóviti
apple	do	corn	future	establish

/ū/   long unstressed

mèhūr	vàzdūh	spòrazūm	lìmūn	ràzūm
bubble	air	agreement	lemon	reason

GD   1.2.5   /o/

/ò/   short 'falling' stress

kò	gòdina	bòca	dòk	jòš
who	year	bottle	while	still

/ȍ/   long 'falling' stress

sȍ	vȍ	gȍst	dȍba	mȍre
salt	ox	guest	period of time	sea

/ó/   short 'rising' stress before a short vowel

dóbiti	govóriti	góveda	bórba	biológija
receive	speak	cattle	struggle	biology

/ó/   short 'rising' stress before a long vowel

dónēti	kólāč	bólī	stómāk	pórtīr
bring	pastry	it hurts	stomach	desk clerk

/o/   after /´/

dómovina	pórodica	uópšte	pónosit	períod
homeland	family	in general	proud	period

/ő/   long 'rising' stress

dőći	gőrak	kőčnica	bőlnica	kőštati
come	bitter	brake	hospital	cost

/ȭ/   after /´/

dévȭjka	bálkȭn	vágȭn	ódbȭjka	kamíȭn
girl	balcony	railroad car	volleyball	truck

/o/   short unstressed

dolína	jàgoda	màlo	domáćica	nàpolje
valley	strawberry	a little	hostess	outside

/ȭ/   long unstressed

mìlȭst	sìnȭć	pòmȭć	svètlȭst
mercy	last night	help	light

GD 1.2.6 /r/

/r̀/ short 'falling' stress

pr̀st	sr̀ce	dr̀vo	gr̀lo	pr̀ljav
finger	heart	wood	throat	dirty

/r̂/   long 'falling' stress

tr̂g	tr̂k	pr̂vo	cr̂n	cr̂kva
square	gallop	first	black	church

/ŕ/   short 'rising' stress before a short vowel

tŕčati	ubŕzati	izdŕžati	ŕđav	dŕžava
run	speed up	endure	bad	state

/ŕ/   short 'rising' stress before a long vowel

pŕvāk	cŕtāč	hŕvānje
champion	draftsman	wrestling

/r/   after /´/

pódrška	póvrće	Úskrs	zágrliti	prévrtati
support	vegetable	Easter	embrace	turn over

/r̃/   long 'rising' stress

svr̃šiti	pr̃ljati	tr̃peti	sr̃dnja	sr̃na
finish	soil	suffer	anger	deer

/r̃/   after /´/

ízvr̃šen	zágr̃ljen	íspr̃ljan	ógr̃nūt	úmr̃vši
carried out	embraced	soiled	covered	having died

/r/   short unstressed

brzína	površína	dovršávati	òstrvo	trgóvati
speed	surface	complete	island	trade

/r̃/   long unstressed

ùmr̃la	prètr̃pan
she dies	crowded

GD 1.2.7 Contrasts in length and stress

The inportance of the differences in stress and vowel length are best
shown by words which differ only in these respects. While such minimal pairs
are not common, a number of them are given here to help the student hear the
differences. Some examples which are otherwise different but which illustrate
the contrast in stress and/or length are also included.

/ ˋ /   and / ˴ /

grȁd	hail	grȁd	city
pȁs	dog	pȁs	belt
sȁd	now	sȁd	planting
Gr̀k	Greek	gr̀k	bitter
bȅg	bey	bȅg	flight
lȕk	onion	lȕk	arch
skȕp	assembly	skȕp	expensive
dȕg	long	dȕg	debt
kȕpljen	gathered	kȕpljen	bought
kȍs	slant	kȍs	blackbird
hrȍm	lame	hrȍm	chrome

/ ˴ /   / ˊ /

rȁvan	plane	rávan	even, flat
rȁdio	radio	rádio	worked
pȅtɪ	fifth	péti se	to climb

/ ˋ /   / ´ /

zèlēn	greens	zélen	green
ùmešan	adroit	úmēšān	involved

27

rùmēn	red color	rúmen	red
gòrē	worse	górē	they're burning
mòći	relics	móći	to be able to
stàjānje	stopping	stájānje	standing

/ ´ /   / ̋ /

rávan	amble	rȁvan	even, flat
slágati	to lie	slȁgati	to arrange
sélo	village	sȅlo	rural get together
svétlo	light	svȅtlo	light (adv.)
némati	a bad mother	nȅmati	not to have
sédeti	to be sitting	sȅditi	to get gray hair
krúnjēnje	crowning	krȕnjēnje	shelling of corn

/ ` /   / ̋ /

pràvo	straight ahead	prȁvo	right (noun)
mlàdež	birth-mark	mlȁdež	youth
kàda	when	kȁda	bathtub
plàvljēnje	flood	plȁvljēnje	blue color
pàrēnje	hot bath	pȁrēnje	mating
prèzānje	startling (noun)	prȅzānje	harnessing
bìlo	pulse	bȉlo	was (n.)
vìšnja	sour cherry	vȉšnja	a kind of green bean
rùka	roar	rȕka	hand, arm
kùpiti	to collect	kȕpiti	to buy
dùga	stave	dȕga	rainbow
gòre	forests, up	gȍre	up

28

Multiple Contrasts

rávan	amble	ràvan	plane	răvan	even, flat

gòre	forests	gòrē	worse	górē	they burn
				gŏre	up

kìrvāv	bloody	kŕvnĭk	murderer	kȑv	blood
				kŕvca	blood (poet.)

GD 1.2.8 Diphthongs: Vowel plus /j/

When a vowel is followed by /j/ the tongue moves further forward and upward than the corresponding English vowel plus /y/. This gives the effect of a more vigorous and intense articulation of the /j/.

gàj	gájtan	pòkušaj	papágāj
grove	cord	attempt	parrot

ájkula	hàjde	bàjka	čàj	čàjnĭk
shark	let's go	fairy tale	tea	tea-pot

bròj	lòj	ròj	vòjnĭ
number	tallow	swarm	military

vójnĭk	vójska	rázbōj
soldier	army	loom

kùjna	rùjno	rùj	bújnōst	čújnōst
kitchen	red	sumac	profusion (plants)	audibility

čùjno	déjstvo	kèj	zéjtin	zéjtinjēnje
audible	effect	quai	oil	oiling

GD 1.2.9 Miscellaneous sequences of vowels

áuto	náuka	páuza	páuk	samóuk
auto	science	pause	spider	self-taught man

pneumátičan	reumatízam	áerodrom	jedánaest	
pneumatic	rheumatism	airport	eleven	
tàoci	kótao	órao	sàobraćaj	saópštiti
hostages	kettle	eagle	traffic	to announce
vèseo	zrèo	pèpeo	meteoróloškī	smèo
gay	ripe	ash	meteorolo- gicaļ	daring

Note 1.4   Consonants.   The consonants as given in Note 1.1 are:

A.   p t k s š c ć č f h

B.   b d g z ž dz đ dž v

C.   r l lj m n nj j

The division into groups A, B and C is based partly on the sound and partly on where the consonants may occur. All of Group A are voiceless (made without vibration of the vocal cords). Those in Group B are voiced (pronounced with simultaneous vibration of the vocal cords) and each one corresponds to a similar voiceless consonant in A (/b/ to /p/, /d/ to /t/, etc.). Those in Group C are voiced but do not pair with voiceless ones.

Some general observations may be made in regard to certain groups of consonants. It may seem that some of the differences pointed out between the Serbo-Croatian sounds and similar English sounds are very slight. This does not mean they are unimportant. The proper pronunciation of such a slight difference will make a great deal of difference to the Serbo-Croatian listener.

/p t k/ in Serbo-Croatian do not have the strong puff of breath found after English p t k in pot, top, cot (this 'aspiration' occurs in English before a stressed vowel when no s precedes the p t or k). They should have very little aspiration, more as in English spot, stop, Scot.

/b d g z ž đ dž v/ in Serbo-Croatian are all voiced, as noted above. At the beginning of a word comparable English sounds such as b d g z j v (bed, dead, gag, zeal, jump, veal) begin like p t k s ch f and then begin voicing. The Serbo-Croatian sounds, on the other hand, are voiced from the beginning.

We might diagram this in this fashion:

| English | b | Serbo-Croatian | b |
| is pronounced | pb | is pronounced | bb |

This difference is particularly hard for the speaker of English to hear.

GD 1.3.1

| pȍ | pólazĭ | pópraviti | pȁr | pȋvo |
| half | leaves | to fix | pair | beer |

| bȍb | bȍrba | bȏl | sȍba | grȍb |
| lima-bean | battle | pain | room | grave |

/t d/ GD 1.3.2

Serbo-Croatian /t/ and /d/ are made by pressure of the tongue against the teeth, not the ridge back of the teeth, as in English. As noted above, Serbo-Croatian /t/ does not have the strong puff of breath the English t has in certain positions (e.g. in top). Nor does Serbo-Croatian /t/ have the great number of variants English t has. Listen to your own t in: top, stop, pot, bottle, button, butter. Each of these is phonetically different. The t of butter or button would sound very strange in Serbo-Croatian and might not be understood.

| tvȓd | sȁt | tȁjna | téle | prȉst |
| hard | hour | secret | calf | finger |

| dȍbar | rȃd | dȃvno | dèlo | glȃd |
| good | work | long time ago | work | hunger |

/c/ GD 1.3.3

/c/ is like t plus s said as a unit. It is also more dental than English t. (The vocal counterpart /dz/ is like d plus z said as a unit.)

| cèo | cȇna | crvēn | cȑkva | cȓnac |
| whole | price | red spot | church | negro · |

| cȑn |
| black |

/ć đ/ GD 1.3.4

Serbo-Croatian /ć đ/ are made on the teeth, as /t/ and /d/. Try making
/t/ plus /j/ (y), then a soft g type of sound in the same position. /ć/ and
/đ/ have relatively high pitch.

ćúrān	vèć	ćūd	úći	ćúmur
turkey	already	disposition	to go in	charcoal

đàk	svàđa	gràđanin	đàvō	ròđāk
pupil	quarrel	citizen	devil	relative

/č dž/ GD 1.3.5

/č/ and /dž/ are made with tongue pressure against the ridge back of the
teeth. They are lower pitched than English ch and j and quite different from
/ć/ and /đ/. Some Yugoslavs use sounds like English ch and j and have no distinction between /ć/ and /č/ or /đ/ and /dž/.

čóvek	čùti	čélik	òbrūč	čȉst
man	to hear	steel	hoop	clean

džȁk	džȉn	džàbē	džámija	dírīndžiti
sack	giant	without pay	mosque	to toil

/š ž/ GD 1.3.6

Serbo-Croatian /š/ and /ž/ are lower in pitch than the English sounds.
The tongue is drawn farther back and the back of the tongue is lower in Serbo-
Croatian than in English.

šátor	šàla	škòla	šljȉva	kòkōš
tent	joke	school	plum	hen

žàlōst	žàba	pážnja	žūt	žȉto
sorrow	frog	attention	yellow	grain

/r/ GD 1.3.7

Serbo-Croatian /r/ is a tongue tip trill. The tongue vibrates against
the back of the teeth. The 'vowel' /r/ is this same trill, accompanied by a
kind of a [ə] (uh) sound. The English r is very different, having no trill and

turning the tip of the tongue back.

rȁd	rȗka	prȇdmet	rȗža	dȁr
work	hand, arm	object	rose	dift

A final /r/, as in /dȁr/ is often voiceless.

/h/   GD 1.3.8

Serbo-Croatian /h/ is not English h English h is a breathing out of air, the position of the tongue depending on the following vowel. the h in he is i height; the h in hoe is o height, etc.

Serbo-Croatian /h/ is a sound made by placing the tongue in a k-like position, humped up nearly touching the back part of the roof of the mouth. It has a slight friction noise similar to that made when clearing the throat. Do not use English h for this sound.

hȍtel	hrȃm	strȁh	hrȃna	hrȃbar
hotel	temple	fear	food	courageous

hvȃla	zȁhvālan	shvȁtati	neshvȃtljivo	hȉljada
thanks	grateful	to comprehend	incompre-hensible	air

dȕh	dȁh	hȉtan	hlȁd	vȁzdūh
spirit	breath	urgent	shade	air

/k g/   GD 1.3.9

Serbo-Croatian /k/ does not have the strong puff of breath often found after English k.

kȍnj	jȁk	kȍrēn	mȅk	krȁtak
horse	strong	root	soft	short

glȍg	gȍvor	mȉg	rȁzgovōr	plȕg
hawthorn	speech	hint	conversa-tion	plough

/k g/ stop the flow of air completely. /h/ restricts the flow but does not stop it. The tongue is relaxed for /h/ but tense for /k g/.

33

/l/   GD 1.3.10

Serbo-Croatian has two /l/ sounds, a lower pitched one, /l/, much like English, and a higher pitched one, /lj/.

làk	làrma	bőlnica	mlȁd	tòpal
light	noise	hospital	young	warm

bȍl	vȁl	òbal	bȁl	kánāl
pain	wave	round	ball	canal

kȁl	svȉla	žȁlōst	zahválnōst	zlònameran
mud	silk	sorrow	gratitude	malicious

/lj/   GD 1.3.11

The /lj/ sound is not /l/ plus /j/ (y). It is an l sound made with the tongue in a similar position to that in saying /j/ (English y).

ljűbav	ljȕt	kèlj	ùgalj	dȑljati
love	angry	kale	coal	to harrow

ljűdi	pòlje	séljāk	póljubac	pȑljav
men	field	peasant	kiss	dirty

/n/   GD 1.3.12

Serbo-Croatian /n/ is made by pressure of the tongue against the teeth, not the ridge back of them.

nòvine	nȍž	sàn	nósāč	pùn
newspaper	knife	dream	porter	full

nā̋da	nèvreme	névolja	néminōvno	neméšānje
hope	bad weather	trouble	unavoidably	non-inter- ference

/nj/   GD 1.3.13

Serbo-Croatian also has two /n/ sounds, one made with the tongue in /j/ position: /nj/. This, like /lj/, has higher pitch than /n/. It is not the n plus y of English canyon.

njégōv	njȉva	sān̋jati	pȁnj	klān̋je
his	field	to dream	stump	slaughtering

manjína	vȉšnja	léčēnje	smétnja	ménjati
minority	sour cherry	medical treat- ment	obstacle	to change

/s/ GD 1.3.14

sȁt	sàv	sètva	glȃs	pràksa
o'clock	all	sowing	voice	practice

/z/ GD 1.3.15

zvézda	zvézdara	zvòno	zlò	zȃrez
star	observatory	bell	evil	notch

/f/ GD 1.3.16

fénjer	jèftin	fúruna	fízika	fèderatīvan
lantern	cheap	stove	physics	federal

/v/ GD 1.3.17

vȋd	véštāk	vèče	glȃva	pȑvȋ
sight	expert	evening	head	first

/j/ GD 1.3.18

Serbo-Croatian /j/ is much like English <u>y</u>. It is generally higher than <u>y</u>, however, just as /i/ is higher than English <u>i</u>. In other words, it does not adjust to the height of the adjacent vowel to the extent English does.

jȁk	jȃje	júnāk	jàbuka	sjȃj
strong	egg	hero	apple	gleam

Note on stress and length symbols

There is a set of symbols devised in the early nineteenth century to indicate primary stress and length. These are widely used and will be found in many grammars and dictionaries. Examples are:

    ˮ short falling   for ˋ   ⌢ long falling   for ˎ
    ˋ short rising   for ˊ   ˊ long rising   for ˴

Secondary stress is not distinguished in this system.

UNIT 2

BASIC SENTENCES

Places and Directions	Mjesto i pravac	Место и правац

A

where is	gdje je	где је
embassy	ambasada	амбасада
Where is the embassy?	3 ˎ 2 |2 ˏ 1# Gdje je ambasada?	3 ˎ 2 |2 ˜ 1# Где је амбасада?

B

right	desno	десно
on the right	na desno	на десно
The embassy is on the right.	2 3ˏ 2 |2 ˎ1 Ambasada je na desno.	2 3˜ 2 |2 ˎ1 Амбасада је на десно.

A

(question word)	li	ли
whether... is?; is?	da li je	да ли је
far	daleko	далеко
from here	odavde	одавде
Is the embassy far from here?	3ˎ 2 ⊥ | Da li je ambasada 2 ˎ ˏ _1 # daleko odavde?	3ˎ 2 ⊥ |2 ˈ Да ли је амбасада далеко ˏ -1 # одавде?

B

| Yes, it is. | 3ˎ2\|2ˎ1
Da, jest. | 3ˎ1\|2ˎ1
Да, јесте. |

36

A

hotel	hotel	хотел
left	lijevo	лево
on the left	na lijevo	на лево
Is the hotel on the left?	3ˋ 2 ˙ |2 Da li je hotel na ˋ1 # lijevo?	3ˋ 2 ˙ |2 ˜1 # Да ли је хотел на лево?

B

Yes, it is.	3ˋ2 |2ˋ1 Da, jest.	3ˋ2|2ˋ1 Да, јесте.
he, it	on	он
near, nearby	blizu	близу
It's nearby.	3ˋ2 |2 ˋ 1 On je blizu.	3˜2 |2 ˜ 1 Он је близу.

A

station	kolodvor (Cr)	станица
Is the station near [here]?	3ˋ 2 ˙ | Da li je kolodvor 2 ˏ 1# blizu?	3ˋ 2 ˙ |2 ˜ 1# Да ли је станица близу?

B

no, not	ne	не
she, it	ona	она
it is not, it isn't	nije	није
No, it isn't near [here].	|2¹ 3ˋ 1 ˩ Ne, on nije blizu.	3ˋ2|2ˋ 3ˋ 1 ˩ Не, она није близу.

that	to	то
restaurant	restoran	ресторан
That's the restaurant.	3ꞈ2 |2 ꞈ -1 To je restoran.	3⁻2 |2 ꞈ -1 То је ресторан.
go	idite	идите
straight	pravo	право
Go straight [ahead].	3ꞈ2 |2 ꞈ1 Idite pravo.	3ꞈ2 |2 ꞈ1 Идите право.
there, over there	tamo	тамо
The station is over there.	3ꞈ2 |2ꞈ1 Tamo je kolodvor.	3ꞈ1 Тамо је станица.

A

theater	kazalište (Cr)	позориште
Where is the theater?	3 ꞈ 2 |2ꞈ 1_ # Gdje je kazalište?	3 ꞈ 2 |2⁻ 1 # Где је позориште?

B

here	ovdje	овде
The theater is here.	23ꞈ 2 |2ꞈ _1 Ovdje je kazalište.	23⁻ 2 |2⁻ 1- Овде је позориште.

A

village	selo	село
Is the village far from here?	2ꞈ 3ꞈ |2 ꞈ 2ꞈ 3 ꞈ |2 Da li je selo daleko Да ли је село далеко ꞈ _1 # ꞈ -1 # odavde? одавде?	

B

it, (rarely: he, she)	ono	оно

It's not far.   3ˎ |2ˌ   ˎ 1   3ˎ |2ˌ   ˎ 1
                             Ono nije daleko.   Оно није далеко.

NOTES

Note 2.1 Noun: Genders

    Da li je hotel na levo? Da, jeste. On je blizu.

    Da li je stanica blizu? Ne, ona nije blizu.

    Da li je kolodvor blizu? Ne, on nije blizu.

    Ovde je pozorište. Ono nije daleko.

    To je restoran.

Serbo-Croatian nouns fall into three classes according to gender: masculine, feminine and neuter. Masculine nouns are replaceable by masculine pronouns (as /ȍn/ 'he [or other masculine referent]' above) feminine (as /óna/ 'she [or other feminine referent]') and neuter by neuter (as /óno/ 'it [or other neuter referent]'). Note that /ȍn/ refers back to /hótel/ and /kȍlodvor/, /óna/ to /stȁnica/, and /óno/ to /pȍzorište/ (or /kázalīšte/). The answer uses /ona/ when /stȁnica/ 'station' is used, but /ȍn/ when /kȍlodvor/ 'station' is used. Some nouns which have occurred so far and their categories are:

Masculine	Feminine	Neuter
dȁn	nȍć	jùtro
gospódin	gòspođa	pȍzorište
hótel	gòspođica	mèsto ('place')
restórān	ambasáda	kázalište
právac ('direction')	stȁnica	
kȍlodvor		

These nouns are all in the nominative singular case. Most masculine nouns (in this case) end in a consonant, most feminine nouns end in /-a/, most neuters in /-o/ or /-e/. There is a separate declension of feminines to which /nȍć/ belongs. (Details of declensions and other variants will be given later.)

Note that /tȍ/ 'that' as pointing out the item, not modifying it, is always the same (neuter singular). In 'that is a restaurant', 'that is a hotel',

<u>'that</u> is a theater', etc., the 'that' is always /tò/.

Note 2.2 Verb: 'is' 'isn't'

    To je restoran.

    Ona nije blizu.

    Da, jest(e).

    There are three forms of the verb 'to be' here: normal, unstressed /je/
'is' (after another word in the clause), the independent stressed form /jèste/
or /jèst/ 'it is, he is, she is', and the negative /nìje/ 'isn't'. Some speakers
also use a stressed /jè/ before /li/ at the beginning of a sentence or clause
/Je li stanica blizu./ (= /Da li je stanica blizu/; see Note 2.3).

Note 2.3 Question words

    Kako ste.

    Gde je ambasada.

    Da li je ambasada daleko odavde.

    The words /kàko/ and /gdè/ (/gdjè/) are question words which usually occur
at the beginning of the sentence or clause. They normally have primary stress.

    The question phrase /dà li/ comes at the beginning of the sentence or
clause. The unstressed /je/ follows immediately. /li/ is a question particle
which is always unstressed and is added to a stressed word or particle.

    Note that the normal stress and pitch of sentences with question words is
the same as for statements. Serbo-Croatian may also use a rising intonation
pattern, as English may, but this is less frequent.

    Answers to yes or no questions are normally brief. Both short and long
answers are given in the drills.

    As indicated in Note 2.2 above, /jè li/ 'is?' may be used instead of
/dà li je/. This usage - the verb first followed by /li/ is less common than
it used to be. (Examples of /dà li je/ alternating with /jè li/ are found in
GD 3.3.2.)

Note 2.4 Abbreviations /g./, /g-đa/, /g-ca/

The abbreviations for /gospodin/, /gospođa/ and /gospođica/ are /g./, /g-đa/ and /g-ca/ respectively. Note that only /g./ 'Mr.' uses a period.

GRAMMATICAL DRILL - GRAMATIČKO VEŽBANJE

The drills are given in the eastern dialect but central words are often added. The instructor who wishes may use central vocabulary and structure throughout. Some examples of conversion are given after / in the drills below.

2.1 Noun - Imenica: Substitution - Zamena

Affirmative sentences - Potvrdne rečenice

Ambasada je daleko odavde.	Restoran je blizu.	Pozorište je pravo.
Stanica je na levo.	Hotel je na desno.	/Kolodvor je ovdje.

Negative sentences - Odrečne rečenice

Ambasada nije daleko odavde.	Ona je blizu.
Hotel nije na desno.	On je na levo.
Stanica nije na levo.	Ona je pravo.
/Kolodvor nije na lijevo.	On je pravo.
Pozorište nije pravo.	Ono je na desno.
/Kazalište nije pravo.	
Restoran nije blizu.	On je daleko.

Affirmative sentence - Potvrdne rečenice

To je ambasada.	To je gospođa Jović.	To je pravo.
To je hotel.	To je gospođica Jović.	To je na levo.
		To je na lijevo.
To je stanica.	Ovde je g. Jović.	To je ovde.
/To je kolodvor.	Ovdje je g. Jović.	To je ovdje.
To je pozorište.		To je daleko odavde.

/To je kazalište.

To je gospodin Jović.   To je restoran.   To je na desno.

Other substitutions - Druge zamene

Idite pravo.   Idite na levo. or Idite levo.
                                                             /lijevo
Idite na desno. or Idite desno.   Idite tamo.

                                       Idite odavde.

Negative sentences - Odrečne rečenice

To nije ambasada. To je stanica.   To nije pravo. To je na levo.
                   /kolodvor   /lijevo

To nije hotel. To je ambasada.   To nije g. Jović.

To nije stanica. To je restoran.   To nije g-đa Jović.

To nije pozorište. To je hotel.   To nije g-ca Jović.
     /kazalište

To nije restoran. To je pozorište.   G. Jović nije ovde.   /ovdje*
                   /kazalište   To nije ovde.   /ovdje

To nije na desno.   To nije daleko odavde.

                                       To nije na levo.   /lijevo

2.2 Questions and Answers - Pitanja i odgovori

Questions - Pitanja (pitanje)   Answers - Odgovori (odgovor)

Gde je ambasada?   Ambasada je na levo. /lijevo. Nije daleko.

Gde je hotel?   Hotel je na desno. On je blizu.

Gde je stanica?   Stanica je pravo. Nije daleko.
    /kolodvor

Gde je pozorište?   Pozorište je tamo. Ono je daleko.
    /kazalište

Gde je restoran?   Restoran je ovde. On je blizu.
                                           /ovdje

---

* maid speaking

Short affirmative reply - Kratak potvrdan odgovor

Da li je ambasada daleko odavde?	Jest(e).	Da li je to pozorište? /kazalište	Jest(e).
Da li je hotel na desno?	Jest(e).	Da li je to restoran?	Jest(e).
Da li je stanica na levo? /kolodvor na lijevo	Jest(e).	Da li je to daleko odavde?	Jest(e).
Da li je pozorište pravo? /kazalište	Jest(e).	Da li je to na desno?	Jest(e).
Da li je restoran blizu?	Jest(e).	Da li je to na levo? /lijevo	Jest(e).
Da li je to ambasada?	Jest(e).	Da li je to pravo?	Jest(e).
Da li je to hotel?	Jest(e).	Da li je to ovde? /ovdje	Jest(e).
Da li je to stanica? /kolodvor	Jest(e).	Da li je to tamo?	Jest(e).

Long affirmative reply - Dug potvrdan odgovor

Da li je restoran blizu?	Da, restoran je blizu.
Da li je ambasada daleko odavde?	Da, ambasada je daleko odavde.
Da li je hotel na desno?	Da, hotel je na desno.
Da li je stanica na levo? /kolodvor na lijevo	Da, stanica je na levo. /kolodvor je na lijevo
Da li je pozorište pravo? /kazalište	Da, pozorište je pravo. /kazalište
Da li je to ambasada?	Da, to je ambasada.
Da li je to hotel?	Da, to je hotel.
Da li je to stanica? /kolodvor	Da, to je stanica. /kolodvor
Da li je to pozorište? /kazalište	Da, to je pozorište. /kazalište
Da li je to restoran?	Da, to je restoran.

Da li je to daleko odavde?   Da, to je daleko odavde.

Da li je to na desno?   Da, to je na desno.

Da li je to na levo?   Da, to je na levo.
      /lijevo   /lijevo

Da li je to pravo?   Da, to je pravo.

Da li je to ovde?   Da, to je ovde.
     /ovdje   /ovdje

Da li je to tamo?   Da, to je tamo.

Short negative reply - Kratak odrečan odgovor

Da li je pozorište pravo?   Ne, nije. Da li je stanica na levo? Ne, nije.

Da li je restoran blizu?   Ne, nije. Da li je to ambasada?   Ne, nije.

Da li je ambasada daleko odavde? Ne, nije. Da li je to hotel?   Ne, nije.

Da li je hotel na desno?   Ne, nije. Da li je to stanica?   Ne, nije.

Da li je to pozorište?   Ne, nije. Da li je to na levo?   Ne, nije.

Da li je to restoran?   Ne, nije. Da li je to pravo?   Ne, nije.

Da li je to daleko odavde?   Ne, nije. Da li je to ovde?   Ne, nije.

Da li je to na desno?   Ne, nije. Da li je to tamo?   Ne, nije.

Expanded short negative reply - Proširen kratak odrečan odgovor

Da li je stanica na levo?   Ne, nije. Ona je na desno.

Da li je pozorište pravo?   Ne, nije. Ono je na levo.

Da li je restoran blizu?   Ne, nije. On je daleko.

Da li je ambasada daleko odavde?   Ne, nije. Ona je blizu.

Da li je hotel na desno?   Ne, nije. On je na levo.

Expanded long negative reply - Dug odrečan odgovor

Da li je hotel na desno?   Ne, hotel nije na desno. On je na levo.

Da li je stanica na levo?   Ne, stanica nije na levo. Ona je pravo.

Da li je pozorište pravo?   Ne, pozorište nije pravo. Ono je na desno.

Da li je restoran blizu?	Ne, restoran nije blizu. On je daleko.
Da li je ambasada daleko odavde?	Ne, ambasada nije daleko odavde. Ona je blizu.
Da li je to ambasada?	Ne, to nije ambasada. To je hotel.
Da li je to hotel?	Ne, to nije hotel. To je ambasada.
Da li je to stanica?	Ne, to nije stanica. To je pozorište.
Da li je to pozorište?	Ne, to nije pozorište. To je stanica.
Da li je to restoran?	Ne, to nije restoran. To je hotel.
Da li je to daleko odavde?	Ne, to nije daleko odavde. To je blizu.
Da li je to na desno?	Ne, to nije na desno. To je na levo.
Da li je to na levo?	Ne, to nije na levo. To je na desno.
Da li je to pravo?	Ne, to nije pravo. To je na levo.
Da li je to ovde?	Ne, to nije ovde. To je pravo.
Da li je to tamo?	Ne, to nije tamo. To je ovde.

2.3 Question and Answer Drill with Prompt

1) The instructor is to say both the statement on the left and the corresponding question on the right and the students are to repeat.

2) After the repetition drill is finished, the questions are to be covered. The first student is to make a question on the basis of the first statement. The second student is to give an appropriate answer and to make a question on the basis of the second statement. The next student gives the answer and makes a new question, etc.

Statement	Question	Statement	Question
Hotel je na levo.	Gde je hotel?	Restoran je na levo.	Gde je restoran?
Stanica je pravo.	Gde je stanica?	Ambasada je desno.	Gde je Ambasada?
Pozorište je na desno.	Gde je pozorište?	To je hotel.	Da li je to hotel?
Stanica je blizu.	Da li je stanica blizu?	Pozorište je daleko odavde.	Da li je pozorište daleko odavde?
Restoran je na levo.	Da li je restoran na levo?	Ambasada je na desno.	Da li je Ambasada na desno?

2.4 Situational Drill

Following is an outline map to practice asking directions.

Assuming first that one is at position A, the students are to ask each other questions such as /Gde je hotel?/, /Da li je hotel na levo?/, etc. The student addressed is to reply appropriately in terms of the diagram.

The relative reference of the adverbs to be used may be diagrammed in two ways -

```
                        pravo

        levo             A              desno


              daleko        tamo
                   tamo
                   blizu
                     A
                   ovde
```

the adverbs within the circle referring to any space within the circle. As indicated, /tamo/ need not be /daleko/ but points out '(over) there'.

2.5 Conversations - Razgovori (razgovor)

2.5.1

A. Da li je to ambasada?   B. Ne, to nije ambasada.

A. Da li je ambasada daleko odavde?   B. Da, jest.

                                       Ambasada je tamo na lijevo.

                                       Idite na lijevo.

A. Da li je hotel blizu?

B. Jest. To je hotel.

A. Hvala. Do viđenja.

B. Molim. Do viđenja.

А. Да ли је то амбасада?

В. Не, то није амбасада.

А. Да ли је амбасада далеко одавде?

В. Да, јесте. Амбасада је тамо, на лево. Идите на лево.

А. Да ли је хотел близу?

В. Јесте. То је хотел.

А. Хвала. До виђења.

В. Молим. До виђења.

2.5.2

A. Da li je hotel daleko?

B. Nije daleko.

A. Da li je to hotel?

B. Nije. To je kazalište.

A. Gdje je hotel?

B. Hotel je tamo, na desno.

Idite na desno.

A. Da li je restoran tamo?

B. Da, jest.

A. Hvala. Do viđenja.

B. Molim. Do viđenja.

А. Да ли је хотел далеко?

В. Није далеко.

А. Да ли је то хотел?

В. Није. То је позориште.

А. Где је хотел?

В. Хотел је тамо, на десно.

Идите на десно.

А. Да ли је ресторан тамо?

В. Да, јесте.

А. Хвала. До виђења.

В. Молим. До виђења.

UNIT 3

BASIC SENTENCES

The Hotel	Hotel	Хотел

A

| what kind, what [is it] like | kákav, kákva, kákvo | ка́кав, ка́ква, ка́кво |
| your | vaš, vaša, vaše | ваш, ваша, ваше |

How is your hotel?
3ˊ 2 ˈ| ˋ1 #
Kakav je vaš hotel?
3ˊ 2 |2ˈ ˋ1 #
Ка́кав је ваш хотел?

Is it good?d
2ˈ 3ˊ ‖
Da li je dobar?
3ˊ 2 |2ˈ 1#
Да ли је добар?

B

my, mine	moj, moja, moje	мо̂ј, мо́ја, мо́је
good	dobar, dobra, dobro	до́бар, до́бра, до́бро
but	ali	али
expensive	skup, skupa, skupo	ску̂п, ску́па, ску́по

My hotel's good, but expensive.
2ʟ ˈ 3ˊ |
Moj hotel je dobar,
2ˈ ʟ1
ali skup.
2ʟ ˈ 3ˊ |2ˈ ˋ1
Мо̂ј хотел је добар, али скуп.

| new | nov, nova, novo | нов, нова, ново |

That's a new hotel.
2ʟ 3ˋ 1ˈ
To je nov hotel.
2ʟ 3ˈ1 ˈ
То је нов хотел.

A

English	Latin	Cyrillic
and (with change of subject or other contrast), but (un-emphatic)	a	а
Tom	Toma / Tomo	Тома / Томо
Tom's	Tomin, Tomina, Tomino / Tomov	Томин, Томина, Томино / Томово
room	soba	соба
And how is Tom's room?	2 3ˎ 2 |2ˎ 1 ˌ # A kakva je Tomina soba?	2 3ˎ 2 |2̄ 1 ˈ # А каква је Томина соба?
great, big, large	velik, velika, veliko	велики, велика, велико
and, also, too	i	и
beautiful, handsome, nice	lijep, lijepa, lijepo	леп, лепа, лепо
Is it large and nice?	2ˌ 3ˌ2 |2 ˌ 1# Da li je velika i lijepa?	3ˌ 2 |3ˌ2 |2 ̄ 1# Да ли је велика и лепа?

B

English	Latin	Cyrillic
his	njegov, njegova, njegovo	његов, његова, његово
wife, woman	žena	жена

satisfied, pleased, happy	zadovoljan, zado-	задовољан, задовољна,
	voljna, zadovoljno	задовољно

His wife is pleased.	2 ˙ 3ˋ 2 | Njegova žena je	3˖2 ˙ |2˖˄ Његова жена је задовољна.
	2˂1 _ zadovoljna.	

A

Zora	Zora	Зора
Zora's	Zorin, Zorina,	Зорин, Зорина, Зорино
	Zorino	
Jovan	Jovan / Ivan	Јован / Иван
Jovan's	Jovanov/Jovanova,	Јованов, Јованова,
	Jovanovo / Ivanov	Јованово / Иванов

How is Zora's and Jovan's hotel?	2˙ 3˴ |2 Kakav je Zorin i	2˙ 3ˉ |2 ˙ Какав је Зорин и Јованов
	˙ ˂1 # Jovanov hotel?	˂1 # хотел?

B

their	njihov, njihova,	њихов, њихова,
	njihovo	њихово
bad	loš, loša, loše	рђав, рђава, рђаво
small, little	mali, mala, malo	мали, мала, мало
clean, pure	čist, čista, čisto	чист, чиста, чисто

Their hotel isn't bad, too. It's small, but clean.

2 3 ˅2   ˎ |2ˎ
I njihov hotel nije

˅1   3ˎ2_ |
loš. Mali je,

2ˎ   ˅1
ali čist.

2 3˅1   �   ˎ   ˎ
И њихов хотел није рђав.

3ˎ2_ |2ˎ   ˅1
Мали је али чист.

also

također

такође

comfortable

udoban, udobna,

udobno

удобан, удобна, удобно

Their room is also comfortable and clean.

2 ˎ   ˉ
Njihova soba je

3ˎ |2ˎ
također udobna i

ˎ 1
čista.

2ˎ   ˎ   3 ˉ |
Њихова соба је такође

2ˎ   ˎ 1
удобна и чиста.

A

And how is Mr. Smith?

2 3˅2 |2
A kako je g. (gos-

ˎ   ˅ ‖
podin) Smit?

2 3˅2 |2   ˎ
А како је г. (господин)

˅1 #
Смит?

Is he pleased?

2ˎ   3˅ _ #
Da li je zadovoljan?

2ˎ   3˅1   #
Да ли је задовољан?

B

Smith's

Smitov, -a, -o

Смитов, Смитова, Смитово

cheap

jeftin, jeftina,

jeftino

јефтин, јефтина, јефтино

although

iako

иако

old

star, -a, -o;

stari, -a, -o

стар, стара, старо;

стари, стара, старо

Smith's hotel isn't cheap, though it's old.	Smitov hotel nije jeftin, iako je star	Смитов хотел није јефтин, иако је стари.
thing, matter, point	stvar f.	ствар
in that	u tome	у томе
But, that's not what's the matter.	Ali stvar nije u tome.	Али, ствар није у томе.

A

in what	u čemu	у чему
What is the matter?	U čemu je stvar?	У чему је ствар?

B

bath, bathroom, bathhouse	kupaona /kupaonica	купатило
rather, fairly	prilično	прилично
dirty	prljav, -a, -o	прљав, прљава, прљаво
His bathroom is rather dirty.	Njegova kupaona je prilično prljava.	Његово купатило је прилично прљаво.
for that, therefore	zato	зато
dissatisfied	nezadovoljan, nezadovoljna, -o	незадовољан, незадовољна, -о
Therefore he is dissatisfied.	On je zato nezadovoljan.	Он је зато незадовољан.

otherwise, moreover, in addition, besides	ínače	иначе
to him	njemu, mu	њему, му
very	jako	врло
Otherwise, his room is very comfortable, and large.	Inače, soba mu je jako udobna i velika.	Иначе, соба му је врло удобна и велика.

NOTES

Note 3.1   Adjectives: Nominative Singular

Kakav je vaš hotel.

Moj hotel je dobar, ali skup.

To je nov hotel.

Mali je, ali čist.

Da li je zadovoljan?

Smitov hotel nije jeftin, iako je stari.

Serbo-Croatian adjectives are declined for three genders. The above examples illustrate the masculine singular. Some adjectives regularly have the ending /-ī/ in the masculine singular, as /mȁlī/; some have no ending. Many adjectives have no ending in what is known as the 'indefinite' but /-ī/ in the 'definite', e.g. /dóbar/ but /dòbrī/. (See below for 'definite' and 'indefinite'.)

Tomina soba je velika i lepa.

Njegova žena je zadovoljna.

Njihova soba je takođe(r) udobna i čista.

Inače soba mu je vrlo udobna i velika.

These illustrate the feminine singular (nominative case only). The ending is /-a/ (/-ā/ when the adjective is definite and has primary stress).

          Njegovo kupatilo je prilično prljavo.

    This example illustrates the neuter singular ending /-o/ (or /-ŏ/; see above under /-a/). After some consonants (such as /j š č/) the ending is /-e/ (/móje/ 'my' /vàše/ 'your').

    Adjectives which have occurred are: (nominative singular forms)

Masculine	Feminine	Neuter	Meaning
-ī			
čìst	čísta	čísto	clean
dóbar	dóbra	dóbro	good
jèftin	jèftina	jèftino	cheap
Jóvanov	Jóvanova	Jóvanovo	Jovan's
làk	làka	làko	light; easy
lĕp	lĕpa	lĕpo	beautiful
/lìjep	/lijépa	/lijépo	
màlī	màlā	màlo	small
lòš	lóša	lóše	bad
mòj	mója	móje	my
nèzadovŏljan	nèzadovŏljna	nèzadovŏljno	dissatisfied
njègov	njègova	njègovo	his
njȋhov	njȋhova	njȋhovo	their
nòv	nóva	nóvo	new
prljav	prljava	prljavo	dirty
r̀đav	r̀đava	r̀đavo	bad
skùp	skúpa	skúpo	expensive
Smȋtov	Smȋtova	Smȋtovo	Smith's
stàr	stára	stáro	old
stărī	stărā	stărŏ	

Tómin	Tómina	Tómino	Tom's
údoban	údŏbna	údŏbno	comfortable
vàš	vàša	vàše	your
vèlik	vèlika	vèliko	big, large
vèlikī	vèlikā	vèlikō	
zàdovŏljan	zàdovŏljna	zàdovŏljno	satisfied
Zórin	Zórina	Zórino	Zorin's

Some, but not all, adjectives have two different forms, called indefinite and definite. The indefinite form has no ending in the masculine and generally has 'rising' / ´/ stress where possible. The definite has /-ī/ as the masculine singular ending, long vowel endings and falling / `/ stress throughout. Compare:

indefinite   lép   lépa   lépo   / lìjep   lìjépa   lìjépo

definite   lèpī   lèpā   lèpō   / lìjepī   lìjepā   lìjepō

Since long vowels which are not themselves stressed are replaced by short vowels when the word has secondary stress, there is no contrast between definite and indefinite under secondary stress except in the masculine singular:

    lȅp   indefinite   ⎫
                      ⎬   lȅpa   lȅpo
    lȅpi   definite   ⎭

The contrast definite/indefinite is therefore largely a matter of whether the adjective has /-ī/ in the masculine singular (nominative - and sometimes accusative). In such a sentence as /moj hotel je skup/ the adjective is generally the indefinite form. Where the adjective precedes the noun, it may be definite or indefinite depending on the meaning: /dobar hotel/ 'a good hotel', /dobri hotel/ 'the good hotel'. The definite is not simply to be equated with the English use of 'the' but with the concept of something specific, known, or the like.

The difference in usage between /stàr/ and /stàrī/ is, however, more complex. /stàr/ is used for people; /stàrī/ may be used either of people or of things. Whether /stàr/ or /stàrī/ is used of a given noun must be learned: /star čovek/

55

'an old man' /stårî gospódin/ 'an old gentleman, the old gentleman'.

The adjectives /moj/, /vaš/, /njegov/ and /njihov/ will be taken up in
Note 4.1.

The adjectives /Jovanov/, /Smitov/, /Tomin/ and /Zorin/ illustrate regular
forms made by adjective endings on noun bases. Nouns in /-a/ have the adjective
ending /-in/: /Toma/ - /Tomin/, /Zora/ - /Zorin/. Nouns ending in a consonant
have the ending /-ov/: /Jovan/ - /Jovanov/, /Smit/ - /Smitov/. These endings
indicate 'pertaining to' and are here translatable as possessives: 'Tom's,
'Zora's', 'Jovan's', 'Smith's'. (These are taken up in more detail in Notes
27.2.2, 27.2.3.)

The pair /zadovoljan/ 'satisfied', /nezadovoljan/ 'dissatisfied' illustrates
the negative prefix /nè-/. This prefix occurs on many adjectives, most of which
also have a form without /nè-/. For the adjectives in the list above the only
other common form in /nè-/ is /nèudoban/ 'uncomfortable'.

GRAMMATICAL DRILLS

3.1   Learning Drill
3.1.1 Single substitution drill, with negative transform.

Following are substitutions with negative transforms. These may be drilled
first in the affirmative and then in the negative, or with the negative added as
a transform after each substitution.

To je veliki hotel.   Tomin hotel je veliki.
(To nije veliki hotel.)   (Tomin hotel nije veliki.)

    mali   rđav /loš   dobar   jeftin

    skup   udoban   neudoban   lep /lijep

    čist   prljav

To je velika soba.   Tomina soba je velika.
(To nije velika soba.)   (Tomina soba nije velika.)

    mala   rđava /loša   dobra   jeftina

    skupa   udobna   neudobna   lepa /lijepa

56

čista   prljava

To je <u>veliko</u> selo.   Tomino selo je <u>veliko</u>.
(To nije <u>veliko</u> selo.)   (Tomino selo nije <u>veliko</u>.)

   malo   lepo /lijepo

   čisto   prljavo

To je <u>Tomin hotel</u>.
(To nije <u>Tomin hotel</u>.)

  Zorin hotel   veliki restoran   udobna soba   lepo selo /lijepo

  nov hotel   Tomina soba   njihova soba   njegov hotel
             /Tomova

  skupa soba   jeftin hotel   staro pozorište   stari restoran
                               /kazalište

<u>Tomin restoran</u> je veliki i lep.   <u>Tomin restoran</u> nije veliki i lep.
              /lijep   Mali je i rđav. /loš   /lijep

  Jovanov hotel   Zorin restoran   njegov hotel   njihov restoran
  /Ivanov

<u>Tomina soba</u> je mala, ali čista i   <u>Tomina soba</u> nije mala. Ona je
  udobna.   velika, ali neudobna.

  njegova soba   Zorina soba   njihov kolodvor

  vaša ambasada   njihova stanica   naša kupaonica

<u>Tomino kupatilo</u> je lepo i čisto.   <u>Tomino kupatilo</u> nije lepo i čisto.
                                 Malo je i prljavo.

           vaše pozorište   Zorino selo
           /kazalište

<u>Tomin hotel</u> je dobar, iako je jeftin.   <u>Tomin hotel</u> nije dobar, iako je skup.

  Jovanov restoran   njegov hotel   njihov hotel   vaš hotel

<u>Tomina soba</u> je prilično udobna, iako   <u>Tomina soba</u> nije udobna, iako je
  je mala.   prilično velika.

  vaša ambasada   njihova stanica   njegova soba   Smitova soba

Tomino kupatilo je prilično dobro,   Tomino kupatilo nije dobro, iako
  iako je staro.   je novo.

    vaše pozorište   njihovo pozorište

Jovan je zadovoljan.   Jovan nije zadovoljan.
Jovan je nezadovoljan.

    Toma   gospodin

    gospodin Jović   gospodin Smit

Zora je zadovoljna.   Zora nije zadovoljna.
Zora je nezadovoljna.

    gospođa   gospođica   gospođa Jović

    Jovanova žena   gospođica Smit

3.1.2 Multiple substitution drill with negative transform.

     The following drill gives two substitutions for the same sentence. On
initial drilling these substitutions are to be made one at a time. Below the
drill outline the complete substitutions which may be made are given. This will
illustrate the order in which substitutions may be made in future drills.

     Two other drills are added. These are to be drilled in the same way.

3.1.2 Multiple

	1	2	
	Zorin	mali	neudoban
<u>Tomin</u> hotel je <u>veliki</u>.	Jovanov	rđav /loš	lep /lijep
1 2	njegov	dobar	čist
	njihov	jeftin	prljav
<u>Tomin</u> hotel nije <u>veliki</u>.	Ivanov	skup	
1 2	Tomov	udoban	

	Tomin hotel je <u>veliki</u>.	Tomin hotel nije <u>veliki</u>.
mali	Tomin hotel je <u>mali</u>.	Tomin hotel nije <u>mali</u>.
rđav	Tomin hotel je <u>rđav</u>. /loš	Tomin hotel nije <u>rđav</u>. /loš
dobar	Tomin hotel je <u>dobar</u>.	Tomin hotel nije <u>dobar</u>.
jeftin	Tomin hotel je <u>jeftin</u>.	Tomin hotel nije <u>jeftin</u>.
skup	Tomin hotel je <u>skup</u>.	Tomin hotel nije <u>skup</u>.
udoban	Tomin hotel je <u>udoban</u>.	Tomin hotel nije <u>udoban</u>.
neudoban	Tomin hotel je <u>neudoban</u>.	Tomin hotel nije <u>neudoban</u>.
lep /lijep	Tomin hotel je <u>lep</u>. /lijep	Tomin hotel nije <u>lep</u>. /lijep
čist	Tomin hotel je <u>čist</u>.	Tomin hotel nije <u>čist</u>.
prljav	Tomin hotel je <u>prljav</u>.	Tomin hotel nije <u>prljav</u>.

	Zorin hotel je <u>veliki</u>.	Zorin hotel nije <u>veliki</u>.
mali	Zorin hotel je <u>mali</u>.	Zorin hotel nije <u>mali</u>.
rđav	Zorin hotel je <u>rđav</u>. /loš	Zorin hotel nije <u>rđav</u>. /loš
dobar	Zorin hotel je <u>dobar</u>.	Zorin hotel nije <u>dobar</u>.
jeftin	Zorin hotel je <u>jeftin</u>.	Zorin hotel nije <u>jeftin</u>.
skup	Zorin hotel je <u>skup</u>.	Zorin hotel nije <u>skup</u>.
udoban	Zorin hotel je <u>udoban</u>.	Zorin hotel nije <u>udoban</u>.
neudoban	Zorin hotel je <u>neudoban</u>.	Zorin hotel nije <u>neudoban</u>.
lep /lijep	Zorin hotel je <u>lep</u>. /lijep	Zorin hotel nije <u>lep</u>. /lijep
čist	Zorin hotel je <u>čist</u>.	Zorin hotel nije <u>čist</u>.
prljav	Zorin hotel je <u>prljav</u>.	Zorin hotel nije <u>prljav</u>.

	Jovanov hotel je <u>veliki</u>.	Jovanov hotel nije <u>veliki</u>.
mali	Jovanov hotel je <u>mali</u>.	Jovanov hotel nije <u>mali</u>.
rđav	Jovanov hotel je <u>rđav</u>. /loš	Jovanov hotel nije <u>rđav</u>. /loš
dobar	Jovanov hotel je <u>dobar</u>.	Jovanov hotel nije <u>dobar</u>.
jeftin	Jovanov hotel je <u>jeftin</u>.	Jovanov hotel nije <u>jeftin</u>.

skup	Jovanov hotel je skup.	Jovanov hotel nije skup.
udoban	Jovanov hotel je udoban.	Jovanov hotel nije udoban.
neudoban	Jovanov hotel je neudoban.	Jovanov hotel nije neudoban.
lep /lijep	Jovanov hotel je lep. /lijep	Jovanov hotel nije lep. /lijep
čist	Jovanov hotel je čist.	Jovanov hotel nije čist.
prljav	Jovanov hotel je prljav.	Jovanov hotel nije prljav.

	Njegov hotel je veliki.	Njegov hotel nije veliki.
mali	Njegov hotel je mali.	Njegov hotel nije mali.
rđav	Njegov hotel je rđav. /loš	Njegov hotel nije rđav. /loš
dobar	Njegov hotel je dobar.	Njegov hotel nije dobar.
jeftin	Njegov hotel je jeftin.	Njegov hotel nije jeftin.
skup	Njegov hotel je skup.	Njegov hotel nije skup.
udoban	Njegov hotel je udoban.	Njegov hotel nije udoban.
neudoban	Njegov hotel je neudoban.	Njegov hotel nije neudoban.
lep /lijep	Njegov hotel je lep. /lijep	Njegov hotel nije lep. /lijep
čist	Njegov hotel je čist.	Njegov hotel nije čist.
prljav	Njegov hotel je prljav.	Njegov hotel nije prljav.

	Njihov hotel je veliki.	Njihov hotel nije veliki.
mali	Njihov hotel je mali.	Njihov hotel nije mali.
rđav	Njihov hotel je rđav. /loš	Njihov hotel nije rđav. /loš
dobar	Njihov hotel je dobar.	Njihov hotel nije dobar.
jeftin	Njihov hotel je jeftin.	Njihov hotel nije jeftin.
skup	Njihov hotel je skup.	Njihov hotel nije skup.
udoban	Njihov hotel je udoban.	Njihov hotel nije udoban.
neudoban	Njihov hotel je neudoban.	Njihov hotel nije neudoban.
lep /lijep	Njihov hotel je lep. /lijep	Njihov hotel nije lep. /lijep
čist	Njihov hotel je čist.	Njihov hotel nije čist.

prljav   Njihov hotel je <u>prljav</u>.   Njihov hotel nije <u>prljav</u>.

<u>Tomina</u> soba je <u>velika</u>.
  1   2

<u>Tomina</u> soba nije <u>velika</u>.
  1   2

1	2	
Zorina	mala	udobna
Jovanova	rđava /loša	neudobna
njegova	dobra	lepa /lijepa
njihova	jeftina	čista
	skupa	prljava

<u>Tomino</u> selo je <u>veliko</u>.
  1   2

<u>Tomino</u> selo nije <u>veliko</u>.
  1   2

1	2
Zorino	malo
Jovanovo	lepo /lijepo
njegovo	čisto
	prljavo

3.2 Substitution-Correlation Drill

To je Tomin hotel.

restoran	žena
soba	kupatilo
	selo

	To je Tomin <u>hotel</u>.
restoran	To je Tomin <u>restoran</u>.
soba	To je Tomina <u>soba</u>.
žena	To je Tomina <u>žena</u>.
kupatilo	To je Tomino <u>kupatilo</u>.
selo	To je Tomino <u>selo</u>.

The following drill is given in full, being a multiple substitution drill. Future drills of this nature will be given in outline only.

      1
To nije moj <u>hotel</u>.

      2
To je <u>Tomin</u> hotel.

1	2
restoran	Jovanov
soba	njegov
kupatilo /kupaona	Smitov
žena	
selo	
mesto /mjesto	
stvar	

	To nije moj <u>hotel</u>.	To je Tomin <u>hotel</u>.
soba	To nije moja <u>soba</u>.	To je Tomina <u>soba</u>.
kupatilo	To nije moje <u>kupatilo</u>.	To je Tomino <u>kupatilo</u>.
žena	To nije moja <u>žena</u>.	To je Tomina <u>žena</u>.
selo	To nije moje <u>selo</u>.	To je Tomino <u>selo</u>.
mesto	To nije moje <u>mesto</u>.	To je Tomino <u>mesto</u>.
stvar	To nije moja <u>stvar</u>.	To je Tomina <u>stvar</u>.

	To nije moj <u>hotel</u>.	To je Jovanov <u>hotel</u>.
soba	To nije moja <u>soba</u>.	To je Jovanova <u>soba</u>.
kupatilo	To nije moje <u>kupatilo</u>.	To je Jovanovo <u>kupatilo</u>.
žena	To nije moja <u>žena</u>.	To je Jovanova <u>žena</u>.
selo	To nije moje <u>selo</u>.	To je Jovanovo <u>selo</u>.
mesto	To nije moje <u>mesto</u>.	To je Jovanovo <u>mesto</u>.
stvar	To nije moja <u>stvar</u>.	To je Jovanova <u>stvar</u>.

	To nije moj <u>hotel</u>.	To je Smitov <u>hotel</u>.
soba	To nije moja <u>soba</u>.	To je Smitova <u>soba</u>.
kupatilo	To nije moje <u>kupatilo</u>.	To je Smitovo <u>kupatilo</u>.
žena	To nije moja <u>žena</u>.	To je Smitova <u>žena</u>.
selo	To nije moje <u>selo</u>.	To je Smitovo <u>selo</u>.
mesto	To nije moje <u>mesto</u>.	To je Smitovo <u>mesto</u>.
stvar	To nije moja <u>stvar</u>.	To je Smitova <u>stvar</u>.

Following are substitutions with negative transforms.

Moj restoran je veliki i lep./lijep   (Moj restoran nije veliki i lep.)

vaša soba   Tomino kupatilo   vaše pozorište
                             /Tomina kupaona   /kazalište

njihova stanica   Jovanov hotel   vaša ambasada

Vaša soba je mala i čista.   (Vaša soba nije mala i čista.)

Tomin hotel   Jovanovo kupatilo   vaša stanica
                             /Jovanova kupaona   /vaš kolodvor

njihovo pozorište   Tomin restoran   Smitov hotel
     /kazališite

Vaše pozorište je lepo i čisto. /lijepo.. (Vaše pozorište nije lepo i čisto.)

Jovanov hotel   njegov restoran   njihova ambasada

naše kazalište   Smitov restoran   vaša stanica

Tomin hotel je lep i čist. /lijep..   (Tomin hotel nije lep i čist.)

kolodvor   soba   restoran

ambasada   pozorište   stanica

kupaonica /kupaona

3.3   Question and Answer Drill

3.3.1   Informational Answers

The following questions require an answer which gives information not contained in the question. There may therefore be many correct answers. The answers given below are examples of correct answers, but classroom drill should allow any correct answer that fits the pattern.

The normal reply to a question is the short answer. For purposes of drill long answers are also included. These would be used under certain circumstances. In addition, the negative answers may be expanded by adding the correct information after stating the negative.

One pattern for the following question and answer drill is as follows:

	1	2
Kakav je Tomin <u>hotel</u>?		<u>Dobar</u> je.
Kakav je Tomin hotel?		Nije dobar.
Kakav je Tomin hotel?		Njegov hotel je dobar.
Kakav je Tomin hotel?		Njegov hotel nije dobar. <u>Rđav</u> je.

Substitute /restoran/ in the above pattern for /hotel/.

For each of the sentences with /hotel/ and /restoran/ substitute the following for /dobar/. The substitutions for /rđav/ are given in parentheses.

mali	(veliki)	neudoban	(udoban)	veliki i lep/lijep	(mali i skup)
veliki	(mali)	lep /lijep	(stari)	udoban i jeftin	(neudoban i skup)
jeftin	(skup)	čist	(prljav)	nov i čist	(stari i prljav)
skup	(jeftin)	prljav	(čist)	dobar i udoban	(loš i neudoban)
udoban	(neudoban)	nov	(stari)	rđav i skup	(dobar i jeftin)

The third column gives a list of combinations of two adjectives which may be substituted for /rđav/. The pattern for such a substitution is:

Sentence: Njegov hotel nije <u>dobar</u>. # Loš je.

Cue: veliki i lep (mali i skup)

Answer: Njegov hotel nije veliki i lep. Mali je i skup.

Note the substitution pattern: Rđav je / Mali je i skup.

The first adjective is followed by /je/, and the second follows, connected by /i/.

In this substitution exercise the answers may be given in turn, rather than every answer for each substitution. For example:

Kakav je Tomin hotel?	Mali je.
Kakav je Tomin hotel?	Nije veliki.
Kakav je Tomin hotel?	Njegov hotel je jeftin.
Kakav je Tomin hotel?	Njegov hotel nije skup. Jeftin je.

The following patterns are to be followed for the feminine and neuter nouns, with the substitutions indicated.

	1		2	
Kakva je	<u>Tomina soba</u>?		<u>Dobra</u> je.	
Kakva je	Tomina soba?		Nije dobra.	
Kakva je	Tomina soba?		Njegova soba je dobra.	
Kakva je	Tomina soba?		Njegova soba nije dobra.	Rđava je.
				/Loše je.

1			2	
Zorina i Jovanova soba.	mala	(velika)	velika i lepa /lijepa	(mala i skupa)
vaša soba	velika	(mala)	udobna i jeftina	(neudobna i skup
	jeftina	(skupa)	rđava i neudobna	(dobra i udobna)
	udobna	(neudobna)	dobra i jeftina	(rđava i skupa)
	čista	(prljava)	prljava i neudobna	(čist i udobna)

	1		2	
Kakvo je	Tomino <u>kupatilo</u>?		<u>Dobro</u> je.	
Kakvo je	Tomino kupatilo?		Nije dobro.	
Kakvo je	Tomino kupatilo?		Njegovo kupatilo je dobro.	
Kakvo je	Tomino kupatilo?		Njegovo kupatilo nije dobro.	Rđavo je.
				/Loše je.

1			2	
pozorište	malo	(veliko)	veliko i lepo	(malo i prljavo)
selo	veliko	(malo)		
	čisto	(prljavo)	čisto i lepo	(prljavo i staro)

Questions and Answers with Substitution-Correlation Drill

Make the substitutions indicated, giving the entire pattern of question and answer as above.

	1		2	
Kakav je	Tomin <u>hotel</u>?		<u>Dobar</u> je.	
Kakav je	Tomin hotel?		Nije dobar.	
Kakav je	Tomin hotel?		Njegov hotel je dobar.	
Kakav je	Tomin hotel?		Njegov hotel nije dobar.	Rđav je.
				/Loše je.

1	2			
soba	mali	(veliki)	veliki i lep/lijep	(mali i rđav)
restoran	veliki	(mali)	dobar i udoban	(rđav i neudoban)
kupatilo	stari	(nov)	prljav i neudoban	(čist i udoban)
ambasada	udoban	(neudoban)	čist i lep	(prljav i stari)
stanica	čist	(prljav)		
kupaona				
kolodvor				

3.3.2 Questions with /da li/ and transform using /li/

Da li je vaš hotel udoban i čist?   Je li vaš hotel udoban i čist.

Da li je vaše pozorište skupo?   Je li vaše pozorište skupo?
    /kazalište   /kazalište
Da li je i vaš restoran prljav i skup?   Je li i vaš restoran prljav i skup?

Da li je vaša Ambasada ovde nova?   Je li vaša Ambasada ovde nova?

Da li je Tomino selo veliko i lepo?   Je li Tomino selo veliko i lepo?
      /lijepo   /lijepo
A da li je vaše kupatilo čisto?   A je li vaše kupatilo čisto?
    /kupaona čista?   /kupaona čista?
Da li je vaša gospođa zadovoljna?   Je li vaša gospođa zadovoljna?

Da li je gospodin Smit zadovoljan?   Je li gospodin Smit zadovoljan?

3.3.3 Yes and No answers

  The following patterns are to be followed, with the substitutions indicated.

Da li je Jovanov hotel veliki?   Da, jeste.

Da li je Jovanov hotel veliki?   Ne, nije.

Da li je Jovanov hotel veliki?   Da, njegov hotel je veliki.

Da li je Jovanov hotel veliki?   Ne, njegov hotel nije veliki. <u>Mali</u>
            je, ali <u>dobar</u>.

  The following questions are to be drilled according to the above pattern.
The substitutions for use in the expanded negative answers are given on the
right.

Da li je Tomina soba velika?   mala, skupa

Da li je vaše pozorište dobro?   rđavo, jeftino

Da li je Zorin i Tomin restoran jeftin?   skup, dobar

Da li je njihova stanica prljava?   čista, mala

Da li je Jovanova soba udobna i lepa?   neudobna, velika
       /lijepa

Pattern

Da li je Jovanov hotel veliki?	Jeste.
Da li je Jovanov hotel veliki?	Nije.
Da li je Jovanov hotel veliki?	Jeste, njegov hotel je veliki.
Da li je Jovanov hotel veliki?	Nije, njegov hotel nije veliki.
	<u>Mali</u> je, iako je <u>skup</u>.

Drill questions

Da li je Jovanova soba skupa?	jeftina, dobra
Da li je Zorin i Tomin restoran jeftin?	skup, stari
Da li je njihova stanica čista? /kolodvor čist?	prljava, nova /prljav, nov
Da li je njegova soba udobna i lepa?	neudobna, skupa
Da li je Tomino kupatilo lepo? /kupaona lijepa?	rđavo, novo /loša, nova

Questions and Answers with Substitution-Correlation Drills

	1	2	
Da li je	<u>Jovanov</u>	<u>hotel veliki</u>?	Da, jeste.
Da li je	Jovanov	hotel veliki?	Ne, nije.

Question and Answer drill with Prompt

GD 3.4

GD 3.4.1

Moj hotel je dobar.	Kakav je vaš hotel?
Tomina soba je velika i lepa. /lijepa	Kakva je Tomina soba?
Zorino kupatilo je malo i prljavo. /Zorina kupaona je mala i prljava.	Kakvo je Zorino kupatilo? /Kakva je Zorina kupaona?
Njegov restoran je jeftin, iako je nov.	Kakav je njegov restoran?
I Tomin restoran je jeftin, iako je nov.	A kakav je Tomin restoran?
Jovanova soba je neudobna i skupa.	Kakva je Jovanova soba?
I naša soba je neudobna, iako je skupa.	A kakva je vaša soba?
Zorin i Jovanov hotel nije dobar, iako je nov.	Kakav je Zorin i Jovanov hotel?

Ja sam dobro, hvala.

I moja žena je dobro, hvala.

Toma je dobro, hvala.

I njegova žena je dobro, hvala.

Tomino selo je veliko i lepo?

Kako ste (vi)?

A kako je vaša gospođa?

Kako je Toma?

A kako je njegova gospođa?

Kakvo je Tomino selo?

GD 3.4.2

Moj hotel je čist.

Njegova soba je udobna i čista.

Njihovo pozorište je vrlo dobro.
    /kazalište

I Tomin hotel je rđav i skup.

Smitov hotel je takođe stari, ali
    udoban.   /također

Njihova stanica je velika.
    /Njihov kolodvor je veliki.

Da li je vaš hotel čist?

Da li je Tomina soba udobna i čista.

Da li je njihovo pozorište dobro?
            /kazalište

Da li je i Tomin hotel rđav i skup?

Da li je Smitov hotel takođe stari,
    ali udoban?   /također

Da li je njihova stanica velika?
    /Da li je njihov kolodvor veliki?

GD 3.5 Conversations - Razgovori

GD 3.5.1   A   B

Kakav je vaš hotel?

Da li je to vaš hotel?

Kakva je vaša soba? Da li je velika?

A da li je čista?

Kakav je Tomin hotel?

Da li je njegova soba čista?

Nije loš.

Jest.

Jest, velika je.

Jest, čista je. Hotel je čist, ali
    skup.

Njegov hotel nije dobar.

Nije. On nije zadovoljan.

Какав је ваш хотел?

Да ли је то ваш хотел?

Каква је ваша соба? Да ли је велика?

А да ли је чиста?

Какав је Томин хотел?

Да ли је његова соба чиста?

Није рђав.

Јесте.

Јесте, велика је.

Јесте, чиста је. Хотел је чист,
    али скуп.

Његов хотел није добар.

Није. Он није задовољан.

GD 3.5.2

Da li je to Tomin hotel?

Gdje je Tomin hotel?

Kakav je Tomin hotel?

Kakva je njegova soba?

Da li je njegov hotel skup?

Da li je Toma zadovoljan?

A da li je Smit zadovoljan?

Ne, to je Smitov hotel.

Njegov hotel je tamo, na lijevo.

Njegov hotel je dobar.

Soba mu je prilično mala, ali je čista.

Nije, iako je nov i lijep.

Da, zadovoljan je.

Da, i Smit je zadovoljan.

Да ли је то Томин хотел?

Где је Томин хотел?

Какав је Томин хотел?

Каква је његова соба?

Да ли је његов хотел скуп?

Да ли је Тома задовољан?

А да ли је Смит задовољан?

Не, то је Смитов хотел.

Његов хотел је тамо, на лево.

Његов хотел је добар.

Соба му је прилично мала, али чиста.

Није, иако је нов и леп.

Да, задовољан је.

Да, и Смит је задовољан.

GD 3.5.3

Kakva je vaša kupaona?
        /kupaonica

Moja kupaona nije dobra. Jako je
  mala i prljava.

Soba nije loša. Prilično je velika
  i udobna.
    A kakva je vaša soba?

Da li je vaš hotel skup?

To je dobro. Moj hotel je skup,
  iako nije dobar.

Moja kupaona je prilično dobra.
    A kakva je vaša kupaona?

A kakva je vaša soba? Da li je dobra?

Moja soba je također dobra. Ja sam
  zadovoljan.

Nije. Moj hotel je jeftin.

Какво је ваше купатило?

Моје купатило је прилично добро.
А какво је ваше купатило?

Моје купатило није добро. Врло је
мало и прљаво.

А каква је ваша соба? Да ли је добра?

Соба није рђава. Прилично је
велика и удобна.
А каква је ваша соба?

Моја соба је такође добра. Ја сам
задовољан.

Да ли је ваш хотел скуп?

Није. Мој хотел је јефтин.

То је добро. Мој хотел је скуп,
иако није добар.

GD 3.5.4

Da li je ovo vaše selo? Jako je
lijepo i veliko.

To nije moje selo. To je Tomino selo.

Da li je vaše selo veliko i lijepo?

Moje selo nije veliko, ali je lijepo.

A da li je vaše selo blizu odavde?

Da, jako je blizu. Moje selo je
tamo na desno.

Da, to nije daleko odavde.

Да ли је ово ваше село? Врло је
лепо и велико.

То није моје село. То је Томино село.

Да ли је ваше село велико и лепо?

Моје село није велико, али је лепо.

А да ли је ваше село близу одавде?

Да, врло је близу.
Моје село је тамо на десно.

Да, то није далеко одавде.

GD 3.6   Home Work - Domaći zadatak

GD 3.6.1 Write out each of the following sentences using each of the
adjectives listed.

Moj restoran je _____.   dobar   jeftin   loš

Zorin hotel nije _____.   rđav   skup

Tomina soba je _____.   čist   lep

Njihova stanica nije _____.   prljav   mali
/Njihov kolodvor
Jovanova kupatilo je _____.   nov   veliki
/Jovanova kupaona
Njihovo pozorište nije _____.   stari   udoban
        /kazalište

GD 3.6.2

Vaš restoran je _____, ali _____.

Vaš restoran je _____, iako je _____.

Tomina soba je _____, ali _____.

Tomina soba je _____, iako je _____.

Zorin hotel je _____, ali je _____.

Zorin hotel je _____, iako je _____.

Vaša stanica je _____, ali _____.

Vaša stanica je _____, iako je _____.

/Vaš kolodvor

Njihovo pozorište je _____, ali _____.

Njihovo pozorište je _____, iako je _____.

/Njihovo kazalište

Fill the above blanks with appropriate adjectives from the list given.

dobar	jeftin	nov	loš
mali	čist	udoban	
veliki	prljav	neudoban	
skup	stari	rđav	

UNIT 4

Basic Sentences - Osnovne rečenice

The Friends	Prijatelji	Пријатељи

A

what	što	шта
he, she, it is working	radi	ради
friend (man)	prijatelj	пријатељ
What's your friend Mr. Smith doing?	Što radi vaš prijatelj, g. (gospodin) Smit?	Шта ради ваш пријатељ, г. (господин) Смит?

B

he, she, it is studying	uči	учи
Serbo-Croatian	srpskohrvatski, -a, -o	српскохрватски, -а, -о
He's studying Serbo-Croatian.	On uči srpskohrvat-ski.	Он учи српскохрватски.

A

| you speak | vi govorite | ви говорите |
| You speak Serbo-Croatian well. | Vi govorite dobro srpskohrvatski. | Ви говорите добро српскохрватски. |

B

| I don't speak | ne govorim | не говорим |

so	tako	тако
No, I don't speak very well.	Ne, ne govorim tako dobro.	Не, не говорим тако добро.
I	ja	ја
now	sada, sad	сада, сад
I'm studying	učim	учим
I'm studying now, too.	I ja sada učim.	И ја сада учим.
we	mi	ми
we're studying	učimo	учимо / учимо
together	zajedno	заједно
We're studying together.	Mi učimo zajedno.	Ми учимо заједно.
does he, she, it know	da li zna	да ли зна
wife (formal)	supruga	супруга
Does your wife know Serbo-Croatian?	Da li zna vaša supruga srpskohrvatski?	Да ли зна ваша супруга српскохрватски?

B

No, she doesn't.	Ne, ne zna.	Не, не зна.
she understands	ona razumije	она разуме
a little	malo	мало
not a bit, not at all	nimalo	нимало

She understands a little.	Ona razumije malo.	Она разуме мало.
/She doesn't understand any at all.	/ Ona ne razumije nimalo.	(Она не разуме, нимало.)

A

yet, still	još	још
some	neki, -a, -o	неки, -а, -о
foreign	stran, strana, -o	стран, страна, -о
	/strani -a, -o	/страни, -а, -о
language, tongue	jezik	језик
Do you and your wife speak any other foreign language?	Da li vi i gospođa govorite još neki strani jezik?	Да ли ви и госпођа говорите још неки стран језик?
we don't speak	ne govorimo	не говоримо
No, we don't.	Ne, ne govorimo.	Не, не говоримо.
her, hers	njen, njena, -o	њен, њена, -о
father	otac	отац
he, she it speaks	govori	говори
German	njemački, -a, -o	немачки, -а, -о
mother	majka	мајка

75

French	francuski, -a, -ō	француски, -а, -о
Her father speaks German well, and her mother French.	Njen otac govori dobro njemački, a njena majka francu-ski.	Њен отац говори добро немачки, а њена мајка француски.
spouse (husband) (formal)	súprug	супруг
husband	mūž	мӯж
English	engleski, -a, -o	енглески, -а, -о
madam!	gospođo	госпођо
Does your husband speak English, madam?	Da li gospođo vaš suprug govori engleski?	Да ли ваш супруг говори енглески, госпођо?

A

weak	slab, -a, -o	слаб, -а, -о
Yes, but poorly.	Da, ali slabo.	Да, али слабо.
no one, any	nijedan, nijedna, nijedno	ниједан, ниједна, ниједно
He doesn't speak any foreign language.	On ne govori nijedan stran jezik.	Он не говори ниједан стран језик.
lazy	lijen, lijena, lijeno	лењ, лења, лењо

76

that he, she, it studies	da uči	да учи
He's [too] lazy to study.	On je lijen, da uči.	Он је лењ, да учи.
for	za	за
our	naš, -a, -e	наш, -a, -e
That's very good for our Serbo-Croatian.	To je jako dobro za naš srpskohrvatski.	То је врло добро за наш српскохрватски.

CULTURAL NOTE

mȕž	man, husband	súprug	husband	gospódin	gentleman, Mr.
žéna	woman, wife	súpruga	wife	góspođa	lady, Mrs.

The usage of these terms does not coincide with standard English use of the words given as translation. Ordinary, informal reference to one's husband or wife uses /mȕž/ or /žéna/ (compare colloquial English 'my man', 'my woman', 'the old man', 'the little woman', etc.). More polite usage is /súprug/, /súpruga/. It is not polite to refer to one's husband or wife as /gospódin/ or /góspođa/ and these titles should never be used in this way. In this respect their usage is more restricted than English 'Mr., Mrs.'.

NOTES

Note 4.1 Pronoun: Personal Pronouns

I ja sada učim.

On je lenj.

Ona razume malo.

Ono nije daleko.

Mi učimo zajedno.

Vi govorite dobro.

These are examples of personal pronouns: /jȁ/ 'I', /mȋ/ 'we', etc. In
the third person there are three different pronouns for the three genders:

/ȍn/   'he (or reference to a masculine noun)'

/óna/   'she (or reference to a feminine noun)'

/óno/   'it (or reference to a neuter noun)'

/ȍn/ and /óna/ are most commonly used with reference to people. /tȍ/ is more
frequent as a neuter referent than /óno/. The plurals are:

/óni/   'they (in general of persons of undesignated gender, of a mixed
            group and of masculine plural)'

/óne/   'they (when only women or females are referred to)'

/óna/   'they (when reference is to neuter plural only)'

As indicated, the common word for 'they' is /óni/. The others are not in
frequent use but may occur.

/vȋ/ is the general word for 'you'. It is used when addressing more than
one person and when speaking to one person under ordinary circumstances. There
is another, familiar, word for 'you': /tȋ/. This is used among intimates, in
rural districts for 'you (singular)' and when addressing the Deity. It should
be avoided in speaking to people unless one is so addressed (as may happen, for
instance, in a rural area).

Note 4.2 Adjective: Pronominal Adjectives

        Moj hotel je dobar.

        Kakav je vaš hotel?

        Njegova žena je zadovoljna.

        Njihov hotel nije rđav.

        Njen otac govori dobro nemački.

        To je vrlo dobro za naš srpskohrvatski.

Among the adjectives discussed in Note 3.1 were many of those illustrated
above. Certain of these are formed on pronoun bases and correspond to these
pronouns. The relationship of the pronoun to the adjective is not clear from
the nominative forms which have been used up to this point, but this aspect will

be clarified in future units. The pronouns and the corresponding adjectives (listing the nominative singular of all genders) are:

	Pronoun		Adjective			
jȁ	I		mȍj	mója	mȏje	my
tȉ	you (familiar)		tvȍj	tvója	tvȏje	your
ȍn	he		njégov	njégova	njégovo	his, its
óno	it					
óna	she		njȅn	njȅna	njȅno	her
			/njézin	njézina	njézino	
mȋ	we		nȁš	nȁša	nȁše	our
vȋ	you (polite or plural)		vȁš	vȁša	vȁše	your
óni	they (masc., mixed, or general)					
óne	they (feminine only)		njȉhov	njȉhova	njȉhove	their
óna	they (neuter only)					

The form /njézin/ 'her' is less used than /njȅn/.

Note 4.3 Verb: Negative - /ne/

Vi govorite dobro.

Ne, ne govorim.

Da li zna vaša gospođa srpskohrvatski?

Ne, ne zna.

/nè/ (stressed) occurs as a separate word, usually forming a separate phrase of its own, meaning 'no'. In addition, there is a /ne/ which occurs before verbs and makes them negative (/ne govorim/, /ne zna/). Although written separately in nearly all cases, /ne/ before a verb is a kind of prefix, it and the word following being a stress unit. (Compare the prefix /ne-/ on adjectives [Note 3.1].) This unit has only one stress, which is on /ne/ with some (short) verbs: /nè zna/. With a few verbs /ne/ has special forms (such as /ni-/ in /nȉje/ 'isn't').

These will be discussed when the forms of these verbs are given in the notes (Notes 7.4, 8.1, 19.1).

Ona ne razume nimalo.

On ne govori nijedan stran jezik.

These sentences are literally 'she does not understand not a bit' and 'he does not speak not one foreign language'. When the verb is negative, certain other words are regularly negative. The adverb /malo/ and the adjective /jedan/ are given negative prefixes when associated with a negative **ver**b. This is the same type of construction as English 'he don't know nothing', but while the English is substandard, the Serbo-Croatian is the only acceptable way of saying it. Double, triple or quadruple negatives are common and required by the structure of the language.

GRAMMATICAL DRILL

GD 4.1 Substitution Learning Drill - Vežba za učenje

Vaš hotel je dobar i nov.	moj
Vaš hotel nije dobar i nov. ·Rđav je i stari.	tvoj
Vaš prijatelj je zadovoljan.	naš
Vaš prijatelj nije zadovoljan. On je nezadovoljan.	njegov
Vaš prijatelj uči srpskohrvatski.	njen
Vaš prijatelj ne uči srpskohrvatski dobro. On je lenj. /lijenj	njihov
Vaš otac govori francuski.	Zorin
Vaš otac ne govori francuski. On ne govori nijedan stran jezik.	

* * * * * * * * * *

Vaša soba je udobna i čista.	moja
Vaša soba nije udobna i čista. Neudobna je i prljava.	tvoja
Vaša majka je nezadovoljna.	naša
Vaša majka nije nezadovoljna. Ona je zadovoljna.	njegova

Vaša majka zna nemački. /njemački.

Vaša majka ne zna nemački. Ona ne zna nijedan stran jezik.

njena

njihova

Tomina

Zorina

Vaše selo je čisto i veliko.

Vaše selo nije čisto i veliko. Malo je i prljavo.

moje	tvoje	naše
njegovo	njeno	njihovo

I moj prijatelj uči srpskohrvatski.

Moj prijatelj takođe uči srpskohrvatski.

vaš otac	vaša majka	Zorin suprug
gospođica Smit	gospodin Smit	gospođa Jović

GD 4.2 Substitution-Correlation Drill - Vežba sa zamenama i izmenama

Make the substitutions indicated, changing the other adjectives as necessary.

Moj restoran je mali i skup.

Moj restoran nije mali i skup. Veliki je i jeftin.

vaša soba

naše pozorište

/kazalište

Naša soba je udobna i čista.

Naša soba nije udobna i čista. Neudobna je i prilično prljava.

njegov hotel	njeno kupatilo /njena kupaona	tvoj restoran
naša ambasada	njihovo pozorište /kazalište	

Vaše kupatilo je staro i neudobna. /Vaša kupaona...

Vaše kupatilo nije staro i neudobno. Novo je i udobno.

tvoj restoran	naša ambasada	Zorin hotel
	njegova soba	

Vaš otac je zadovoljan.

Vaš otac nije zadovoljan.

moja majka   njegova gospođa   njen suprug

tvoja žena   gospođa Jović   gospođica Smit

GD 4.3 Question and Answer Drill

GD 4.3.1 Informational Answers

Substitution-Learning Drill

Kako govori srpskohrvatski vaš   Govori prilično dobro.

  prijatelj?   Ne govori dobro. On sada uči.

vaš otac   g. Jović   njegov otac

g. Smit   Zorin otac   Zorin muž

vaš suprug

Šta radi vaša gospođa?   Ona uči nemački. /njemački.

Šta uči vaša gospođa?   Ona uči nemački. /njemački

Kako govori nemački vaša gospođa?   Govori prilično dobro.

               /njemački   Ne govori dobro. Ona sada uči.

vaša majka   g-đa Smit

g-ca Smit   vaša žena

Kakav je vaš hotel?   Dobar je.
                                        Nije dobar.
                                        Moj hotel je dobar.
                                        Moj hotel nije dobar. Nije čist.

Kakva je vaša soba.   Dobra je.
                                        Nije dobra.
                                        Moja soba je dobra.
                                        Moja soba nije dobra. Nije čista.

Kakvo je <u>vaše</u> selo?

Malo je.

Nije malo.

Moje selo je malo.

Moje selo nije malo.

tvoj	njegov	njen
njihov	Zorin	Tomin

Substitution-Correlation Drill

Šta radi <u>vaš prijatelj</u>? /što...

On uči srpskohrvatski.

Šta uči <u>vaš</u> prijatelj?

On uči francuski.

Kako govori srpskohrvatski <u>vaš
prijatelj</u>?

Govori prilično dobro.

Ne govori dobro. On sada uči.

vaš otac	tvoja žena	g-ca Smit
Zorin suprug	vaša majka	tvoj prijatelj
g. Smit	g-đa Smit	

      1   2

Kakav je <u>vaš</u> <u>hotel</u>?

Dobar je.

Nije dobar.

Moj hotel je dobar.

Moj hotel nije dobar. Mali je i
prljav.

1		2	
tvoj	njegov	soba	kupatilo
njen	njihov	restoran	ambasada
Zorin	Jovanov	stanica	pozorište
		kolodvor	kazalište

GD 4.3.2 Yes and No answers

Substitution Learning Drill

         1   2

Da li <u>vaš prijatelj</u> <u>uči</u> srpskohrvatski?

Da, uči.

Ne, ne uči.

Da, moj prijatelj uči
srpskohrvatski.

                                    Ne, moj prijatelj na uči
                                    srpskohrvatski. On uči francuski.

          1   2
vaš otac   Zorin muž   govori   zna
vaš suprug   g. Smit   razume
  /vaša supruga

     1   2
Da li vaša gospođa govori nemački?   Da, govori.
                /njemački?   Ne, ne govori.
                                            Da, moja žena govori nemački.
                                            Ne, moja žena ne govori nemački.
                                              Ona ne govori nijedan stran jezik.

         1   2
tvoja žena   vaša majka   zna
g-đa Smit   Zorina majka

The above drill may be repeated using the pattern:

              2   1
                Uči li vaš prijatelj srpskohrvatski?

Substitution-Correlation Drill

Da li vaš prijatelj uči   Da, uči.
  srpskohrvatski?   Ne, ne uči.
                                            Da, moj prijatelj uči
                                              srpskohrvatski.

                                    (a)   Ne, moj prijatelj ne uči
                                            srpskohrvatski. On uči francuski.

                                    (b)   Ne, moj prijatelj ne uči
                                            srpskohrvatski. On ne uči
                                            nijedan stran jezik.

         1   2
tvoja žena   vaš otac   govori   zna
Zorin muž   vaša majka   razume
                                      /razumije
vaš suprug   g-đa Smit

    The students have the choice of giving a negative answer following either
(a) or (b).

Repeat the above drill, using the pattern:

<pre>
       2   1
  Uči li vaš prijatelj srpskohrvatski?
</pre>

GD 4.4   Question and Answer Drill with Prompt

GD 4.4.1

Moj prijatelj govori dobro
  srpskohrvatski.

Kako vaš prijatelj govori
  srpskohrvatski?

Ja govorim slabo srpskohrvatski.

Kako (vi) govorite srpskohrvatski?

Moja žena slabo govori, ali dobro
  razume nemački. /razumije njemački

Kako vaša gospođa govori i razume
  nemački? /razumije njemački?

Mi učimo ovde srpskohrvatski. /ovdje

Gde (vi) učite srpskohrvatski? /Gdje

I moj prijatelj uči ovde srpskohrvatski. /ovdje

A gde vaš prijatelj uči srpskohrvatski?
  /gdje

Gospođa Smit govori dobro francuski.

Kako gospođa Smit govori francuski?

I gospodin Smit govori dobro francuski.

A kako gospodin Smit govori francuski?

Moj prijatelj gospodin Smit sada uči
  nemački. /njemački

Šta radi sada vaš prijatelj gospodin
  Smit? /što

Moja majka je dobro, hvala.

Kako je vaša majka? Šta radi? /što

GD 4.4.2

Moja žena govori srpskohrvatski.

Da li vaša supruga govori srpskohrvatski?

Ja učim srpskohrvatski.

Da li vi učite srpskohrvatski?

I gospodin Smit uči srpskohrvatski.

Da li i gospodin Smit uči srpskohrvatski?

Mi učimo zajedno srpskohrvatski.

Da li vi učite zajedno srpskohrvatski?

Zorin otac govori nemački. /njemački

Da li Zorin otac govori nemački. /njemač

Njena majka razume, ali ne govori
  nemački. /razumije...njemački

Da li Zorina majka razume i govori
  nemački? /razumije...njemački

Ja znam malo francuski.

Da li vi znate francuski?

GD 4.5 Conversations - Razgovori

GD 4.5.1

A	B

Da li govorite srpskohrvatski?

Kako govorite?

A razumijete li srpskohrvatski?

Da li govori vaš prijatelj
srpskohrvatski?

Da li vi učite srpskohrvatski?

Gdje učite?

Da, govorim.

Ne govorim dobro.

Da, razumijem, ali ne dobro.

Ne, ne govori.
On sada uči.

Da, učim.

Učim ovdje.

Moj prijatelj i ja učimo zajedno.

Да ли говорите, српскохрватски?

Како говорите?

А разумете ли српскохрватски?

Да ли говори ваш пријатељ
српскохрватски?

Да ли ви учите српскохрватски?

Где учите?

Да, говорим.

Не говорим добро.

Да, разумем, али не добро.

Не, не говори.
Он сада учи.

Да, учим.

Учим овде.
Мој пријатељ и ја учимо заједно.

4.5.2

Da li vaš prijatelj g. Smit zna
srpskohrvatski?

A zna li g-đa Smit naš jezik?

Da li ona uči srpskohrvatski?

Gdje uči g. Smit srpskohrvatski?

Zna malo.

I ona zna malo.

Ne, ona ne uči vaš jezik, ali g. Smit
uči.

I on uči ovdje.

Mi učimo zajedno.

Да ли ваш пријатељ г. Смит зна
српскохрватски?

Зна мало.

А зна ли г-ђа Смит наш језик?

И она зна мало.

Да ли она учи српскохрватски?

Не, она не учи ваш језик, али г. Смит учи.

Где учи г. Смит српскохрватски?

И он учи овде.
Ми учимо заједно.

4.5.3

Da li vaš prijatelj govori srpskohrvatski, gospodine?

Da, govori.

Kako on govori.

On govori i razumije jako dobro.

Da li on govori još neki stran
jezik?

Da on govori još njemački i francuski.

Da li vaša gospođa govori neki stran
jezik?

Ne, ona ne govori nijedan stran jezik.
Ona sada uči njemački.

Da li vi govorite njemački?

Da, govorim, ali slabo.

Да ли ваш пријатељ говори српскохрватски, господине?

Да, говори.

Како он говори?

Он говори и разуме врло добро.

Да ли он говори још неки стран језик?

Да, он говори још немачки и француски.

Да ли ваша госпођа говори неки стран
језик?

Не, она не говори ниједан стран језик.
Она сада учи немачки.

Да ли ви говорите немачки?

Да, говорим, али слабо.

GD 4.6   Home Work - Domaći zadatak
GD 4.6.1   Answers to questions

1. Kako govori srpskohrvatski vaša gospođa?

2. Kako vaš prijatelj razume francuski? /razumije

3. Zna li Zorin suprug engleski?

4. Da li vaš prijatelj govori nemački? /njemački

5. Šta uči g-ca (gospođica) Smit? /što

6. Šta radi ovde g. Smit? /Što

    Give full answers both affirmative and negative for 1-4, and affirmative only for 5 and 6.

GD 4.6.2 Question transforms

Moja majka govori srpskohrvatski.

Zorin muž razume nemački. /razumije njemački

Moj prijatelj uči srpskohrvatski.

Gospođa Smit zna francuski.

Moja žena uči nemački. /njemački

Gospođica Smit govori i razume dobro srpskohrvatski. /razumije

    Make questions with /da li/ and give full answers both affirmative and negative.

UNIT 5

Basic Sentences - Osnovne rečenice

Going Out	Izlazak	Излазак

A

do you travel	da li putujete	да ли путујете
much, many	mnogo	много
Do you travel a lot, Mr. Smith?	Da li mnogo putujete,	Да ли путујете много,
	g. (gospodine) Smite?	г. (господине) Смите?

B

| Yes, I do. | Da, putujem. | Да, путујем. |

A

| Where do you travel? | Gdje putujete? | Где путујете? |

B

frequently, often	često	често
Zagreb	Zagreb	Загреб
Split	Split	Сплит
I often go to Zagreb and Split.	Putujem često za	Путујем често у Загреб
	Zagreb i Split.	и Сплит.

A

| you spend (time) | provodite | проводите |

89

time, weather	vrijeme G vremena	време, Г времена

How do you spend [your] time here?	Kako provodite vrijeme ovdje?	Како проводите време овде?
do you go out	izlazite li	излазите ли
somewhere, someplace	negdje	негде
in the evening	uveče	увече
Do you go out anywhere in the evening?	Idete li negdje uveče?	Излазите ли негде увече?

B

/ nowhere	/ nigdje	/ нигде
/No, nowhere.	/Ne, nigdje.	/Не, нигде.
we go, we're going	idemo / idemo	идемо / идемо
rarely, seldom	rijetko	ретко
Yes, we go to the theater, but not very often.	Da, idemo u kazalište ali rijetko.	Да, идемо у позориште, али ретко.
approximately	otprilike	отприлике
once, one time	jedanput	једанпут
not any time, not at all	nijedanput	ниједанпут
or	ili	или

twice	dvaput / dva puta	двапут/два пута
monthly	mjesečno	месечно
About once or twice a month.	Otprilike jedanput ili dvaput mjesečno.	Отприлике једанпут или двапут, месечно.
/Maybe once or not even that often a month.	/Otprilike jedanput ili nijedanput mjesečno.	/Отприлике једанпут или ниједанпут месечно.)

A

more frequently	češće	чешће
movie theater, movies	kino	биоскоп
Do you go to the movies more often?	Da li idete češće u kino?	Да ли идете чешће у биоскоп?

B

perhaps, maybe	možda	можда
weekly	nedjeljno	недељно
Yes, maybe once a week.	Da , možda jedanput nedjeljno.	Да , можда, једанпут недељно.

A

they go out, they're going out	izlaze	излазе
every	svaki, -a, -o	сваки, -а, -о

91

evening	večer G večeri f.	вече̄
Do Tom and John go out every evening?	Da li Toma i Jovan izlaze svake večeri?	Да ли Тома и Јован излазе свако вече?

B

they (masculine)	oni	они
they go, they're going	oni idu	они иду
usually	obično	обично
They go usually to the hotel Metropol.	Da, oni obično idu u hotel Metropol.	Да, они обично иду у хотел Метропол.

A

they are working, they work, they are engaged in some activity	oni rade	они раде
What do they do there?	Što oni rade tamo?	Шта они раде тамо?

B

nothing	ništa	ништа
They don't do anything.	Ne rade ništa.	Не раде ништа.
something	nešto	нешто
they drink, they are drinking	piju	пију
they are sitting	sjede	седе

they are conversing, talking	razgovaraju	разговарају
They drink something, sit and talk.	Nešto piju, sjede i razgovaraju.	Нешто пију, седе и разговарају.
they have	oni imaju	они имају
their own	svoj, svoja, svoje	свој, своја, своје
company, society	društvo	друштво
pleasant	ugodan, ugodna ugodno	пријатан, пријатна, пријатно
pleasantly	ugodno	пријатно
They have their own circle of friends and have a nice time.	Oni imaju svoje društvo i provode vrijeme ugodno.	Они имају своје друштво и проводе време пријатно.

A

going out		излазак
Is going out expensive here?		Да ли је излазак овде скуп?
is necessary	treba	треба
money	novac G nȏvca	нȏвац, нȏвца
a lot of money	mnogo novaca	много новаца
entertainment	razonoda	разонода

93

English	Latin (Croatian)	Cyrillic (Serbian)
Does entertainment take a lot of money here? ('is a lot of money necessary for entertainment')	Da li ovdje treba mnogo novaca za razonodu?	(Да ли овде треба много новаца за разоноду?)

B

| No, the theater is cheap. | Ne, kazalište je jeftino. | Није, позориште је јефтино. |
| And so are the movies ('movies also'). | Kino, također. | Биоскоп, такође. |

---

outside	vani	напољу
How's the weather outside?	Kakvo je vrijeme vani?	Какво је време напољу?
clear (of weather)	vedar, vedra, -o	ведар, ведра, -о
cloudy	oblačan, oblačna, -o	облачан, облачно, -о
The weather is nice and clear.	Vrijeme je lijepo i vedro.	Време је лепо и ведро.
The weather is cloudy.	Vrijeme je oblačno.	Време је облачно.
it falls	pada	пада
rain	kiša	киша
to rain	kišiti, kiši /kišjeti	кишити, киши

It's raining.   3ˋ2- 2ˋ1   3ˋ2-|2ˋ1
           Pada kiša.   Пада киша.
     or,   23ˊ1-   23ˌ ˍ1)
           Kiši.   (Киши.)

Juncture

Beginning with this unit, the single bar will be omitted when the juncture is also represented by a comma.

NOTES

Note 5.1 Verb: Present

I ja sada učim.   Toma i Jovan izlaze svako veče.

On uči srpskohrvatski.   Idemo u pozorište.

Mi učimo zajedno.   Oni obično idu u hotel Metropol.

Izlazite li negde uveče.   Oni imaju svoje društvo.

Serbo-Croatian verbs have endings for person and number. /účīm/ means 'I'm studying.' /-m/ indicates 'I'. The addition of /jȁ/ is a type of emphasis. The endings as illustrated above are:

-m	I	-mo	we
		-te	you
-zero	he, she, it	-ē	
		-ū	they
		-jū	

The /-te/ ending is for 'you' either plural or polite singular. The familiar second person ending is /-š/ : /účīš/. This is used to members of one's family, intimate friends, in addressing the Deity, etc. It should be avoided by the learner as its use implies too great familiarity. It should be noted, however, that it is used very commonly in rural areas as the normal way to address one person. (See /tȉ/, Note 4.1)

From the examples /učīm/, /ídēmo/, /znȁ/ we see that three vowels are possible before these endings. (These are usually long when the verb has primary stress.) Verbs having the vowel /i/ in the other forms (that is before /-m/, /-š/ etc.) have /-ē/ for 'they'; those having /e/ in the other forms have /ū/ for 'they'; those having /a/ have /-jū/ for 'they' (/ímām/ 'I have', /ímajū/ 'they have' - /a/ is always short before /-jū/. There are a few exceptions to this, such as /razúmēm/ - /razúmejū/.

Following are the forms of three typical verbs:

účĭm		ĭdēm		ímām	
účĭš		ĭdēš		ímāš	
účĭ		ĭdē		ímā	
učĭmo	/účĭmo	idémo	/ĭdēmo	imámo	/ímāmo
učĭte	/účĭte	idéte	/ĭdete	imáte	/ímāte
účē		ĭdū		ímajū	

The stress patterns vary. There are a few very frequent ones and also many which apply to only a few verbs. (Some of these patterns are discussed in Note 22.2.)

Following are verbs which have occured which pattern in the same way as the three given above (stress not being considered):

i	e	a
rȁdĭm	pútujēm	znȁm
góvorĭm	pĭjēm	pȁdām
próvodĭm	razúmijēm	ímām
ízlazĭm		razgóvārām
sèdĭm /sjèdĭm		

The verb /razúmēm/ has the third person plural ending like the verbs with /a/. The central dialect form is perfectly regular.

razúmēm	razumémo	razúmijēm	razúmijēmo
razúmēš	razuméte	razúmijēš	razumijēte
razúmē	razúmejū	razúmijē	razúmijū

All of the above verbs may be freely used in situations corresponding to English present progressive forms: 'I'm going, I'm eating, I'm working' etc.

Some English equivalents use the simple present: 'I know', 'I like', but these indicate a state of being, a continuing situation or quality. Nearly every Serbo-Croatian verb has two forms, one corresponding to the English progressive or state of being forms, the other indicating the termination of the action or its completion. All of the verbs discussed above are of the former, imperfective, type. Perfective verbs will be taken up in a later note. This is a matter of usage and is not regularly reflected in the form of the verb. Both types take the same endings.

Note 5.2 Adjective-Adverb Relationship: Ending /-o/

> Moj hotel je dobar.
>
> Hvala, dobro sam.
>
> Vi govorite dobro srpskohrvatski.

The adjective /dóbar/ has a neuter form /dóbro/. This has the same ending as the adverb /dóbro/, illustrated in the examples on the right. Many adverbs have the same ending as the neuter singular of the adjective, though many of these differ in stress from the adjective. Compare:

Adjective	(m. sg)	n. sg.	Adverb	
lȅp /lȉjep	beautiful	lȇpo /lȉjépo	lȅpo /lȉjepo	beautifully, nicely
r̀dav	bad	r̀davo	r̀davo	badly
údoban	comfortable	údobno	údobno	comfortably
lȅnj/lȉjen	lazy	lȇnjo /lȉjéno	lȅnjo /lȉjeno	lazily
rȇdak /rijédak	rare	rȇtko /rijétko	rȇtko /rȉjétko	rarely, seldom
čȅst	frequent	čȇsto	čȅsto	frequently
prȉjatan	pleasant	prȉjatno	prȉjatno	pleasantly
óbičan	ordinary, customary	óbično	óbično	ordinarily, usually

There may be other differences between the adjective and the adverb:

mȁlī	small	mȁlō	màlo	a little bit

The adjective and adverb will often be introduced together in the build-up in later units.

Where the adjective neuter ending is /-e/ (or -ě), the adverb is also /-e/:

čèšćī   more frequent   čèšćě   čèšće   more frequently

The adverb ending /-o/ (/-e/) si only one of many adverb formatives.

GRAMMATICAL DRILL

GD 5.1   Substitution-Correlation Drill
GD 5.1.1   Substitution-Correlation Drill with Negative Transforms

     Following is a substitution-correlation drill with negative transforms.
The key words on the left include pronouns in parentheses. The parentheses
indicate that the verb is to be changed to this person but that the pronoun
itself is not to be used. The first drill is given in full.

Putuje<u>m</u> često u Zagreb i Split.   /za

(ti)	(mi)	oni
on	otac i ja	Toma i Jovan
g. Jović	vi	one
ona	vi i Toma	majka i žena

	Putuje<u>m</u> često u Zagreb i Split.	Ne putujem često u Zagreb i Split.
(ti)	Putuje<u>š</u> često u Zagreb i Split.	Ne putuješ često u Zagreb i Split.
on	<u>On</u> putuje često u Zagreb i Split.	On ne putuje često u Zagreb i Split.
g. Jović	<u>G. Jović</u> putuje često u Zagreb i Split.	G. Jović ne putuje često u Zagreb i Split.
ona	<u>Ona</u> putuje često u Zagreb i Split.	Ona ne putuje često u Zagreb i Split.
(mi)	Putujemo često u Zagreb i Split.	Ne putujemo često u Zagreb i Split.

otac i ja	<u>Otac i ja</u> putujemo često u Zagreb i Split.	Otac i ja ne putujema često u Zagreb i Split.
vi	<u>Vi</u> putujete često u Zagreb i Split.	Vi ne putujete često u Zagreb i Split.
vi i Toma	<u>Vi i Toma</u> putujete često u Zagreb i Split.	Vi i Toma ne putujete često u Zagreb i Split.
oni	<u>Oni</u> putuju često u Zagreb i Split.	Oni ne putuju često u Zagreb i Split.
Toma i Jovan	<u>Toma i Jovan</u> putuju često u Zagreb i Split.	Toma i Jovan ne putuju često u Zagreb i Split.
one	<u>One</u> putuju često u Zagreb i Split.	One ne putuju često u Zagreb i Split.
majka i žena	<u>Majka i žena</u> putuju često u Zagreb i Split.	Majka i žena ne putuju često u Zagreb i Split.

The following sentences are to be drilled with the same substitutions and transforms:

Provodim vreme ovde prijatno.   /vrijeme ovdje

Govorim engleski i srpskohrvatski dobro.

Idem u pozorište otprilike jedanput mesečno.   /kazalište, mjesečno

Izlazim svako veče u hotel Metropol.   /Idem svake večeri

Imam svoje društvo.

Razumem nemački dobro.   /Razumijem njemački

Učim francuski mnogo.

Make the indicated substitutions with negative transforms:

<u>Toma</u> uči srpskohrvatski svaki dan.

(ja)	(mi)
Toma i ja	vi i vaš prijatelj
Zora i njen muž	g. i g-đa Smit

Further sentences for drill according to the above pattern are:

Moj prijatelj govori dobro francuski.

Zora razume nemački.   /razumije njemački

On provodi vreme prijatno.   /vrijeme ugodno

G. Smit putuje retko u Zagreb.   /rijetko

GD 5.1.2   Substitution with Plural Transforms

     The following drill is substitution with plural transforms. The initial substitution is that of the singular form. The plural of this is to be supplied by the student without further cue.

Izlazim retko uveče.   /rijetko uveče

    (ti)

    on

    ona

	Izlazim retko uveče.	Izlazimo retko uveče.
(ti)	Izlaziš retko uveče.	Izlazite retko uveče.
on	On izlazi retko uveče.	Oni izlaze retko uveče.
ona	Ona izlazi retko uveče.	One izlaze retko uveče.

     The following sentences are to be drilled with the same substitutions and transforms:

Govorim i razumem srpskohrvatski, ali rđavo.   /razumijem

Idem u bioskop možda jedanput nedeljno.   /nedjeljno

Imam svoje društvo.

Putujem u Zagreb, ali ne često.   /za

Razumem francuski dobro, iako ne govorim dobro.   /razumijem

Izlazim negde svako veče.   /Idem negdje svake večeri.

GD 5.1.3 Substitution-correlation drill with pronoun transform. Each sentence of the following drill is to be repeated replacing the subject by the appropriate pronoun.

G. Jović radi mnogo.   On radi mnogo.

    g-đa Smit   g. Smit i ja

    Toma i Jovan   g. i g-đa Smit

    g-đa i g-ca Smit   g-ca Smit i njena majka

g-đa Smit	G-đa Smit radi mnogo.	Ona radi mnogo.
g. Smit i ja	G. Smit i ja radimo mnogo.	Mi radimo mnogo.
Toma i Jovan	Toma i Jovan rade mnogo.	Oni rade mnogo.
g. i g-đa Smit	G. i g-đa Smit rade mnogo.	Oni rade mnogo.
g-đa i g-ca Smit	G-đa i g-ca Smit rade mnogo.	One rade mnogo.
g-ca Smit i njena majka	G-ca Smit i njena majka rade mnogo.	One rade mnogo.

The following sentences are to be drilled with the same substitutions and transforms:

G. Smit zna dobro srpskohrvatski.

G. Jović razume dobro engleski, ali govori rđavo.   /razumije

Toma sedi, nešto pije i razgovara.   /sjedi

G. Jović ide u pozorište, ali retko.   /kazalište, rijetko

G. Smit ide u bioskop često.   /kino

G. Jović ima svoje društvo.

G. Smit provodi vreme prijatno.   /vrijeme ugodno

Make the indicated substitutions with pronoun transforms:

Toma i Jovan idu u bioskop jedanput nedeljno.

    g. Jović i ja   g-đa Smit

    moj prijatelj   g-đa i g. Jović

g-đa i g-ca Smit   vi i vaša gospođa

Further sentences for drill according to the above pattern are:

Moj prijatelj i njegova žena izlaze vrlo mnogo. /jako

G-đa Jović i njena majka svako jutro sede, razgovaraju i nešto piju.   /sjede

Toma i Jovan razumeju francuski, ali rđavo govore.   /razumiju

Moja žena i ja idemo u pozorište otprilike jedanput mesečno.   /kazalište,
                                                                        mjesečno

Vi i vaš prijatelj govorite dobro srpskohrvatski.

Toma i Zora uče dobro nemački.   /njemački

GD 5.2   Question and Answer Drill
GD 5.2.1   Informational Answers

    Substitution-Correlation Drill
    Use the items listed as the subject of both question and answer.

Gde izlaz<u>ite</u> uveče?   /Gdje idete   Obično izlazim u bioskop.   /idem,
  uvečer.   kino

Kako provod<u>ite</u> vreme ovde? /vrijeme   Provodim vreme vrlo prijatno.   /vrijeme
                              ovdje   ugodno
Kako govor<u>ite</u> srpskohrvatski?   Ne govorim dobro, ja sada učim.

Kako razum<u>ete</u> nemački i francuski?   Nemački razumem dobro, a francuski
  /razumijete njemački   rđavo.   /Njemački razumijem

Šta rad<u>ite</u> uveče? /Što, uvečer   Sedim i učim srpskohrvatski. /Sjedim

(t1)   on   ona   vi i vaša gospođa   oni
        Jovan   Zora   vi i vaša majka   Toma i Jovan
        g. Smit   g-ca Smit   g. i g-đa Smit
        vaš muž   vaša supruga   vaša žena i majka

                            one
                            g-đa i g-ca Jović
                            vaša majka i žena

GD 5.2.2 Yes and No Answers

Da li putuje<u>te</u> često u Zagreb i   Da, putujem.
  Split?   /za
                                                Ne, ne putujem.

                                                Da, putujem vrlo često u Zagreb i Split. /za

                                                Ne, ne putujem često u Zagreb i Split. /za

(ti)   on   ona   vi i vaša gospođa   oni
        Jovan   Zora   vaša majka i vi   Toma i Jovan
        g. Smit   g-ca Smit   g. i g-đa Smit
        Zorin muž   Tomina žena   Toma i njegov
                                                              prijatelj

                            one
                            g-đa i g-ca Jović
                            vaša majka i supruga
                            njegova žena i njena majka

The sentences for drill:

Da li govorite francuski?

Da li idete često u pozorište?   /kazalište

Da li izlazite uveče?   /uvečer

Da li imate svoje društvo?

Da li razumete nemački?   /razumijete njemački

Da li učite srpskohrvatski?

Da li znate gde je hotel Metropol?   /gdje

Repeat the above drills, using the pattern:

        Putujete li često u Zagreb i Split?   /za

GD 5.3 Question and Answer with Prompt

Oni (Toma i Jovan) idu često u bioskop.   Da li Toma i Jovan idu često u
  /kino   bioskop? /kino

Oni izlaze negde uveče. /idu negdje   Da li oni izlaze negde uveče? /idu
  uvečer   negdje uvečer

Mi ne izlazimo nigde uveče.   Da li vi izlazite negde uveče?
  /idemo nigdje uvečer

Oni (Toma i Jovan) mnogo putuju.   Da li Toma i Jovan mnogo putuju?

Oni provode ovde vreme prijatno.   Kako oni provode vreme ovde?
  /ovdje vrijeme ugodno   /vrijeme ovdje

Oni uveče sede, nešto piju i razgo- Šta oni rade uveče?   /Što, uvečer
  varaju.   /uvečer sjede

Gospodin i gospođa Smit uče srpsko- Da li gospodin i gospođa Smit uče
  hrvatski?   srpskohrvatski?

Ja sam lenj i ne radim ništa uveče. Šta vi radite uveče?   /Što, uvečer
  /lijen , uvečer

Toma i Jovan imaju svoje društvo.   Da li Toma i Jovan imaju svoje
                                       društvo?

Oni malo uče i malo znaju.   Da li oni znaju nešto?

Oni (Gospodin i gospođa Smit)   Da li g. i g-đa Smit govore srpsko-
  razumeju prilično srpskohrvatski,   hrvatski?
  ali ne govore dobro.   /razumiju

Jovan i Toma idu retko u pozorište. Da li Jovan i Toma idu često u
  /rijetko, kazalište   pozorište? /kazalište

Vreme je lepo i vedro. /vrijeme, lijepo Kakvo je vreme napolju? /vrijeme,
Napolju je oblačno.   vani

Još pada kiša.   Da li još pada kiša?

GD 5.4 Conversations - Razgovori
GD 5.4.1

                    A   B

Kako provodite vrijeme ovdje, g. Smite? Ja mnogo radim i putujem.

Gdje putujete?   Putujem obično u Zagreb i Split.

Da li putujete tamo često?   Da, putujem.

Kako govorite srpskohrvatski?   Govorim prilično slabo.

A kako razumijete?   Razumijem prilično dobro.

To je dobro.   Hvala.

Како проводите време овде, г. Смите?   Ја много радим и путујем.

Где путујете?   Путујем обично у Загреб и Сплит.

Да ли путујете тамо често?   Да, путујем.

Како говорите српскохрватски?   Говорим прилично слабо.

А како разумете?   Разумем прилично добро.

То је добро.   Хвала.

GD 5.4.2

Da li izlazite negdje uvečer?   Da, izlazim.

Gdje izlazite?   Idemo u kazalište.

Da li idete često u kazalište?   Ne. Idemo otprilike jedanput ili
                                            dvaput mjesečno.

Da li idete u kino?   Da, idemo.

Da li idete često u kino?   Da, idemo jedanput ili dvaput nedjeljno.

Vrlo dobro.

Да ли излазите негде увече?   Да, излазим.

Где излазите?   Идемо у позориште.

Да ли идете често у позориште?   Не. Идемо отприлике једанпут или
                                            двапут месечно.

Да ли идете у биоскоп?   Да, идемо.

Да ли идете често у биоскоп?   Да, идемо једанпут или двапут недељно.

Врло добро.

GD 5.4.3

Šta radite uvečer, gospodine Smite?   Obično sjedimo i nešto radimo ili
                                            razgovaramo.

Što radite?   Ja učim srpskohrvatski, a moja žena
                                               francuski.

Vi govorite dobro srpskohrvatski.   Da razumijem prilično dobro, ali još ne
                                               govorim dobro.

Da li znate francuski?   Da, znam prilično dobro.

Kako govori vaša gospođa francuski?   I ona govori dobro.

Da li vi učite francuski?   Ne, sada ne učim.

Do viđenja, g. Smite.   Do viđenja, g. Joviću.

Шта радите увече, господине Смите?   Обично седимо и нешто радимо или
                                               разговарамо.

Шта радите?   Ја учим српскохрватски, а моја жена
                                               француски.

Ви говорите добро српскохрватски.   Ја разумем прилично добро, али још не
                                               говорим добро.

Да ли знате француски?   Да, знам прилично добро.

Како говори ваша госпођа француски?   И она говори добро.

Да ли ви учите француски?   Не, сада не учим.

До виђена, г. Смите.   До виђена, г. Јовићу.

GD 5.4   Homework - Domaći zadatak

GD 5.4.1 Re-write the Conversations changing the subject of the verb in the
first sentence (and correspondingly throughout) to:

>   Conversation 1   vaš prijatelj
>
>   Conversation 2   Toma i Jovan
>
>   Conversation 3   Toma i njegova žena

GD 5.4.2 Re-write the following questions using the items in parentheses to
the right of each as the subject. Write out short affirmative and negative
answers to the first five, long affirmative and negative answers to the second
five.

Da li putujete često?   (Toma i Jovan)

Da li provodite vreme ovde prijatno?   (g. i g-đa Smit)

Da li idete često u pozorište?   (g-đa i g-ca Smit)

Da li govorite francuski?   (vaš prijatelj i njegova žena)

Da li izlazite uveče?   (Toma i njegova žena)

Da li znate gde je hotel Metropol?   (vaš otac i majka)

Da li sedite i razgovarate uveče?   (Toma i Jovan)

Da li imate lepo društvo ovde?   (vaša majka i žena)

Da li razumete dobro srpskohrvatski?   (g. i g-đa Smit)

Da li učite mnogo?   (g. Smit i njegov prijatelj)

UNIT 6

Basic Sentences - Osnovne rečenice

At the Restaurant	U restoranu	У ресторану

A

| to wish, want, I wish, want | Željeti, želīm | желети, желим |
| What do you want, sir? | Što želite, gospodine? | Шта желите, господине? |

B

| to eat an evening meal; I'm eating an evening meal | večerati, véčerām | вечерати, вечерам |
| I want to eat. | Želim večerati. | Желим да вечерам. |

A

| What do you want to eat? | Što želite večerati? | Шта желите да вечерате? |

B

to eat, I'm eating	jèsti, jèdēm	јести, једем
soup	jùha	супа
veal (adj.)	télećī, -ā, -ē	телећи, -а, -е
meat	mȇso	месо
if	àko	ако
black	cȓn, cȓna, cȓno;	црн, црна, црно;
	cȓnī, -ā, -ō	црни, -а, -о

bread	krùh	хле̏б
some black bread	cȓnog krùha	цр̏ног хле̏ба
I want to eat, (/I'd like [some]) soup, veal, and, if you have [any], some black bread.	Želîm juhu, teleće meso i, ako imate crnog kruha.	Желим да једем супу, теле̑ће месо, и ако имате црни хле̑б.

A

What does your friend want?	Što želi vaš prijatelj? #	Шта жели ваш пријатељ? #

B

coffee	kàva	ка̀фа
He'd like [some] coffee.	On želi kavu.	Он жели кафу.
to give, that I give	dàti, da dȁm	да̀ти, да да̏м
give	dȁjte	да̏јте
glass	čàša	ча̀ша
water	vóda	вода
of water	vódē	во̑де̄
you	vȁs, vas	ва̏с, вас
Please give him coffee and a glass of water.	Dajte mu kavu i čašu vode, prosim.	Да̑јте му кафу и ча̏шу во̑де, мо̑лӣм вас.
thirsty	žédan, žédna, -o	жедан, жедна, -дно

109

/ hungry	/ gládan, gládna, -o	гла̑дан, гла̑дна, -дно
He's thirsty.	On je žedan.	Он је же̏дан.

A

sweeter; with more sugar	slàđī, -ā, -ē	сла̏ђи, -а̄, -е̄
bitterer, with less sugar	gòrčī, -ā, -ō	го̏рчи, -а̄, -е̄
What kind of coffee do you want, sir, with more or less sugar?	Kakvu kavu želite, gospodine? Slađu ili gorču?	Какву кафу желите, господине, слађу или горчу?

C

completely	pótpuno	по̀тпуно
quite	sàsvīm	сасви̏м
bitter	górak, górka, -o	го̀рак, го̀рка, -о
sweet	sládak, slátka, -o	сла̀дак, сла̀тка, -о
Without sugar, please. I don't drink coffee with sugar.	Sasvim gorku, molim. Ja ne pijem slatku kavu.	Потпуно горку, молим. Ја не пијем слатку кафу.

B

in the morning	ùjutro	у̏јутру
What do you drink in the morning?	Što pijete ujutro?	Шта пијете ујутру?

C

white	bȉjel, bijéla, -o,	бе̏о, бе́ла, -о;
	bȉjelī, -ā, -ō	бе̏ли, -а, -о

| ('I drink') café au lait. | Pȉjem bȉjelu kavu. | Пи́jем бе̏лу ка́фу. |

B

| when | kàd /kàda | ка̏д |

| When do Tom and John drink coffee? | Kada pȉju Toma i Jovan kavu? | Ка̏д пи́jу Тома и Jован ка́фу? |

C

| strong | jȁk, jáka, jáko | jа̏к, jа́ка, jа́ко |
| tea | čàj, pl. čàjevi | ча̏j ча̏jеви |

| They drink strong, bitter coffee or tea in the evening. | Oni pȉju uvečer jáku, gorku kavu ili čaj. | Они пи́jу уве́че jа́ку, горку ка́фу или ча̏j. |

| /never | /nȉkada | никад |

| /They never drink coffee in the evening. | /Oni nȉkada ne pȉju kavu uvečer. | Они никад не пи́jу ка́фу уве́че. |

B

| waiter | kónobār G konobára (Cr.) | ке̏лнер |
| this | óvāj, óvā, óvō | ова̏j, ова, ово |

111

cold	hlȃdan, hlȃdna, -o	хла́дан, хла́дна, -о
Waiter, this coffee is cold.	Konobar, ova kava je hladna.	Келнер, ова кафа је хладна.
to like, I like	vóljeti, vòlīm	волети, волим
I don't like	nè volīm	не волим
I don't like cold coffee.	Ja ne volīm hladnu kavu.	Ја не волим хладну кафу.
to bring, that I bring	dónijeti, da donésēm	донети, да донесем
bring!	donésite	донесите
to me	mèni, mi	мени, ми
other, second	drùgī, -ā, -ō	други, -а, -о
hot	vrȕć, vrúća, vrúće	врућ, врућа, вруће
Please bring me another hot [cup of] coffee.	Molim donesite mi drugu, vruću kavu.	Молим донесите ми другу, врућу кафу.

A

immediately, at once	òdmāh	одмах
Yes sir, right away.	Prosim, odmāh.	Молим, одмах.

B

only	sàmo	само

beer	pȉvo	пиво
wine	víno	вино
I drink only cold beer, wine, and water, (/but) not coffee.	Ja pijem samo hladno pivo, vino i vodu, (ali) ne kavu.	Ја пијем само хладно пиво, вино и воду, не кафу.
(Later)	(Kàsnijē)	(Касније)

B

one	jédan, jédna, jédno	један, једна, једно
Waiter, please bring me ('yet') another [cup of] coffee.	Konobar, donesite mi molim još jednu kavu.	Келнер, донесите ми молим још једну кафу.
(Later)	(Kasnije)	(Касније)
to pay, that I pay	plátiti, da plàtīm	платити, да платим
The bill please. ('Please that I pay' /'Please to pay').	Prosim, platiti.	Молим, да платим.

Note: The numbers indicating pitch are omitted in Units 6 following unless an unfamiliar pattern occurs.

NOTES

Note 6.1   Noun: Accusative Singular

Note 6.1.1 Noun: Accusative Singular Form

	Nominative	Accusative
Masculine	hleb	Želim da jedem hleb.
	čaj	Oni piju čaj.
	bioskop	U bioskop idemo češće.
	hotel	Oni obično idu u hotel.
	jezik	Govorite li neki stran(i) jezik?
Neuter	meso	Želim da jedem teleće meso.
	pivo	Ja pijem samo hladno pivo i vino.
	vino	
	vreme	Kako provodite vreme ovde.
	pozorište /kazalište	Idemo u pozorište. /kazalište
	društvo	Oni imaju svoje društvo.
Feminine	supa	Želim da jedem supu.
	juha	Želio bih juhu.
	kafa (kava)	Dajte mu kafu (/kavu) i čašu vode.
	čaša	
	voda	Ja pijem samo vodu.

The object of a verb is most frequently in the accusative case. Examples of objects in the accusative both of verbs and of the preposition /u/ 'into', are given above (see also below). The masculine nouns shown all have the same form for both nominative and accusative singular. Note, however, that all of these nouns designate things which do not have animal life. Such, inanimate, masculine nouns have the same form for nominative and accusative singular. Masculine nouns denoting people or animals of any sort (things having animal life) are known as 'animate' nouns. The accusative singular of such nouns is discussed in Note 12.1. Suffice it to say here that such nouns have a suffix /-a/ in the accusative: N /gospódin/, A /gospódina/.

Neuter nouns always have the same form for nominative and accusative. Note /vreme/ 'time, weather'. This noun has special forms which will be taken up later.

Feminine nouns with nominative singular in /-a/ have /-u/ in the accusative singular. Feminine nouns of the /nòć/ type have, with a few exceptions, the same form for nominative and accusative singular. Without exception nouns of this type which end in a consonant in the nominative have the same form for the accusative. /nòć/ is the only noun of this type which has occurred. They will be referred to as feminine /-i/ nouns (for reasons to appear later).

In summary:

	Masculine Inanimate	Masculine Animate	Neuter	Feminine	Feminine
Nom.	jezik	gospodin	meso	stanica	noć
Acc.	jezik	gospodina	meso	stanicu	noć

Note 6.1.2   Noun: Use of accusative

a.   Oni piju čaj.

b.   Idemo u pozorište.

The accusative case may be used as (a) the object of a verb of (b) the object of a preposition. It is also used in expressions indicating duration of time (equivalent to sentences such as 'he was there a month', 'I stayed a year' etc.). The only time expression with the accusative which has occurred is /laku noć/, 'a light night!'.

The accusative with the preposition /u/ indicates direction towards, often literally spatial, as /u pozorište/ 'to (that is, into) the theater'. Compare also /Mi putujemo često u Zagreb i Split/, that is 'into Zagreb and Split'. (Note, however, that /za/ 'to, for' is used here in the other dialect.) The preposition /na/ with the accusative indicates direction towards in a way very parallel to /u/, /na/ plus accusative usually meaning 'onto'.

Another example of /za/ with the accusative is in /To je dobro za vaš srpskohrvatski/, with the meaning 'for'.

What case follows a given preposition and what meaning the combination
has must be learned. The object of a verb may also be in another case, as
/crnog kruha/ in the Basic Sentences. Here the latin version uses the genitive
(Note 11.1), while the cyrillic uses the accusative.

Note 6.2 Adjective: Accusative Singular

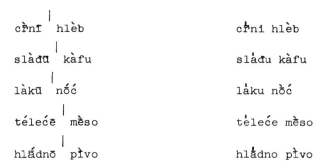

crnī hlèb	crni hlèb
slàđu kàfu	slàđu kàfu
làkū nőć	làku nőć
télećē mèso	téleće mèso
hlắdnō pȉvo	hlắdno pȉvo

These are examples of adjectives plus noun in the accusative. On the
left the adjectives are stressed as if said by themselves, so that each adjective plus noun group is made up of two phrases. This shows the stresses and
vowel lengths of the adjectives when fully differentiated. When the adjective
has secondary stress the endings, being unstressed, are all short.

It may be seen from these few examples that adjectives modifying inanimate
masculine nouns (/hlèb/) or neuter nouns (/mèso/, /pȉvo/) have the same form as
in the nominative. (The endings with animate masculine nouns are discussed in
Note 12.2.) Adjectives modifying feminine nouns (of either type) have /-u/
(or /-ū/) in the accusative singular.

Some of the adjectives introduced in this unit are:

	m.		f.		n.	
indefinite	bèo	/bȉjel	béla	/bijéla	bélo	/bijélo
definite	bèlī	/bȉjelī	bèlā	/bȉjelā	bèlō	/bȉjelō
indefinite	cȑn		cȑna		cȑno	
definite	cȑnī		cȑnā		cȑnō	
indefinite	gőrak		gőrka		gőrko	
definite	gòrkī		gòrkā		gòrkō	

indefinite	hládan	hládna	hládno
definite	hlȁdnī	hlȁdnā	hlȁdnō
indefinite	vrȗć	vrúća	vrúće
	vrȗćī	vrȗća	vrȗćē
definite	gòrčī	gòrčā	gòrčē
only	slàdī	slàdā	slàdē
Pronominal	óvāj	óvā	óvō

Note the variation of stress between indefinite and definite forms.

Note 6.3 Verb: /žélīm/ and /vòlīm/

    Želim da jedem.

    Ne volim hladnu kafu.

    /žélīm/ means 'I want, I wish, I desire'. /vòlīm/ means 'I like, I prefer'. The normal English equivalent of /žélīm/ is often 'I'd like', but this should not be confused with 'I like', /vòlīm/.

Note 6.4 Verb: Infinitive

    Žélīm večerati   Žélīm da večerām

    As noted in Unit 1, there are some differences of grammatical construction between eastern and central Serbo-Croatian. One of the most common is illustrated above. The central dialect uses the infinitive after words such as 'want', similar to English 'I want to eat dinner'. The eastern dialect uses a clause intorduced by /da/, 'I want that I eat dinner'.

    The infinitive is the form used when talking about the verb (e.g. 'the present of [the verb] /jèsti/') and is the form which is used in dictionaries. Beginning with this unit the infinitive will be given whenever a new verb is introduced. The first person singular of the verb will also be given, as the forms are often not predictable, one from the other. Other forms will be given in the notes as necessary.

If a verb is perfective (see Note 5.1), /da/ will be used before the present tense form. This indicates that the perfective present rarely occurs without some clause introducer such as /da/. (It does not mean that it always follows /da/.)

The following list gives the infinitive of most of the verbs which have been used in units 1-6, as well as the first person singular and the third person plural of the present. The imperative is given when it has occurred in the units.

	Infinitive	1st. Sg.	3 Pl.	Imperative
to be	bìti	sam /jésam	su /jèsu	
to bring	dóněti	da donésěm	donésů	donésite
to be speaking	govóriti	góvorīm	góvorě	
to be going	ìći	ìděm	ìdū	ìdite /ìdite
to have	ìmati	ìmām	ìmajū	
to be going out	ìzlaziti	ìzlazīm	ìzlazě	
to excuse	izvíniti /izvínjeti	da ìzvīnīm	ìzvīně	izvínite
to excuse	izvóleti /izvóljeti	da ìzvolīm	ìzvolě	izvólte /izvólite
to be drinking	pìti	pìjěm	pìjū	
to be travelling	putóvati	pútujěm	pútujū	
to be working	ráditi	ràdīm	ràdě	
to be conversing	razgovárati	razgóvārām	razgováraju	
to understand	razúmeti /razúmjeti	razúmēm /razúmijěm	razúmejū /razúmijū	
to be sitting	sédeti /sjéditi	sédīm /sjédīm	sédě /sjédě	sédite /sjédite
to sit down	sèsti /sjèsti	da sèdněm /da sjedněm	sèdnū /sjèdnū	
to be learning	účiti	účīm	účě	

to be eating an evening meal	véčerati	véčerām	véčerajū
to like	vóleti /vóljeti	vòlīm	vòlē
to know	znàti	znȁm	znàjū

GRAMMATICAL DRILL

The conversations will be the only drills given with central dialect variants from Unit 6 on, though vocabulary items are used for substitution in some drills. Obviously the instructor may use either dialect in going through the drills.

GD 6.1 Controlled Adaptation Drill

In this drill the nouns listed for substitution are all given in the nominative form. The noun used in the sentence is given at the head of the list, also in the nominative, to show whether or not any change of form is necessary. Some place names are added for additional practice.

Moj prijatelj želi da ide u <u>restoran.</u>

<u>restoran</u>
hotel
Zagreb
Beograd
pozorište
Skoplje
Sarajevo
selo

Moj prijatelj želi da ide u <u>ambasadu.</u>

<u>ambasada</u>
Ljubljana
Amerika
Jugoslavija

Ja volim <u>moj hotel.</u>

<u>moj hotel</u>

Ne volim <u>moj hotel.</u>

mali restoran
crno pivo
belo vino

                                                        crni hleb

                                                        vruć čaj

                                                        bijeli kruh

Ja volim <u>vruću kafu.</u>   <u>vruća kafa</u>

Ne volim <u>vruću kafu.</u>   hladna voda slađa kafa

                                                        gorča kafa

                                                        velika soba

                                                        naša ambasada

Dajte mi još <u>jedan čaj.</u>   <u>jedan čaj</u>

                                                        jedno pivo

                                                        jedno belo vino

Dajte mi još <u>jednu kafu.</u>   <u>jedna kafa</u>

                                                        jedna slađa kafa

                                                        jedna gorča kafa

                                                        jedna potpuno gorka kafa

                                                        jedna čaša vode

GD 6.2 Adaptation Drill with negative transform

    Make the substitutions indicated, changing the form when necessary, then
give the negative of the statement.

Toma i Jovan žele da idu u <u>restoran.</u>   soba   Beograd

                                                 hotel   Zagreb

                                                 selo   Skoplje

                                                 ambasada   Ljubljana

                                                 bioskop   Sarajevo

                                                               Jugoslavija

Oni vole <u>svoj hotel.</u>   mali restoran   vruć čaj

                                                 velika soba   naša ambasada

                                                 vruća kafa   njihovo pozorište

GD 6.3   Substitution Correlation Drill

GD 6.3.1 Adjective substitution

Ova kafa je <u>hladna</u>.	Ja volim <u>hladnu</u> kafu.
dobar	gorak
sladak	vruć
jak	

Ovo pivo je <u>vruće</u>.	Ja ne volim <u>vruće</u> pivo.
sladak	slab
jak	hladan
rđav	

Ovaj čaj je <u>hladan</u>.	Ja ne volim <u>hladan</u> čaj.
gorak	vruć
rđav	jak

<u>Moja</u> kafa je slatka.	Ja ne pijem slatku kafu.
<u>Moje</u> pivo nije hladno.	Ja ne pijem vruće pivo.
Moj čaj je gorak.	Ja pijem sladak čaj.
vaš	njihov
naš	
njegov	Tomin
njen	Zorin

GD 6.3.2 Verb subject substitution

Substitution of verb subject with negative transform. Use each of the subjects indicated, changing the verb as necessary.

<u>Ja</u> volim svoj (/moj) hotel.

on	ona	mi	vi	oni
Jovan	moja žena	otac i ja	vi i vaša gospođa	Toma i Jovan
otac	majka	moja žena i ja	vi i Jovan	g. i g-đa Jović

             ti   one
                       moja majka i žena
                       g-đa i g-ca Smit

Moj prijatelj pije kafu ujutru.

             majka   ti
             vi   oni
             Tomina žena   vi i vaša žena
             moja žena i ja   on i njegov otac
             Toma i Jovan   g-đa i g-ca Jović

Use the items listed as subjects of the verb in each sentence, changing both verbs to the correct form. Then give the negative transform of the sentence. For example:

Želim da idem u restoran.

G-ca Jović želi da ide u restoran.

G-ca Jović ne želi da ide u restoran.

Želim da idem u restoran.

             on   (mi)
             ona   moja majka i ja
             vaša majka   oni
             vi   g. i g-đa Jović
             vi i vaš otac   one

GD 6.3.3 Verb substitution (/želeti/, /voleti/)

In this drill the underlined verb phrase is to be changed in the next sentence. The Serbo-Croatian of the latter is to be covered and the cue is given by the next English sentence. The drill is on the distinction between the verbs /želeti/ 'to want to' and /voleti/ 'to like, prefer'.

Moj prijatelj želi jaku crnu kafu.	My friend would like a strong black [cup of] coffee.
On voli jaku crnu kafu.	He likes strong black coffee.
Toma i Jovan piju jaku crnu kafu.	Tom and John drink strong black coffee.

Toma i Jovan vole jaku crnu kafu.	Tom and John like strong black coffee.
Oni žele jaku crnu kafu.	They would like strong black coffee.
Moja žena voli da ide u pozorište.	My wife likes to go to the theater.
Ona želi da ide u pozorište.	She'd like to go to the theater.
I ja želim da idem u pozorište.	I'd like to go to the theater, too.
Ja takođe volim pozorište.	I also like the theater.

GD 6.4   Questions and Answers - Pitanja i odgovori
GD 6.4.1 Informational Answers
            Substitution-Correlation Drill

This is a pair drill. Change both the question and the answer as indicated
by the substitutions indicated.

1	2
Gde idete?	Idem u našu ambasadu.

```
        on.................svoja soba
        vi i gospođa.......moja soba
        oni................restoran
        Toma i Jovan.......Jovanova soba
        g. i. g-đa Jović...bioskop
```

1	2
Gde putuju g. i g-đa Smit?	Oni putuju u Jugoslaviju.

```
        vaš prijatelj..............Skoplje
        Tomina majka...............Ljubljana
        vaš otac i majka...........Dalmacija
        vaša majka i žena..........Sarajevo
        vaša žena i njena majka....Beograd
        vi.........................nigde
```

1	2
Gde izlazite uveče?	Obično idem u pozorište.

```
        g. i g-đa Smit......bioskop
        Toma...............hotel Metropol
        Zora i njen muž.....nigde
```

123

Šta pijete ujutru?   Pijem kafu.

       vaša gospođa.........crna kafa

       Tomin otac..........bela kafa

       Zora................vruć čaj

       vaš otac i majka.....topal čaj

Kakav hotel imate?   Imam dobar hotel.

       restoran......oni

       soba..........g. i g-đa Smit

       kupatilo......vi i gospođa

Kad pijete kafu?   Pijem uveče.

       Zorin otac............čaj

       Tomina majka.........bela kafa

       Zora i njen otac......pivo

       g-đa i g-ca Jović.....belo vino

     Make the substitutions as indicated. The adjectives to be used in the answers are given in parentheses.

Kakvu kafu pijete?   Pijem belu kafu.

       čaj   (jak)........Toma

       pivo   (crn)........Zora

       vino   (beo)........Toma i Zora

       pivo   (hladan).....Zora i njen otac

       vino   (crn)........Zora i njena majka

GD 6.4.2   Yes and No Answers

     Make the indicated substitutions.

Da li (vi) idete često u pozorište?   Da, idem.

                                             Ne, ne idem.

                                             Da, idem često u pozorište.

                                             Ne, ne idem često u pozorište.

```
Toma.........................kafana
vi i gospođa..................bioskop
vaš prijatelj i njegova žena....selo
g. i g-đa Jović...............Zagreb
```

$$\overset{1}{\underline{\text{Da li (vi) putuj}\underline{\text{ete}}}} \text{ često u } \overset{2}{\underline{\text{Dalmaciju}}}?$$

Da li (vi) putuj**ete** često u Dalmaciju? Da, putujem.

Ne, ne putujem.

Da, putujem često u Dalmaciju.

Ne, ne putujem često u Dalmaciju.

```
g. Smit....................Sarajevo
Zora i njen muž.............Makedonija
vi i g. Jović..............Bosna
Zora i njena majka.........Hercegovina
Toma i njegov prijatelj.....Crna Gora
```

GD 6.5 Question and Answer Drill with Prompt

Želim da pijem crnu kafu.	Šta želite da pijete?
Ja pijem slatku kafu.	Kakvu kafu pijete?
Oni (piju jak čaj).	Kakav čaj oni piju?
Mi želimo belo vino.	Kakvo vino želite?
On (Moj prijatelj) voli crnu kafu.	Da li vaš prijatelj voli crnu kafu?
I ja volim crnu kafu.	A da li vi volite crnu kafu?
Ja pijem kafu ujutru.	Kad pijete kafu? /Šta pijete ujutru?
Moja kafa je dobra.	Kakva je vaša kafa? Da li je dobra?
I moj čaj je dobar.	A kakav je vaš čaj? Da li je dobar?
Moja žena pije slatku kafu.	Kakvu kafu pije vaša gospođa? /Da li vaša gospođa pije slatku kafu?
On (Moj prijatelj) želi da pije pivo.	Šta želi da pije vaš prijatelj?
I ja želim da pijem pivo.	A šta vi želite da pijete?
Ja ne volim hladnu kafu.	Da li vi volite hladnu kafu?
Ova kafa je hladna. Donesite mi drugu kafu.	Šta želite, gospodine?

Donesite mi još jedno pivo.   Da li želite još jedno pivo?

Donesite mi jedan vruć čaj.   Da li želite još nešto, gospodine?

/Ne želim ništa, hvala.

Ja sam žedan. Želim da pijem   Da li ste žedni? Želite li da pijete
    nešto.   nešto?

/Nisam žedan. Ne želim da pijem
    ništa.

On (Jovan) je gladan i žedan.   Da li Jovan želi nešto da jede ili pije?

I ja sam žedan.   Da li ste i vi žedni?
  /Ni ja nisam žedan

On (Moj otac) pije kafu uveče.   Kad vaš otac pije kafu?
  /Moj otac nikad ne pije kafu.

Ja pijem kafu uveče.   Šta vi pijete uveče? /Da li pijete
                                  kafu uveče?

Oni imaju lepu sobu.   Kakvu sobu oni imaju?
                               /Da li oni imaju lepu sobu?

Oni putuju često u Dalmaciju.   Da li oni često putuju?

GD 6.6 Conversations - Razgovori
GD 6.6.1

             A   B

Šta pijete ujutru?   Pijem kafu.

Kakvu kafu pijete?   Pijem jaku gorku kafu.

Da li vaša gospođa pije kafu?   Ne, moja žena ne pije kafu.

Šta ona pije?   Ona pije čaj. Ona voli čaj.

Kakav čaj ona pije?   Ona pije sladak, vrlo jak čaj.

Шта пијете ујутру?   **Пијем кафу.**

Какву кафу пијете?   **Пијем јаку горку кафу.**

Дали ваша госпођа пије кафу?   **Не, моја жена не пије кафу.**

Шта она пије?   Она пије чај. Она воли чај.

Какав чај она пије?   Она пије сладак, врло јак чај.
....

GD 6.6.2

Gde idu Toma i Jovan.   Idu u ambasadu.

Da li vi idete u ambasadu?   Ne, moja žena i ja idemo u restoran.

Zašto[1] idete u restoran?   Ja želim da jedem, a moja žena želi
da pije čaj.

Kakav je vaš restoran? Je li skup?   Mi idemo u jedan mali restoran. On
je dobar i nije skup.

Где иду Тома и Јован?   Иду у амбасаду.

Да ли ви идете у амбасаду?   Не, моја жена и ја идемо у ресторан.

Зашто[1] идете у ресторан?   Ја желим да једем, а моја жена жели
да пије чај.

Какав је ваш ресторан? Је ли скуп?   Ми идемо у један мали ресторан. Он је
добар и није скуп.

---
[1] /zašto/ - 'why'

GD 6.6.3

Šta želite, gospodine?   Želim da jedem.

Šta želite da jedete?   Donesite mi supu, teleće meso i ako
imate crni hleb.

Želite li nešto da pijete?   Jeste, donesite mi jedno hladno pivo.

Šta želi gospođa?   Ona ne želi da jede. Ona želi da pije
čaj.

Kakav čaj gospođa želi.   Ona pije sladak, ali jak čaj.

Molim, gospodine.

Шта желите господине?   Желим да једем.

Шта желите да једете?   Донесите ми супу, телеће месо и ако
имате црни хлеб.

Желите ли нешто да пијете?   Јесте, донесите ми једно хладно пиво.

Шта жели госпођа?   Она не жели да једе.   Она жели да пије чај.

Какав чај госпођа жели?   Она пије сладак, али јак чај.

Молим, господине.

GD 6.7   Homework - Domaći zadatak

GD 6.7.1 Make questions to which the following sentences are appropriate answers. The questions to sentences 1-4 are to be made with /kakav/ (in the proper form), sentences 5-7 with /gde/, sentences 8-10 with /kad/.

1. Moj prijatelj ima lepu i veliku sobu.

2. Toma i Jovan piju jaku, slatku kafu.

3. Ja pijem slab, gorak čaj.

4. Zora i njen muž imaju malo i prljavo kupatilo.

5. Toma i njegov prijatelj izlaze svako veče u hotel Metropol.

6. Gospodin i gospođa Jović idu u pozorište.

7. Moj prijatelj ne ide svaki dan u bioskop.

8. Kafu pijem uveče.

9. Moja žena pije čaj uveče.

10. Želim da pijem kafu.

GD 6.7.2 Make another set of questions for the above sentences, using /da li/ for sentences 1-5, /li/ alone for sentences 6-10.

    Make short affirmative answers to 1-5, long to 6-10. Make long negative answers to 6-10.

UNIT 7

Basic Sentences - Osnovne rečenice

Asking For Information	Traženje obaveštenja	Тражење обавештења

A

How are the hotels here?	Kakvi su ovdje hoteli?	Какви су овде хотели?
are they	dà li su	дà ли су
or,	jésu li	jéсу ли
Are they good?	Da li su dobri?	Да ли су добри?

B

| Our hotels are clean and comfortable. | Naši hoteli su čisti i udobni. | Наши хотели су чисти и удобни. |

A

| That's fine. | To je dobro. | То је добро. |

B

why	zàšto /štò	зàшто /штò
to ask	pítati, pìtām	пӣта̄ти, пѝта̄м
Why do you ask?	Zašto pitate?	Зашто питате?
both...and	i...i	и...и
neither...nor	ni...ni	ни...ни

We have very comfortable (both) hotels and restaurants.	Mȉ ȉmamo vrlo udobne hotele ȉ restorane.	Ми имамо врло удобне и хотеле и ресторане.

A

information	obavješténje	обавештење
Excuse me, [I'd like] just one more [bit of] information.	Oprostite, samo jȍš jedno obavještenje.	Извините, само још једно обавештење.

B

ask!	pȉtājte	питајте
everything, all	svè	свè
that, which	štȍ	штȍ
Please, ask whatever ('all that') you want.	Izvolite, pȉtajte svè štȍ želite.	Изволте, питајте све што желите.

A

How are the bathrooms?	Kakve su kupaone?	Каква су купатила?
in good order, correct, honest (of people)	ȉsprāvan, ȉsprāvna, -o	исправан, исправна, -о
order, now	rȇd, pl. rèdovi	рȇд, рèдови
all right, O.K.	u rédu	у рȇду
Are they perfectly all right?	Da li su sasvim u redu?	Да ли су исправна?

B

naturally, of course	ná̄ravno	на̏равно
all	sȁv, svȁ, svȅ	са̏в, сва̏, све̏
Of course. All the bath-rooms are all right.	Naravno. Sve su kupaone u redu.	На̏равно. Сва̏ купатила су у ре̄ду.

A

| warm | tȍpal / tȍpao, tȍpla, -o | то̏пал / то̏пао, то̏пла, -о |
| Do they have hot and cold water? | Da li imaju toplu i hladnu vodu? | Да ли има̄ју то̏плу и хладну воду? |

B

Yes, they do.	Da, imaju.	Да̏# има̄ју.
one should not	nè trebā	не̏ треба̄
reflexive pronoun	sèbe, se	се̏бе се
to worry	brìnuti (se), brìnēm [se]	бри̏нути (се), бри̏нем (се)
You should not worry about anything.	Ne treba ništa brinuti.	Не̏ треба̄ ништа да бри̏не̄те.

A

| truth | ìstina | и̏стина |
| he, she, it doesn't have; there isn't | nȅmā | не̏ма̄ |

131

Is it true that not every
room has its own bath?

Da li je istina, da

Да ли је истина, да свака

svaka soba nema

соба нема своје купатило?

svoju kupaonicu?

B

Yes, it is.

Da, istina je.

Да, истина је.

bed   póstelja   кревет

chair   stólica   столица

table   stȍl G. stóla   стȍ, стола стȍлови
                       pl. stólovi

mirror   zȑcalo (Cr.)   огледало

But all their rooms
have comfortable beds,
nice chairs, tables,
and mirrors.

Ali sve sobe imaju

Али све собе имају удобне

udobne postelje,

кревете, лепе столице,

lijepe stolice,

столове и огледала.

stolove i zrcala.

A

to maintain, keep   održávati, održávām   одржавати, одржавам

is maintained, is kept   održáva se   одржава се

cleanliness   čistóća   чистоћа

How is the cleanliness
(maintained) here?

Kako se ovdje održava

Како се овде одржава

čistóća?

чистоћа?

132

B

Very good.	Vrlo dobro.	Врло добро.
Belgrade	Beógrad	Београд
park	pàrk, pl. pàrkovi	па̀рк, па̀ркови
like, as	kào	као
as well as	kào i	као и
street	ùlica	у̀лица
square	tȑg, pl. tȓgovi	тр̏г, тр̑гови
Both Belgrade and Zagreb have beautiful parks as well as clean streets and squares.	I Beograd i Zagreb imaju lijepe parkove, čiste ulice i tȓgove.	И Београд и Загреб имају лепе паркове, као и чисте улице и тргове.

A

| coffeehouse, coffee shop | kavána | кафа́на |
| Are all the coffeehouses nice and clean? | Da li su sve kavane dobre i čiste? | Да ли су све кафане добре и чисте? |

B

sadness, grief, affliction	žàlōst f.	жа̀ло̄ст
unfortunately	nà žalōst	на̀ жало̄ст
they are not	nísu	нису

133

Unfortunately, they are not. Na žalost, nisu.   На жалост, нису.

I'm sorry ('sorry   Žao mi je   жао ми је
   is to me')

to hear   čuti, čujēm   чути, чујем

I'm sorry to hear that.   Žao mi je to čuti.   Жао ми је што чујем то.

GRAMMATICAL NOTES

Note 7.1 Noun/Adjective: Nominative and Accusative Plural

   Naši hoteli su čisti i udobni.

   Mi imamo vrlo udobne i hotele i restorane.

   Ali sve sobe imaju udobne krevete (postelje), lepe stolice, stolove i
      ogledala (zrcala).

   Da li su sve kafane dobre i čiste.

   Sva kupatila su u redu.

These sentences illustrate nouns of all genders in the plural, both nominative
and accusative. Compare:

Masculine   Adjective

Sing.	NA	hótel	restórān	pàrk	stȍ	krèvet	čȉst	údoban
Plural	N	hóteli	restoráni	pàrkovi	stólovi	krèveti	čȉsti	údōbni
	A	hótele	restoráne	pàrkove	stólove	krèvete	čȉste	údōbne

Feminine /-i/

Sing.	NA	nȍć	žàlōst	vèčēr
Plural	NA	nȍći	žàlōsti	vèčeri

134

Neuter

Sing.	NA		ogledalo	zȑcalo	kupátilo	sélo	čȉsto	údōbno
Plural	NA		oglédala	zȑcala	kupátila	sèla	čȉsta	údōbna

These illustrate common endings:

Sing.	Masc.	Fem.	Fem. /-i/	Neut.	Pl.	Masc.	Fem.	Fem. /-i/	Neut.
N	-zero	-a	-zero	-o		-i	-e	-i	-a
A	-zero	-u	-zero	-o		-e	-e	-i	-a

There are variations of some of these (such as /-e/ for neuter singular), but these are typical endings. The adjective endings are nearly the same, with the addition of /-i/ or /-ī/ for the masculine NA singular, noting that the other endings may be long when the adjective is definite and has primary stress (for example, /dòbrā/).

Some masculine nouns have an extended stem in the plural (/tȓgovi/, /stólovi/, /pàrkovi/). Most such nouns have one syllable stems in the singular. /stȍ/ has the /l/ of the stem /stȍl/ replaced by /-o/, resulting in long /-ȏ/.

Note 7.2 Adjective: Agreement with Multiple Nouns

Mi imamo vrlo udobne i hotele i restorane.

Imaju prilično čiste ulice i trgove.

In these sentences the adjective pertains to both of the following nouns. It so happens that the endings are the same for the adjectives and nouns concerned. Were the nouns in the second sentence in the nominative (/ulice i trgovi/), the endings would be different and the adjective could agree with only one of them: /čiste ulice i trgovi/. Were the nouns reversed, the form would be: /čisti trgovi i ulice/. In other words, where an adjective goes with two or more nouns, it usually agrees in form with the nearer (or nearest) of the nouns.

Should the nouns be singular and indicate people, the adjective may agree with the nearer or it may be plural:

Njegov otac i majka.

Njegova majka i sin.

Njegovi brat i sestra.

When the adjective is in the predicate and refers back to the noun, it is masculine plural when

1) the subject is masculine plural

Naši gradovi su lepi.

2) the subject consists of two masculine nouns

Naš park i trg su lepi.

3) the subject consists of singular nouns of mixed genders

Naš krevet i ogledalo su lepi.

Naša soba i krevet su udobni.

Naš brat i sestra su mali.

4) the subject consists of two neuters

Naše ogledalo i kupalilo su čisti.

The adjective is feminine plural if both subjects are feminine.

Naše večeri i noći su lepe.

Naše ulice i kafane su čiste.

The adjective is neuter plural if both subjects are neuter plural.

Naša ogledala i kupatila su čista

Note 7.3 Noun: Singular and Plural - Special Cases (/vèče/ and /vèčēr/)

Occasional nouns in Serbo-Croatian occur only in the singular or only in the plural (compare <u>scissors</u> in English). Examples of such will be noted when they occur. /vèče/ (of /dobro veče/) occurs only in the singular. When the plural 'evenings' is spoken of the plural of the feminine /i/ noun /vèčēr/ is used: /vèčeri/.

Note 7.4   Verb /ímatí/:   negative present

Da li je istina da svaka soba nema svoje kupatilo?

In Note 4.3 special negative verb forms such as /nije/ were mentioned. Three verbs have such forms, in which the negative prefix combines with the following verb. The negative present of /ímatí/ is one of these. Compare:

ímām	imámo	ímāmo	nèmām	nèmāmo
ímāš	imáte	ímāte	nèmāš	nèmāte
ímā	ímaju		nèmā	némajū

An explanatory spelling with double vowels for length clarifies the structure: /ímaam/, negative /neemaam/ (that is, /ímaam/ has the shape /-emaam/ after /ne-/).

Grammatical Drills - Grammatička vežba

GD 7.1 Substitution-Learning Drill - Zamena, vežba za učenje
GD 7.1.1 Nominative Plural - Nominativ množine

Make the indicated substitutions.

Naši hoteli su lepi i čisti.	restorani	parkovi
Naši hoteli nisu lepi i čisti.	kreveti	trgovi
Rđavi su i prljavi.	stolovi	

Njihove sobe su velike i čiste.	kafane	stanice
Njihove sobe nisu velike i čiste.	postelje	ulice
Male su i prljave.	kupaonice /kupaone	

Naša sela su mala, ali lepa.	pozorišta	ogledala
Naša nisu mala. Velika su, ali nisu čista.	kazališta	kupatila

GD 7.1.2 Accusative Singular and Plural - Akuzativ jednine i množine

Oni imaju velike i čiste <u>krevete.</u>

Oni nemaju velike i čiste <u>krevete.</u>

  Njihovi kreveti su mali i nisu čisti.

restorane   hotele   parkove

trgove   stolove

Moji prijatelji imaju velike i čiste <u>sobe.</u>

Moji prijatelji nemaju velike i čiste <u>sobe.</u>

  Njihove sobe su male i prljave.

kafane   postelje   stolice

GD 7.2 Substitution Learning Drill

GD 7.2.1 Several subjects (in singular and plural) of the same gender.

Moj   hotel i restoran su <u>čisti.</u>   prljav

Naši hoteli i restorani su <u>čisti.</u>   lep

Moja soba i kafana su <u>čiste.</u>   veliki

Naše sobe i kafane su <u>čiste.</u>   mali

Moje kupatilo i ogledalo su <u>čisti.</u>

Naša kupatila i ogledala su <u>čista.</u>

GD 7.2.2 Several subjects (in singular and plural) of different genders.

Moja Soba i krevet su <u>čisti.</u>   prljav

Naše Sobe i kreveti su <u>čisti.</u>   veliki

Moja Soba i kupatilo su <u>čisti.</u>   mali

Naše Sobe i kupatila su <u>čisti.</u>   lep

GD 7.2.3 Several objects (in singular and plural) of different genders.

On ima <u>čistu</u> sobu i kupatilo.   Hotel ima <u>čiste</u> sobe i kupatila.

Ja imam <u>čist</u> krevet i sobu.   Hotel ima <u>čiste</u> krevete i sobe.

Mi imamo <u>čisto</u> kupatilo i krevet.   Hotel ima <u>čista</u> kupatila i krevete.

    udoban   veliki

    prljav   neudoban

GD 7.3 Substitution-Correlation Drill - Vežba sa zamenama i izmenama
GD 7.3.1 Substitution-Correlation Drill with negative transform

<u>Njihovi kreveti</u> su udobni i čisti.

naš hotel	naš park	moja stolica
njihova stanica	vaš restoran	naša ambasada

<u>Naše kafane</u> su male i čiste.

njihova ulica	njeno kupatilo	njegov trg
naš park	naše pozorište	Zorino ogledalo
naše selo	naša kupaonica /kupaona	

Imamo lepe i čiste <u>sobe</u>.

krevet /postelja	ogledalo	park
ulica	pozorište /kazalište	stolica
sto		kupaonica /kupaona

GD 7.3.2 Substitution-Correlation Drill with nominative plural transform.

    The following drill is substitution with nominative plural transforms. The initial substitution is that of the singular form. The plural of this is to be supplied by the student without further cue.

Naš restoran je veliki i lep.   Naši restorani su veliki i lepi.

Tomina soba je lepa, iako je jeftina.

Ovde je hotel dobar, iako je mali.

Kupatilo je dobro, iako je staro.

Naša ulica je mala, ali čista.

Naš trg je veliki, ali nije čist.

Naša stanica je mala i prljava.

Zorino ogledalo je malo, ali dobro.

Njihov trg je veliki i lep.

Stolica je velika i udobna.

Naš sto je mali, ali vrlo lep.

Naše selo je veliko i lepo.

Noć je lepa i vedra.

Dan je lep i topal.

Jutro je lepo, ali hladno.

Veče je lepo, ali toplo. /Večer

GD 7.3.3 Substitution-Correlation Drill with accusative plural transform.

Imam veliki i čist krevet.   Imam velike i čiste krevete.

Moji prijatelji nemaju dobru sobu.

Ne volim mali hotel.

Moj prijatelj voli svoju sobu.

Volim našu ulicu.

Mi imamo dobro i veliko pozorište.

Zagreb ima dobar hotel.

Beograd ima veliki i lep trg.

Oni imaju malu, ali čistu stanicu.

Mi imamo lep park.

Oni nemaju čisto kupatilo.

GD 7.3.4 Substitution-Correlation Adjective Drill

Make the substitutions as indicated, changing the form of the adjective as necessary.

Moj krevet je <u>udoban.</u>

Njegova stolica je <u>udobna.</u>

neudoban	mali	čist
prljav	jeftin	lep
skup		

Njihov hotel je <u>nov.</u>

Naša postelja je <u>nova.</u>

Ovde su stanice <u>nove.</u>

Sva ogledala su <u>nova.</u>

Sve sobe imaju <u>nove</u> krevete.

Mi imamo <u>nove</u> krevete.

Oni imaju novo ogledalo.

čist	stari	prljav

Vaša sela su <u>velika.</u>

Svi stolovi su <u>veliki.</u>

Moj krevet je <u>veliki.</u>

Vaš hotel ima <u>velike</u> sobe.

Vaš prijatelj ima <u>veliku</u> sobu.

Vi imate velika <u>sela.</u>

čist   mali   prljav

lep

Make all 2 substitutions with the original sentence, then with each 1 substitution:

                1   2
Beograd ima nove trgove 1 parkove.

                    1   2
čist   prljav   hotel 1 restoran

mali   veliki   kafana 1 hotel pozorište 1 bioskop

stari   lep   ulica 1 park

                2   1
Njihovi kreveti 1 sobe nisu dobri.

                    1   2
udoban   neudoban   soba 1 kupatilo

rđav   stari   hotel 1 kafana

nov   stolica 1 sto

GD 7.4 Questions and Answers - Pitanja 1 odgovori
GD 7.4.1 Informational Answers
                    Controlled Substitution-Learning Drill

        Make the indicated substitutions. Nominative plural.

Kakvi su vaši kreveti?   Dobri su.
                                          Nisu dobri.
                                          Naši kreveti su dobri.
                                          Naši kreveti nisu dobri.
                                              Rđavi su.

krevet

hotel   restoran   park   trg

Kakve su vaše sobe?   Velike su.
                                          Nisu velike.
                                          Naše sobe su velike.
                                          Naše sobe nisu velike.

Male su i prljave.

soba

kafana   ulica   stanica

stolica   postelja

Kakva su vaša pozorišta?   Dobra su.
                                          Nisu dobra.
                                          Naša pozorišta su dobra.
                                          Naša pozorišta nisu dobra.

selo   kazalište

ogledalo /zrcalo

Make the indicated substitutions. Accusative plural.

Kakve hotele imaju Beograd i Zagreb?   Imaju lepe hotele.
                                          Nemaju lepe hotele.
                                          Oni imaju lepe hotele.
                                          Oni nemaju lepe hotele.
                                            Njihovi hoteli su mali i prljavi.

hotel

restoran   trg   park

Kakve sobe imate?   Imamo lepe sobe.
                                          Nemamo lepe sobe.
                                          Naše sobe su male i prljave.

soba

ulica   kafana   stolica

stanica   postelja

Substitution-Correlation Drill

    Make the indicated substitutions with the necessary adaptations. Nominative
plural.

Kakvi su vaši hoteli?   Dobri su.
                                          Nisu dobri.

143

                              Naši hoteli su dobri.

                              Naši hoteli nisu dobri.

                                Rđavi su i skupi.

njihovo pozorište   njena soba   njegova kafana

vaše pozorište   njihov bioskop

Kakve su <u>vaše ulice?</u>   Lepe su.

                                        Nisu lepe.

                                        Naše ulice su lepe i čiste.

                                        Naše ulice nisu lepe. One su prljave

                                          i male.

njegov bioskop   vaš trg   njihov park

                          vaše selo

    Make the indicated substitutions and adaptations. Accusative plural.

Kakve <u>sobe</u> ima hotel Metropol?   Ima dobre sobe.

                                        Nema dobre sobe.

                                        On ima dobre sobe.

                                        On nema dobre sobe, iako je nov i skup.

ogledalo   krevet /postelja

Kakve <u>hotele</u> imaju Beograd i Zagreb?   Imaju dobre <u>hotele</u>.

                                        Nemaju dobre <u>hotele</u>.

                                        Oni imaju dobre <u>hotele</u>.

                                        Oni nemaju dobre <u>hotele</u>.

ulica   trg   pozorište /kazalište

kafana   bioskop   park

GD 7.4.2 Yes and No Answers

Controlled Substitution-Correlation Drill

    Make the indicated substitutions. Nominative plural.

Da li su njihovi <u>kreveti</u> čisti?   Da, čisti su.

                                        Ne, nisu čisti.

Da, njihovi <u>kreveti</u> su čisti.

Ne, njihovi <u>kreveti</u> nisu čisti. Oni su prljavi i neudobni.

<u>krevet</u>

hotel   restoran   bioskop /kino

Da li su <u>Tomine i Jovanove</u> sobe dobre?   Da, dobre su.

Ne, nisu dobre.

Da, njihove sobe su dobre.

Ne, njihove sobe nisu dobre. Male su i prljave.

<u>Tomina i Jovanova soba</u>

vaša kafana   njihova ulica

Tomina stolica   vaša stanica

Da li su njihova pozorišta dobra?   Da, dobra su.

/kazališta   Ne, nisu dobra.

Da, njihova pozorišta su dobra.

Ne, njihova pozorišta nisu dobra. Mala su i prljava.

<u>njihovo pozorište</u>

vaše kupatilo   njeno ogledalo

Make the indicated substitutions. Accusative plural.

Da li Beograd i Zagreb imaju <u>lepe i velike hotele?</u>   Da, imaju.

Ne, nemaju.

Da, Beograd i Zagreb imaju lepe i velike hotele.

Ne, Beograd i Zagreb nemaju lepe i velike hotele. Njihovi hoteli su mali i prljavi.

<u>lep i veliki hotel</u>

dobar i jeftin restoran   veliki i čist trg   veliki i čist park

dobar i jeftin bioskop

Da li imate <u>dobre i čiste sobe?</u>   Da, imamo.

                                     Ne, nemamo.

                                     Da, imamo dobre i čiste sobe.

                                     Ne, nemamo dobre i čiste sobe.

                                          Naše sobe su male i prljave.

<u>dobra i čista soba</u>

lepa i prava ulica   velika i čista kafana

velika i udobna stolica   velika i čista stanica

Da li imate <u>lepa i ispravna kupatila?</u>   Da, imamo.

                                     Ne, nemamo.

                                     Da, imamo dobra i ispravna kupatila.

                                     Ne, nemamo dobra i ispravna kupatila.

                                       Naša kupatila su rđava i neispravna.

<u>lepo i ispravno kupatilo</u>

dobro i jeftino pozorište   lepo i veliko ogledalo

lepo i čisto selo

Repeat the above drills, using pattern:

Jesu li njihovi kreveti čist?   Jesu, čisti su.

                                   Nisu čisti. Prljavi su.

                                   Jeste, njihovi kreveti su čisti.

                                   Ne, njihovi kreveti nisu čisti, ali

                                       neki su.

                                     Oni su neudobni i prljavi.

pozorište   soba   kafana

bioskop   postelja

Da li su <u>vaše ulice čiste?</u>   Da, čiste su.

                                     Ne, nisu čiste.

                                     Da, naše ulice su čiste.

                                   Ne, naše ulice nisu čiste.

njihov bioskop skup   vaš trg lep

vaše pozorište dobro

Make the indicated substitutions with transforms. Accusative plural.

Da li Beograd i Zagreb imaju   Da, imaju.
  velike i lepe hotele?   Ne, nemaju.
  _____   Da, Zagreb i Beograd imaju lepe i
                         velike hotele.
                       Ne, Beograd i Zagreb nemaju lepe i
                         velike hotele. Njihovi hoteli su
                         mali i neudobni.

lepa i prava ulica	dobro i jeftino pozorište	veliki i lep trg
velika i udobna kafana	dobar i jeftin bioskup	lep i veliki park

Repeat the above drills, using the pattern:

    Jesu li hoteli udobni i čisti?   Jesu.
                               etc.

GD 7.5 Question and Answer Drill with Prompt

Naši restorani i hoteli su udobni   Kakvi su vaši restorani i hoteli?
  i čisti.   Da li su udobni i čisti?

Tomina soba je udobna i čista.   Kakva je Tomina soba? Da li je
                               udobna i čista.

Naše sobe nisu udobne i čiste.   Kakve su vaše sobe? Da li su udobne
                               i čiste?

Moje kupatilo je dobro.   Kakvo je vaše kupatilo?

Naša kupatila su takođe dobra i u redu.   Kakva su vaša kupatila? Da li su
                               ispravna?

Beograd i Zagreb imaju lepe i velike   Kakve parkove i trgove imaju Beograd
  parkove i trgove.   i Zagreb? /Da li Beograd i Zagreb
                               imaju...

Mi imamo dobre i restorane i kafane.   Kakve restorane i kafane imate?
  /Mi nemamo dobre ni restorane
    ni kafane.

Ja imam lepu sobu i kupatilo i vrlo   Kakvu sobu i kupatilo imate? Da li
  sam zadovoljan.   ste zadovoljni?

Toma i Jovan nemaju dobre sobe i   Kakve sobe i kupatila imaju Toma i
  kupatila i vrlo su nezadovoljni.   Jovan? Da li su zadovoljni?

/Da li Toma i Jovan imaju.....

Moja soba i kupatilo su čisti.

Da li su vaša (/vaši) soba i kupatilo čisti?

Naše sobe i kreveti su udobni i čisti.

Kakve su vaše sobe i kreveti? Da li su udobni i čisti?

Moj hotel i restoran su čisti.

Kakvi su vaši hotel i restoran? Da li su čisti?

Hotel ima čiste krevete i sobe.

Kakve krevete i sobe ima hotel? /Da li hotel ima čiste krevete i sobe?

Hotel ima čista kupatila i sobe.

Kakva kupatila i sobe ima hotel? /Da li hotel ima čista kupatila i sobe?

GD 7.5 Conversations - Razgovori
7.5.1

A	B
Kakvi su ovde hoteli?	Ovde su hoteli dobri.
Kakve su sobe i kupatila. Da li su čisti?	Jesu. I sobe i kupatila su čisti.
A kakvi su kreveti?	Kreveti su takođe dobri i udobni.
Da li su vaša kupatila u redu?	Jesu. Sva kupatila su u redu.
Da li su vaše sobe skupe?	Jesu.
Da li je vaš restoran skup.	Jeste, skup je, ali dobar.
To je dobro. Moj restoran je skup, iako nije dobar.	Žao mi je.

Какви су овде хотели?	Овде су хотели добри.
Какве су собе и купатила. Да ли су чисти?	Jесу. И собе и купатила су чисти.
А какви су кревети?	Кревети су такође добри и удобни.
Да ли су ваша купатила у реду?	Jесу. Сва купатила су у реду.
Да ли су ваше собе скупе?	Jесу.
Да ли је ваш ресторан скуп?	Jесте, скуп је, али добар.

То је добро. , Мој ресторан је скуп, Жао ми је.
 јако није добар.

GD 7.5.2

Da li idete ovde u kafanu?	Da, idem.
Kad idete u kafanu?	Idem svako drugo veče.
Kakve su kafane ovde?	Prilično su dobre.
U koju kafanu idete?	Idem u jednu malu, ali čistu kafanu.
Da li je vaša kafana skupa?	Nije. Ona je jeftina.
Da li su sve kafane ovde jeftine?	Nisu. Neke su vrlo skupe.
Da li vi idete u skupe kafane?	Da, idem, ali retko. Ja ne volim skupe kafane.

Да ли идете овде у кафану?	Да, идем.
Кад идете у кафану?	Идем свако друго вече.
Какве су кафане овде?	Прилично су добре.
У коју кафану идете?	Идем у једну малу, али чисту кафану.
Да ли је ваша кафана скупа?	Није. Она је јефтина.
Да ли су све кафене овде јефтине?	Нису. Неке су врло скупе.
Да ли ви идете у скупе кафане?	Да, идем, али ретко. Ја не волим скупе кафане.

GD 7.5.3

Kakve hotele imaju Beograd i Zagreb?	Oni imaju dobre i čiste hotele.
Da li idete često u Zagreb?	Da, idem vrlo često. Jedanput ili dvaput mesečno.
Kakve ulice ima Zagreb?	On ima lepe i prave ulice.
Da li Zagreb ima lepe trgove, kao Beograd?	Naravno, Zagreb ima vrlo lepe i velike trgove.
Da li Beograd i Zagreb imaju lepa pozorišta?	Jeste, imaju. I Beograd i Zagreb imaju lepa pozorišta i bioskope.
Da li vaši prijatelji idu često u pozorište?	Idu, ali ne često. Otpr edanput mjesečno.

Zašto oni ne idu češće u kazalište?   Oni ne znaju dobro srpskohrvatski.

Da li vi znate dobro srpskohrvatski?   Znam prilično dobro.

                                             Ja idem često i u kazalište i u
                                             kino.

Какве хотеле имају Београд и Загреб?   Они имају добре и чисте хотеле.

Да ли идете често у Загреб?   Да, идем врло често. Једанпут или
                                             двапут месечно.

Какве улице има Загреб?   Он има лепе и праве улице.

Да ли Загреб има лепе тргове, као   Наравно, Загреб има врло лепе и
Београд?   велике тргове.

Да ли Београд и Загреб имају лепа   Јесте. И Београд и Загреб имају
позоришта?   лепа позоришта и биоскопе.

Да ли ваши пријатељи иду често у   Иду, али не често. Отприлике
позориште?   једанпут месечно.

Зашто они не иду чешће у позориште?   Они не знају добро српскохрватски.

Да ли ви знате добро српскохрватски?   Знам прилично добро.

                                             Ја идем често и у позориште и у
                                             биоскоп.

GD 7.6 Homework - Domaći zadatak

1. Write out each of these sentences using each of the adjectives listed.

Naši hoteli su _____ i _____.	dobar čist
Njihove sobe su _____ i _____.	veliki udoban
Naše ulice su _____ i _____.	lep prav
Njena pozorišta su _____, iako su _____.	rđav skup
Naša kupatila su _____, iako su _____.	neispravan nov
Zorine stolice su _____, ali _____.	lep neudoban
Ovde su parkovi i trgovi _____ i _____.	veliki lep
Trgovi i ulice su _____.	čist

Krevet i soba su _____.   udoban

Soba i kupatilo su _____.   čist

2. Change the objects in these sentences to plural.

Zagreb ima lep i veliki hotel.

Imam lepu i veliku sobu.

Moje selo ima lepu i pravu ulicu.

Ljubljana ima veliko i lepo pozorište i bioskop.

Hotel Metropol nema neispravno kupatilo.

Zora ima malu i čistu sobu.

Zagreb ima lep i veliki park i trg.

Sarajevo ima čist i lep trg i ulicu.

Toma ima čistu sobu i kupatilo.

UNIT 8

Basic Sentences - Osnovne rečenice

Meeting People	Upoznavanje	Упознавање

A

Hello, Mr. Jović.	Dobar dan, gospodine Joviću.	Добар дан, господине Јовићу.
How are you, what are you doing?	[Kako ste, što radite?]	Како сте, шта радите?
of new	nóva / nòvoga	
How are you, what's new ('what is there of new')?	Kako ste, što ima novoga?	Како сте, шта има ново?

B

| question | pítanje | питање |
| Thanks (for the question), I'm fine. How are you? | Hvala na pitanju dobro sam. Kako ste vi? | Хвала на питању добро сам. Како сте ви? |

A

I'm fine, too, thank you.	Hvala. I ja sam dobro.	Хвала. И ја сам добро.
to allow, permit	dozvóliti, da dózvolīm	дозволити, да дозволим
allow!	dozvólite	дозволите
to become acquainted, introduce	upóznati, da upóznām	упознати, да упознам

152

May I introduce you.	Dozvolite da vas upoznam.	Дозволите да вас упознам.
this, these (pron.)	óvo	ово
These are my friends Bob and Tom.	Ovo su moji prijatelji Bob i Tom.	Ово су моји пријатељи Боб и Том.

B

I'm glad	drȁgo mi je	мило ми је
gentlemen	gospóda	господа
gentlemen!	gòspodo	господо
I'm glad to meet you, gentlemen.	Drago mi je vas upoznati gospodo.	Мило ми је господо да се упознамо.
surely	sȉgūrno	сигурно
American (man)	Amerikánac, pl. Amerikánci	Американац, Американци
American (woman)	Ameríkānka	Американка
(interrogative particle expressing surprise)	zar	зар
(interrogative sentence final), is it not so?	zar nè	је л'те
is that so?	jé l'te	jé л'те
You are surely Americans, aren't you?	Vi ste sigurno Amerikanci, zar ne?	Ви сте сигурно Американци, је л'те?

C

| [Yes], we are. | Jèsmo. | Jȅсмо. |

A

brothers	bràća	бра̏ħа
They're brothers.	Òni su braća.	О̀ни су бра̏ħа.
brother	bràt	бра̏т
young	mlȁd, mláda, -o;	мла̄̏д, мла́да, -о;
	mlȁdī	мла̄̏ди, -а̄, -о̄
attractive, likable, nice	simpátičan,	симпатичан,
	simpátična, -čno	симпатична, -о
man	čóvjek, pl. ljȕdi	чове̄к, љӯ̏ди
Bob and his brother are very nice young people.	Bob i njegov brat su mladi i simpatični ljudi.	Боб и његов бра̏т су| мла́ди и симпатични љӯди.

C

tourist	túrist / túrista	ту́рист / ту́риста
We're here as tourists.	Ovdje smo kao turisti.	О̏вде смо | као ту́ристи.
through	kròz	кро̏з
Europe	Evrópa	Евро̄́па
Greece	Grčka	Грчка

154

We're travelling through Europe to Greece.	Mȋ putujemo kroz Evropu, za Gȑčku.	Мӣ путу̀је̄мо кроз Евро̏пу за Гр̀чку.

A

to see	vȉdjeti, vȉdīm	ви̏дети, ви̏дӣм
Yugoslavia	Jugoslávija	Југосла̏ви ја
Now they'd like to see Yugoslavia and get acquainted with it.	Sada žele vidjeti i upoznati Jugoslaviju.	Сада̀ же̏ле да ви̏де̄ и упо̏знају Југосла̏вију.
pertaining to business	pòslōvan, pòslōvna, -o	посло̏ван, посло̏вна, -о
business man	pòslōvan čòvjek /bȋznismen	посло̏ван чо̏век /би́знисмен
artist	úmjetnik, pl. úmjetnici	уметни̏к, уметни̏ци
Bob is a business man, and his brother is an artist.	Bob je poslovan čòvjek a njegov brat je úmjetnik.	Бо̏б је посло̏ван чо̏век, а ѣегов бра̏т је уметни̏к.

B

where to, whither	kúdā /kùd	куда̄ / ку̏д
to be leaving, to leave	ódlaziti, ódlazīm	о̏длазити, о̏длазӣм
Where are you going from here, gentlemen?	Kud odlāzite ódavde, gospodo?#	Куда̄ о̏длазите о̏да̄вде, господо?#

155

C

tomorrow	sùtra	сутра
Athens	Aténa	Атина
We're travelling to Athens, (to) Greece, tomorrow.	Sutra putujemo za Atenu, u Grčku.	Сутра путујемо у Атину, у Грчку.
Greek	grčkī, -ā, -ō	грчки, -ā, -ō
monument	spòmenīk, pl. spòmenīci	спомоник, спомоници
My brother would like to see the old Greek monuments.	Moj brat želi vidjeti stare grčke spomenike.	Мој брат жели да види старе грчке споменике.

B

I'm glad [to hear it] gentlemen.	Drago mi je gospodo.	Мило ми је господо.
to you	vàma, vam	вама, вам
happy, fortunate, lucky	srètan, srètna, -o	сретан, сретна, -o /срећан, срећна, -о
way, road, trip	pùt, pl. pútevi	пут, путеви
I wish you a nice trip.	Želim vam sretan put.	Желим вам сретан пут.

Note: Croatian uses both /cèsta/ and /pùt/. /cèsta/ is 'road' while /pùt/ may be used for 'road', 'way', or 'trip'. In the above expression only /pùt/ may be used.

Supplement - Peoples and Places

Following is a brief list of places, illustrating some typical forms of place names and the words for the inhabitants. Note that the person must be either masculine or feminine. There is no word for an 'American', only 'an American (male)' and 'an American (female)'. The adjective for 'American' is not given here and is not used in this connection.

Place	Person (m)	Person (f)
Amérika	Amerikánac (G Amerikánca)	Ameríkānka
(Sjédīnjenē Amérīčkē Dŕžave - S.A.D.)		
Jugoslávija	Jugoslóvēɲ /Jugoslávēn	Jugoslóvēɲka /Jugoslávēnka
Cŕna Góra	Crnogórac (G Crnógōrca)	Crnógōrka
Bòsna	Bosánac (G Bosánca)	Bósānka
Hèrcegovina	Hèrcegovac (G Hércegovca)	Hèrcegōvka
Makédōnija	Makédónac (G Makédónca)	Makédōnka
Slóvēnija	Slovénac (G Slovēnca)	Slóvēnka
Hŕvātska	Hŕvāt	Hrvática
Sŕbija	Sŕbin	Sŕpkinja
Evrópa	Evrópljanin	Evrópljanka
Gŕčka	Gŕk	Gŕkinja
Bùgarska	Bùgarin	Bùgārka
Mádžarska / Mádarska	Mádžār / Mádār	Madžárica / Madarica
Ítalija	Italíjan / Talíjan	Italíjanka / Talíjanka
Énglēska	Énglēz (G. Engléza)	Énglēskinja
Fráncūska	Fráncūz	Fráncūskinja
Rúsija	Rùs	Rùskinja
Némačka	Némac (G Nemca)	Nèmica
Švájcārska / Švìcarska	Švájcárac / Švìcarac (G Svajcárca / Svìcarca	Švájcárkinja / Švìcarka
Áustrija	Austrijánac (G Austrijánca)	Austríjānka

157

Grammatical Notes

Note 8.1 Verb: Present of 'to be'

I Ja sam dobro.   Da, jeste.

Njegov brat je umetnik.   Jesmo.

Jè li ambasada daleko odavde.   Ovde smo kao turisti.

Stvar nije u tome.   Kako ste vi?

                                           Neke su prljave.

                                           Jesu li dobri?

                                           Nisu sve kafane dobre.

The verb 'to be' has three sets of forms in the present. The most frequent is an enclitic set, occurring after a stressed word at the beginning of a clause. Examples above are /sam/, /je/, /smo/, /ste/, /su/. None of these are stressed, and they always follow some other word.

The second set has, except for /je/, longer forms. Examples above are /jè/, /jèste/, /jèsu/. Note that there is an enclitic, unstressed /je/ and a stressed /jè/. (See below.)

The third set of forms, also stressed, is the negative. /nije/ and /nísu/ are examples. The negative occurs only stressed.

The full set of forms is:

Unstressed		Stressed Affirmative	
sam	smo	jèsam	jèsmo
si	ste	jèsi	jèste
je	su	jèste, jèst, jè	jèsu

Stressed Negative	
nísam	nísmo
nísi	níste
níje	nísu

Stressed /jè/ is used before /li/, as /jè li/ 'is (it)?'. Stressed /jèste/ and /jèst/ 'is' are often used for 'yes' as well as for 'he, she, it is'. The other stressed affirmative forms are used before /li/ and as emphatic forms 'I am!', 'he is!', etc. They are also used in answers to questions: /Jeste li vi gospodin Jović?/ -- /Da, jesam./. (For the use of these present forms in connection with the past see Notes 17.1 and 18.1)

The unstressed forms are enclitic, that is, they are suffixed to the previous (stressed) word. There are a number of enclitics in Serbo-Croatian and the order in which they occur is fixed. Compare:

Da li su dobra?

Žao mi je.

/li/, /mi/, /su/, /je/ are all enclitics. That is, whenever two or more enclitics occur next to each other, they must occur in the order here given. The order of the enclitics which have occurred so far is:

1	2	3	4	5
li	sam	mi	vas	je
	si	mu	nas	
	smo		ih	
	ste			
	su			

Not more than one enclitic from each slot may occur. Note that the present of 'to be' is in slot 2, except for /je/, which occurs last. This also means that if one of the forms from slot 2 occurs, then /je/ 'is' may not occur, and vice versa. (/nas/ and /ih/ have been added from Note 8.2.)

Note 8.2 Pronoun, Personal: Nominative and Accusative Plural

Mi putujemo kroz Evropu.

Kako ste vi?

Dozvolite da vas upoznam.

Oni su takođe(r) čisti.

Oni su braća.

Ona imaju toplu i hladnu vodu.

/mȉ/, /vȉ/, /óni/, /óne/ and /óna/ have already been introduced in connection with the pronominal adjectives (see Note 4.1). /vas/ is an enclitic
accusative. The pronouns have in several cases both stressed and enclitic
forms. The stressed form of 'you' is /vȁs/. The full set of plural personal
pronouns, nominative and accusative, is:

					m (etc.)		f		n
N	mȉ	we	vȉ	you	óni		óne		óna
A	nȁs	us	vȁs	you	njȉh				
or,	nas		vas		ih				

Note that the accusative forms are close to the corresponding adjectives:
/nȁs/ - /nȁš/, /vȁs/ - /vȁš/, /njȉh/ - /njȉhov/.

Grammatical Drill

GD 8.1   Substitution-Correlation Drill

In drilling with nouns indicating persons of a given area, the appropriate
gender should always be used. For example in a sentence /Ja sam _____ / the
form used should be masculine or feminine according to the speaker. Similarly,
/On je _____ / must have a masculine noun filling the blank, /Ona je ____ /
a feminine one.

GD 8.1.1   Substitution-Correlation drill with negative transform.

These drills are given in full in the affirmative.

	Ja sam Amerikanac. Ja nisam Amerikanac.
on	On je Amerikanac.
Jovanov prijatelj	On je Jovanov prijatelj.
mi	Mi smo Jovanovi prijatelji.
poslovan čovek/ biznismen	Mi smo poslovni ljudi. / ... biznismeni

160

oni	Oni su <u>poslovni ljudi.</u> / ... biznismeni
Jugosloven	<u>Oni</u> su Jugosloveni.
vi (polite form)	<u>Vi</u> ste Jugosloven.
moji prijatelji	Moji prijatelji su <u>Jugosloveni.</u>
turist	Moji prijatelji su <u>turisti.</u>
umetnik	<u>Moji prijatelji</u> su umetnici.
g. Smit	Gospodin Smit je umetnik.
	<u>Zora</u> je Jugoslovenka.
one	<u>One</u> su Jugoslovenke.
ovo	<u>Ovo</u> su <u>Jugoslovenke.</u>
moje kćeri	<u>Ovo</u> su moje kćeri.
Nada i Zora	Nada i Zora su <u>moje kćeri.</u>
Jugoslovenke	<u>Nada i Zora</u> su Jugoslovenke.
mi (f.)	Mi smo <u>Jugoslovenke.</u>
Amerikanke	<u>Mi</u> smo Amerikanke.
ona	Ona je <u>Amerikanka.</u>
turist	Ona je turist.
	Zora i Jovan su <u>Jugosloveni.</u>
naš prijatelj	<u>Zora i Jovan</u> su naši prijatelji.
ona	Ona je <u>naš prijatelj.</u>
zadovoljan	<u>Ona</u> je zadovoljna.
g. i g-đa Jović	G. i g-đa Jović su <u>zadovoljni.</u>
još mlad	<u>G. i g-đa Jović</u> su još mladi.
one	One su <u>još mlade.</u>
turist	One su <u>turisti.</u>
već nezadovoljan	<u>One</u> su već nezadovoljne.
naši prijatelji	Naši prijatelji su već nezadovoljni.

161

	Moj otac je dobro, hvala.
Ja	I ja sam dobro.
on	I on je dobro.
takođe	On je takođe dobro.
g. i g-đa Jović	G. i g-đa Jović su takođe dobro.
i	I g. i g-đa Jović su dobro.
mi	I mi smo dobro.

GD 8.1.2 Substitution-Correlation Drill

Oni žele da vide i upoznaju Jugoslaviju.

(ja)	on	ona	vi	moji prijatelji	one
(ti)	moj prijatelj	moja žena		Toma i Jovan	g-đa i g-ca Jović

Sentences for drill with the same substitutions.

Oni putuju kroz Evropu.

Oni žele da vide stare grčke spomenike.

Oni sutra odlaze odavde.

Oni putuju sutra u Atinu, u Grčku.

GD 8.1.3 Substitution-Correlation Drill with plural transforms.

    Type sentences are given first. These are to be drilled as pairs. The sentences for drill follow.

Masculine

Ja sam Amerikanac. ⟶ Mi smo Amerikanci.

Ti si Amerikanac.   ⟶ Vi ste Amerikanci.

Vi ste Amerikanac.

On je Amerikanac. ⟶ Oni su Amerikanci.

162

Sentences for drill:

Ja sam njihov prijatelj.

Ja sam poslovan čovek. /biznismen

Ja nisam mlad čovek.

Ja sam dobar otac.

Ja sam takođe dobro.

Feminine

Ja sam Amerikanka.   ⟶   Mi smo Amerikanke.

Ti si Amerikanka. ⟩

   ⟶   Vi ste Amerikanke.

Vi ste Amerikanka. ⟩

Ona je Amerikanka.   ⟶   One su Amerikanke.

Sentence for drill:

Ja sam Jovanova majka.

GD 8.2 Questions and Answers

GD 8.2.1 Informational Answers

      Substitution-Correlation Drill

    Use the items listed as the subject of both questions and answers.

Kako <u>ste</u>, šta rad<u>ite</u>?   Hvala, dobro sam.

                               Hvala, nisam dobro.

Kuda (vi) putu<u>jete</u> odavde?   Putujem u Beograd, u Jugoslaviji.

(ti)	on	ona	oni
	Jovan / Ivan	Zora	one
	g. Smit	g-ca Smit	
	vaš suprug	vaša supruga	

Kuda putuju <u>Toma i Jovan</u> odavde?   Oni putuju u Atinu, u Grčku.

vi i vaša gospoda	g. i g-ca Smit	g-đa i g-ca Smit
vi i vaš prijatelj	vaši prijatelji	vaša majka i žena
	Zora i njen otac	Zora i njena majka

GD 8.2.2 Yes and No Answers

Da li ste <u>vi</u> Amerikanac?   Jesam.

Nisam.

Jeste, ja sam Amerikanac.

Ne, ja nisam Amerikanac.

(ti)	on	vi (plural)	oni
	vaš brat	vi i gospoda	g. i g-đa Jović
			gospoda

Sentences for drill:

Da li ste <u>vi</u> Tomin prijatelj?

Da li ste <u>vi</u> Jugosloven? /Jugoslaven

Da li ste <u>vi</u> Francuz?

Da li ste <u>vi</u> zadovoljni?

Repeat this drill with /Jeste li/.

Da li ste <u>vi</u> Amerikanka?   Jesam.

Da li ste <u>vi</u> Amerikanka?   Nisam.

Jeste, ja sam Amerikanka.

Ne, ja nisam Amerikanka.

(ti)	ona	vi (plural)	one
	Tomina majka	vi i vaša majka	gospođe
			gospođice
			g-đa i g-ca Smit

Sentences for drill:

Da li ste <u>vi</u> Hrvatica?

Da li ste <u>vi</u> Srpkinja?

Da li ste <u>vi</u> Slovenka?

Da li je <u>vaš prijatelj</u> ovde kao turist?   Da, jeste.

Ne, nije.

Da, on je ovde kao turist.

Ne, on nije ovde kao turist.

ti	on	ona	vi (pol.)	oni
	Jovan	g-đa Smit	vi (pl.)	vaši prijatelji
	g. Smit	gospođica	vi i gospođa	gospoda

one

gospođe

Sentences for drill:

Da li je <u>vaš prijatelj</u> dobro?

Da li je <u>vaš prijatelj</u> zadovoljan?

Da li su i <u>vaši prijatelji</u> Amerikanci?   Da, jesu.

Ne, nisu.

Jeste, i oni su Amerikanci.

Ne, oni nisu Amerikanci.

on	gospodin Smit	gospodin i gospođa Smit
vi (pol.)	vi (plural)	gospoda

Sentences for drill:

Da li su i <u>vaši prijatelji</u> zadovoljni?

Da li su i <u>vaši prijatelji</u> Jugosloveni?   /Jugoslaveni

Da li su i <u>vaši prijatelji</u> turisti?

Repeat the above drills (8.2.2 1-4), using the pattern:

Jeste li vi Amerikanac?   Jesam.   itd.

                                 Nisam.

                                 Jeste, ja sam Amerikanac.

                                 Ne, ja nisam Amerikanac.

                                              etc.

<u>Vi</u> ste gospodine Amerikanac, zar ne?   Da, jesam.
                        /je l'te
                                             Ne, nisam.

                                             Da, ja sam Amerikanac.

                                             Ne, ja nisam Amerikanac.

on   oni

vaš brat   g. i g-đa Jović

Toma   Zora i Toma

Sentences for drill:

<u>Vi</u> ste Jovanov prijatelj, zar ne? /je l'te

<u>Vi</u> ste gospodine zadovoljni, zar ne? /je l'te

<u>Vi</u> ste ovde kao turist, zar ne? /je l'te

Zar ste <u>vi</u> gospodine Amerikanac?   Da, jesam.

                                             Da, ja sam Amerikanac.

Zar <u>vi</u> gospodine niste Amerikanac?   Ne, nisam.

                                             Ne, ja nisam Amerikanac.

on   oni

vaš prijatelj   vaši prijatelji

Toma   vi (plural)

166

Sentences for drill:

Zar ste vi Jovanov prijatelj?

Zar ste vi gospodine zadovoljni?

Zar ste vi ovde kao turist?

Zar ste vi gospođo, Amerikanka?   Da, jesam.

                                        Da, ja sam Amerikanka.

Zar vi gospođo niste Amerikanka?   Ne, nisam.

                                        Ne, ja nisam Amerikanka.

ona   one

vaša majka   Zora i njena majka

Zora   vi (plural)

Sentences for drill:

Zar ste vi gospođo zadovoljni?

Zar ste vi gospođo ovde kao turist?

Zar ste vi gospođo Jugoslovenka? /Jugoslavenka

GD 8.3 Question and Answer Drill with Prompt

Tomini prijatelji su Amerikanci.   Da li su Tomini prijatelji Amerikanci?

Moj prijatelj je Amerikanac, a nje-   Da li su vaš prijatelj i njegova žena
   gova žena je Jugoslovenka.   Amerikanci?

Oni su ovde kao turisti.   Šta oni rade ovde?

Oni žele da vide stare spomenike.   Šta oni žele da vide?

Oni odlaze odavde u Grčku.   Gde (/Kuda) oni odlaze odavde?

Toma je poslovan čovek, a njegov   Da li su Toma i njegov brat poslovni
   brat je umetnik. /biznismen   ljudi? /biznismeni

Oni sutra putuju u Grčku.   Kad oni putuju u Grčku?

   /Ne znam, kad oni putuju u Grčku.

Oni žele da upoznaju Grčku i njene
   spomenike.

Moj prijatelj i njegov brat su
   nezadovoljni.

Oni nemaju lepu sobu i kupatilo.

Moj otac i majka su zadovoljni, ali
   sestra nije.

Jovan pita kakve su vaše sobe.
   /Jovan pita da li ste zadovoljni.

Da li oni žele da upoznaju Grčku?
   /Zašto oni putuju u Grčku?

Da li su vaš prijatelj i njegov brat
   zadovoljni?

Zašto (/Što) su oni nezadovoljni?

Da li su vaši (otac, majka i sestra)
   zadovoljni?

Šta pita Jovan?

GD 8.4   Conversations - Razgovori
GD 8.4.1

                    A   B

Jeste li vi gospodine, Amerikanac?   Da, jesam.

I vaš prijatelj je sigurno   Jest.   I on je Amerikanac.
   Amerikanac, zar ne?

Jeste li vi ovdje kao turisti,   Da, jesmo. Mi putujemo kao turisti.
   gospodo?

Gdje putujete odavde?   Putujemo za Split i Dubrovnik.
                                          Želimo vidjeti Dalmaciju.

Kad putujete za Dalmaciju?   Putujemo sutra.
                                          Sada želimo vidjeti i upoznati Beograd.

Drago mi je gospodo.

Да ли сте ви господине, Американац?   Да, јесам.

И ваш пријатељ је сигурно Американац,   Јесте. И он је Американац.
   је л те?

Да ли сте ви овде као туристи, господо?   Да, јесмо. Ми путујемо као туристи.

Где путујете одавде?   Путујемо у Сплит и Дубровник.
                                          Желимо да видимо Далмацију.

Кад путујете у Далмацију?   Путујемо сутра. Сада желимо да видимо
                                          и упознамо Београд.

Мило ми је господо.

GD 8.4.2

Vaši prijatelji Bob i Tom su vrlo simpatični ljudi.	Jesu.
Oni su poslovni ljudi, zar ne? / biznismeni	Bob jest, a Tom nije.
Šta radi Tom?	On je umjetnik.
Oni putuju kao turisti, zar ne?	Jest. Sada žele upoznati Dalmaciju.
Kad putuju Dalmaciju?	Sutra putuju za Split.

Ваши пријатељи Боб и Том су врло симпатични људи.	Јесу.
Они су пословни људи, зар не? / бизнисмени	Боб јесте, а Том није.
Ста ради Том?	Он је уметник.
Они путују као туристи, је л'те?	Јесте. Сада желе да упознају Далмацију.
Кад путују у Далмацију?	Сутра путују у Сплит.

GD 8.4.3

Kakav hotel imate, gospodine? Da li ste zadovoljni?	Da, i moja žena i ja smo zadovoljni. Naš hotel je dobar. Mi imamo lepu sobu i kupaonu.
Da li su vaš prijatelj i njegova žena zadovoljni? Kakvu sobu i kupaonu / kupaonicu oni imaju?	Na žalost, moj prijatelj i njegova žena nisu zadovoljni.
U čemu je stvar? Zašto nisu zadovoljni?	Njihova soba je mala i nije čista. Postelje također nisu udobne.
Je li njihova kupaona u redu? / kupaonica	Jest, ali je mala i prljava. I soba i kupaona su male i prljave.
Žao mi je.	I meni je žao.

Какав хотел имате, господине?

Да ли сте задовољни?

Да ли су ваш пријатељ и његова жена
задовољни? Какву собу и купатило
они имају?

У чему је ствар? Зашто нису
задовољни?

Да ли је њихово купатило исправно?

Жао ми је.

Да, и моја жена и ја смо задовољни.

Наш хотел је добар.

Ми имамо лепу собу и купатило.

На жалост, мој пријатељ и његова жена
нису задовољни.

Њихова соба је мала и није чиста.

Кревети такође нису удобни.

Јесте, али је мало и прљаво.

И соба и купатило су мали и прљави.

И мени је жао.

GD 8.5 Homework - Domaći zadatak

1. Make questions for which the following sentences are appropriate
answers. The questions are to be made both with /li/ and /da li/ for each
sentence.

1. Moj prijatelj i njegova žena su Amerikanci.

2. Moja žena i ja smo vrlo zadovoljni.

3. Ovde sam kao turist.

4. Moja žena je dobra majka.

5. Moj prijatelj je umetnik.

6. Toma i Jovan su poslovni ljudi.

7. To su moji prijatelji Tom i Bob.

8. G. i g-đa Jović su Jugosloveni.

2. Make another set of questions for the above sentences, using /zar ne/.
Make short affirmative answers to 1-4. Make long affirmative answers for 5-8.

Unit 9

Basic Sentences - Osnovne rečenice

Looking for Someone	Traženje nekoga	Тражење некога
	A	
house, home	dȍm	кӳћа
at home	dòma	код кӯћē
Is Tom at home, ma'am?	Da li je Toma doma gospođo?	Да ли је Тома код кӯћē, госпођо?
	B	
I'm afraid ('unfortunately') he isn't.	Na žalost nije.	На жалост није.
	A	
to disturb	uznemirívati, uznemírujēm	узнемиравати, узнемиравам
or,	smètati, smȅtām	сметати, сметам
Excuse me for disturbing you, but do you know where he is?	Izvinite što vam smetam, (ali) da li znate gdje je?	Извините што вас узнемиравам, али, да ли знате где је?
urgent	hìtan, hìtna, -o	хитан, хитна, -о
urgently	hìtno	хитно
I need him urgently.	Trebā mi hitno.	Треба ми хитно.
	B	
time point, period of time	dȍba (n. pl. indecl.)	дȍба

He's usually at home at this time.	U ovo doba on je obično doma.	У ово̄ до̄ба̀ о̀н је о̀бично ко̀д кӯђе̄.
simple, vulgar	pròst, -a, -o	про̀ст, -а, -о
simply	pròsto	про̀сто
to be able	mо́ći, mо́gu	мо́ђи, мо́гу
he, she, it can	mòže	мо̀же
I simply don't know where he can be.	Prosto ne znam gdje može biti.	Про̀сто не зна̄м гдѐ мо̀же бѝти.

A

by chance, casually, accidentally	slùčajno	слу̀ча̄јно
Is he by any chance in the restaurant?	Da nije slùčajno u restoranu? /Da nije	Да нѝје слу̀ча̄јно у ресто̄ра̀ну?
or,	u restoranu?	/Да нѝје у ресто̄ра̀ну?

B

to think	mìsliti, mìslīm	мѝслити, мѝслӣм
already, but (contrastive) [in eastern Yugoslavia]	vèć	вѐђ
than, but (contrastive)	nègo	нѐго
I don't think he's in the restaurant but in the coffee shop.	Mislim da nije u restoranu, nego u kavani.	Мѝслӣм да нѝје у ресто̄ра̀ну, вѐђ у ка̀фани.

172

		/Мислим да није у ресторану, него у кафани.
to look	pógledati, da pógledām	погледати, да погледам
look!	pógledājte	погледајте
first	pȑvī, -ā, -ō	први, -ā, -ō
first, at first	pȑvo	прво
(clause initial particle, continuative), and	pà	па
and then	pa ònda	па онда
Look in the coffee shop first, and then in the restaurant.	Pogledajte prvo u kavanu, pa onda u restoran.	Погледајте прво у кафани, па онда у ресторану.

A

to be coming, to come	dólaziti, dólazī	долазити, долазӣ
home (direction towards)	dòma	кући
When does he come home?	Kad on dolazi doma?	Кад он долази кући?

B

around, about	òko	око
seven	sèdam	седам
About seven.	Oko sedam.	Око седам.
Where are you now?	Gdje ste vi sada?	Где сте ви сада?

173

A

consulate	konzúlāt	кȯнзулȃт
office	úred	канцелариja
I'm in the consulate, in [my] office.	Jȃ sam u konzulatu,	Jȃ сам у конзулȃту, у
	u uredu.	канцеларији.

B

to say	kázati, da kȁžem	кȃзати, да кȁжēм
to come	dóći, da dȍđēm	дȏћи, да дȍђē
What should I tell Tom when he comes?	Štȍ da kažem Tomi,	Шта да кȃжем Томи, кад дȍђē?
	kad dođe?	
message	pòruka	пȍрука
Do you have any message?	Da li ímate neku	Да ли имȁте неку поруку?
	poruku?	

A

to say, tell	réći, da rèčēm	рȅћи, да речēм
tell him!	récite mu	рȅците му
to report	jáviti se, da se jāvī	jȃвити се, да се jȁвȋ
counsellor, advisor	sávjetnīk, sávjetnīci	сȃветнȋк, сȃветнȋци

174

as soon as	čim	чим
Will you please tell him to phone me ('report to me') or counsellor Smith as soon as he comes.	Molim vas, recite mu čim dođe, da se javi meni ili savjetniku Smitu.	Молим вас, реците му да се јави мени или саветнику Смиту, чим дође.
to finish	svršiti, da svršīm	свршити, да свршим
this evening	večeras	вечерас
work, job	posao m. Gsg. posla, pl. poslovi	посао, посла, послови
We have urgent work to finish this evening.	Treba svršiti večeras jedan hitan posao.	Треба да свршимо вечерас један хитан посао.

B

Very well. Good-by, sir.	Vrlo dobro. Do viđenja, gospodine.	Врло добро. До виђења, господине.

A

Good-by, ma'am.	Do viđenja, gospođo.	До виђења, госпођо.

Note: /kȁd dȍđē/ is /kadȍđē/. When two identical consonants come next to each other, one drops. This is not shown by the spelling when the two consonants are spelled with a space between them.

Grammatical Notes

Note 9.1   Noun: Dative Case

Note 9.1.1   Dative Case Form

Mislim da nije u restoranu već u kafani.

Ja sam u konzulatu, u kancelariji.

Hvala na pitanju, dobro sam.

Šta da kažem Tomi, kad dođe?

Recite mu da se javi meni ili savetniku Smitu, čim dođe.

The above sentences show typical nouns in the dative case, masculine, neuter and feminine a-nouns.

Masculine and neuter nouns have the ending /-u/ in the dative singular: m. /restoránu/, /konzulátu/, /sávetnīku/, n. /pítānju/. The plural ending for these nouns is /-ima/: /restoránima/, /konzulátima/, /sávetnīcima/, /pítānjima/.

Feminine a-nouns have /-i/ in the singular (/kanceláriji/), /-ama/ in the plural (/kancelárijama/). /kùći/ '(to) home' is a special use of the dative.

Feminine i-nouns have /-i/ in the singular, /-ima/ in the plural: /nòći/, /nóćima/. (Grammarians distinguish D /nòći/ L /nóći/.)

The dative plural /sávetnīcima/ shows a change of /k/ to /c/ before /i/. This is a regular change (there being few exceptions) before the dative singular ending /-i/ (f., a-nouns), the dative plural ending /-ima/ (m. and n.), the masculine nominative plural /-i/ (Note 7.1), the imperative /-i(te)/ (/recite/, for example) and some less common forms. Further examples will occur in later units.

Untill recently a distinction between dative and locative was made. The dative was used as indirect object and after a few prepositions, particularly /k/. The locative was used after certain other prepositions, including /u/ and /na/. These two cases are here considered as one and called 'dative'. With some speakers there is still a distinction between the dative and locative cases of certain words, the difference in the noun being one of stress. /gràd/ 'city' is one of these words. Such speakers say /gràdu/ for the dative and /grádu/ for

the locative.   There are no differences of noun or adjective endings for thr two
cases in the standard language.

Note 9.1.2   Use of Dative

Two uses of the dative case are illustrated above: after prepositions
(/u/ 'in', /na/ 'on, at' [here 'on the occasion of', 'for']) and indirect object
(/Tomi/ 'to Tom', /mu/ 'to him', /meni/ 'to me', /savetniku/ 'to the counsellor',
/Smitu/ 'to Smith').   Only the noun forms will be discussed at this time.   See
Notes 10.1-4 for pronoun and adjective forms, as well as further notes on usage.

Both the dative and the accusative cases may occur after the prepositions
/u/ and /na/.   The basic distinction here (and with certain other prepositions)
is that the accusative indicates the goal or direction towards, while the dative
indicates place where.   One says, therefore, /idem u kafanu/ 'I'm going to
(that is, into) the coffee shop' but /ja sam u kafani/ 'I am in the coffee shop'.
The fundamental difference of meaning between /u/ and /na/ is that /u/ indicates
'into' with the accusative and 'inside of' with the dative, while /na/ indicates
'onto' with the accusative and 'on' with the dative.   Compare /u kuću/ 'into the
house' /u kući/ 'in(side) the house', /na trg/ '(on)to the square', /na trgu/
'on the square'.   (Cf Note 6.1.2)   This basic difference has been somewhat
obscured, primarily through the change of meaning of some of the nouns involved.
It is therefore necessary to learn which of these two prepositions is used with
certain words.   For example, /na/ is normally used with /stanica/:   /na stanicu/
'to the station', /na stanici/ 'at the station'.   The basic meaning of /stanica/
is the place where the stopping and standing is done.   It also means '(bus) stop'
so that /na/ as 'on' is appropriate from an overall point of view.   The usage
of /na/ cannot always be so easily rationalized.   Compare /na univeritétu/ 'at
the university'.

An interesting instance of the difference of meaning is found in the two
versions of the same basic sentence:

Pogledajte prvo u kavanu,   Pogledajte prvo u kafani,
    pa onda u restoran.   pa onda u restoranu.

The sentence to the left uses the accusative, as the speaker has in mind the
goal or direction.   The speaker saying that on the right has in mind the place
where the looking is to be done.   Another usage to be noted, though not used by
all speakers, is /na/ in /na kafi/ in the sense 'at coffee', 'having coffee':

177

/On je na kafi/ 'He's [out] having a cup of coffee' (or the like).

Note 9.2 Verb: Use of Negative

   Mislim da nije u restoranu.

   Serbo-Croatian negates what is thought, not the thinking, in constructions such as the above. English negates the 'think'. Compare:

Mislim da je u restoranu.	I think he's in the restaurant.
Mislim da nije u restoranu.	I don't think he's in the restaurant.

Grammar Drill - Gramatička vežba

GD 9.1   Substitution-Learning Drill - Vežba za učenje sa zamenom

GD 9.1.1 The place of location of persons and/or things - Mesto gde se lica
                                                            ili stvari nalaze

Toma je u restoranu.	hotelu	Beogradu
Toma nije u restoranu već u hotelu.	parku	Zagrebu
	bioskopu	Splitu
	konzulatu	Dubrovniku
	. . .	
	pozorištu	Sarajevu
	kupatilu	Skoplju
. . .		
Moj prijatelj je u sobi.	kafani	Ljubljani
Moj prijatelj nije u sobi nego	ambasadi	Dalmaciji
u kafani.	kancelariji	Srbiji
		Americi
		Jugoslaviji

/kod kuće/ and /doma/ may also be substituted for /u sobi/.

Make the substitutions indicated and give negative transforms.

Moji prijatelji su na trgu.	putu (trip)	stanici	kafi
	pivu	ulici	

178

Toma sedi na krevetu.   stolici

Stolica je u sobi.   kancelariji   hotelu

                                             kući   kupatilu

U sobi je sve čisto i u redu.   ambasadi

                                             kući

                                             kafani

                                             kancelariji

U sobama je lepo, ali nije udobno.   ambasadama   kućama

                                             kafanama   kancelarijama

U hotelu je sve čisto, ali nije   parku
lepo.
                                             restoranu

                                             bioskopu

                                             konzulatu

                                             pozorištu

U hotelima   se čistoća dobro   parkovima   restoranima
održava.
                                             bioskopima   konzulatima

                                             pozorištima   kupatilima

Na stanici je prilično prljavo.   ulici   trgu

                                             stanicama   ulicama

                                             trgovima

Pair drill.
              1   1   2
Vidite prvo u restoranu, pa onda   konzulatu   ambasadi
     2
  u kafani.   parku   kancelariji

                                             restoranu   sobi

GD 9.1.2   Indirect Object

    Make the substitutions indicated.

Ne želimo da smetamo <u>Jovanu</u>. / ... Ivanu

Dajte <u>Jovanu</u> kafu.	Tomi
Recite <u>Jovanu</u> da dođe u ambasadu.	gospodinu Joviću
Kažite <u>Jovanu</u> da se javi savetniku Smitu, čim dođe.	gospodi Jović
Javite <u>Jovanu</u> da dođe u ambasadu.	gospodici Jović

Jovan treba da se javi <u>savetniku Smitu,</u> čim dođe.

Make all number 1 substitutions with the original sentence, then with each
number 2 substitution.

       1   2

<u>Savetniku Smitu</u> treba hitno <u>Jovan</u>.

1			2	
gospodinu Joviću	Tomi		soba	gospođa Smit
gospodi	Zori			
gospodi Jović	gospodici Jović			

GD 9.2   Substitution-Transformation Drill - Vežbanje sa zamenenama i izmenama

            The place of location of persons and/or things - Mesto gde se lica ili

                                                   stvari nalaze

    Make the substitutions indicated with necessary changes of form.

Toma je u <u>restoranu</u>. /Tomo	bioskop	Zagreb
Toma nije u <u>restoranu</u> već u <u>hotelu</u>.	kafana	Ljubljana
	pozorište	Beograd
Substitute /bioskop/ for	soba	Skoplje
/restoran/, /kafana/ for	kancelarija	Srbija
/hotel/, then /kafana/ for	konzulat	Makedonija
/restoran/, /pozorište/	ambasada	Dalmacija
for /hotel/, etc.		

Make the substitutions indicated with negative transforms.

Moji prijatelji su na <u>trgu.</u>	stanica	kafa /kava
	put (trip)	pivo

Toma sedi na <u>krevetu.</u>	stolica
	ulica

Tomina stolica je u <u>sobi.</u>	hotel	kupatilo
	kancelarija	ured
	kuća	kupaona /kupaonica

U <u>sobi</u> je sve čisto i u redu.

U <u>sobama</u> je sve čisto i u redu.

ambasada	hotel
kuća	konzulat
kafana	pozorište
ambasada	kazalište

GD 9.2.1 Indirect Object

Make the substitutions indicated with necessary transforms.

Dajte <u>Tomi</u> kafu.	gospodin Jović
Donesite <u>Tomi</u> kafu.	gospođa Jović
Recite <u>Tomi</u> da dođe u ambasadu.	gospođica Jović
Kažite <u>Tomi</u> da se javi savetniku Smitu, čim dođe.	Jovan
Javite <u>Tomi</u> da dođe u konzulat.	Zora

Toma treba da se javi <u>savetniku Smitu</u> čim dođe.

GD 9.3 Questions and Answers

GD 9.3.1 Informational Answers

GD 9.3.1.1 Adaptation Drill - Vežba sa zamenama i izmenama

Make the substitutions indicated as well as other necessary changes.

Gde su Jovan i Toma?   U <u>restoranu.</u>
/Ivan i Tomo

Oni su u restoranu.

hotel	park	bioskop	konzulat
Beograd	Zagreb	Split	stanica
kafana	soba	kolodvor	ured

Gde je g-ca Smit?

U restoranu.

Ona je u restoranu.

Kako se održava čistoća u restoranu?

Vrlo dobro. U restoranu je sve lepo i čisto.

Ne održave se dobro.

pozorište	kupatilo	Sarajevo	Skoplje
kafana	ambasada	kancelarija	Ljubljana
Dalmacija	Srbija	Amerika	Jugoslavija

Gde su vaši prijatelji?

Na putu.

Oni su na putu.

stanica	kafa

pivo

Gde pijete češće kafu, kod kuće ili u restoranu?

Kod kuće.

Pijem češće kafu kod kuće nego u restoranu.

U restoranu pijem kafu retko.

kafana	kancelarija	konzulat	ambasada

GD 9.3.2 Yes and No Answers

Da li je vaš suprug u restoranu, gospođo?

Da, jeste.

Ne, nije.

Da, on je u restoranu.

Ne, on nije u restoranu, već u kafani.

Da li Toma i Jovan rade u <u>restoranu</u>,   Da, rade.
  gospodine?

Ne, ne rade.

Da, oni rade u <u>restoranu</u>.

Ne, oni ne rade u <u>restoranu</u>, već
  u <u>kafani</u>.

kafana	hotel	ambasada	konzulat
kancelarija	Beograd	Subotica	Kragujevac
Ljubljana	Skoplje		
Priština	Celje		

Da li je u <u>sobi</u> sve čisto i u redu?   Da, jeste.

Ne, nije.

Da, u <u>sobi</u> je sve čisto i u redu.

Ne, u <u>sobi</u> nije sve čisto i u redu.

Da li je u <u>sobama</u> sve čisto i u redu? Da, jeste.

Ne, nije.

Da, u <u>sobama</u> je sve čisto i u redu.

Ne, u <u>sobama</u> nije sve čisto i u redu.

| hotel | kafana | restoran | kupatilo |

Repeat the above drills, using the pattern:

Je li vaš suprug u <u>restoranu,</u> gospođo?   Jeste.

Nije.

Jeste, on je u <u>restoranu</u>.

Ne, on nije u <u>restoranu</u>, već u <u>kafani</u>.

GD 9.4 Question and Answer Drill with Prompt

Moj otac je u Dalmaciji.	Gde je vaš otac?
Moj otac nije kod kuće. On je u Dalmaciji.	Da li je vaš otac kod kuće? /Zar vaš otac nije kod kuće?
Moj (/Moji) otac i majka su u Splitu.	Gde su vaši (/vaš) otac i majka?
Toma i Jovan provode večeri u kafani.	Gde Toma i Jovan provode večeri?
Oni sede u kafani svako veče.	Zar oni sede svako veče u kafani?
Toma i Jovan su u sobi, nešto razgovaraju.	Gde su Toma i Jovan? /Da li su Toma i Jovan u sobi?
Toma nije kod kuće.	Da li je Toma kod kuće?
Ne znam gde je Toma.	Da li znate gde je Toma?
Treba mi Toma.	Ko vam treba? /Da li vam treba Toma?
Trebaju mi Toma i Jovan.	Ko vam treba? /Da li vam trebaju Toma i Jovan?
Savetniku Smitu trebaju Toma i Jovan.	Kome trebaju Toma i Jovan?
Mislim da Toma nije u restoranu, već u kafani.	Da nije Toma (slučajno) u restoranu? /Da li je Toma u restoranu?
Pogledajte prvo u kafani, pa onda u restoranu.	Gde je Toma? Da nije u restoranu?
U ovo doba Toma može biti kod kuće.	Gde Toma može biti u ovo doba?
Ne znam gde Toma može biti u ovo doba.	
U ovo doba Toma je obično u kafani, a ne kod kuće.	Zar Toma nije kod kuće u ovo doba?
Imam jednu poruku za Tomu.	Da li imate neku poruku za Tomu?
Recite Tomi da se javi savetniku Smitu čim dođe.	Kakvu poruku imate za Tomu? /Šta da kažem Tomi kad dođe?
Večeras treba da svršimo jedan hitan posao.	Da li imate nešto da radite večeras?
U Beogradu je lepo vreme. Ne pada kiša.	Kakvo je vreme u Beogradu? Da li pada kiša?

GD 9.4 Conversations - Razgovori

GD 9.4.1

A	B
Gdje je vaš prijatelj Toma?	On je u kinu.
Da li vi idete često u kino.	Ne, ja idem češće u kazalište nego u kino.
Kakva su kina i kazališta u Beogradu?	Nisu loša.
Kako ljudi provode vrijeme ovdje?	Obično kod kuće ili u kinu, kazalištu, parkovima ili kavani.
Ovdje ljudi idu često u kavane, zar ne?	Idu često. To je istina, ali ne samo u kavane.
	Idu također u kazališta i kina.
Šta rade u kavanama.	Obično sjede, nešto piju, jedu i razgovaraju.

Где је ваш пријатељ Тома?	Он је у биоскопу.
Да ли ви идете често у биоскоп?	Не, ја идем чешће у позориште него у биоскоп.
Какви су биоскопи и позоришта у Београду?	Нису рђави.
Како људи проводе време овде?	Обично код куће, или у биоскопу, позоришту, парковима или кафани.
Овде људи иду често у кафане, зар не?	Иду често. То је истина, али не само у кафане.
	Иду такође у позоришта и биоскопе.
Шта раде у кафанама?	Обично седе, нешто пију, једу и разговарају.

GD 9.4.2

Da li je g. Jović doma?	Ne, nije.
Da li znate gdje je?	On je u ovo doba obično u kavani.
	Vidite u kavani.
Izvinite što vam smetam, gospođo.	Ne, ne, vi me ne smetate. To nije ništa.
Kad g. Jović dolazi doma?	On dolazi doma kući oko sedam.
	Želite li da mu nešto kažem kad dođe
	doma.
Prosim vas, recite mu da mi se javi	Prosim, gospodine.
čim dođe.	
Do viđenja, godpođo.	Do viđenja, gospodine.

Да ли је г. Јовић код куће?	Не, није.
Да ли знате где је?	Он је у ово доба обично у кафани.
	Видите у кафани.
Извините што вас узнемиравам, госпођо.	Не, не, ви ме не узнемиравате. То није ништа.
Кад г. Јовић долази кући?	Он долази кући око седам.
	Желите да му нешто кажем кад дође кући.
Молим вас, реците му да ми се јави	Молим господине.
чим дође.	
До виђена, госпођо.	До виђена, господине.

GD 9.4.3

Da li su vaši prijatelji još na putu?	Da, jesu.
Gdje su oni sada?	Sada su u Dubrovniku, u Dalmaciji.
Putujete li vi često.	Da, putujem.
Vi putujete često u Zagreb, zar ne?	Ne samo u Zagreb. Ja putujem također mnogo.
Zašto putujete tako mnogo?	Prvo, ja volim putovati.
	A drugo, želim upoznati Jugoslaviju.
Kakvi su putevi u Jugoslaviji?	Neki putevi su jako dobri, ali ne svi.
Kakvi su putevi u Bosni i Makedoniji?	Neki su dobri, a neki nisu.

Да ли су ваши пријатељи још на путу?	Да, jесу.
Где су они сада?	Сада су у Дубровнику, у Далмацији.
Путујете ли ви често?	Да, путујем.
Ви путујете често у Загреб, је л'те?	Не само у Загреб. Ја путујем такође много.
Зашто путујете тако много?	Прво, ја волим да путујем.
	А друго, желим да упознам Југославију.
Какви су путеви у Југославији?	Неки путеви су врло добри, али не сви.
Какви су путеви у Босни и Македонији?	Неки су добри а неки нису.

GD 9.5 Homework - Domaći zadatak

1.   Write out each of these sentences changing underlined subjects, and objects
of prepositions, to plural.

Moj prijatelj sedi u kafani i pije kafu.   (Gde...)

Ja provodim vreme u kafani, bioskopu i pozorištu.   (Gde...)

Krevet u sobi je lep i udoban.   (Kakav...)

Soba u hotelu je lepa, iako je jeftina.   (Gde...)

On voli da ide u kafanu i pozorište.   (Da li...)

Na trgu i ulici sve je lepo i čisto.   (...li...)

On sedi na krevetu, a ne na stolici.   (...li...)

Stolica i krevet su u sobi.   (Gde...)

2.   Make questions to which the above sentences are appropriate answers.   The
question words are given in parentheses.   Make short affirmative answers to each
question.

UNIT 10

Basic Sentences - Osnovne rečenice

Where do you Live	Gde stanujete	Где станујете

A

American	américkī, -ā, -ō	амерички, -ā, -ō
Your husband works in the American Embassy, doesn't he, ma'am?	Vaš suprug, gospođo, radi u Američkoj ambasadi, zar ne?	Ваш муж, госпођо, ради у Америчкој амбасади, јел'те?#

B

Yes, that's right.	Da, tako je.	Да,# тако је.

A

to be living, dwelling	stanóvati, stánujēm	становати, станујēм
city, town	grȁd, pl. grȁdovi	грȁд, грȁдови
suburbs	prédgrađe	предгрāђе
outskirts	perifêrija	периферија
Do you live in the city or the suburbs?	Da li stanujete u gradu ili u predgrađu?	Да ли станујете у грȁду или на периферији грȁда.

B

We have a nice house in the suburbs.	Imamo lijepu kuću u predgrađu.	Имамо лепу кућу на периферији грȁда.

189

difficult, heavy, hard	téžak, téška, -o	тȇжак, тȇшка, -о
with difficulty	tèško	тȅшко
to live	žívjeti, žìvīm	жи́вети, жи́вим
It's hard to live in the city.	Teško je žívjeti u gradu.	Тȅшко је жи́вети у гра́ду.

A

which	kójī, -ā, -ō	ко̀јӣ, -а̄, -ē
in which	u kòm	у ко̑м
or,	u kójēm	у ко̀је̄м
end, part, region	dìo, G dijéla pl. dijélovi	кра̑ј, кра̀ја, кра̀јеви
Where do you live?	U kom dijelu vi stanujete?	У ком кра̑ју ста́нујете?

B

Topchider Hill	Tòpčidersko brdo	То̀пчидерско бр̏до
We live on Topchider Hill.	Stanujemo na Topčiderskom brdu.	Ста́нујемо на То̀пчидерском бр̏ду.

A

On which street?	U kojoj ulici?	У ко̀јо̄ј у̏лици?

B

Shakespeare Street	Šèkspīrova ùlica	Шекспӣрова улица
comma	zárez	зарез
number	bròj, pl. bròjevi	брȏj, брȍјеви
four	čètiri	четири
On Shakespeare Street, number 4.	U Šèkspirovoj, broj 4.	У Шекспӣровој, брȏj 4.

A

to yours	vášima, vášim	вашима, вашим
to please	dópadati se, dópadā se	допадати се, допадā се
or,	svíđati se, svída se	свиђати се, свиђа се
Well, how do you and your family like Belgrade, madam?	(Pa) kako se vama i vašima dopada Beograd, gospođo?	Па како се вама и вашима допада Београд, госпођо?

B

to my	mòm	мȏм
or,	mójēm	мојēм
Both my husband and I like Belgrade very much.	(I) mom mužu i meni Beograd se jako dopada.	И мȏм мужу и мени Београд се много допада.

to my	mójīm	мојим
parent	róditelj, pl. róditelji	родитељ, родитељи
more	vȉše	више
My parents like Zagreb better than Belgrade.	Mojīm roditeljīma se vȉše svȉđa Zagreb nego Beograd.	Мојим родитељима се више допада Загреб него Београд.

A

constant, permanent	stálan, stálna, -o, stȁlnī, -ā, -ō	сталан, стална, -о; сталнӣ, -ā, -ō
constantly, permanently	stȁlno	стално
Where do your parents live?	Gdje stalno žȉve vašī roditelji?	Где стално живе ваши родитељи?[#]

B

New York	Njȕjork	Њујорк
They live in America, in New York.	Onȉ žȉve u Americi, u Njujorku.	Они живе у Америци, у Њујорку.
family	obítelj (Cr.)	породица
Kragujevac	Krȁgujevac	Крагујевац

English	Latin	Cyrillic
Our friend Mr. Popović and his family live in Kragujevac, Serbia.	Naš prijatelj gospodin Popović i njegova obitelj žive u Kragujevcu, u Srbiji.	Наш пријатељ господин Поповић и његова породица живе у Крагујевцу, у Србији.

<u>In the Living Room</u> U sobi za boravak danju У соби за седење

English	Latin	Cyrillic
that, the (afore-mentioned)	tãj, tà, tò	тāj, тā, тō
Anna, give that [cup of] coffee to my mother.	Ana, molim dajte tu kavu mojoj majci.	Ана, дајте ту кафу мојој мајци.
cup	šólja	шоља
for whom	za kògā	за когā
There is also a [cup of] tea, sir. Who is it for?	Ima i jedna šolja čaja, gospodine. Za koga je?	Има и један чај, господине. За когā је?
sister	séstra	сестра
My sister drinks tea.	Moja sestra pije čaj.	Моја сестра пије чај.
to her	njòj, joj	њоj, joj
Give her the tea.	Njoj dajte čaj.	Њоj дајте чај.
to my friends, for my friends	mòjim prijatéljima	мојим пријатељима
(distributive particle), per, [to] each	pò	по

193

Bring a glass of wine for each of my friends and myself.	Mojim prijateljima i meni donesite po jedno vino.	Мојим пријатељима и мени донесите по једно вино.
Yes, sir.	Molim, gospodine.	Молим, господине.

Grammatical Notes

Note 10.1 Adjective: Dative Case

Vaš muž radi u Američkoj ambasadi, jel'te?	Pa kako se vama i vašima dopada Beograd?
U kom kraju vi stanujete?	I mom mužu i meni Beograd se mnogo dopada.
Stanujemo na Topčiderskom brdu.	Mojim roditeljima se više dopada Zagreb nego Beograd.
U kojoj ulici?	Dajte tu kafu mojoj majci.
U Šekspirovoj, broj 4.	

The above sentences illustrate some dative forms of adjectives, including pronominal adjectives.

Masculine and neuter adjectives have the ending /-ōm/ (or /-ēm/) in the singular, /-Im/ in the plural. There are also longer variants /-ōme/ ~ /-ēme/, /-Ima/. The last is in common use with certain pronominal adjectives. The vowel of each ending is long if the adjective has primary stress. Examples: /Topčiderskōm/ (m. sg.), /vàšima/, /mójIm/ (m. pl.). /kȍm/ and /mȍm/ are masculine singular dative forms but are short forms, there being also the rather archaic /kójēm/ and /mójēm/.

Feminine adjectives have the ending /-ōj/ in the singular, /-Im/ in the plural (the vowel long when the adjective has primary stress). Only /-ōj/ has occurred: /Américkōj/, /kójōj/, for example.

Note the use of the adjective without the noun in /u Šekspirovoj, broj 4/.

Note 10.2 Pronoun: Dative Case

Dajte mu kafu molim.

Donesite mi drugu, vruću kafu.

Milo mi je gospodo.

Želim vam sretan put.

Treba mi hitno.

Recite mu da se javi meni ili savetniku
Smitu, čim dođe.

Pa kako se vama i vašima dopada
Beograd, gospođo?

I mom mužu i meni Beograd se mnogo
dopada.

Njoj dajte čaj.

Mojim prijateljima i meni donesite
po jedno vino.

There are both long (stressed) and short (unstressed, enclitic) forms of
the personal pronouns in the dative case (and also for the accusative, which is
added here for comparison, see Note 12.2). Compare:

N	jȁ		tȉ		ȍn, óno		óna	
A	méne	me	tébe	te	njéga	ga	njȕ	je (ju)
D	méni	mi	tébi	ti	njému	mu	njȏj	joj

N	mȉ		vȉ		óni, óna, óne			
A	nȁs	nas	vȁs	vas	njȉh	ih		
D	nàma	nam	vàma	vam	njȉma	im		

The longer forms are used where there is emphasis or contrast. In /i mȏm mȕžu
i méni/ 'to both my husband and myself' the stressed /méni/ must be used to
parallel the stressed noun phrase /mȏm mȕžu/.

Other examples are similar. Note, for example, /méni ili sȁvetniku Smȉtu/,
/vàma i vášima/, /mȍjim prijatéljima i méni/. In one instance the stressed
pronoun is put first in the sentence - /njȏj/ '(give) her (tea)'. The unstressed forms are much more frequently used, though never first in a sentence.

These examples illustrate further the use of the dative without any preposition. The general meaning is one of reference, indicating the person concerned
or in whose interest something is done, but who is not himself taking part in

the action, if any, described by the sentence. While many datives without
prepositions are equivalent to English 'indirect objects' ('give <u>him</u> coffee',
'give <u>her</u> tea', etc.), it is better to take a broader view of the basic meaning
of the dative, since many other examples can in no way be 'indirect objects'.
Compare the following:

Indirect object:	dajte mu
	donesite mi
	recite mu
	njoj dajte čaj
	želim vam sretan put
Impersonal type construction:	milo mi je (neuter plus 'is')
	drago mi je
With /treba/	treba mi hitno
With verbs using /se/	da se javi meni
	kako se vama i vašima dopada /sviđa

The verbs /jàvī se/ 'is informing', /dópadā se/ 'is pleasing' are examples of the
use of the reflexive pronoun /se/ (short, unstressed, enclitic with a verb).
Such combinations are known as 'reflexive verbs'. The dative is frequently used
with reflexive verbs. /jàvī se/ is parallel to /récite/ in usage, that is, the
dative may be considered as 'indirect object' as it may be further stated what
the person is to be informed of. On the other hand, a phrase such as /Beograd
mi se dopada/ 'I like Belgrade' might be translated more literally 'Belgrade, so
far as my personal interest is concerned, is pleasing'.

The dative is also used with /trèbā/. In the above instance it is literally
'he is needed with reference to my welfare urgently'. /trèbā mi/ is frequently
translatable 'I need'.

The pronoun /kò/ 'who' has dative /kóme/; /tò/ 'that' has /tòme/. /štà/
(/štò/) 'what' has /čému/ as in /u čému je stvār?/. See below for the adjectives
/kójī/ and /tàj/.

Note 10.3 Pronominal Adjectives: Dative Case

The pronominal adjectives were included in the discussion found in Note 10.1.
See also Note 4.2. The present note summarizes these pronominal adjective forms.
(The masculine animate accusative forms are not considered here, as they are not
fully discussed until Note 12.1.)

	'my'	'your' (sg.)	'his, its'	'her'
N	mòɟ	tvòɟ	nɟégov	nɟěn
A	mòɟ	tvòɟ	nɟégov	nɟěn
D	mòm (móɟēm)	tvòm (tvóɟēm)	nɟégovom	nɟěnom

	'our'	'your'	'their'
N	nàš	vàš	nɟìhov
A	nàš	vàš	nɟìhov
D	nàšem	vàšem	nɟìhovom

The examples listed above in Note 10.1 give two other pronominal adjectives:
/tàɟ/, 'that, the aforementioned' and /kóɟ I/ 'which'.

/tàɟ/ has an ending /-āɟ/ in the masculine singular nominative (and inanimate
accusative). Compare:

	m.	n.	f.
N	tàɟ	tò	tà
A	tàɟ (inan.)	tò	tù
D	tòm	tòm	tòɟ

N	kóɟ I	kóɟē	kóɟā
A	kóɟ I (inan.)	kóɟē	kóɟū
D	kòm (kóɟēm)	kòm (kóɟēm)	kóɟòɟ

Note 10.4 Pronoun and Pronominal Adjective: Parallel use

Inače, soba mu je lepa i udobna.

/sòba mu/ here is translated by 'his room'. Another phrase so translatable is
/ngégova sòba/. The first uses the dative of the short pronoun, the meaning

being the same as in the examples in Note 10.2. above, that of reference to a given person, indicating his personal involvement, etc. This is a very frequent (and colloquial) pattern corresponding to the English use of a possessive adjective ('my', 'his', etc.). The pronominal adjectives /mȏj/, /njégov/ are either more emphatic or more general.

It should also be noted that the words /ótac/ and /mȁjka/ are normally used alone when the reference is to 'my father' and 'my mother', as in the English sentence 'Father has gone for the day'.

Note 10.5 Question Expressions /jé l'te/, /zar nè/

    Vaš muž, gospođo, radi u američkoj ambasadi, je l'te

    Vaš muž, gospođo, radi u američkoj ambasadi, zar ne?

/jé l'te/ or /zar nè/ is added to form a question anticipating an affirmative reply. The corresponding English adds a substitute verb in a question type of construction: 'he works, doesn't he?', 'he's there, isn't he?', 'he went, didn't he?'. Serbo-Croatian uses /je l'te/ or /zar ne/ for all such constructions.

    In such a construction the sentence is the same as the simple statement, but is followed by /jé l'te/ or /zar nè/. Other examples:

    Tomina soba je velika i lepa, je l'te? (/zar ne)

    On želi da pije kafu, je l'te? (/zar ne)

    Oni piju jaku, ali gorku kafu, je l'te? (/zar **ne**)

/jé l'te/ and /zar **ne**/ correspond to 'isn't it', 'doesn't he', 'don't they' in these sentences.

Grammar Drill - Gramatička vežba

GD 10.1 Dative of nouns accompanied by adjective (singular and plural) -
      Dativ/Lokativ imenica sa pridevima u jednini i množini

GD 10.1.1 Substitution-Learning Drill - Vežba za učenje sa zamenom

Singular

    Make the substitutions indicated and give the negative transform.

Toma je u <u>svom restoranu.</u>

Toma nije u <u>svom restoranu.</u>

mom hotelu / mojem hotelu   našem parku

svom bioskopu   Američkom konzulatu

našem pozorištu   vašem uredu

Moj prijatelj je u <u>svojoj sobi.</u>

Tominoj sobi   Nemačkoj ambasadi

Jovanovoj kancelariji   svojoj kafani

Stanjemo na <u>Topčiderskom brdu.</u>

Malom Kalemegdanu (Mali Kalemegdan)   Cvetnom trgu (Cvetni trg)

Zelenom vencu (Zeleni venac)   Banovom brdu (Banovo brdo)

Stanujemo u <u>Miloševoj ulici.</u>

Jovanovoj ulici (Jovanova ulica)   Zorinoj ulici (Zorina ulica)

Šekspirovoj ulici   Knez-Mihailovoj ulici (Knez-Mihailova
                                          ulica. Note that /Knez-Mihailov is
                                          a unit, /Knez/ does not change.)

Oni žive u <u>Novom Sadu.</u>

Gornjem Milanovcu (Gornji Milanovac)   Gorskom kotaru (Gorski kotar)

Generalskom Stolu (Generalski Stol)

Oni žive u <u>Staroj Pazovi.</u>

Rogaškoj Slatini (Rogaška Slatina)   Vrnjačkoj Banji (Vrnjačka Banja)

Niškoj Banji (Niška Banja)

Make the indicated substitutions.

Molim vas dajte tu kafu <u>mom ocu.</u>

Beograd se dopada <u>mom ocu.</u>   /sviđa

Beograd se ne dopada <u>mom ocu.</u>

mom prijatelju   mojoj majci

Tominom bratu   Tominoj sestri

Zorinom mužu   Jovanovoj supruzi

Plural

Make the indicated substitutions with negative transforms.

U ovo doba oni su sigurno u <u>svojim</u>   U ovo doba oni sigurno nisu u svojim
  <u>sobama.</u>   sobama.

svojim hotelima   njihovim restoranima

svojim kućama   njihovim kancelarijama

svojim krevetima   njihovim uredima

Make the indicated substitutions.

Dajte te kafe <u>našim prijateljima.</u>

Beograd se dopada <u>našim prijateljima.</u> /sviđa

Donesite po jedno pivo nama i <u>našim prijateljima.</u>

našim majkama   našim roditeljima

Tominim sestrama

GD 10.1.2 Controlled Adaptation Drill

Vaš prijatelj je u <u>svom hotelu.</u>

                    <u>svom kupatilu</u>

                    <u>svojoj sobi</u>

svoj hotel   svoje kupatilo   svoja soba

američki konzulat   naše pozorište   Američka ambasada

naš bioskop   svoje selo   njegova kancelarija

svoj ured   to kazalište   svoja kafana

Stanujemo na Cvetnom trgu. Cvetni trg   Banovo brdo.

                Banovom brdu.   Mali Kalemegdan   Topčidersko brdo

                            Zeleni venac   Dedinje

                            Avalski put

Stanujemo u Puškinovoj ulici.   Puškinova ulica.

                                        Miloševa ulica

                                        Knez-Mihailova ulica

                                        Maglajska ulica

                                        Šekspirova ulica

                                        Jovanova ulica

Moji roditelji žive u Novom Sadu.   Novi Sad   Stara Pazova

                Staroj Pazovi   Gornji Milanovac   Rogaška Slatina

                                    Gorski kotar   Vrnjačka Banja

                                    Generalski Stol   Niška Banja

Beograd se sviđa mom bratu.   moj brat   moja sestra

                mojoj sestri   vaš prijatelj   naša majka

Mom bratu se sviđa Beograd.   Zorin suprug   moja žena

Mojoj sestri   naš otac   Tomina braća

Jugoslavija se sviđa <u>našim prijateljima</u>.   <u>naši prijatelji</u>   <u>naše sestre</u>

       <u>našim sestrama</u>   naši roditelji   naše majke

                                    naši ljudi   naše žene

GD 10.1.2 Substitution-Adaptation Drill - Vežbanje sa zamenama i izmenama

Make the indicated substitutions, adapting the form to the context.

Toma je u <u>svom hotelu</u>.   svoja kafana

Toma nije u <u>svom hotelu</u> nego vašem.   njihovo pozorište

Moji prijatelji su u <u>svojoj sobi</u>.   Jovanova kuća

Moji prijatelji nisu u <u>svojoj sobi</u>, već u našoj.   njegova kancelarija

                                              Nemačka ambasada

                                              taj ured

Pair drill.

                   1

Stanujemo na <u>Topčiderskom brdu</u>.

                    1   2

Mi ne stanujemo na <u>Topčiderskom brdu</u>, već u <u>Miloševoj ulici</u>.

                       1   2

                    Mali Kalemegdan.........Jovanova ulica

                    Cvetni trg..............Knez-Mihailova ulica

                    Zeleni venac............Zorina ulica

                    Banovo brdo.............Maglajska ulica

                    Avaliski put............Puškinova ulica

                         1

Moji prijatelji žive u <u>Novom Sadu</u>.

                       1   2

Moji prijatelji ne žive u <u>Novom Sadu</u>, nego u <u>Staroj Pazovi</u>.

                       1   2

                    Gornji Milanovac........Rogaška Slatina

                    Gorski kotar............Vrnjačka Banja

                    Generalski Stol.........Niška Banja

Make the indicated substitutions and necessary adaptations. Singular

Molim vas dajte tu kafu <u>mojoj sestri</u>.

Beograd i Zagreb se dopadaju <u>mojoj sestri</u>. /sviđaju

Beograd se dopada, a Zagreb se ne dopada <u>mojoj sestri</u>.

naš otac	Tomina majka
vaša supruga	njen muž
Zorin otac	vaš prijatelj
Jovanov brat	vaša braća

Make the indicated substitutions with necessary adaptations.   Plural

Moji prijatelji su u ovo doba sigurno u <u>svojim sobama</u>.

Moji prijatelji u ovo doba sigurno nisu u <u>svojim sobama</u>.

njihov hotel	svoja kancelarija
njihov krevet	

Donesite po jedno pivo <u>našim prijateljima</u>.

<u>Našim prijateljima</u> se ne dopada Beograd.   /sviđa

<u>Našim prijateljima</u> se dopada Zagreb više nego Beograd.

naše žene	njihove majke
Jovanovi roditelji	Tomine sestre
njihovi muževi	vaši očevi

GD 10.2   Dative of the personal pronouns - Dativ ličnih zamenica
GD 10.2.1 Substitution-Learning Drill - Vežba sa učenje sa zamenom

<u>Plain</u>

Dajte <u>mi</u> kafu.	mu (Jovanu)	nam (ocu i meni)
	joj (Zori)	im (mojim roditeljima)

Emphatic

Dajte meni kafu.   njemu (Jovanu)   nama (ocu i meni)

                          njoj (Zori)   njima (mojim roditeljima)

Plain

Treba mi soba.   ti   nam

Milo mi je. /Drago   mu   vam

Žao mi je.   joj   im

Emphatic

Meni treba soba.   tebi   nama

Meni je milo. /drago   njemu   vama

Meni je vrlo žao.   njoj   njima

GD 10.2.2 Substitution-Adaptation Drill – Vežba sa zamenama i izmenama

Dajte mi jednu jaku kafu.   on   mi

Dajte Jovanu tu kafu.   ona   oni

Treba mi lepa i velika soba.   on   mi

Mnogo mi je žao što imate rđavu sobu.   ti   vi

Milo mi je što imate lepu i čistu sobu.   ona   oni
 /Drago mi je...

GD 10.2.3 Adjective Drill with Pronoun Transform

In the sentences on the left a pronominal adjective with a noun is used. In those on the right the dative of the corresponding (short) personal pronoun is substituted for the adjective. The meaning of the sentences is roughly the same, those on the right being more colloquial.

Moja kuća je lepa i udobna.	Kuća mi je lepa i udobna.
Tvoja kuća je lepa i udobna.	Kuća ti je lepa i udobna.
Njegova kuća je lepa i udobna.	Kuća mu je lepa i udobna.
Njena kuća je lepa i udobna.	Kuća joj je lepa i udobna.
Naša kuća je lepa i udobna.	Kuća nam je lepa i udobna.
Vaša kuća je lepa i udobna.	Kuća vam je lepa i udobna.
Njihova kuća je lepa i udobna.	Kuća im je lepa i udobna.

GD 10.3 Random Substitution Drill

	Jovan radi u jednom velikom restoranu.
ići	Jovan ide u jedan veliki restoran.
Miloševa ulica	Jovan ide u Miloševu ulicu.
stanovati	Jovan stanuje u Miloševoj ulici.
lep kraj grada	Jovan stanuje u lepom kraju grada.
lepa i velika kuća	Jovan stanuje u lepoj i velikoj kući.
imati	Jovan ima lepu i veliku kuću.
trebati	Jovanu treba lepa i velika kuća.
jedno obaveštenje	Jovanu treba jedno obaveštenje.
oni	Njima treba jedno obaveštenje.
ova soba	Njima treba ova soba.
dopadati se	Njima se dopada ova soba.
voleti	Oni vole ovu sobu.
živeti	Oni žive u ovoj sobi.

GD 10.4 Questions and Answers
GD 10.4.1 Informational Answers

Pair Drill

Gde je Beograd?	U Jugoslaviji.
	Beograd je u Jugoslaviji.

Gde živite?   U Beogradu, u Jugoslaviji.

                               Živim u Beogradu, u Jugoslaviji.

                         or Živimo u Beogradu, u Jugoslaviji.

Njujork.......Amerika   Mostar......Hercegovina

Ljubljana.....Slovenija   Skoplje.....Makedonija

Zagreb........Hrvatska (adj. decl.) Titograd....Crna Gora

Kragujevac....Srbija   Priština....Kosovo i Metohija

Novi Sad......Vojvodina   Split.......Dalmacija

Sarajevo......Bosna   Osijek......Slavonija

U kom gradu žive Jovan i Toma.   U Zagrebu.

                                     Oni žive u Zagrebu.

                                     Jovan i Toma žive u Zagrebu.

Beograd   Priština

Kragujevac   Varaždin

Ljubljana   Topola

Skoplje   Titovo Užice

Tuzla   Novi Sad

Sarajevo   Gornji Milanovac

Titograd   Bosanska Gradiška

Substitution Drill

Gde stanujete?
                                            1
                                     U Miloševoj ulici.
                                                 1
                                     Stanujem u Miloševoj ulici.
                                                  1
                                     Stanujemo u Miloševoj ulici.
                                          2
                                     Na Malom Kalemegdanu.
                                              2
                                     Stanujem na Malom Kalemegdanu.

U kojoj ulici stanujete?

U Miloševoj ulici.

Stanujem u Miloševoj ulici.

1 (with /u/)	2 (with /na/)
grad	Cvetni trg
predgrade	Zeleni venac
Jovanova ulica	Topčidersko brdo
Zorina ulica	Dedinje
Knez-Mihailova ulica	periferija grada

Make the substitutions as indicated.

Kako se Zori dopada Beograd? /sviđa

Dopada joj se mnogo.

Ne dopada joj se.

Njoj se Beograd mnogo dopada.

Njoj se Beograd ne dopada.

Jovanu	njemu, mu
g. i g-đi Smit	njima, im
Zori i vama	nama, nam

Kakva soba treba Zori?

Treba joj lepa i velika soba.

Njoj treba lepa i velika soba.

Šta treba Zori?

Make the substitutions indicated, using in the answers the appropriate form of the pronoun for each substituted item.

Kako se vašem suprugu sviđa Zagreb?

Sviđa mu se mnogo.

Ne sviđa mu se.

Njemu se mnogo sviđa Zagreb.

Njemu se ne sviđa Zagreb.

Tomina sestra	Vaša majka	vi i vaš otac
vaši prijatelji	Zorin brat	

Make the substitutions indicated, using the proper form of the pronoun for both question and answer.

Kakva soba vam treba?	Treba mi lepa i velika soba.
	/ Meni treba lepa i velika soba.
Kako vam se sviđaju Beograd i Zagreb?	Sviđaju mi se mnogo.
	Ne sviđaju mi se.
	Meni se mnogo sviđaju i Beograd i Zagreb.
	Meni se mnogo ne sviđaju ni Beograd ni Zagreb.

on	ona	vi (plural)
oni		

GD 10.4.2 Yes and No Answers

Substitution-Adaptation Correlation Drill - Vežbanje sa zamenama i izmenama

    Make all 2 substitutions with the original question, then with each 1 substitution.

1	2	
Da li vaš brat živi u Novom Sadu?		Da, živi.
		Ne, ne živi.
		Da, on živi u Novom Sadu.
		Ne, on ne živi u Novom Sadu.

1	2	
vi	Stara Pazova	Niška Banja
vaši roditelji	Gornji Milanovac	
porodica Jović	Rogaška Slatina	
vi i vaša porodica /obitelj	Gorski Kotar	
	Vrnjačka Banja	

           1   2

Da li <u>Toma i Jovan</u> stanuju na <u>Topčiderskom brdu?</u>   Da, stanuju.

                                               Ne, ne stanuju.

                                               Da, oni stanuju na

                                                   <u>Topčiderskom brdu.</u>

                                               Ne, oni ne stanuju na

                                                   <u>Topčiderskom brdu.</u>

        1   2

porodica Jović   Cvetni trg   periferija grada

vi   Zeleni venac

vi (plural)   Banovo brdu

ti   Dedinje

          1   2

Da li <u>Toma</u> treba da se javi <u>savetniku Smitu?</u>   Da, treba.

                                               Ne, ne treba.

    1   2

(ja)   Američka ambasada

(mi)   naš konzulat

(vi)   svoja kancelarija

oni   g. i g-đa Jović

Da li <u>vam</u> treba soba?   Da, treba.

                                           Ne, ne treba.

                                           Da, treba mi soba.

                                           Ne, ne treba mi soba.

Da li <u>vam</u> se sviđaju Beograd i Zagreb?   Da, sviđaju se.

                                           Ne, ne sviđaju se.

                                           Da, sviđaju mi se i Beograd i

                                               Zagreb.

Da li se <u>vama</u> sviđaju Beograd i Zagreb?   Da, sviđaju se.

                                        Ne, ne sviđaju se.

                                        Da, meni se sviđaju i Beograd i
                                                 Zagreb.

vi (plural)   on   ona

oni

Da li se Beograd dopada <u>vašem ocu?</u>   Da, dopada.

                                        Ne, ne dopada.

                                        Da, Beograd se dopada mom ocu.

                                        Ne, Beograd se ne dopada mom ocu.

Tomina majka   Jovanov brat   vaša sestra

naš prijatelj   vaš muž

Repeat the above drill with the following plural items.

moji roditelji   vaši prijatelji   naše majke

Tomine sestre   vaši muževi

     The items for the substitutions in the following drill are given in the proper form. Each item is to be used in the question, and the appropriate form of it also in the answer.

Da li se Beograd i Zagreb sviđaju   Da, sviđaju joj se.
    <u>vašoj majci?</u>

                                      Ne, ne sviđaju joj se.

                                      Da, njoj se sviđaju i Beograd i
                                               Zagreb.

joj   njoj   vam

vama   vašem bratu   mu

njemu   vašim roditeljima   gospodi i gospodici Jović

im   njima

Repeat the substitutions at the beginning of GD 10.4.2 with:

Živi li vaš brat u Novom Sadu?   Da, živi.

                                        Ne, ne živi.

                                        Da, moj brat živi u Novom Sadu.

                                        Ne, moj brat ne živi u Novom Sadu.

GD 10.5 Question and Answer Drill with Prompt

Ja radim u Američkoj ambasadi.   Gde radite, gospodine?

Stanujemo u gradu.   Gde stanujete. /Da li stanujete u
                                        gradu?

Mi ne stanujemo u gradu, već na   Da li stanujete u gradu? /Zar ne
  periferiji grada.   stanujete u gradu?

Imamo lepu kuću na periferiji.   Kakvu kuću imate?

Teško je živeti u gradu. Vrlo je   Kako je živeti u gradu?
  toplo.

Naša kuća je na Topčiderskom brdu.   U kom (/kojem) kraju je vaša kuća?

Nama je vrlo prijatno u našoj kući.   Sigurno je vrlo prijatno stanovati na
                                        Topčiderskom brdu?

Naša kuća je u Puškinovoj ulici.   U kojoj ulici je vaša kuća?

Meni se dopada Beograd mnogo.   Da li vam se dopada Beograd?

Mom ocu se ne sviđa Beograd.   Da li se vašem ocu sviđa Beograd?

Mom ocu se više sviđaju Zagreb i   Koji gradovi se sviđaju vašem ocu?
  Ljubljana.

Moj prijatelj i njegova porodica   Gde žive vaš prijatelj i njegova
  žive u Kragujevcu, u Srbiji.   porodica?

Tomini roditelji žive u jednom malom   Gde žive Tomini roditelji?
  mestu u Gorskom kotaru u Hrvatskoj.

Kuća nam je mala i neudobna.   Kakva vam je kuća.

Treba nam velika i udobna kuća.   Kakva kuća vam treba?

Recite Tominoj majci da je Toma   Šta da kažem Tominoj majci?
  dobro i da ne brine.

Dajte tu kafu mojoj sestri.   Kome da dam ova kafu?   /Za koga je
                                           ova kafa?

Mi obično pijemo kafu u jednoj   Gde vi obično pijete kafu?
  maloj kafani.

GD 10.4   Conversations - Razgovori
GD 10.4.1

                A   B

Gdje radite, gospodine Popoviću?   Radim u Beogradu.

Da li stanujete u Beogradu?   Ne, ne stanujem.

Gdje stanujete?   Stanujem u Staroj Pazovi.

Zašto ne stanujete u Beogradu već   Moja žena ima kuću u Staroj Pazovi.
  u Staroj Pazovi?   Zato stanujemo tamo.

To je druga stvar. Kakvu kuću ima   Ima vrlo lijepu i udobnu kuću.
  vaša gospođa?

To je lijepo.   Da, mi smo zadovoljni.

Где радите, господине Поповићу?   Радим у Београду.

Да ли станујете у Београду?   Не, не станујем.

Где станујете?   Станујем у Старој Пазови.

Зашто не станујете у Београду већ   Моја жена има кућу у Старој Пазови.
  у Старој Пазови?   Зато станујемо тамо.

То је друга ствар. Какву кућу има   Има врло лепу и удобну кућу.
  ваша госпођа?

То је лепо.   Да, ми смо задовољни.

GD 10.4.2

Vi radite u američkoj ambasadi,   Da, radim.
  gospodine, zar ne?

Gdje je američka ambasada?   Ona je u Miloševoj ulici.

Da li stanujete u gradu ili predgrađu?   Stanujemo u predgrađu.

U kom (/kojem) dijelu stanujete?

Moja žena ne voli živeti u gradu.

U kojoj ulici stanujete?

Stanujemo na Topčiderskom Brdu.

Da, znam.

Znate li gdje je Šekspirova ulica?

Kakvu kuću imate?

Mi stanujemo u Šekspirovoj ulici broj 4.

Da li je vaša gospođa zadovoljna?

Imamo prilično veliku i vrlo udobnu kuću.

Jest, i ona i ja smo vrlo zadovoljni.

Ви радите у америчкој амбасади,
  господине, јел'те?

Да, радим.

Где је америчка амбасада?

Она је у Милошевој улици.

Да ли станујете у граду или на
  периферији.

Станујемо на периферији.

Моја жена не воли да живи у граду.

У ком (/којем) крају станујете?

Станујемо на Топчидерском Брду.

У којој улици станујете?

Знате ли где је Шекспирова улица?

Да, знам.

Ми станујемо у Шекспировој улици број 4.

Какву кућу имате?

Имамо прилично велику и врло удобну кућу.

Да ли је ваша госпођа задовољна?

Јесте, и она и ја смо врло задовољни.

GD 10.4.3

Kako vam se dopada Beograd, gospodine
  Smite?

On mi se mnogo dopada.

A dopada li se Beograd vašoj gospođi?

Da, njoj se također Beograd dopada
  jako mnogo.

U Beogradu su sada njeni roditelji,
  zar ne?

Da, jesu.

Kako se njima sviđa Jugoslavija.

Oni vole Jugoslaviju. Ali Zagreb im se
  više dopada nego Beograd, a Split
  više nego Zagreb.

To razumijem. I ja volim Zagreb i
  Split. Ali, meni se više dopada
  Gorski kotar nego Dalmacija.

Gde je Gorski kotar?

Gorski kotar je u Hrvatskoj.

Znate li gdje je Rijeka?   Da, znam.

Tamo je Gorski kotar.

Kako se vama i gospođi Smit dopadaju   Oni nam se jako dopadaju. I moja žena
   Dedinje i Topčidersko brdo?   i ja mnogo volimo Jugoslaviju.

Hvala gospodine. To mi je milo. I
   mi Jugoslaveni volimo Ameriku.

Како вам се допада Београд, господине   Он ми се много допада.
   Смите?

А допада ли се Београд вашој госпођи?   Да, њој се такође Београд допада
                                                     врло много.

У Београду су сада њени родитељи,   Да, јесу.
   јел'те?

Како се њима свиђа Југославија.   Они воле Југославију. Али Загреб им се
                                                     више допада него Београд, а Сплит
                                                     више него Загреб.

То разумем. И ја волим Загреб и Сплит. Где је Горски котар?
   Али, мени се више допада Горски котар
   него Далмација.

Горски отар је у Хрватској.

Знате ли где је Ријека?   Да, знам.

Тамо је Горски котар.

Како се вама и госпођи Смит допадају   Они нам се допадају врло много.
   Дедиње и Топчидерско брдо?   И моја жена и ја много волимо
                                                     Југославију.

Хвала господине. То ми је мило.
   И ми Југословени волимо Америку.

GD 10.5 Homework - Domaći zadatak

1.   Fill the blanks in 1-3 with the proper form of the item to the right of
the sentence. In 4-10 fill the blanks with a proper item from those listed to
the right of each sentence.

1. Moj prijatelj živi u..........   (Slavonski Brod)

2. Slavonski Brod je u ....   (Hrvatska)

3. Mi imamo lepu kuću u ....br. 4.   (Zagrebačka ulica)

4. Trebaju.........lepe i velike sobe. (mom prijatelju, njemu, mu)

5. ....trebaju lepe i velike sobe. (savetniku Smitu, njemu, mu)

6. ....se dopada Beograd vrlo mnogo. (mojoj ženi, njoj, joj)

7. Jovan treba da.........se javi.   (savetniku Smitu, njemu, mu)

8. Recite.........da mi se javi čim dođe kući. (Jovanu, mu)

9. ....je milo što imate lepu sobu. (mojoj ženi i meni, nama, nam)

10. Milo.........je što ste zadovoljni.
    /Drago   (g-nu i g-đi Jović, njima, im)

2. Make questions to which the above sentences will be appropriate answers.

UNIT 11

Basic Sentences - Osnovne rečenice

Where are you From?	Odakle ste?	Одакле сте?

A

whose	čȉjȋ, -ā, -ē	чѝјӣ, -ā, -ē
that	ónāj, ónā, ónō	òнāј, òнā, òнō
that (pronominal)	ónō	òно
Whose monument is that?	Čȉjȋ je ȍno spòmenȋk?	Чѝјӣ је ȍно споменӣк?#

B

prince	knȇz, pl. knèževi	кнȇз, кнèжеви
	/knèzovi	/ кнèзови
Michael	Miháilo	Михáило
That's the Prince Michael monument.	Tȍ je spòmenȋk Knèza	Tȍ је споменӣк Кнèза
	Miháila.	Михáила.

A

building	zgràda	згрàда
across (with G)	prèko	прèко
across from (with G)	preko púta	преко пýта
What building is that across from the monument?	Kòja je ȍno zgràda	Kòjā је ȍно згрàда прèко
	prèko púta spòmenȋka?	пýта споменӣка?#

216

B

national	národnī, -ā, -ō	на̑родни̅, -а̅, -о̅
museum	múzēj	му́зеј
That's the National Museum.	Tȍ je Národnī múzēj.	То̑ је на̑родни̅ музе̑ј.

A

| from where | òdākle | ода̄кле |
| Where is your friend from? | Òdākle je vȁš prȉjatelj? | Ода̄кле је ваш прӣјатељ?# |

B

| from, out of (with G) | iz | из |
| He's from Split [in] Dalmacia. | Ȍn je iz Splȉta, iz Dálmācijē. | О̑н је из Сплита, из Далма̄ције̄. |

A

with us	kod nȁs	код на̑с
visit	pòsjeta	посета
He's coming to visit us ('He's coming to us on a visit'), isn't he?	Ȍn dȍlazi kod nȁs u pòsjetu, zȁr nè?	О̑н долази код нас у посету, је л'те?#

B

| probably | vjerojátno | веро̀ватно |
| Saturday | súbota | су̀бота |

Sunday, week	nédjelja	нéдеља
Yes, probably on Saturday or Sunday.	Jèst. Vjerojátno u súbotu ili nédjelju.	Јèсте. Вероватно у суботу или недељу.

A

today	dánas	данас
post office, mail	pòšta	пòшта
Is there any mail today?	Dà li ima dánas pòštē?	Да ли има данас пòштē?#

B

| Yes, there is. | Dà, imā. | Да,# имā. |

A

how big	kóliki, -ā, -ō	колики, -ā, -ō / колики
how much, how many	kóliko	колико / колико
letter	písmo Gpl. pìsāmā	писмо, пūсāмā
How many letter are there?	Kóliko pìsāmā ima?	Колико пūсāмā има?#

B

several	nèkoliko	неколико
There are several letters.	Ima nèkoliko pìsama.	Има неколико писама.
for me	za méne	за мене
from (with G)	od	од

from my father	od mȍg(a) óca	од мȍг(а) о́ца
One is for me from home, from my mother and father.	Jȅdno je za mȅne od kȕćē, od mȍg(a) óca i mȁjkē.	Јȅдно је за мȅне од кȕћē, од мȍг(а) о́ца и мȁјкē.

A

How are they?	Kàko su òni?	Ка́ко су о́ни?#

B

God	Bȍg, G. Bȍga, pl., bȍgovi	Бȍг, Бȍга, бȍгови
Thank God, they are fine.	Hvȁla Bȍgu, dòbro su.	Хва̄ла Бȍгу, дȍбро су.
next, going, coming, (week, month)	ídūćī, -ā, -ō	идӯћи, -ā, -ē
summer	ljȅto	лȅто
vacation (during summer)	ljȅtovānje	лȅтова̄ње
They're leaving Novi Sad next week on vacation.	Òni òdlaze ídućē nèdjelje iz Nòvog Sáda na ljȅtovānje.	Они одлазе идӯће недеље из Нȍвог Са̄да на лȅтова̄ње.

A

who	kò	ко̀
from whom	od kóga	од кога̄

Who is the other letter from?	Od kógā je drùgo písmo?	Од кога̄ је̍ друго пи̍смо?#

B

The other letter is from our friends the Jovanović's.	Drùgo písmo je od nàšíh prijatéljā Jovánovíćā.	Друго пи̍смо је од на̍ших прија̍те̍ља Јовановиһа̄.
to be returning, to return	vràćati se, vràćajū se	враһати се, враһаjȳ се
the day after tomorrow	prèkosutra /prèksutra	прекосутра /прексутра
western	zàpadnī, -ā, -ō	за̍паднӣ, -а̄, -о̄
They're coming back from West Germany the day after tomorrow.	Òni se vràćaju prèkosutra iz Zàpadne Njèmačkē.	Они се враһају прекосутра из За̍падне Нема̍чке.

A

baggage	pŕtljāga	пртља̄г
brought	dònijet /donésen	доне̄т / доне́сен
from, from off, out of (vehicle) (with G)	s, sa	с, са
pertaining to a railroad	žèljeznìčkī, -ā, -ō	железничкӣ, -а̄, -о̄
railroad station	kòlodvōr (Cr)	железничка станица

| Has your friend's baggage been brought from the railroad station? | Dà li je prtljága vašeg prijatelja doneséna sa kòlodvora? | Да ли је пртљаг вашег пријатеља донёт са железничке станице?# |

B

| Not ('isn't') yet. | Nìje jòš. | Није још. |

A

| Do you know who can bring it? | Dà li znáte kò ga mòže dónijeti? | Да ли знате ко може да га донесе?# |

B

| desk clerk | pórtīr | портӣр |
| Ask the desk clerk. | Pítājte portíra. | Питајте портӣра. |

Grammatical Notes

Note 11.1 Noun/Adjective: Genitive
Note 11.1.1 Genitive: Form

On je iz Splita, iz Dalmacije.

Jedno je za mene od kuće, od moga oca i majke.

Oni odlaze iduće nedelje iz Novog Sada na letovanje.

Je li prtljag vašeg prijatelja donet sa železničke stanice?

The genitive singular ending for masculine and neuter nouns is /-a/. The adjective ending is /-ōg/ (/-ēg/) or /-ōga/ (/-ēga/). The genitive singular ending for feminine /a/ nouns is /-ē/, as is the adjective ending. Feminine /i/ nouns have /i/: /nòć/ G. /nòći/.

221

Ima nekoliko pisama.

Drugo pismo je od naših prijatelja Jovanovića.

The genitive plural ending for neuter nouns is /-ā/. A preceding vowel is lengthened: /pìsāmā/. In this word the preceding vowel is moveable /a/. The base of the word is /pis(a)ma/. The (a) is lost before all other endings: /pismo/ G. /pisma/ D. /pismu/, etc. The genitive plural /-ā/ lengthens the preceding (a): /pìsāmā/.

The genitive plural ending for masculine nouns is usually /-ā/ but some nouns have /-ī/. /-ā/ lengthens the preceding vowel if it is not already long: /prìjatēljā/, /Jóvīćā/. /-ī/ has no effect on the preceding vowel.

The genitive plural ending for feminine /i/ nouns is always /-ī/ /nòćī/. The ending for /a/ nouns may be /-ā/ or /-ī/: /màjkī/, /sestárā/ (with moveable /a/), /nèdēljā/, /stànīcā/, /-ā/ being the more frequent.

The genitive plural ending for all adjectives is /-īh/.

Note 11.1.2 Genitive: Use

a)   On je iz Splita, iz Dalmacije.

       Jedno je za mene od kuće, od mog oca i majke.

       On nije kod kuće.

       Je li vaš prtljag donet sa železničke stanice.

       Koja je ono zgrada preko puta spomenika?

       On dolazi kod nas u posetu.

       Oni odlaze iduće nedelje iz Novog Sada.

b)   Ima li danas pošte?

       Da, ima nekoliko pisama.

       Koliko pisama ima?

c)   Oni odlaze iduće nedelje iz Novog Sada na letovanje.

d)   To je spomenik Kneza Mihaila.

Da li je prtljag vašeg prijatelja donet sa stanice?

The genitive case is most frequently used with prepositions, as in a)
above. Some prepositions are used with one case only. /iz/, /od/ and /kod/
are always followed by the genitive. Other prepositions may be used with two,
and some even three, cases. /sa/ may be used with two cases, genitive and instrumental; with the genitive the basic meaning is 'down from on top of'. In
the example above it is simply 'from'. When a preposition may be used with more
than one case, the meaning is different with each case. (Compare /u/ and /na/
with dative or accusative.)

Of the prepositions which are regularly followed by the genitive, the following have been used so far: /blízu/ 'near', /do/ 'up to, as far as, next to'
(/do viđénja/ is 'up to [that is, 'until'] seeing [again]'), /iz/ 'out of, from',
/kod/ 'at (the place of)' (e.g. /kòd kućē/ 'at home' /kòd nās/ 'at our house')
/od/ 'from, away from', /oko/ 'about, around', /prèko/ 'across' (the phrase
/prèko púta/ is also followed by a genitive after the /puta/: 'across the road
from _____').

The sentences in b) illustrate the use of the genitive with regard to
quantity. It indicates 'some of': 'is there any mail today', 'is there some
mail today'. The genitive of quantity may be used in other constructions, as
the object of a verb, for example: /on želi da pije vode/ 'he wants to drink
some water'. This usage of the genitive alone for quantity is restricted to
nouns indicating an indeterminate 'mass' or quantity of the item in question.
These are frequently called 'mass nouns'. The genitive singular of the 'mass
noun' is used in this meaning.

The genitive is also used after certain words indicating quantity, such
as /kolíko/ 'how much, how many?', /nèkoliko/ 'several'. The examples are of
items in the plural, so the genitive plural is used. (See also Note 13.1 on the
use of the genitive plural after certain numerals.)

The sentence in c) illustrates the genitive of time, expressing the time
within which something may occur. They are going sometime within the period of
time 'next week'. This contrasts with the accusative of time, which indicates
the extent of time: /jèdan sàt/ 'for an hour'. Only nouns with some sort of
modifier occur in genitive of time expressions.

The sentences in d) illustrate the genitive as indicating possession. When the noun is compound, as /Knez Mihailo/, or is modified by an adjective, it is used in the genitive for possession. Another example is /kuća njihovog prijatelja/ 'their friend's house'. (/Smitov/ 'Smith's' is an example of the suffix /-ov/, which also corresponds to English possessive expressions; compare /njihov/ 'their'. This type of suffix is discussed in Note 27.2.)

Note 11.2 Pronoun: /ónō/

Koja je ono zgrada?　　　　　Čiji je ono spomenik?

To je Narodni muzej.　　　　　To je spomenik Kneza Mihaila.

/ónō/ refers to something at a distance. /tò/ refers to something pointed out or mentioned previously. There is a third, /óvo/ 'this' (compare /óvde/ 'here') which refers to something at hand. There are corresponding adjectives to each (cf Note 10.3):

Pronoun	Adjective		
óvō	óvāj	óvā	óvō
ónō	ónāj	ónā	ónō
tò	tàj	tà	tò

Grammatical Drill

GD 11.1　　Learning Drill - Vežba za učenje

GD 11.1.1　Genitive with Preposition - Genitiv sa predlogom

Singular without Adjective - Jednina bez prideva

Pair Drill

　　　　　　　　　　　1　　　　　　2
Moj prijatelj je iz Splita, iz Dalmacije.

　　　1　　　　　　　　　　2
Zagreba ....Hrvatske

Kragujevca ....Srbije

Čikaga ....Amerike

Sarajeva ....Bosne

Skoplja ....Makedonije

Alternative Drill

Ima pismo od <u>oca</u> iz Čikaga.

Nema pismo od <u>oca</u>, već od <u>brata</u>.

Mi odlazimo sutra u posetu kod <u>oca</u>.

Mi ne odlazimo sutra u posetu kod <u>oca</u>, već kod <u>brata</u>.

brata	majke
prijatelja	sestre
Jovana	Zore
gospodina Jovića	gospođe Jović

Singular with Adjective - Jednina sa pridevom

Moj prijatelj je iz <u>Novog Sada.</u>

	Gornjeg Milanovca	Stare Pazove
	Generalskog Stola	Vrnjačke Banje
	Gorskog kotara	Crne Gore
		Niške Banje

Alternative Drill

Ima pismo od <u>mog oca,</u> iz Čikaga.

Nema pismo od <u>mog oca,</u> već od <u>mog brata.</u>

mog(a) brata	moje majke
vašeg prijatelja	vaše sestre
vašeg supruga	Tomine žene
Zorinog muža	naše braće

Plural - Množina

Ima pismo od <u>naših roditelja.</u>

naših prijatelja	naših majki
vaših sestara	Jovanovih sinova

GD 11.1.2 Genitive of Quantity - Partitivni genitiv (za količinu)
GD 11.1.2.1 With Mass Nouns - Sa gradivnim imenicama

Without Adjectives - Bez prideva

Ima vina.	mesa	kafe
Ima mnogo vina.	piva	pošte
	hleba	vode
	čaja	
Moj prijatelj pije mnogo vina.	piva	kafe
	čaja	vode
Jugosloveni jedu mnogo mesa.	hleba	
	kruha	

With Adjectives - Sa pridevom

Ima crnog vina.	telećeg mesa	bele kafe
Ima mnogo crnog vina.	belog vina	hladne vode
	crnog hleba	tople vode
	toplog čaja	
Moj prijatelj pije mnogo crnog vina.	hladnog piva	crne kafe
	toplog čaja	hladne vode

GD 11.1.2.2 Genitive of Quantity with Count Nouns - Partitivni genitiv sa stvarnim imenicama

Without Adjective - Bez prideva

Ovde ima nekoliko bioskopa.	portira	ljudi
Ovde nema mnogo bioskopa.	trgova	obitelji
	parkova	
	pozorišta /kazališta	

soba

kafana

With Adjective - Sa pridevom

Ovde ima nekoliko <u>lepih spomenika.</u>

Ovde neme mnogo <u>lepih spomenika.</u>

dobrih restorana	dobrih ljudi
lepih parkova	velikih obitelji
velikih muzeja	
velikih pozorišta	
lepih soba	
dobrih kafana	
udobnih kuća	

GD 11.1.3 Genitive of Time - Temporalni genitiv

Oni odlaze <u>iduće nedelje</u> iz Novog Sada na letovanje.

ove subote

ove nedelje

iduće subote

Jovan ide <u>svake subote</u> u kafanu.

iduće subote	svakog dana
svake nedelje	
svake noći	

GD 11.1.4 Genitive of Possession - Possesivni genitiv

Prtljag <u>moga prijatelja</u> je donet sa
   železničke stanice.

Kuća <u>moga prijatelja</u> je vrlo lepa.

Pismo <u>moga prijatelja</u> je vrlo lepo.

Zorinog brata	vaše majke
vašeg oca	njihove sestre
Tominog sina	moje žene
njenog muža	vaše gospođe

227

Zgrada <u>Narodnog muzeja</u> je lepa   vašeg hotela   naše Ambasade
    i velika.   našeg bioskopa   Železničke stanice

                                          našeg pozorišta
                                          Narodnog pozorišta

GD 11.2 Controlled Adaptation Drill

    In this drill the nouns for substitution are given in the nominative form.
Each item listed for the substitution follows the pattern of the noun heading
the list.

GD 11.2.1 Genitive with Preposition - Genitiv sa **predlogom**
Singular without Adjective - Jednina, bez prideva

<u>Pair Drill</u>

Naši prijatelji se vraćaju prekosutra iz <u>Dalmacije</u>, iz <u>Splita</u>.

                        Dalmacija   Split

                        Hrvatska............Zagreb
                        Srbija..............Kragujevac
                        Amerika.............Čikago
                        Bosna...............Sarajevo
                        Makedonija..........Skoplje

<u>Alternative Drill</u>

Ima jedno pismo od kuće od <u>oca</u>.

                        <u>majke</u>

Oni odlaze prekosutra u posetu kod <u>oca</u>.

                        <u>majke</u>

        otac   majka

        brat   sestra

        prijatelj   Zora

228

Jovan /Ivan   gospođa Jović

gospodin Jović   gospođica Jović

Singular with Adjective-Jednina sa pridevom

Alternative Drill

Moja kuća je preko puta Narodnog muzeja.

Moja kuća nije preko puta Narodnog muzeja, nego preko puta jedne kafane.

Moji prijatelji stanuju blizu Narodnog muzeja.

Mi stanujemo do Narodnog muzeja.

Narodni muzej   jedna kafana

jedan spomenik   Američka ambasada

lep park   železnička stanica

Engleski konzulat

Narodno pozorište

Ima pismo od Zorinog oca.

        Tomine majke

Zorin otac   Tomina majka

vaš prijatelj   naša sestra

Jovanov brat /Ivanov   Jovanova supruga /Ivanova

Zorin muž   vaša porodica

Plural - Množina

Drugo pismo je od naših prijatelja.

        naših majki

naš prijatelj   naša majka

naša sestra   ti ljudi

naši roditelji   njihova majka

GD 11.2.2 Genitive of Quantity - Partitivni genitiv

GD 11.2.2.1 With Mass Nouns - Sa gradivnim imenicama

Without Adjectives - Bez prideva

U kući ima <u>vina.</u>

        <u>kafe</u>

<u>vino</u>	<u>kafa</u>
pivo	voda
meso	
čaj	
hleb /kruh	

Ja pijem malo <u>vina.</u>

         <u>kafe</u>

Ja ne pijem mnogo <u>vina.</u>

         <u>kafe</u>

<u>vino</u>	<u>kafa</u>
pivo	voda
čaj	

With Adjectives - Sa pridevom

Ako želite imamo <u>crnog vina.</u>

         <u>tople vode</u>

<u>crno vino</u>	<u>topla voda</u>
hladno pivo	vruća kafa /vruća kava
teleće meso	hladna voda
topal čaj	
crni hleb /crni kruh	

Mi pijemo mnogo <u>crnog vina.</u>

              <u>hladne vode.</u>

<u>crno vino</u>	<u>hladna voda</u>
hladno pivo	vruća kafa
topal čaj	

GD 11.2.2.2 With Count Nouns - Sa stvarnim imenicama

<u>Without Adjective - Bez prideva</u>

U gradu ima nekoliko <u>restorana.</u>

U gradu nema mnogo <u>restorana.</u>

             <u>kafana</u>

<u>restoran</u>	<u>kafana</u>
hotel	ulica
bioskop /kino	kuća
park	zgrada
trg	
spomenik	
pozorište /kazalište	

U ovoj kući stanuje nekoliko <u>porodica.</u>

             <u>ljudi</u>

<u>porodica</u>	<u>čovek</u>
žena	obitelj

<u>With Adjectives - Sa pridevom</u>

U gradu ima nekoliko <u>dobrih hotela.</u>

             <u>dobrih ljudi</u>

dobar hotel   dobar čovek

dobra kafana

lepa zgrada

velika ulica

lepa kuća

dobro pozorište

U toj kući ima nekoliko velikih soba.

velika soba

udoban krevet

veliki sto

udobna stolica

GD 11.2.3 Genitive of Time - Temporalni genitiv

Moji roditelji odlaze iduće nedelje na letovanje.

iduća nedelja

ova subota

druga nedelja

iduća subota

druga subota

Jovan ide svakog dana u grad u sedam.

       svake subote

svaki dan   svaka subota

svaki drugi dan   ova subota

                      druga nedelja

                      iduća subota

GD 11.2.4 Genitive of Possession - Possesivni genitiv

Soba <u>vašeg prijatelja</u> je lepa, iako je jeftina.

    <u>vaše sestre</u>

Hotel <u>vašeg prijatelja</u> je vrlo dobar, ali skup.

    <u>vaše sestre</u>

Kuća <u>vašeg prijatelja</u> je prilično mala, inače je lepa i udobna.

    <u>vaše sestre</u>

<u>vaš prijatelj</u>	<u>vaša sestra</u>
Zorin brat	Jovanova majka
Tomin otac	Tomina žena
Zorin muž	njegova porodica
njen otac	njihova sestra

<u>Plural - Množina</u>

Hotel <u>vaših prijatelja</u> je rđav, iako je skup.

Kuće <u>vaših prijatelja</u> su velike i lepe.

Porodice <u>vaših prijatelja</u> putuju danas u Ljubljanu.

<u>vaš prijatelj</u>

vaša sestra

GD 11.3 Adaptation Drill

In this drill the nouns for substitution are given in the nominative form without any indication of the form which is to be used in the sentence. Use the appropriate form and then give the negative transform. (The negative transform is given if it is not completely predictable.)

GD 11.3.1 Genitive with Preposition - Genitiv sa predlogom
         Singular, without Adjective - Jednina, bez prideva

Moji roditelji se vraćaju prekosutra iz <u>Dalmacije</u>.

Zagreb	Sarajevo	Bosna
Makedonija	Čikago	Amerika
Kragujevac	Hrvatska	Srbija
Skoplje	Jugoslavija	

Ima pismo od <u>oca</u>.

Naši prijatelji odlaze danas u posetu kod <u>oca</u>.

sestra	brat	majka
Jovan	Zora	gospodin Jović
gospođa Jović		

         Singular with Adjective - Jednina sa pridevom

Mi smo iz <u>Novog Sada</u>.

Stara Pazova	Gornji Milanovac	Vrnjačka Banja
Generalski Stol	Crna Gora	Rogaška Slatina

Ima lepo pismo od <u>Jovanovog sina</u>.

njegova majka	vaš prijatelj	Tomin otac
Jovanova žena	Zorina sestra	moj brat
njen muž		

<u>Alternative Drill</u>

Moj prijatelj stanuje preko puta <u>Američke ambasade</u>.

Moj prijatelj ne stanuje preko puta <u>Američke ambasade</u> nego preko puta <u>Nemačke ambasade</u>.

Moj hotel je blizu <u>Američke ambasade</u>.

Narodni muzej   Železnička stanica   Jovanov hotel

Engleski konzulat   jedan park   Narodno pozorište

jedna velika kuća

<u>Plural - Množina</u>

<u>Alternative Drill</u>

Ima pismo od <u>naših roditelja</u>.

Nema pismo od <u>naših roditelja</u>, već od <u>naših prijatelja</u>.

I jedno i drugo pismo je od <u>naših roditelja</u>.

Tomina sestra   naša majka

naš otac   Ivanova sestra

Moja žena je u poseti kod <u>mojih roditelja</u>.

Moja žena nije u poseti kod <u>mojih roditelja</u>, nego kod <u>njenih roditelja</u>.

naš prijatelj   moja sestra   njena sestra

Zorini roditelji   Jovanova sestra   njihova majka

GD 11.3.2   Genitive of Quantity - Partitivni genitiv
GD 11.3.2.1 With Mass Nouns - Sa gradivnim imenicama

<u>Without Adjective - Bez prideva</u>

Ima <u>vina</u>.

Imamo <u>vina</u>.

U kući ima <u>vina</u>.   hleb /kruh   meso   voda

Ima mnogo <u>vina</u>.   čaj   kafa /kava   pivo

Ima malo <u>vina</u>.

Nema nimalo <u>vina</u>.

Jugosloveni piju mnogo <u>vina</u>.

kafa   čaj   voda

pivo

Moj prijatelj jede mnogo <u>mesa</u>.

hleb /kruh

With Adjectives - Sa pridevima

Ima <u>crnog vina</u>.

Ima malo <u>crnog vina</u>.

Nema nimalo <u>crnog vina</u>.

Ako želite, imamo <u>crnog vina</u>.

Žao mi je, ali nemamo <u>crnog vina</u>.

belo vino   hladna voda   crni hleb /kruh

topla voda   teleće meso   hladno pivo

Oni piju mnogo <u>hladnog piva</u>.

hladna voda   belo vino   vruć čaj

GD 11.3.2.2 With Count Nouns - Sa stvarnim imenicama

Without Adjectives - Bez prideva

Ovde ima nekoliko <u>parkova</u>.

Ovde nema nekoliko <u>parkova</u>, već jedan.

Ovde nema mnogo <u>parkova</u>.

U gradu ima nekoliko <u>parkova</u>.

U gradu nema nekoliko <u>parkova</u>, već samo jedan.

kafana   trg   kazalište

pozorište   spomenik

U sobi ima nekoliko <u>stolica</u>.

U sobi nema nekoliko <u>stolica</u>, već koliko ja znam samo jedna.

ogledalo   krevet   sto

čovek   postelja

With Adjectives - Sa pridevima

U gradu ima nekoliko <u>dobrih hotela</u>.

U gradu nema nekoliko <u>dobrih hotela</u>, nego samo jedan.

U gradu nema mnogo <u>dobrih hotela</u>.

U gradu ima malo <u>dobrih hotela</u>.

lep park   lepa zgrada

lep spomenik   veliki trg

veliki muzej   lepa ulica

čista kafana   udobna kuća

U ovoj kući ima nekoliko <u>udobnih soba</u>.

Koliko ja znam u ovoj kući nema nekoliko <u>udobnih soba</u>, već samo jedna.

ispravno kupatilo   mlad čovek

udoban krevet   veliki sto

udobna stolica   stara žena

GD 11.3.3 Genitive of Time - Temporalni genitiv

Mi odlazimo <u>iduće nedelje</u> na letovanje.   ova subota

                                                         druga nedelja

                                                         iduća subota

                                                         ova nedelja

                                                         druga subota

Ovde ljudi idu u kafanu <u>svake subote</u>.

svaki dan

svaka noć

svaka nedelja

svaki drugi dan

svaka druga noć

GD 11.3.4 Genitive of Possession - Posesivni genitiv

Prtljag <u>vašeg prijatelja</u> je težak.

Kuća <u>vašeg prijatelja</u> je udobna, ali skupa.

Kuća <u>vašeg prijatelja</u> nije udobna, iako je skupa.

Soba <u>vašeg prijatelja</u> je samo mala, inače je i lepa i čista.

Pismo <u>vašeg prijatelja</u> je vrlo lepo.

Jovanova sestra	njen muž	njegova porodica /obitelj
vaš otac		njegov brat
Tomina žena		njihova sestra

Zgrada <u>Narodnog muzeja</u> je lepa i velika.

Narodno pozorište

Američka ambasada

vaš hotel

železnička stanica

naš bioskop

<u>Plural - Množina</u>

Hotel <u>vaših prijatelja</u> je rđav, iako je skup.

Kuće <u>vaših prijatelja</u> su velike i lepe.

Porodice <u>vaših prijatelja</u> putuju danas u Ljubljanu.

vaša sestra

ovaj čovek

taj čovek

njihova majka

GD 11.4   Questions and Answers

GD 11.4.1 Informational Answers

Singular without Adjectives

Pair Drill

Odakle je vaš prijatelj?

Iz Jugoslavije, iz Beograda.

On je iz Jugoslavije, iz Beograda.

1	2
Dalmacija	Split
Hrvatska	Zagreb
Srbija	Kragujevac
Amerika	Čikago
Bosna	Sarajevo
Slovenija	Ljubljana
Makedonija	Skoplje

Kad se vaši prijatelji vraćaju iz Dalmacije?

Iduće nedelje.

Oni se vraćaju iz Dalmacije iduće nedelje.

Zagreb

Sarajevo

Skoplje

Ljubljana

Slovenija

Hercegovina

Mostar

Od koga je pismo?

Od oca.

Pismo je od oca.

Kod koga idete sutra u posetu?

Kod oca.

Sutra idemo u posetu kod oca.

majka

brat

sestra

gospođa Jović

gospodin Jović

gospođica Jović

Koliko vaš prijatelj pije <u>vina</u>?   Pije mnogo.

Ne pije mnogo.

On pije mnogo <u>vina</u>.

On ne pije mnogo <u>vina</u>.

pivo

kafa

čaj

voda

GD 11.4.2 With Adjectives

Odakle su vaši prijatelji?   Iz <u>Novog Sada</u>.

Oni su iz <u>Novog Sada</u>.

Stara Pazova

Gornji Milanovac

Niška Banja

Gorski Kotar

Vrnjačka Banja

Crna Gora

Od koga ima pismo?   Od <u>vašeg oca</u>.

Ima pismo od <u>vašeg oca</u>.

Nema pismo ni od koga.

moja majka

Tomin brat /Tomov

Jovanova sestra /Ivanov

Tomina porodica   /obitelj

Kod koga idete u posetu?   Kod <u>našeg prijatelja</u>.

                                            Idemo u posetu kod <u>našeg prijatelja</u>.

naš otac i majka

Zorin brat

moja sestra

Gde stanujete?   Preko puta <u>Narodnog muzeja</u>.

                                            Stanujem preko puta <u>Narodnog muzeja</u>.

Ko stanuje preko puta <u>Narodnog muzeja</u>?

Ko stanuje blizu <u>Narodnog muzeja</u>?

Narodno pozorište

Američka ambasada

Nemački konzulat

Železnička stanica

GD   11.4.3   Plural

Od koga ima pismo?   Od <u>naših roditelja</u>.

                                            Ima pismo od <u>naših roditelja</u>.

Kad idete u posetu kod <u>vaših</u>   Ove subote.
   <u>roditelja.</u>   Idemo u posetu ove subote.

naša majka

naša sestra

naš sin

241

Koliko parkova ima u gradu?   Ima nekoliko.

                                            Ima nekoliko parkova.

                                            Nema nijedan park.

kafana

bioskop /kino

trg

pozorište /kazalište

Koliko dobrih muzeja ima u gradu?   Ima nekoliko dobrih muzeja.

                                            Nema nijedan dobar muzej.

dobra kafana

velika ulica

lep trg

dobro pozorište /kazalište

Koliko stolica ima u sobi?   Ima nekoliko stolica.

                                            Ne znam koliko stolica ima u sobi.

sto

ogledalo /zrcalo

krevet   /postelja

čovek

žena

Od koga su pisma?   Od naših roditelja.

                                            I jedno i drugo pismo je od naših roditelja.

naš prijatelj

naša sestra

Jovanov sin

naše žene

naši muževi

naše majke

GD 11.4.2 Yes and No Answers

Singular without Adjective

Pair Drill

                         1
Jeste (li) vi iz Jugoslavije?   Jesam.

                                       Nisam.

                                                                  2
                                       Jeste, ja sam iz Jugoslavije, iz Beograda.

                                       Ne, ja nisam iz Jugoslavije.

Da li je vaš prijatelj iz   Jeste.
   Jugoslavije?
                                       Nije.

                                       Jeste, on je iz Jugoslavije, iz Beograda.

                                       Ne, on nije iz Jugoslavije.

      1   2
   Hrvatska .... Zagreb

   Slovenija .... Ljubljana

   Srbija .... Kragujevac

   Bosna .... Sarajevo

   Hercegovina .... Mostar

   Makedonija .... Skoplje

Alternative Drill

Da li ima pismo od oca?   Da, ima.

                                       Ne, nema.

                                       Da, ima pismo od oca.

                                       Ne, nema pismo od oca već od majke.

brat   gospodin Jović   Zora

sestra   gospođica Jović   gospođa Jović

Substitution Drill

Da li ima <u>vina</u>?   Da, ima.

                                                 Ne, nema.

                                                 Da, ima vina.

                                                 Ne, nema vina.

Da li imate <u>vina</u>?   Da, imamo.

                                                 Ne, nemamo.

                                                 Da, imamo vina.

                                                 Ne, nemamo vina.

hleb

kafa

pivo

voda

čaj

Da li Jugosloveni piju mnogo <u>vina</u>?   Da, piju.

                                                 Ne, ne piju.

                                                 Da, oni piju mnogo vina.

                                                 Ne, oni ne piju mnogo vina.

pivo

kafa

čaj

Da li vi jedete mnogo mesa?   Da, jedem.

                                                 Ne, ne jedem.

                                                 Da, jedem mnogo mesa.

                                                 Ne, ne jedem mnogo mesa.

hleb /kruh

Singular with Adjective

Alternative Drill

Da li ste vi iz Novog Sada?   Jesam.

                                               Nisam.

                                               Jeste, ja sam iz Novog Sada.

                                               Ne, ja nisam iz Novog Sada, nego iz
                                                   Stare Pazove.

Gornji Milanovac

Vrnjačka Banja

Generalski Stol

Crna Gora

Gorski Kotar

Niška Banja

Substitution Drill

Da li ima danas pošte?   Da, ima pismo od mog oca.

                                               Ne, nema pošte.

vaš otac

moja majka

naš brat

Jovanova sestra

Tomina porodica

Alternative Drill

Da li vaši prijatelji stanuju   Da, stanuju.
    preko puta Američke ambasade?
                                               Ne, ne stanuju.

                                               Da, oni stanuju preko puta Američke
                                                   ambasade.

                                               Ne, oni ne stanuju preko puta Američke

ambasade, već preko puta Narodnog
muzeja.

Narodno pozorište

Engleska ambasada

Nemački konzulat

Železnička stanica

The following sentences are for the same type of drill:

Da li vi stanujite blizu Američke ambasade?

Ima li crnog vina?   Da, ima.

Ne, nema.

Da, ima crnog vina.

Ne, nema crnog vina.

hladna voda

belo vino

topla voda

crni hleb

teleće meso

Da li je prtljag vašeg prijatelja težak?   Jeste.

Nije.

Jeste, prtljag moga prijatelja je
vrlo težak.

Ne, njegov prtljag nije težak, već
lak.

vaš otac   njegova žena

Zorina sestra   njegov brat

Zorin muž   vaša majka

Following are sentences for the same type of drill:

Da li je kuća <u>vašeg prijatelja</u> udobna?

Da li je soba <u>vašeg prijatelja</u> mala?

Da li je pismo <u>vašeg prijatelja</u> lepo?

Da li idete <u>svakog dana</u> u Staru Pazovu?　　　Da, idem.

Ne, ne idem.

Da, idem <u>svakog dana</u> u Staru Pazovu.

Ne, ne idem <u>svakog dana</u>, već <u>svakog drugog dana</u>.

svaka subota

svaka nedelja

ova nedelja

ova subota

Plural - Without Adjectives

Da li ima <u>hotela</u> u gradu?　　　Da, ima.

Ne, nema.

Da, ima <u>hotela</u> u gradu.

Ne, nema <u>hotela</u> u gradu.

Žao mi je, ali ne znam koliko <u>**hotela**</u> **ima** u gradu.

kafana

bioskop　/kino

park

pozorište　/kazalište

trg

čovek

Following are questions for the same type of drill:

Da li ima mnogo <u>hotela</u> u gradu?

Da li ima mnogo ljudi u <u>hotelu</u>?

With Adjectives

Da li ima ovde <u>dobrih hotela</u>?　　　Da, ima.

Ne, nema.

Da, ima <u>dobrih hotela.</u>

Ne, nema <u>dobrih hotela.</u>

Ne znam da li ovde ima <u>dobrih hotela.</u>

dobra kafana

dobar restoran

velika ulica

lep trg

dobro pozorište

lep spomenik

Da li ima pismo od <u>naših roditelja?</u>   Da, ima.

Ne, nema.

Da, ima pismo od <u>naših roditelja.</u>

Ne, nema pismo od <u>naših roditelja.</u>

naša majka

naša sestra

vaš prijatelj

Da li je hotel <u>vaših prijatelja</u> udoban   Jeste.

  i lep?   Nije.

Jeste, hotel mojih prijatelja je

  udoban i lep.

Ne, njihov hotel nije udoban i lep.

Žao mi je, ali ne znam kakav je

  njihov hotel.

vaši roditelji

vaša sestra

taj čovek

ta žena

The following sentences are for the same type of drill:

Da li su kuće <u>vaših prijatelja</u> udobne i lepe?

Da li porodice <u>vaših prijatelja</u> putuju danas u Ljubljanu?

Repeat the above drills using the pattern:

   Jeste li vi iz Jugoslavije?

248

GD 11.5 Question and Answer Drill with Prompt

Ovo je kuća moga oca.	Čija je ovo kuća?
Ja stanujem u kući moga oca.	U čijoj kući vi stanujete?
Ona zgrada preko puta spomenika je Narodni muzej.	Koja je ono zgrada preko puta spomenika?
Do naše kuće (/Do nas) stanuje g. Jović.	Ko stanuje do vaše kuće (/do vas)?
Blizu naših kuća ima jedan veliki park.	Da li ima neki park blizu vaših kuća?
Od naših kuća do parka nije daleko.	Da li je daleko od vaših kuća do parka?
Ima pismo od mog oca iz Čikaga.	Da li ima pošte? /Od koga ima pismo?
Pismo nije od mog oca, već od moje majke.	Zar pismo nije od vašeg oca!
Jugosloveni jedu mnogo mesa.	Da li Jugosloveni jedu mnogo mesa?
Jugosloveni ne jedu mnogo mesa, već hleba.	Zar Jugosloveni ne jedu mnogo mesa?
Ima mnogo crnog vina.	Koliko ima crnog vina?
Ovde ima nekoliko dobrih hotela.	Da li ima ovde dobrih hotela?
Moji prijatelji odlaze ove nedelje na letovanje.	Kad vaši prijatelji odlaze na letovanje?
Toma se vraća sa letovanja iduće nedelje.	Kad se Toma vraća sa letovanja?

GD 11.6 Conversations - Razgovori

11.6.1

A	B
Da li vi stanujete u ovoj ulici?	Da, stanujem. Ovo je moja kuća.
Čija je ono kuća preko puta vaše?	To je kuća moga prijatelja gospodina Jovanovića.
Ova kuća do vaše također je jako lijepa. Ko stanuje u njoj?	U toj kuća stanuje brat gospođe Jovanović.

Ovo je jako lijep kraj grada.

Sve kuće u ovoj ulici su jako lijepe
i blizu parka.

Da, vidim.

Jest. I moja žena i ja volimo našu
kuću jako mnogo.

Da, ovdje je jako lijepo i prijatno.

Kao što vidite, mi imamo mali park oko
kuće.

Да ли ви станујете у овој улици?

Чија је оно кућа преко пута ваше?

Ова кућа до ваше такође је врло лепа.

Ко станује у њој?

Ово је врло леп крај града.

Све куће у овој улици су врло лепе и
близу парка.

Да, видим.

Да, станујем. Ово је моја кућа.

То је кућа мога пријатеља господина
Јовановића.

У тој кући станује брат госпође
Јовановоћ.

Јесте. И моја жена и ја волимо нашу
кућу врло много.

Да, овде је врло лепо и пријатно.

Као што видите, ми имамо мали парк
око куће.

GD 11.6.2

Da li ima danas pošte?

Od koga su?

Gdje su oni na ljetovanju.

U Dubrovniku je sada sigurno lijepo
i prijatno.

Kad se oni vraćuju kući iz
Dubrovnika?

Od koga je drugo pismo?

Da, ima nekoliko pisama.

Ima jedno pismo od mog brata i sestre
sa ljetovanja.

Pismo je iz Dalmacije, iz Dubrovnika.

Da, oni kažu u pismu, da im je jako
lijepo i prijatno.

Oni se vraćaju kući iduće subote ili
nedjelje.

Drugo pismo je od mojih roditelja.

Da li su i oni na ljetovanju?

Ne, nisu. Oni idu na ljetovanje čim brat i sestra dođu kući.

Да ли има данас поште?

Да, има неколико писама.

Од кога су?

Има једно писмо од мог брата и сестре са летовања.

Где су они на летовању?

Писмо је из Далмације, из Дубровника.

У Дубровнику је сада сигурно лепо и пријатно.

Да, они кажу у писму да им је врло лепо и пријатно.

Кад се они враћају кући из Дубровника?

Они се враћају кући идуће суботе или недеље.

Од кога је друго писмо?

Друго писмо је од мојих родитеља.

Да ли су и они на летовању?

Не, нису. Они иду на летовање чим брат и сестра дођу кући.

GD 11.6.3

Gdje je ovdje Narodni muzej?

Vidite li onaj spomenik, tamo?

Vidim. Čiji je to spomenik?

To je spomenik Kneza Mihaila.

Ona zgrada preko puta spomenika je je Narodni muzej.

A koja je ona druga zgrada?

To je Narodno kazalište.

I jedna i druga zgrada su lijepe i velike.

Da li ima ovdje mnogo muzeja?

Da, ima.

A kazališta?

Ima i kazališta.

Spomenika nema mnogo, to već vidim.

Nema u gradu, ali ima na Kalemegdanu.

Šta je Kalemegdan?

Kalemegdan je brdo na kome je park.

Где је овде Народни музеј?

Видите ли онај споменик, тамо?

Видим. Чији је то споменик?

То је споменик Кнеза Михаила.

Она зграда преко пута споменика је
Народни музеј.

А која је она друга зграда?   То је Народно позориште.

И једна друга зграда су лепе и велике.

Да ли има овде много музеја?   Да, има.

А позоришта?   Има и позоришта.

Споменика нема много, то већ видим.   Нема у граду, али има на Калемегдану.

Шта је Калемегдан?   Калемегдан је брдо на коме је парк.

GD 11.7 Homework - Domaći zadatak

1. Write out each of these sentences using the items listed.

Moj prijatelj nije iz _____ već iz _____.   (Skoplje...Ljubljana)

Ima pismo od _____ i _____.   (moj otac...moja majka)

Mi stanujemo preko puta _____.   (jedan lep park)

Kuća moga prijatelja je do _____.   (Francuska ambasada)

Njegova kuća je blizu _____.   (naša)

Ja ne pijem mnogo ni _____ ni _____.   (pivo...vino)

Moj prijatelj ne ide u kafanu _____ već ____.   (svaki dan...svaka subota)

Prtljag _____ već je donet sa železničke   (vaši rodetilji)
   stanice.

Vaš prtljag je donet na železničku stanicu   (vaš hotel)
   iz _____.

2. Make questions for the following sentences. Question words are given in
parentheses. Give a negative answer to each question wherever possible.

Ima pismo od oca iz Čikaga.   (.../koga/...)

Mi odlazimo sutra u posetu kod majke.   (.../koga/...)

Ima vina.	(/da li/...
Ovde ima nekoliko dobrih hotela.	.(.../li/...
U Beogradu ima dobrih hotela.	(/kakav/...
Iduće nedelje idem u Zagreb.	(/da li/...
Prtljag moje majke je donet sa železničke stanice u hotel.	(/da li/...
Ovo je kuća gospodina Jovanovića.	(/čiji/...
Zgrada Narodnog pozorišta je vrlo lepa.	(/kakav/...
Ovo je zgrada Narodnog muzeja.	(/koji/...

UNIT 12

Basic Sentences - Osnove rečenice

The Family -I	O obitelji -I	О породици -I

A

| What relatives ('whom') does your friend have? | Kóga ima vaš prijatelj? | Кога има ваш пријатељ?# |

B

| son | sȋn pl. sȉnovi Gpl. sinóvā | сȋн, синови, синовā |

| He has a wife and a son. | Ima žénu i jèdnog sȋna. | Има жену и једног сȋна. |

A

to call	zváti, zóvēm	звати, зовȇм
he is called ('he calls himself')	ȍn se zóvē	он се зовȇ
What's his name?	Kàko se ȍn zóvē?	Како се ȍн зове?#

B

| His name is Marko Savić. | Ȍn se zóvē Mȁrko Sávić. | Он се зове Мȁрко Савић. |

or,

| name | ȉme G. ȉmena pl. iména G. iménā | име, имена именā, именā |

| | Njègovo ȉme je Mȁrko Sávić. | Његово име је Мȁрко Савић. |

A

| to know | poznávati, póznājēm | познāвати, познајȇм |
| somebody, some one | nèko | неко |

Do you know anyone of his family ('someone of his')?	Dà li póznajete nèkoga od njègovíh?	Да ли познајете неког од његових?#

B

a long time ago	odávno	одавно
Yes, I've known his brother and his sister for a long time.	Dà, póznajem odávno njègovog bràta i séstru.	Да, познајем одавно његовог брата и сестру.

A

And do you know his wife?	A póznajête li njègovu žénu?	А познајете ли његову жену?#

B

her	njû	њу
Yes, I know her, too.	Dà, póznajem i njû.	Да, познајем и њу.
them	njîh, ih	њих, их
I know them all.	Póznajêm ih svè.	Познајем их све.
His wife knows you.	Njègova žéna póznajê vâs.	Његова жена познаје вас.
to remember	sjèćati se, sjèćâm se	сећати се, сећам се
of her	njê, je	њē, је
Don't you remember her ('of her')?	Zâr se vî ne sjèćâte njê?	Зар се ви не сећате њē?

A

No, I don't remember her.	Nè, ne sjèćâm je se.	Не,# не сећам је се.
no one	nìko	нико

255

I don't know anyone of them.	Ne poznajem nikoga od njih.	Не познајем никога од њих.

At Home	Kód kućē	Код куће
here	tu	тӯ
There is a man here, ma'am.	Tu je jedan čovjek, gospođo.	Тӯ је један човек, госпођо.
to be looking for	trážiti, tràžīm	тражити, тражим
He's looking for Mr. Smith.	Tràžī gospodina Smìta.	Тражи господина Смита.

B

to let	pústiti, da pùstīm	пустити, да пустӣм
let!	pústite	пустите
inside	unútra	унӯтра / унӯтра
Let him in.	Pústite ga unútra.	Пустите га унӯтра.

D

Good afternoon, ma'am.	Dòbar dằn, gospođo.	Добар дằн, госпођо.

B

Good afternoon, sir.	Dòbar dằn, gospodine.	Добар дằн, господине.
but		
I'm sorry, my husband isn't at home. He's still at the office.	Žào mi je, àli mòj mùž níje kod kùćē. Jòš je u úredu.	Жао ми је, али мӧј муж није код куће. Још је у канцеларији.

D

hour, o'clock	sằt Gpl. sátī /ùra	сằт, сāтӣ
at what time	u kòliko sátī	у колико сāтӣ

What time does he come home?	U kòliko sàti òn dòlazi kùći?	У колико сати он долази кући?

B

half	pòla	пола
He usually comes home at six thirty.	On òbično dòlazi kùći u pòla sèdam.	Он обично долази кући у пола седам.
to wait up to the point of arrival	sáčekati, da sáčekām	сачекати, да сачекам
or,	príčekati, da príčekam	причекати, да причекам
If you have the time, you can wait until he comes.	Àko ìmate vrèmena mòžete ga príčekati.	Ако имате времена можете га сачекати.

D

long	dùg, -a, -o	дуг, -а, -о
long(adv.)	dùgo	дуго
to be waiting for	čèkati, čèkām	чекати, чекам
I'm sorry, but it's too long for me to wait.	Izvínite, àli dùgo mi je čèkati.	Извините, али дуго ми је да чекам.

A

spring	próljeće	пролеће
always	ùvijek	увек
this kind	ovákav, ovákva, -o, /ovákī, ováka, -o	овакав, оваква, -о / оваки, овака, -о
thus, this way	ováko	овако

257

Is spring always this beautiful in your country ('with you')?	Dà li je pròljeće kod vȁs ùvijek ovȁko lijépo?	Dȁ ли је прȍлеће кȍд вȃс увек овȁко лȇпо?

B

the most beautiful	nȁjljepšī, -ā, -ē	нȁјлȇпшȳ, -ā, -ē
yearly, annual	gódišnjī, -ā, -ē	гȍдишњȳ, -ā, -ē
Yes, spring is the most beautiful season of the year here ('with us').	Dà, pròljeće je kod nȁs nȁjljepše gódišnje dȍba.	Dȁ, прȍлеће је кȍд нȃс нȁјлȇпше гȍдишње дȍба.
pertaining to spring	próljetnjī, -ā, -ē /próljećnjī, -ā, -ē /próljetnī, -ā, -õ	прȍлетнȳ, -ā, -ē /прȍлећнȳ, -ā, -õ /прȍлетнȳ, -ā, -õ
fresh, cool	svjȅž, svjèža /svjéža, -e	свȅж, -a, -e
Both the spring days and nights are pleasant and fresh.	Pròljetni dȃni i nȍći su prȉjatni i svjȅžī.	Прȍлетнȳ и дȃни и нȍћи су прȉјатни и свȅжи.

Grammatical Notes

Note 12.1 Noun: Accusative of Masculine Animate Noun

> Ima ženu i jednog sina.
> Da, poznajem odavno njegovog brata i sestru.
> Traži gospodina Smita.

/sȉna/, /bràta/, /gospódina/ are all forms identical with the genitive but occurring as direct objects of verbs, parallel with the accusatives /ženu/ and /séstru/. All three nouns are masculine and share a particular feature: they refer to animate (living) beings. The masculine nouns which have the accusative the same as the nominative (as /grȁd/, /hòtel/, /bȉoskop/, /jézik/) refer to objects in themselves inanimate. (Parts of living beings, such as /jézik/ 'tongue' are not classified as animate.) Only beings which have animal life are classified as animate. Trees and other plants are treated as inanimate.

Compare, for example,

	Animate				Inanimate			
N	prìjatelj	sȉn	ótac	čóvek	dȁn	grȁd	spòmenīk	pȕt
A	prìjatelja	sȉna	óca	čovéka	dȁn	grȁd	spòmenīk	pȕt
G	prìjatelja	sȉna	óca	čovéka	dȁna	grȁda	spòmenīka	púta
D	prìjatelju	sȉnu	ócu	čovéku	dȁnu	grȁdu	spòmenīku	pútu
					/dánu	/grádu		

Note 12.2 Pronoun: Accusative and Genitive

Njegova žena poznaje vas.

Pustite ga unutra.

Možete ga sačekati.

Poznajem ih sve.

Poznajem i nju.

Zar se vi ne sećate nje?

Ne, ne sećam je se.

Ne poznajem nikoga od njih.

Koga ima vaš prijatelj.

Da li poznajete nekoga od njegovih?

Most of the pronouns have the same forms for accusative and genitive. This is not so apparent as with the nouns, as the most frequent forms used are in general different for the two. Compare:

Personal Pronouns

N	jȁ	tȉ	ȍn,	óna
A	méne me	tébe te	njéga ga	njȕ je, ju
G	méne me	tébe te	njéga ga	njȅ je

N	mȉ	vȉ	óni, óne, óna	
A	nȁs nas	vȁs vas	njȉh ih	
G	nȁs nas	vȁs vas	njȉh ih	

The feminine /njȕ, ju/ are the only forms not identical with the genitive. (/ju/ is given here for the sake of completeness. For its use see Note 17.1.2).

As the object of verbs, the unstressed forms of the accusative are far more frequent than the stressed, as in most cases there is no emphasis on the pronoun object. After prepositions which take the accusative (such as /za/) the long form is normal (/za méne/). The genitive is most frequently used after prepositions (such as /od/), and the stressed form is normal there, also. Examples of stressed accusative (njȕ/) and of unstressed genitive (/je/ in /sèćām je se/) are given above. They are normal forms in normal use. (Note the use of the genitive as the direct object of /sèćati se/ ꞌto rememberꞌ.)

Other pronouns

N	kȍ	nèko	nȉko	tȍ	štȁ
A	kóga	nèkoga	nȉkoga	tȍ	štȁ
G	kóga	nèkoga	nȉkoga	tòga	čéga

Note the prefix forms of /kȍ/ ꞌwhoꞌ: /nèko/ ꞌsomeoneꞌ /nȉko/ ꞌno oneꞌ. The last, /nȉko/, does not occur after prepositions. Instead, the negative /ni/ precedes the preposition and the proper form of /kȍ/ follows it: /ni od kóga/ ꞌfrom no oneꞌ. /ni/ is the negative of /i/ ꞌalso, even, andꞌ.

Words such as /tȃj/ ꞌthatꞌ /mȏj/ ꞌmyꞌ, etc. follow the pattern of the noun they modify. NA /moj hotel/ but AG /moga prijatelja/. They are pronominal adjectives and are given separate treatment in the notes.

Note 12.3   Syntax: Case and Word Order

       Jedan čovek čeka vašeg brata.

       Vašeg brata čeka jedan čovek.

These examples are from the Grammatical Drill. The different forms of nominative and accusative make possible both word orders: Subject - Verb - Object /and/ Object - Verb - Subject. The latter order is used for emphasis or other stylistic effect but is perfectly normal and unambiguous. Thorough familiarity with case forms and their relationship to the verb will facilitate understanding of such not infrequent constructions.

Note 12.4   Enclitics: Review

       The pronoun forms in Notes 10.2 and 12.2 provide a more complete list of enclitics. Following the order in Note 8.1 we have:

1	2	3	4	5
li	sam	mi	me	je
	si	ti	te	se
	smo	mu	ga	
	ste	joj	je/ju	
	su	nam	nas	
		vam	vas	
		im	ih	

(A still more complete listing is found in Note 20.2.)

Grammatical Drill

GD 12.1   Adaptation Drill

GD 12.1.1 Without Adjectives

Ima jedno pismo iz Jugoslavije, za brata.   otac

Nema nijedno pismo is Jugoslavije, za brata.   Jovan

                                                           gospodin Popović

Moj prijatelj ima brata u Jugoslaviji.   otac

Moj prijatelj nema brata u Jugoslaviji, nego sestru.   sin

Mi čekamo brata, koji dolazi iz Zagreba.   otac

Mi ne čekamo brata, već sestru, koja dolazi iz Zagreba.   sin

                                                            prijatelj

Pustite brata unutra.   Jovan

                                                         otac

                                                         gospodin Jović

Majka zove brata da dođe kod nje.   otac

Majka ne zove brata da dođe kod nje, već sestru.   sin

                                                           Marko

                                                           Jovan

GD 12.1.2 <u>With Adjectives</u>

Oni poznaju odavno <u>Zorinog brata.</u>   Tomin otac /Tomov
Oni ne poznaju odavno <u>Zorinog brata.</u>   vaš prijatelj gospodin
                                                            Popović

Ovaj čovek traži <u>Zorinog brata.</u>   Zorin muž gospodin
                                                            Jovanović
Ovaj čovek ne traži <u>Zorinog brata,</u> već vašeg oca.   njen brat Toma /Tomov

Ova gospođica čeka <u>Zorinog brata.</u>
Ova gospođica ne čeka <u>Zorinog brata,</u> već vas.

GD 12.1.3 Genitive of the Personal Pronouns

    Use the genitive form of the pronouns listed for substitution.

<u>Stressed Forms:</u>

Gospodin i gospođa Jović stanuju blizu <u>mene</u>. / ... Ivić ...
Gospodin i gospođa Jović ne stanuju blizu <u>mene</u> nego blizu Narodnog muzeja.

Moji roditelji dolaze sutra u posetu kod <u>mene</u>.
Moji roditelji ne dolaze sutra u posetu kod <u>mene</u> već prekosutra.

Jovan radi i zna više od <u>mene</u>. /Ivan
Jovan ne radi i ne zna više od <u>mene</u>.

Jovići se sećaju <u>mene</u>, ali se ne sećaju gospodina Smita.
Jovići se ne sećaju <u>mene</u>, ali se sećaju gospodina Smita.

Smitovi stanuju preko puta <u>mene</u>.
Smitovi ne stanuju preko puta <u>mene</u>, već preko puta Američke ambasade.

         ti   on   ona   mi   vi   oni

<u>Unstressed Forms</u> - <u>Enclitics</u>

Jovan <u>me</u> se seća, ali njegova sestra <u>me</u> se ne seća.   ti
Jovan <u>me</u> se ne seća, ali njegova sestra <u>me</u> se seća.   on

Oni <u>me</u> se sećaju s letovanja.   ona
Oni <u>me</u> se ne sećaju s letovanja.   mi

Sećaju <u>me</u> se.   vi
Ne sećaju <u>me</u> se.   oni

Noun-Pronoun Drill

In the sentence a noun in the genitive is used. The corresponding pronoun should be substituted for the noun, as illustrated in parentheses for the first sentence.

Jovići stanuju blizu mog brata.   (Jovići stanuju blizu njega.)

Jovići stanuju blizu moje majke.

Jovići stanuju blizu mene i mog brata.

Jovići stanuju blizu vas i vaše sestre.

Jovići stanuju blizu mojih roditelja.

Following are sentences for the same drill:

Oni dolaze sutra u posetu kod mog brata.

Gospodica Smit uči i zna više od mog brata.

Oni stanuju preko puta mog brata.

Zora sedi u pozorištu do mog brata.

Sećam se Jovana.   (Sećam ga se.)

Sećam se Zore.

On se seća mene i moje žene.

On se seća vas i vaše gospođe.

Sećamo se Jovana i njegovih.

GD 12.1.4 Accusative of the Personal Pronouns

Make the indicated substitutions, using the correct form of the pronoun.

Stressed Forms:

Ima jedno pismo za mene, iz Čikaga.	ti
Nema nijedno pismo za mene, iz Čikaga.	on
Gospodin Jović poznaje i mene i Zoru.	ona
Gospodin Jović ne poznaje ni mene ni Zoru.	mi
Ti ljudi traže mene, a ne vas.	vi
Ti ljudi ne traže mene, već vas.	oni

Otac zove mene, a ne Jovana.

Otac ne zove mene, nego Jovana.

Unstressed Forms - Enclitics:

Gospodin Jović me dobro poznaje.   ti

Gospodin Jović me ne poznaje dobro.   on

Otac me mnogo voli.   ona

Otac me ne voli mnogo.   mi

Jovan i Zora me traže.   vi

Jovan i Zora me ne traže.   oni

Ako brat ima vremena može me sačekati.

Ako brat nema vremena ne treba da me čeka.

Ako brat nema vremena neka me ne čeka.

Brat me zove da stanujem kod njega.

Brat me ne zove da stanujem kod njega.

GD 12.1.5 Noun-Pronoun Drill

Ima pismo za Jovana.   (Ima pismo za njega.)

Ima pismo za Zoru.

Ima pismo za mene i Jovana.

Ima pismo za vas i vašeg brata.

Ima pismo za Joviće.

Other sentences for drill:

Gospoda poznaju Jovana, a ne Tomu.

Ovi ljudi traže Zoru, a ne Tomu.

Ovaj gospodin zove vašeg brata, a ne Tomu.

Ti ljudi čekaju vašu majku, ne Tomu.

Gospoda poznaju Jovana.   (Gospoda ga poznaju.)

Gospoda poznaju našu sestru.

Gospoda poznaju oca i mene.

Gospoda poznaju vas i vašeg brata.

Gospoda poznaju vaše roditelje.

Sentences for drill:

Ovi ljudi traže Jovana.

Ovaj gospodin zove Jovana.

Gospodin Jović ne voli Jovana.

Jedan čovek čeka Jovana.

GD 12.2 Word Order Inversion Drill

Make a new sentence, putting the underlined items first.

Jedan čovek čeka gospođu i gospodina Smita.	Gospođu i gospodina Smita čeka jedan čovek.
Jedan čovek čeka vašeg brata.	Vašeg brata čeka jedan čovek.
Jedan čovek čeka vašeg oca i majku.	Vašeg oca i majku čeka jedan čovek.
Jedan čovek čeka vašu sestru i brata.	Vašu sestru i brata čeka jedan čovek.

The following sentences are to be drilled in the same way:

Poznajem dobro i gospodina i gospođu Smit.

Jedan gospodin traži gospođu i gospodina Smita.

Neko iz ambasade zove gospođu i gospodina Smita.

GD 12.3 Questions and Answers

GD 12.3.1 Informational Answers

GD 12.3.1.1 For Masculine Animate Nouns in Accusative Singular

Koga ima vaš prijatelj u Jugoslaviji?   Ima oca.

Nema nikoga.

Moj prijatelj ima oca u Jugoslaviji.

Moj prijatelj nema nikoga u Jugoslaviji

Ne znam da li on ima koga (/nekoga)

u Jugoslaviji. Možda ima.

brat   sin   star otac

For additional drill: Koga čeka Jovan na železničkoj stanici?

Za koga ima pismo?   Za oca.

Ima pismo za oca.

Nema pismo ni za koga.

Ne znam da li ima pismo za nekoga.
Verovatno da nema.

brat   vaš sin Toma   Jovan
Zorin otac   gospodin Jović

Da li vi čekate nekoga ili putujete,   Čekam oca, ne putujem.
  Jovane?   Ne čekam nikoga. Putujem u Zagreb.

svoj brat   otac i majka   jedan prijatelj

Koga ima ovde Zora?   Ima muža.
                                        Nema nikoga.
                                        Ona ima ovde muža.
                                        Ona nema ovde nikoga.
                                        Ne znam da li ona ima koga ovde.
                                          Verovatno ima nekoga.

otac   brat   sin   suprug

For additional drill:

Koga traži Zora?
Koga zove Zora?

Koga čekaju g. i g-đa Jović?   Čekaju njihovog sina.
                                        Ne čekaju nikoga.
                                        Traže neka obaveštenja za put u
                                          Nemačku.

Tomin otac   njihov prijatelj g. Jovanović

For additional drill:

Koga traže Jovan i Zora?

Ko traži gospodina Jovića?   Savetnik Američke ambasade g. Smit.
                                        Traži ga savetnik Američke ambasade
                                          g. Smit.
                                        Ne traži ga niko.
                                        Ne znam ko ga traži.

moj brat Toma   moj muž   gospodin i gospoda Savić

For additional drill:

Ko zove gospodina Jovića?

GD 12.3.1.2 Genitive of the Personal Pronouns

Ko od naših prijatelja stanuje <u>blizu vas</u>?   Jovići stanuju blizu mene.
                                                           Niko od naših prijatelja ne
                                                              stanuje blizu mene.

Jovan   Zora
vi i vaš otac   Jovan i Toma

For additional drill:

Ko stanuje do <u>vas</u>?
Ko stanuje preko puta <u>vas</u>?
Ko sedi u pozorištu do <u>vas</u>.

Ko se još seća <u>g. Smita</u> u Beogradu?   Toma ga se još seća.
                                                    Niko ga se više ne seća.
                                                    Ne znam da li ga se još neko seća.

Zora   ja i moja žena   Zora i Jovan

Ko <u>me</u> se još seća u Beogradu?   Toma vas se još seća.
                                              Niko vas se više ne seća.
                                              Ne znam da li vas se još neko seća.
                                                 Verovatno, da.

ti   on   ona   mi   vi   oni

GD 12.3.1.3 Accusative of the Personal Pronouns

Za koga ima pismo?   Ima pismo za <u>mene</u>.
                                  Nema pismo ni za koga.
                                  Ne znam da li ima pošte za koga.
                                  Ne znam da li ima pošte za nekoga.
                                     Verovatno da nema.

mi   vi   Toma i ja   vi i vaša žena

Koga traže ovi ljudi? | Traže _mene_.
Ne traže nikoga.
Oni sigurno traže _mene_.
Ne znam koga oni traže.
Izvinite, ali ne znam koga oni traže.

Koga poznaju g. i g-đa Smit u Beogradu? | Poznaju _mene_.
Ne žalost ne poznaju nikoga.
G. i g-đa Smit poznaju _mene_.
Ne znam da li oni poznaju koga ovde. Verovatno da ne poznaju nikoga.

Koga čekaju vaši prijatelji g. i g-đa Jović? | Čekaju _mene_.
Ne čekaju nikoga. Oni sigurno putuju.
Oni sigurno čekaju _mene_.
Ne znam koga oni čekaju.

Ko _vas_ ovde poznaje, gospodine? | Poznaje me g. Jovanović.
Na žalost, ne poznaje me niko.

Ko poznaje ovde vašeg brata, gospodine? | Poznaje ga g. Jovanović.
Na žalost, niko ga ne poznaje.

on	Jovan	ona	vaša majka
mi	vi i vaš otac	oni	Toma i Jovan

For additional drill:

Ko _vas_ čeka na stanici, gospodo?
Ko _vas_ zove, gospođice?
Ko _vas_ traži, gospodo?

GD 12.3.2 _Yes and No Answers_

GD 12.3.2.1 _For Masculine Animate Nouns in Accusative Singular_

Da li Jovan ima koga u Jugoslaviji? | Da, ima _oca_.
Ne, nema nikoga.
Da, Jovan ima _oca_ u Jugoslaviji.

Ne, Jovan nema nikoga u
Jugoslaviji.

Ne znam da li Jovan ima koga u
Jugoslaviji. Verovatno nema
nikoga.

jedan prijatelj   brat   sin

Da li g. i g-đa Jović poznaju <u>Jovanovog</u>   Da, poznaju ga.
  <u>brata</u>?   Ne, ne poznaju ga.

Da, oni poznaju dobro <u>Jovanovog</u>
  <u>brata</u>.

Ne, oni ne poznaju <u>Jovanovog brata</u>.

vaš otac   vi i vaš prijatelj   moj otac i majka

Da li neko čeka <u>mog brata</u>?   Da, čeka ga.

Ne, ne čeka ga.

Da, jedan čovek čeka <u>vašeg brata</u>.

Ne, niko ne čeka <u>vašeg brata</u>.

moj otac i ja   vas prijatelj   vi i vaš prijatelj   Jovan i Toma

Da li neko traži <u>mog brata</u>?

Da li neko zove <u>mog brata</u>?

GD 12.3.2.2 Genitive of the Personal Pronouns

Da li vaši prijatelji stanuju blizu <u>vas</u>?   Da, stanuju.

Ne, ne stanuju.

Da, moji prijatelji stanuju blizu
  mene.

Ne, moji prijatelji ne stanuju
  blizu mene.

Jovan   Zora   vi i vaš brat   Jovan i Zora
on   ona   vi (pl.)   oni

Da li Jovan uči i zna više od <u>vas</u>?

Da li vaši roditelji dolaze sutra u posetu kod <u>vas</u>?

Da li porodica Smit stanuje preko puta <u>vas</u>?

Da li gospođica Jović sedi u pozorištu do <u>vas</u>?

Da li _me_ se sećate?   Da, sećam vas se.

                                                   Ne, ne sećam vas se.

                                                   Naravno, sećam vas se vrlo dobro.

                                                   Žao mi je, ali ne sećam vas se.

on   ona   mi   oni

Jovan

Zora

Jovan i Zora

GD 12.3.2.3 Accusative of the Personal Pronouns

Da li ima pošte za _Jovana?_   Da, ima.

                                                   Ne, nema.

                                                   Na, ima jedno pismo za njega.

                                                   Ne, nema pošte za njega.

ja   Zora   Zora i Toma   Zora i ja   g. i g-đa Jović

Da li vi tražite _moga brata Jovana,_   Da, tražim ga.

   gospodine?   Ne, ne tražim ga.

                                                   Da, ja tražim vašeg brata Jovana.

                                                   Ne, ja ne tražim njega nego vas.

moj muž   moja sestra   ja i moja žena   moji roditelji

Da li g. Smit poznaje _moga brata Jovana,_ gospođo?

The above drills may be repeated using the following pattern and making the
necessary adaptations:

        Ima li Jovan koga u Jugoslaviji?

GD 12.4   Question and Answer Drill with Prompt

Moj prijatelj ima porodicu ovde.   Da li vaš prijatelj ima porodicu ovde?

On ima ženu i jednog sina.   Koga on ima?

Njegov sin se zove Marko.   Kako se zove njegov sin?

  /Sin mu se zove Marko.   /Kako mu se zove sin?

Ja imam jednog prijatelja u Beogradu.

Nemam nikoga u Beogradu.

Poznajem g. Jovića. On je jedan
od mojih prijatelja.

Mi se sećamo naših prijatelja u
Jugoslaviji.

Ja tražim gospodina Smita.

Gospodina Smita traži jedan čovek.

Pustite toga gospodina unutra.

Izvinite, ali ja vas se ne sećam,
gospodine.

Ja se sećam vašeg brata.

Hvala ali ne mogu da sedim.

Žao mi je ali nemam vremena da čekam
gospodina Smita.

On dolazi kući oko sedam sati.

Kod nas je proleće uvek lepo.

Kod njih su noći uvek sveže.

Kod nas često pada kiša.

Da li imate prijatelja u Beogradu?

Da li imate nekoga u Beogradu?

Da li poznajete g. Jovića?

Da li se sećate vaših prijatelja u
Jugoslaviji?

Koga tražite, gospodine? /Šta želite,
gospodine?

Ko traži gospodina Smita?

Da li da pustim toga čoveka unutra?

Da li me se sećate, gospođo?

Da li se sećate moga brata?

Izvolte sesti, gospodine.

Da li imate vremena da sačekate moga
muža?

Kad on dolazi kući?

Da li je u Jugoslaviji proleće uvek lepo?

Da li su kod njih noći uvek sveže?

Da li kod vas često pada kiša?

GD 12.5 <u>Conversations - Razgovori</u>
GD 12.5.1

A	B
Kako se zove vaš prijatelj?	On se zove Sava Popović.
Odakle je on?	On je iz jednog mjesta blizu Novog Sada.
Kako se zove to mjesto?	To mjesto se zove Kamenica.
Je li to veliko mjesto.	Nije, ali je jako lijepo.
Da li vaš prijatelj ima porodicu?	Jest, ima ženu i sina.
Kako se zove njegova žena?	Zovu je Zora, ali njeno ime je Zorka.

Da li mu je sin veliki?   Nije, Mali je.

Kako se zove njegov sin?   Zove se Marko.

Како се зове ваш пријатељ?   Он се зове Сава Поповић.

Одакле је он?   Он је из једног места близу Новог Сада.

Како се зове то место?   То место се зове Каменица.

Је ли то велико место?   Није, али је врло лепо.

Да ли ваш пријатељ има породицу?   Јесте, има жену и сина.

Како се зове његова жена?   Зову је Зора, али њено име је Зорка.

Да ли му је син велики?   Није. Мали је.

Како му се зове син?   Зове се Марко.

GD 12.5.2

Poznajete li vi gospodina Savića?   Da, poznajem ga.

A poznajete li njegovu ženu gospođu   Da, poznajem i nju i njega.
    Savić?

Kakvi su oni ljudi?   Jako su dobri ljudi.

Da li ih dobro poznajete? Oni stanuju   Da, mi se poznajemo odavno. Zašto
    preko puta nas.   pitate?

Moja žena poznaje gospođu Savić i   Ne treba ništa da brinete.

    odlazi kod nje.   Savići su dobro društvo za vas i vašu
                                                ženu.

Milo mi je. Hvala na obavještenju.

Познајете ли ви господина Савића?   Да, познајем га.

А познајете ли његову жену госпођу   Да, познајем и њу и њега.
    Савић?

Какви су они људи?   Врло су добри људи.

Да ли их добро познајете? Они
   станују преко пута нас.

Да, Ми се познајемо одавно.
   Зашто питате?

Моја жена познаје госпођу Савић и
   и одлази код ње.

Не треба ништа да бринете. Савићи су
   добро друштво за вас и вашу жену.

Мило ми је. Хвала на обавештењу.

GD 12.5.3

Dobar dan, Jovane.

Dobar dan, Tomo.

Šta radite vi na kolodvoru? Da
   ne putujete?

Ne, čekam oca i majku.

Gdje su vaši roditelji?

Oni danas dolaze iz Splita, s ljetovanja.

Koga vi čekate?

Ne čekam nikoga. Ja putujem.

Gdje putujete?

Putujem u Dalmaciju na ljetovanje.

U koje mjesto idete?

Idem u Makarsku.

Idete li sad prvi put u Makarsku?

Da, prvi put. Poznajete li vi
   Makarsku?

Da, poznajem je vrlo dobro.

Da li je Makarska lijepo mjesto za
   ljetovanje?

Jeste. U Makarskoj je ljetovanje
   jako prijatno.

Milo mi je. Hvala na obavještenju.

Добар дан, Јоване.

Добар дан, Томо.

Шта радите ви на станици?
   Да не путујете?

Не, чекам оца и мајку.

Где су ваши родитељи?

Они данас долазе из Сплита, с летовања.
   Кога ви чекате?

Не чеким никога. Ја путујем.

Где путујете?

Путујем у Далмацију на летовање.

У које место идете?

Идем у Макарску.

Идете ли сад први пут у Макарску?

Да, први пут. Познајете ли ви Макарску?

Да, познајем је врло добро.

Да ли је Макарска лепо место за летовање?

Јесте. У Макарској је летовање врло пријатно.

Мило ми је. Хвала на обавештењу.

GD 12.6 Homework - Domaći zadatak

GD 12.6.1 Complete the following sentences using the words in parentheses.

Otac _____ zove se Vladimir.   (Marko i Sava Savić)

Kuća _____ je lepa i udobna.   (moj brat Vladimir)

Gospođo, ima jedna poruka za _____.   (vaš suprug)

Ovaj čovek čeka _____.   (vi i gospodin Savić)

Ovi ljudi ne traže _____ već _____.   (ja _____ vi)

Poznajem dobro i _____ i _____.   (vaš brat _____ vaš otac)

_____ traži jedan gospodin.   (ona)

Oni stanuju blizu _____.   (mi)

Sećam se dobro i _____ i _____.   (vaš otac _____ vaš brat)

Ne sećamo _____ se.   (on)

GD 12.6.2 Write out sentences 1 - 4 with the object at the beginning of each sentence. In sentences 5 - 10 substitute the corresponding pronouns for the underlined nouns.

1.   Neki ljudi traže Jovana i Tomu.

2.   Gospodin Savić čeka savetnika Smita.

3.   Jedna gospođa zove gospodina Smita.

4.   Neki ljudi ih čekaju.

5.   On poznaje Jovana, ali ne poznaje Zoru.

6.   Tražimo Jovana i Zoru.

7. Otac voli <u>sestru</u> više nego <u>mene i brata</u>.

8. Otac voli mnogo <u>sestru</u>.

9. Oni se sećaju <u>gospodina Smita</u>.

10. Jovan čeka <u>roditelje</u> na železničkoj stanici.

UNIT 13

Basic Sentences - Osnovne rečenice

Going Out	Izlazak	Излазак

A

We're going to the movies this evening.	Večeras idemo u kino.	Вечерас идемо у биоскоп.
to be giving	dávati, dájēm	давати, дајēм
is given, is being given	dájē se	даје се
Yugoslav	jugoslávēnskī, -ā, -ō	југословēнскӣ, -ā, -ō
film, picture	fȉlm, pl. fȉlmovi	филм, филмови
A Yugoslav picture is being shown ('given').	Dáje se jèdan jugo-slávēnskī fȉlm.	Даје се један југо-словенскӣ филм.

B

to cost	kȏštati, kȍštā	кȏштати, кȍштā
or,	stájati, stójī	стајати, стаје
ticket	úlaznica	улазница
How much does the ticket cost?	Kòliko kȍštā úlaznica?	Колико кȍштā улазница? #
or,	Kòliko stòjī úlaznica?	Колико стајē улазница? #

A

hundred	stȍ	стȍ
dinar	dínār / dȉnār	динāр / динар
(The ticket costs) one hundred dinars.	Úlaznica stójī stȍ dȉnārā.	Улазница кȍшта стȍ динāра.
to will, want	htjèti, hóću	хтети, хоħу

you will, you want	hóćete	хоћете
with	s / sa	с, са
with us	s nàma	с нама
free	slòbodan, slòbodna, -o	слободан, слободна, -о
Would you like to go with us (if you're free)?	Hóćete li ići s nàma, ako ste slòbodni?	Да ли хоћете да идете с нама, ако сте слободни?#

B

willingly, gladly	ràdo	радо
I'd be glad to, but I need some Yugoslav money.	Hóću jáko ràdo,# ali treba mi nešto Jugoslávēnskōg nóvca.	Хоћу врло радо,# али треба ми нешто југословēнскōг новца.
to exchange, change	promijéniti, da prómijenīm	променити, да променим
five	pȅt	пȇт
dollar	dòlar	долар
Can you change five dollars into dinars for me?	Dà li mi mòžete promijéniti pȅt dòlara u dìnare?	Да ли можете да ми промените пȇт долара у динаре?#

A

to have to, must	mórati, mòrām	морати, морам
official	zváničan, zvánična, -o /slúžben, -a, -o	званичан, зв.нична, -о /службен, -а, -о
No, you have to change dollars through official channels ('by official way').	Nè, vi mòrate promijéniti dòlare službenim pútem.	Не, ви морате да промените доларе званичним путем.

B

to loan	pozájmiti, da pózajmīm	позајмити, да позајмим
or,	posúditi, da pósūdīm	посудити, да посудим
a couple (with feminine nouns)	dvìje-trì / dvijétrī	двȅ-трȋ /двȅтрȋ
a couple (with masculine nouns)	dvà-trì / dvátrī)	двȁ-трȋ / двȁтрȋ
thousand	tìsuća	хиљада
Can you lend me two or three thousand dinars?	Dà li mi mòžete posúditi dvìje-trì tìsuće dìnārā?	Да ли можете да ми позајмите две-три хиљаде динара?#

A

that big	tolíkī, -ā, -ō	толикӣ, -ā, -ō
that much, that many	tòliko	толико
ever	gòd	год
whatever	kàko gòd	како год
Yes, I can. I have that many ('dinars').	Jèst, mógu. Tòliko dìnara ìmām.	да, могу. Толико динара имам.
Whatever you like.	Kàko gòd hóćete.	Како год хоћете.

B

enough	dòvoljno	довољно
All right, that's enough for this evening.	U rédu. Tò je dòvoljno za večéras.	У реду. То је довољно за вечерас.
What time is it?	Kòliko je sátī?	Колико је сати?#

278

A

two (with masculine and neuter nouns)	dvȁ	двȁ
ten	dèsēt	дѐсет
It's ten past two.	Sàda su dvȁ i dèset.	Сада је два и десет.
or,		
minute	mȋnūt, Gpl minútā	минут, минута
to pass by	prȍći, da prȍđem	проћи, да прођем
passed	prȍšao, prȍšla, -o	прошао, прошла, -о
It's now ten past two. ('two o'clock and ten minutes'/ 'ten minutes have passed two')	Sàda su dvȁ sȁta i dèset minútā.	Сада је десет минута прошло двȁ.

B

| to be beginning, begin | pȍčinjati, pȍčinjē | почивати, почиње |
| What time does the movie start? | U kòliko sȁti pȍčinje kȋno? | У колико сати почиње биоскоп? |

A

eight	òsam	осам
The movie starts at eight.	Kȋno pȍčinje u òsam.	Биоскоп почиње у осам.
schedule	ràsporēd	распоред
after	pòslije	после
before	prȉje	пре
noon	pȍdne (n. indecl.)	подне
afternoon, P.M.	pòslije pȍdne	после подне
before noon, A.M.	prȉje pȍdne	пре подне

279

What's your schedule for this afternoon?	Kàkav je vȁš ràsporēd za pȍslije pȍdne?	Какав је ваш распоред за после подне?#

B

to go, leave	òtīći, da òdēm	отићи, да одем
duty	dȕžnōst (f.)	дужност
First, I have to go to the embassy to report for duty.	Prvo mȍram òtīći u ambasȃdu, da se jȁvim na dȕžnōst.	Прво треба да одем у амбасаду, да се јавим на дужност.
Then I have to go to the railroad station to see about my luggage.	Ȍnda mȍram òtīći na kòlodvōr, da vȉdim mȏj prtljag.	Онда треба да одем на железничку станицу да видим за мој пртљаг.

A

You have plenty of time.	Ȉmate dòvoljno vrȅmena.	Имате довољно времена.

Grammatical Notes

Note 13.1   Cardinal Numerals - Obični brojevi
Note 13.1.1 Cardinal Numerals Form - Obični brojevi: oblik

1	jédan, jédna, jédno	13	trínaest	40	četrdésēt
2	dvȁ, dvȅ /dvȉje	14	četŕnaest	50	pedésēt
3	trȋ	15	pétnaest	60	šezdésēt / šéset
4	čétiri	16	šésnaest	70	sedamdésēt
5	pȅt	17	sedámnaest	80	osamdésēt
6	šȅst	18	osámnaest	90	devedésēt
7	sèdam	19	devétnaest	100	stȏ / stòtina
8	òsam	20	dvȃdesēt	200	dvȅsta / dvȅ stòtine
9	dèvēt	21	dvȃdesēt jédan	300	trȉsta / trȉ stòtine
10	dèsēt	22	dvȃdesēt dvȁ	400	čétiristo / čétiri stòtine
11	jedánaest	23	dvȃdesēt trȉ	500	pȅtstȏ / pȅt stòtīnā
12	dvánaest	30	trídesēt		

600	šȅststō / šȅst stòtīnā
700	sȅdamstō / sȅdam stòtīnā
800	òsamstō / òsam stòtīnā
900	dȅvetstō / dȅvēt stòtīnā
1.000	hȋljada / tȉsuća
1,000.000	milíōn / milijún

Note use of period for thousand where English uses a comma.

Note 13.1.2 Cardinal Numbers: Usage - Obični brojevi: upotreba

1.   Daje se jedan jugoslovenski film.

Mojim prijateljima i meni donesite po jedno vino.

Kelner, donesite mi molim još jednu kafu.

On ne govori nijedan stran jezik.

Ima ženu i jednog sina.

2.   Sada je dva sata.

2-3(000)   Mogu da vam pozajmim dve-tri hiljade dinara.

5   Možete li da mi promenite pet dolara u dinare?

100   Ulaznica košta sto dinara.

The numeral 1 is an adjective and agrees with the noun - /jédan fȉlm/, /jédno vȋno/, /jédno pȉvo/, /jédnu kàfu/, /jédnog sȉna/. All numbers ending in /jédan/ are followed by the singular form of the noun (if there is a singular). 'One man' is /jédan čȍvek/. The next number ending in /jédan/ is 'twenty-one' so 'twenty-one men' is /dvádeset i jèdan čȍvek/. Any number ending in /jédan/, no matter how high, has the same pattern: /hȋljadu i jèdan čȍvek/ '1001 men', /hȋljadu i jèdna nȍć/ '1001 nights'. The noun may, of course, be in any case, and the case of /jedan/ is determined by that of the noun it modifies: /od jédnog čovéka/ 'from one man' (genitive), /vȉdeo sam hȋljadu i jèdnog čovéka/ 'I saw 1001 men' (accusative). If the noun has only a plural form, as /kòla/ 'car' (neuter plural), /jédan/ agrees with it: /jédna kòla/ 'a car' and a verb used with it is also plural. (/jédan/ may also be used in the plural in the sense of 'individual (so-and-sos), certain ones', '(one and) the same'.)

The number two has two forms: /dvà/, used before masculine and neuter nouns (or to refer to them), and /dvȅ/ (/dvȉje/) used with feminine nouns (or to refer to them). The form of the noun (and modifying adjectives) is according to the following pattern:

dvȁ čovéka	dvȁ oglédala
dvȁ stára čovéka	dvȁ vélika oglédala
dvȅ žéne	dvȅ nòći
dvȅ lȅpe žéne	dvȅ lȅpe nòći

The ending on feminine /a/ nouns is a short /-e/. The agreeing adjective has the same ending. Feminine /i/ nouns have /-i/. The ending on masculine and neuter nouns, and accompanying adjectives, is /-a/. For convenience we may call this ending the 'dual'. Contrast the dual and the genitive singular endings:

	Masculine and Neuter		Feminine /a/		Feminine /i/	
	Adj.	Noun	Adj.	Noun	Adj.	Noun
Genitive	-ōg	-a	-ē	-ē	-ē	-i
Dual	-a	-a	-e	-e	-e	-i

The dual endings are used after /dvȁ/, /dvȅ/, /trȉ/, /čétiri/ or any number ending in one of these. They are also used after /dvȁ-trȉ/, /dvȅ-trȉ/ 'a couple; two or three', as well as /òba/ f. /òbe/ (or /òbadvā/, /òbadvē/ ~ /òbadvije/) 'both'. For example, /sto i čétiri čoveka/ '104 men'.

Any number not ending in /jédan/, /dvȁ/, /dvȅ/, /trȉ/, /čétiri/ is followed by the genitive plural of both adjective and noun. Compare:

jedan čòvek	jedna žéna
dva čovéka	dve žéne
tri čovéka	tri žéne
četiri čovéka	četiri žéne
pet ljúdī	pet žénā
devetnaest ljúdī	devetnaest žénā
dvadeset ljúdī	dvadeset žénā
dvadeset i jedan čòvek	dvadeset i jedna žéna
dvadeset i dva čovéka	dvadeset i dve žéne
hiljadu velikih ljúdī	hiljadu lepih žénā

282

Note the use of /po/ in /po jedno vino/. This particle has a distribu-
tive meaning: 'one [serving of] wine for each [of us]'.

Of the numerals given in Note 13.1.1, /jédan/ is an adjective, /stotina/,
/híljada/, and /tìsuća/ are feminine nouns. After numerals they have the regular case endings: /trî híljade/, /trî tìsuće/, /pêt híljadā/, /pêt tìsūćā/.
When beginning a number, they are invariable: /hiljadu i jedan čovjek/, /tisuću
i jedna noć/, /došao sam sa hiljadu i jednim čovekom/, /došao sam sa tisuću i
pedeset knjiga/. /milíōn/ or /milíjūn/ is a masculine noun. /dvà/ and /dvè/
vary according to gender but rarely for case. All other numerals of this list
are invariable and are treated as neuters where gender is called for. Except
for the verb /ímā/ (discussed in Note 13.3 and 23.1.1), the numerals /dvà/
(/dvè/), /trî/ and /cétiri/ as subjects are used with a plural verb. Numerals
above five may be used with either a singular or plural verb.

Although /dvà/, /dvè/ (/dvìje/) and /trî/ are usually invariable, occasional
use is made of older case forms. Genitive forms are /dvájū/ (m., n.) /dvéjū/
(/dvíjū/, f.) and /tríjū/. An example occurs in Unit 22: /Videli smo sudar
dvaju kola./ 'we saw the collision of two cars'. Of other forms /dvéma/
(/dvjéma/, f.), /obéma/ (/objéma/) and /tríma/ are sometimes found. These are
both dative and instrumental (see Note 15.1). /dvéma/ must be used in the
sentence /Ja sam predao pismo dvema ženama/ 'I gave the letter to two women'
(indirect object). It is optional in /Dete se igralo sa dvema loptama/ 'the
child was playing with two balls' (with preposition /sa/). More common is
/Dete se igralo sa dve lopte/.

Note the adjective /nijédan/ 'not one, not a single'. Compare /kò/ 'who',
/nìko/ 'no one', /štà/ 'what', /nìšta/ 'nothing'.

Note 13.2 Other Quantity Words - Druge reči za količinu

    Toliko dinara imam.
    Koliko pisama ima?
    Ima nekoliko pisama.

In addition to the numerals, there are many other words expressing
quantity, such as /màlo/, /mnògo/, /kolíko/, /nèkolíko/, /tolíko/. Nouns following these are also in the genitive plural. The quantity words themselves are
neuter singular.

Note the elements which make up certain of these: /k-olík-o/, /t-olík-o/,
/ne-k-olík-o/. The /k-/ is the /k-/ of /ko/, the /t-/ is the /t-/ of /to/.
/-o/ is the neuter ending.

Note 13.3 Verb /ímati/ - Glagol /ímati/

> Ima i jedan čaj, gospodine.
> Ima ženu i jednog sina.

The verb /ímati/ has two usages of the present tense forms /ímā/ and
/ímajū/. They may be used as 'has, have', as in 'he has a wife and son' or as
'there is, there are' as 'there's also a [cup of] tea, sir'.

The noun (or nouns) associated with /ímā/ 'there is, there are' is usually
the subject of /ímā/. Collective subjects (including numerals /pèt/ on) are
usually used with /ímā/, though the reference is to a plurality of objects. For
more detail see Note 23.1.1.

Note 13.4 Verb: /hóću/, /mógu/ - Glagoli /hóću/ i /mógu/

> Hoću vrlo rado.
> Hoćete li da idete s nama?
> Kako god hoćete.
> Mogu da vam pozajmim dve-tri hiljade dinara.
> Možete li da mi promenite pet dolara?

The verbs /hóću/ 'I will' and /mógu/ 'I can' are the only verbs in Serbo-
Croatian which have /-u/ for 'I'. They are also different (from each other as
well) in the third person plural:

hóću	hóćemo	mógu	mòžemo
hòćeš	hóćete	mòžeš	mòžete
hòće	hóćē	mòže	mògū

The verb /hoću/ is used in the sense of 'will, want', as well as 'will' for future (discussed in Note 19.1).

Grammatical Drill - Gramatička vežba

GD 13.1   Cardinal Numerals - Obični brojevi
GD 13.1.1 /dva/, /dve/, /tri/, /četiri/, and their compounds /dvadeset dva/,
            /dvadeset tri/, /dvadeset četiri/ etc.

Without Adjectives

Sada je <u>dva</u> sata.   tri   dvadeset tri
                                            četiri   dvadeset četiri
                                            dvadeset dva

Ne mogu da vam promenim <u>dva</u> dolara u dinare.   tri   pedeset tri
                                                       četiri   sto četiri
                                                       dvadeset dva   hiljadu dva

Masculine to Feminine Transform
    Substitute the noun in parentheses for the one underlined.

Jovan ima samo dva <u>brata.</u>   (sestra)   Jovan ima samo dve sestre.
Kuća ima samo dva <u>stola.</u>   (soba)
Soba ima samo dva <u>kreveta.</u>   (stolica)
Grad ima samo dva <u>restorana.</u>   (kafana)
Grad ima samo dva <u>trga.</u>   (ulica)
Kuća ima samo dva <u>kupatila.</u>   (kancelarija)
Još samo dva <u>čoveka</u> čekaju.   (žena)
Toma ima dva <u>hotela.</u>   (kuća)

Masculine to Feminine with Negative Transform: e.g.

Moj prijatelj ima dva <u>brata.</u>   (sestra)   Moj prijatelj nema dva brata,
                                                          već dve sestre.

Naša soba ima dva <u>stola.</u>   (stolica)
Kuća ima dva <u>kreveta.</u>   (soba)
Grad ima dva <u>parka.</u>   (kafana)
Kuća ima dva <u>kupatila.</u>   (kancelarija)
Dva <u>čoveka</u> čekaju.   (žena)

Moj prijatelj ima dva <u>hotela.</u>   (kuća)

In the following drill make all 2 substitutions, using /dve/ when required, then repeat the drill with the 1 substitutions.

	1	2		1		2	
Jovan ima	<u>dva</u>	<u>brata.</u>	tri	dolar	ogledalo	sestra
			četiri	prijatelj	kupatilo	stolica
				dinar	pismo	soba
				sto		kancelarija
				krevet		kuća

	1	2		1		2	
Naš grad ima	<u>dva</u>	<u>hotela.</u>	tri	hotel	kafana
			četiri	spomenik	ulica
			dvadeset dva	park	kuća
			trideset tri	trg	kazalište
			pedeset četiri	restoran	pozorište
			sto četiri	muzej	
			dvesta dva		

With Adjectives

Repeat each sentence using the number indicated with the underlined adjective noun phrase.

Moja kuća je blizu <u>jednog velikog parka.</u>	dva	Moja kuća je blizu dva velika parka.
Soba ima <u>jedan udoban krevet.</u>	tri	Soba ima tri udobna kreveta.
Ima pismo od <u>mog starog prijatelja.</u>	dva	Ima pismo od moja dva stara prijatelja.
Moja kuća ima samo <u>jednu veliku i lepu sobu.</u>	četiri	Moja kuća ima četiri velike i lepe sobe.
U sobi ima <u>jedna udobna stolica.</u>	dve	U sobi imaju dve udobne stolice
Grad ima <u>jednu veliku ulicu.</u>	dve	Grad ima dve velike ulice.
Grad ima <u>jedan veliki i lep hotel.</u>	dva	Grad ima dva velika i lepa hotela.
Sutra idemo u posetu kod <u>jednog starog prijatelja.</u>	dva	Sutra idemo u posetu kod dva stara prijatelja.

286

Repeat the above drill with negative transform, according to the model:

Moja kuća je blizu <u>jednog velikog</u>
<u>parka.</u>

Moja kuća nije blizu jednog već blizu
dva velika parka.

or,

Moja kuća nije blizu jednog velikog
parka, već blizu dva velika parka.

<u>Controlled Adaptation Drill with negative transform.</u>

Naš grad ima <u>dva¹ dobra hotela.²</u>
          <u>dve dobre kafane</u>

1		2
tri	<u>dobar hotel</u>	<u>dobra kafana</u>
četiri	lepo pozorište	velika i lepa ulica
	veliki trg	nova železnička stanica
	lep park	mala, ali čista ulica
	dobar restoran	mala železnička stanica
	lep i veliki muzej	
	lep i veliki spomenik	

<u>Adaptation Drill with negative transform.</u>

Jovan ima <u>**dva** velika brata.</u>

1		2
tri	čist i udoban krevet	čisto kupatilo
četiri	udobna soba	vrlo lepa i velika kuća
	lepo i veliko ogledalo	prljava i neudobna soba
	mala i neudobna stolica	lepa i udobna stolica

GD 13.1.2 Genitive plural with numbers /pet/, etc.

Ovde ima <u>**pet** velikih zgrada.</u>

Ovde nema <u>**pet** velikih zgrada</u> već samo dva.

	1		2	
šest	dvanaest	mala soba	dobra kafana
devet	osamnaest	lep muzej	lepo pozorište
deset	dvadeset pet	veliki bioskop	veliki trg

Treba da odem na železničku stanicu u pet sati.

šest	osam	deset	dvanaest
sedam	devet	jedanaest	

GD 13.1.3   Dual and Genitive with various numbers

     Substitute the numbers at the right of each sentence for those underlined.

Kafa košta dvadeset dva dinara.	18	50	75
Vino košta trideset pet dinara.	31	90	125
Pivo staje četrdeset četiri dinara.	15	150	60
Hleb staje petnaest dinara.	35	25	45
Meso košta četiri stotine dinara,			
kako koje.[1]	280	350	375
Ulaznica za bioskop staje sto dinara.	250	280	105
Ulaznica za posorište staje dvesta			
pedeset dinara.	320	575	201
Soba košta hiljadu petsto dinara.	2.005	1.122	2.504

GD 13.2   Agreement of verbs with numerals and associated nouns

GD 13.2.1   Verb /imati/ - Glagol /imati/

     This is a learning drill contrasting the numerals plus noun as object of /ima/ 'has' with the numeral plus noun as subject of /ima/ 'there is' or 'there are' (also /imaju/).

1	Naša kuća ima jednu sobu.	U našoj kući ima jedna velika soba.
2	Naša kuća ima dve velike sobe.	U našoj kući imaju dve velike sobe.
3	Naša kuća ima pet velikih soba.	U našoj kući ima pet velikih soba.

Repeat sentences   2   with /tri/ and /četiri/.

Repeat sentences   2   (on right only) with /ima/.

Repeat sentences   3   with /osam/ and /jedanaest/.

---

[1]   /kako koje/ 'depending on what kind it is' ('how which').

/ima/ ᵗthere is, there areᵗ

U gradu ima <u>jedan</u> hotel.

U gradu imaju <u>dva</u> hotela.

U gradu ima <u>pet</u> hotela.

Use the following sentences for the above drill:

Ima <u>jedno</u> pismo za vas, gospodine.

Ima <u>jedan</u> dobar put do Beograda.

Ima <u>jedan</u> lep park preko puta moje kuće.

Ima <u>jedna</u> poruka za vas.

GD 13.2.2 With other verbs - S drugim glagolima

U ovoj kući stanuje <u>jedan</u> čovek.

U ovoj kući stanuju <u>dva</u> čoveka.

U ovoj kući stanuje <u>pet</u> ljudi.

U ovoj kući stanuju <u>pet</u> ljudi.

Use the following sentences for the above drill:

U kancelariji čeka <u>jedan</u> čovek.

<u>Jedan</u> čovek traži gospodina Smita.

Gospodina Smita traži <u>jedna</u> žena.

Treba mi <u>jedna</u> soba.

GD 13.3 Verbs /hóću/ and /mógu/

Hoć<u>u</u> da idem u bioskop, ako se daje dobar film.

Neć<u>u</u> da idem u bioskop, ako se ne daje dobar film.

Ne mog<u>u</u> da vam promenim deset dolara u dinare.

Mog<u>u</u> da vam pozajmim nekoliko hilada dinara.

on	ona	(vi)	oni	one
Jovan	Zora	vi (pl)	Jovan i Toma	majka i sestra
moj otac	moja majka	vi i Toma	moji prijatelji	moje sestre

GD 13.4   Questions and Answers - Pitanja i odgovori

GD 13.4.1 Informational Answers

    Make all 1 substitutions with all 2 combinations thereof. Use /dve/ where appropriate.

1	2
Koliko velikih hotela ima u gradu?	Ima dva.
	Nema nijedan.
	Ima dva velika hotela.
	Nema nijedan veliki hotel.

1		2	
pozorište	trg	tri	sedam
park	bioskop /kino	četiri	devet
muzej	kafana /kavana	pet	jedanaest
spomenik	stanica	šest	četrnaest
zgrada	ulica	osam	

Ko traži gospodina Smita?	Traži ga jedan čovek.	dva
	Niko ga ne traži.	tri
	Gospodina Smita traži jedan čovek.	četiri
		pet
Ko stanuje u ovoj kući?	U ovoj kući stanuje jedna mala porodica.	šest
		osam
	U ovoj kući niko ne stanuje.	

Ko čeka gospodina Jovića?	Čeka ga jedna žena.
	Koliko ja znam niko ga ne čeka.
	Gospodina Jovića čeka jedna žena.

Koliko dobrih puteva ima do vašeg mesta?	Ima jedan dobar put.
	Nema nijedan.
	Ima jedan dobar put do moga mesta.
	Nema nijedan dobar put do moga mesta.

Answer the following questions with the numbers on the right.

Koliko spomenika ima u gradu?	21	9	17
Koliko velikih zgrada ima u gradu?	501	366	1.623
Koliko kafana ima u gradu?	13	110	155
Koliko pozorišta ima u gradu?	7	10	13
Koliko dobrih hotela ima ovde?	2	14	133
Koliko košta kafa?	22	15	55
Koliko staje vino?	11	18	26
Koliko košta hleb?	35	42	54
Koliko staje meso?	280	292	755
Koliko košta ulaznica?	110	225	380
Koliko staje soba u hotel Metropolu?	950	1.200	2.315
Koliko dinara možete da mi pozajmite?	5.200	15.300	100.000

U koliko sati odlazite odavde?   1 3 7 10 2 5 11 8 4 12 6 9

GD 13.4.2 _Yes and No Answers_

1	2
Da li ima <u>velikih parkova</u> u gradu?	Da, ima <u>dva</u> velika parka. Ne, nema nijedan veliki park u gradu.

1		2	
dobar hotel	lep spomenik	tri	devet
lep trg	dobra kafana	pet	četiri
dobar bioskop	lepa ulica		

Da li neko stanuje u ovoj zgradi?	Da, stanuju <u>dve</u> velike porodice.	tri
	Ne, niko ne stanuje u toj zgradi.	šest četiri deset

Da li to neko traži gospodina Smita?

Da, traže ga <u>dva</u> čoveka.
Ne, ne traži ga niko.

Da li neko čeka moga muža?

Da, čekaju ga <u>dve</u> žene.
Ne, niko ga ne čeka.

Da li ima dobrih puteva do vašeg grada?

Da, ima <u>dva</u> dobra puta.
Ne, nema nijedan dobar put do nas.

	Da li je kafa ovde skupa?	Ne, nije skupa. Kafa košta	1	2
		petnaest dinara.	12	60
		1	14	90
		Da, skupa je. Kafa košta	13	70
		pedeset dinara.	16	80
		2	17	110
			21	120
			25	140

	Da li možete da mi promenite	Žao mi je, ali ne mogu.		pet	
	pet dolara u dinare?	Vi morate da promenite	3	4
		dolare zvaničnim putem.	10	15
			19	32
			21	45

Da li možete da mi pozajmite   Da, mogu.
  dve hiljade dinara do sutra?   Ne, ne mogu.

Da, mogu da vam pozajmim
  dve hiljade dinara.

Žao mi je, ali ne mogu da
  vam pozajmim dve hiljade dinara.

3.000	10.200	101.000
4.500	55.500	200.000

Repeat the above drills with the pattern:

    Ima li velikih restorana u gradu?

GD 13.5 Question and Answer Drill with Prompt

Večeras idemo u bioskop.	Da li idete večeras u bioskop?
Večeras ne idemo nigde.	Da li idete negde večeras?
Daje se jedan jugoslovenski film.	Šta se daje u bioskopu?
Ovde se obično daju strani filmovi.	Kakvi se filmovi daju ovde?
Ulaznica staje 250 dinara.	Koliko staje ulaznica?
Bioskop počinje u osam sati.	U koliko sati počinje bioskop?
Sada je četiri i pet.	Koliko je sati?
/Sada je pet minuta prošlo četiri.	

Ja nemam jugoslovenskog novca.

Treba mi 2.500 dinara.

Mogu da vam promenim 5 dolara u
dinare.
/Ne mogu da vam promenim nijedan
dolar u dinare.

Vi morate da promenite dolare zva-
ničnim putem.

Mogu da vam pozajmim dve-tri
hiljade dinara.

Dva čoveka čekaju g. Smita.

U ovoj kući stanuju tri porodice.

U sobi imaju dva kreveta i dve
stolice.

Ima (/imaju) dve poruke za vas.

Sviđa mi se nekoliko zgrada preko
puta pošte.

Da li imate jugoslovenskog novca?

Koliko dinara vam treba?

Da li možete da mi promenite 5 dolara
u dinare?

Zašto ne možete da mi promenite dolare?

Da li možete da mi pozajmite nešto
dinara?

Da li neko (/ko/) čeka gospodina Smita?

Koliko porodica stanuje u ovoj kući?

Koliko kreveta i stolica ima u sobi?

Da li ima neka poruka za mene?

Kako vam se sviđaju zgrade preko
puta pošte?

GD 13.6 Conversations - Razgovori
GD 13.6.1

A

Da li ima u Beogradu mnogo kazališta.

To je dovoljno veliki broj, samo
ako su dobra?

Koliko ima kina.

Kakvi se filmovi daju u kinima?

Da li se daju američki filmovi?

Kakvi su jugoslavenski filmovi?

Da li idete često u kino i kazalište?

A u kazalište?

B

Mislim da ima četiri ili pet.

Dobra su.

Kina ima oko četrdeset, a možda i više.

Daju se jugoslavenski i strani filmovi.

Naravno, daje se mnogo američkih
filmova.

Neki su jako dobri.

Idemo jako često u kino.

Samo kad se daje nešto dobro.

Да ли има у Београду много позоришта?   Мислим да има четири или пет.

То је прилично велики број, само ако   Добра су.
су добра?

Колико има биоскопа?   Биоскопа има око четрдесет, а можда
и више.

Какви се филмови дају у биоскопима?   Дају се југословенски и страни филмови.

Да ли се дају амерички филмови?   Наравно, даје се много америчких
филмова.

Какви су југословенски филмови?   Неки су врло добри.

Да ли идете често у биоскоп и   Идемо врло често у биоскоп.
позориште?

А у позориште?   Само кад се даје нешто добро.

GD 13.6.2

Da li ste slobodni večeras?   Jesam. Zašto pitate?

Da li hoćete da idete s nama u kino?   Hoću jako rado. Šta se daje?

Daje se jedan jugoslavenski film.   Da li su kina ovdje skupa?

Nisu, jeftina su.   Koliko stoji ulaznica?

Ulaznica stoji sto dinara.   Da li možete da mi promijenite nekoliko
dolara u dinare?

Ne mogu da vam promijenim. Vi   Možete li mi posuditi nešto dinara.
morate da promijenite dolare
službenim putem.

Koliko dinara vam treba?   Treba mi pet tisuća dinara.

Toliko mogu da vam posudim.   Dobro, hvala.

Да ли сте слободни вечерас?   Јесам. Зашто питате?

Да ли хоћете да идете с нама   Хоћу врло радо. Шта се даје?
у биоскоп?

Даје се један југословенски филм.   Да ли су биоскопи овде скупи?

Нису, јефтини су.   Колико стаје улазника?

Улазника стаје сто динара.

Не могу да вам променим. Ви морате да
променете доларе званичним путем.

Колико динара вам треба?

Толико могу да вам позајмим.

Да ли можете да ми промените неколико
долара у динаре?

Да ли можете да ми позајмите нешто
динара.

Треба ми пет хиљада динара.

Добро, хвала.

GD 13.6.3

Čujem da vaš prijatelj traži kuću. Da
   li je to istina?
Koliko soba mu treba?
U kom dijelu grada on želi stanovati?

Ima jedna kuća sa pet lijepih,
   velikih soba, ali nije u tom dijelu.
Ta kuća je na Avalskom putu.
Ne, ne stanuje niko. Kuća je nova.

Da, ima dve velike i lijepe kupaone.
Ta kuća je na Avalskom puta br. 42.
Koliko vaš prijatelj želi da plati
   mjesečno za kuću?

Da, tako je.

Trebaju mu četiri sobe.
On želi stanovati na Topčiderskom
   brdu ili Dedinju.
Gdje je ta kuća?

Da li neko stanuje u toj kući?
Vrlo dobro. To je kuća za mog
   prijatelja. Ima li kuća kupaonu?
Koji je broj te kuće?

On može da plati do 70.000 dinara
   mjesečno. Više ne.

Чујем да ваш пријатељ тражи кућу.

Да ли је то истина?

Колико соба му треба?

У ком крају града он жели да станује?

Има једна кућа са пет лепих, великих
   соба, али није у том крају.

Та кућа је на Авалском путу.

Не, не станује нико. Кућа је нова.

Да, има два велика и лепа купатила.

Та кућа је на Авалском путу бр. 42.
Колико ваш пријатељ жели да плати
   месечно за кућу?

Да, тако је.

Требају му четири собе.

Он жели да станује на Топчидерском брду
   или Дедињу.

Где је та кућа?

Да ли неко станује у тој кући?

Врло добро. То је кућа за мог
   пријатеља. Има ли кућа купатило?

Који је број те куће?

Он може да плати до 70.000 динара
   месечно. Више не.

GD 13.7 Homework - Domaći zadatak

1. Fill the blanks in 1-6 with the proper form of the items listed to the right of each sentence. In 7-10 fill the blanks with the proper item of those listed to the right of each sentence.

1. Jovanova soba ima dva _____ i tri _____.   (krevet ____ stolica)

2. Grad ima tri _____.   (dobar restoran)

3. Kuća ima _____ _____.   (2   mala soba)

4. U ovoj kući stanuje pet _____.   (čovek)

5. U gradu ima četiri _____.   (veliki lep spomenik)

6. Moja kuća je blizu dva _____.   (veliki park)

7. Dva čoveka _____ gospodina Smita.   (traži - traže)

8. Pet ljudi vas _____, gospodine.   (čeka - čekaju)

9. Moja dva prijatelja _____ u ovoj kući.   (stanuje - stanuju)

10. Gospodinu Smitu _____ dve velike sobe.   (treba - trebaju)

2. Answer these questions using the numbers and numbers and nouns listed to the right of each sentence.

1. Koliko soba ima vaša kuća?   (2)

2. Koliko dobrih hotela ima u gradu?   (6)

3. Koliko košta hleb?   (22 - dinar)

4. Koliko lepih parkova ima u gradu?   (3)

5. Ko traži gospodina Smita?   (2 - čovek)

6. Ko me čeka?   (2 - žena)

7. Ko stanuje u ovoj kući?   (5 - velika porodica)

8. Koliko dinara možete da mi pozajmite?   (31.000 - dinar)

9. Koliko vaš prijatelj može da plati mesečno za kuću?   (50 - 52.000 - dinar)

10. Od koliko soba vam treba kuća, gospodine?   (4 - 5 - soba)

UNIT 14

Basic Sentences - Osnovne rečenice

The Family -II	O obitelji -II	О породици -II

A

| children | djéca | деца |
| Do you have any children? | Ìmāte li djécē? | Да ли имате деце?# |

B

child	dijéte G djéteta	дете детета
daughter	kćî f. A kćềr, G kćèri Gpl kćérī	кћи кћềр, кћèри кћéрū
Yes, I have two children, a son and a daughter.	Dà, ìmam dvȃ djéteta, sîna i kćềr.	Да, имам двȃ детета, сина и кћềр.

A

| year | gòdina | година |
| How old are your children
('How many years have
your children')? | Kòliko gòdina ìmaju
vaša djéca? | Колико годинā имају ваша
деца?# |

B

My son is five years old, and my daughter two.	Sîn ìma pềt gòdina, a kćî dvìje.	Син има пềт годинā, а кћи двề.
married (of a man)	òženjen, -a, -o	ожењен, -a, -o
Are you married?	Dà li ste vî òženjeni?	Да ли сте ви ожењени?#

A

| No, I'm not. | Nè, nísam. | Не, нисам. |

B

relative	sròdnīk pl sròdnīci	сро̀днūк сро̀днūци
or,	ròđāk pl ròđāci	ро̀ђāк ро̀ђāци
Do you have any relatives ('of relatives')?	Dà li ìmate ròđāke?	Да ли има̀те сро̀днūкā?#

A

| I have brothers and sisters in America. | Ìmam bràću i séstre u Américi. | Ѝмам бра̀ħу и се̑стре у Америци. |
| I have no one here. | Óvdje nèmam nìkoga. | О̑вдје не̏мам нѝкога. |

B

| How many brothers and sisters do you have? | Kòliko bràće i sestárā ìmāte? | Ко̀лико бра̀ħе и сеста̑ра има̑те?# |

A

I have three brothers and two sisters.	Ìmam trī bràta i dvìje séstre.	Ѝмам три̑ бра̀та и двē се̏стре.
married (of a woman)	ùdāta	у̀да̑та
My brothers and sisters are married.	Bràća su òženjena, a séstre su ùdāte.	Бра̀ħа су о̀жењена, а сестре су у̀да̑те.

B

get, be getting	dobíjati, dóbījām	доби̑јати, до̏би̑jа̑м
to be receiving, accepting	prímati, prīmām	при̑мати, при̏ма̑м
orderly, tidy	úredan, úredna, -o	у́редан, у́редна, -о
regularly	úredno	у́редно

298

Does your mail from America come regularly ('do you receive mail from America in orderly fashion')?	Dà li prìmate ùredno pòštu ìz Àmerikē?	Да ли добијате уредно пошту из Америке?#

A

Yes, I do.	Dà, prìmām.	Да,# добијам.

B

How long does it take a letter to come from America to Belgrade?	Kòliko vrémena pùtuje pìsmo od Àmerike do Beógrada?	Колико времена путује писмо од Америке до Београда?#

A

to get	dòbiti, da dòbijēm	добити, да добијам
to receive, accept	prímiti, da prìmīm	примити, да примим
state	dr̀žava	држава
I get a letter from [my] parents in Michigan ('out of the state of M.') in three or four days.	Ja prìmīm pìsmo od ròditēljā ìz dr̀žave Mìčigan za trì-čètiri dàna.	Ја добијем писмо од родитеља из државе Мичиган за три-четири дана.

B

fast, quick	br̀z, br̀za, br̀zo	брз, брза, брзо
fast, quickly	br̀zo	брзо
That's pretty fast.	Tò je prílično br̀zo.	То је прилично брзо.

A

However, that's not always [the case].	Ìstina, tò nìje ùvijek.	Истина, то није увек.
sometimes	kàtkad / kátkada	неки пут
to be detained, retained	zadr̀žati se, da se zadr̀žīm	задржати се, да се задржим

longer	dùžī, -ā, -ō	дужи, -ā, -ō
Sometimes it takes longer ('a letter is retained longer'), five to seven days.	Kàdkad se pȉsmo zadȑžī dùžē, pȇt do sȅdam dȃnā.	Неки пут се писмо задржи дуже, пет до седам дана.
to happen, occur; it happens, occurs	dešávati se, dȅšāvā se	дешавати се, дȅшāвā се
or,	dogáđati se, dȍgāđā se	догађати се, догāђā се
during winter, in winter	zȉmi	зими
rarely ever, hardly ever	rijétko kàda	ретко кад
in summer	ljèti	лети
That usually happens during winter, rarely in summer.	Tȏ se ȍbīčno dȍgađa zȉmi, rijétko kada ljèti.	То се обично дешава зими, ретко кад лети.

B

nevertheless, however	ȉpāk, ȉpak	ипāк, ипак
That still isn't bad.	Tȏ ȉpak nȉje lȍše.	То ипак није рђаво.

A

pertaining to airplane	avíōnskī, -ā, -ō	авиōнскӣ, -ā, -ō
It can be said that an airmail letter takes ('travels') three days to one week ('seven days'/ a week of days').	Mȍže se rȅćī da avionsko pȉsmo pùtuje od trȉ do sȅdam dȃnā.	Може се рећи да авионско писмо путује од три до недељу дāнā.

Notes

Note 14.1   Noun: Special Forms

Note 14.1.1   Noun: /déte/

    Imate li déce?

    Da, imam dva deteta, sina i kćer.

    Koliko godina imaju vaša deca?

/déte/~/dijéte/ 'child' is a neuter noun. The stem is /detet-/~/djetet-/,
the final /-t-/ of which is lost in the nominative-accusative. It is kept before
the endings /-a/, etc: Gen. /déteta/ Dat. /détetu/ (/djéteta/, /djétetu/). The
plural is a feminine singular noun in form, /déca/~/djéca/, taking a plural verb
but feminine adjectives: /moja deca su ovde/. There are a number of neuter
nouns of this type, with shortened stem in the nominative-accusative. Neuter
nouns denoting living beings regularly have a feminine singular form as plural,
(either an /a/ noun [as /déca/] or an /i/ noun). See further Note.

Note 14.1.2 Noun: /bràt/ , /gospódin/

    Koliko braće i sestara imate?

    Imam tri brata i dve sestre.

    Braća su oženjena, a sestre su udate.

/bràt/, a regular masculine animate noun in the singular, has as its
plural /bràća/. /bràća/, like /déca/, is a feminine /a/ noun in form, with adjectives agreeing with it (as /òženjena/) but with plural verb forms.

/gospódin/ 'gentleman' also has an /a/ noun as plural: /gospóda/.

Note 14.1.3 Noun: /kćî/

    Imam dva deteta, sina i kćer.

    Sin ima pet godina, a kći dve.

/kćî/ is a feminine /i/ noun, of the same general type as /nôć/. The
nominative singular is irregular. The other forms have the stem /kćer-/.
Compare:

301

	sg.	pl.	sg.	pl.
N	kćî	kćèri	nòć	nòći
A	kćȇr	kćèri	nȍć	nȍći
G	kćèri	kćèrî	nòći	nócî
D	kćèri	kćèrima	nóći	nócima

Note 14.2　Numerals:　Collective Numerals and Numerical Adjectives

In addition to the cardinal numbers, there are also collective numbers, used in certain situations (see below).　For example:

2	dvòje		8	òsmoro
3	tròje	'a group of three'	9	dèvetoro
4	čètvoro	'a group of four'	10	dèsetoro
5	pètoro	etc.	11	jedánaestoro
6	šèstoro		20	dvádesetoro
7	sèdmoro		50	pedésetoro
				etc.

The collective numerals are used a) with plurals of feminine singular form. The noun is in the genitive:

dvòje déce̅	two children
pètoro bràće̅	five brothers

b) with words indicating a group of persons or animals of various kinds, such as of mixed gender or age:

šèstoro ljúdȋ	six people (of mixed type)

/dvȁ/, /trȋ/, /čétiri/ may be used (with the dual) instead of /dvòje/, /tròje/, /čètvoro/, but for numbers of persons (ending in) five and up the collectives must be used:

Optional:	dvòje déce̅	dvȁ déteta
	tròje bràće	trȋ bràta
	čètvoro teládȋ	čétiri téleta
Obligatory:	pètoro déce̅	
	šèstoro bràće	
	òsmoro teládȋ	

302

In addition to the collective numerals there are also adjectives with numeral bases which are used in certain situations. These adjectives agree with the nouns they modify. The nouns are generally those which occur only in the plural. For example:

dvòja kòla	two cars
dvòje pantalóne	two pairs of pants
dvòji svàtovi	two wedding parties

These adjectives are regularly used for 2, 3, 4, but their use is optional for five on:

pètora kòla	or	pèt kòlā
šèstore pantalóne		šést pantalónā
sèdmora vrátā		sèdam vrátā

The noun /svàt/, used as an example above, is interesting in illustrating these uses. /svàt/ means 'wedding guest'. The plural /svàtovi/ means 'a wedding party'. The use of the adjective /dvòji/ is quite rare but occurs, as given above, with this plural. There are two genitive plurals, /svátā/ 'of wedding guests' and /svatóvā/ 'of wedding parties'. We may have:

pèt svátā	five wedding guests
pèt svatóvā or pètori svàtovi	five wedding parties

Note the use of the genitive after /pèt/ but the use of the nominative plural with the numerical adjectives.

The forms of the collective numerals and those of the numerical adjectives sometimes coincide, but they must not be confused. Contrast:

Collective numeral plus genitive:	dvòje décē
Numerical adjective (nominative plural):	dvòje pantalóne

Grammatical Drill

GD 14.1   Learning Drill
GD 14.1.1 Nouns: /déca/, /bràća/, /gospóda/, and /kćĭ/.

In the first column a phrase with a feminine a-noun is used. In the second the nouns: /déca/, /bràća/, /gospóda/, and /kćĭ/ are used.

303

Type Sentences

To je <u>moja majka.</u>   To su moja <u>braća.</u>

To je <u>moja žena.</u>   To su <u>moja deca.</u>

Ko je <u>ta gospoda?</u>   Ko su <u>ta gospoda?</u>

To je <u>moja sestra.</u>   To je <u>moja kći.</u>

Substitution Drill

Ima pismo od <u>moje majke.</u>   Ima pismo od <u>moje braće.</u>

      moje žene   moje dece

      te gospođe   te gospode

      moje sestre   moje kćeri

Dajte novac <u>mojoj majci.</u>   Dajte novac <u>mojoj braći.</u>

      mojoj ženi   mojoj deci

      toj gospođi   toj gospodi

      mojoj sestri   mojoj kćeri

Mi poznajemo <u>vašu majku.</u>   Mi poznajemo <u>vašu braću.</u>

      vašu ženu   vašu decu

      tu gospođu   tu gospodu

      vašu sestru   vašu kćer

GD 14.1.2 Nouns /déca/, /bràća/, and /gospóda/ with numbers

The following type sentences are to be drilled first. They set the pattern for the sentences which follow and are for substitution drill. The adjective numeral /jédan/ is used in the first type sentence for contrast, though it is not drilled in the substitution sentences.

Ja imam samo <u>jedno dete.</u>

Imam <u>dva deteta.</u>   Imam <u>dvoje dece.</u>

Imam <u>tri deteta.</u>   Imam <u>troje dece.</u>

Imam <u>četiri deteta.</u>   Imam <u>četvoro dece.</u>

             Imam <u>petoro dece.</u>

             Imam <u>šestoro dece.</u>

             Imam <u>desetoro dece.</u>

             Imam <u>dvanaestoro dece.</u>

Substitution Drill:

Ona ima <u>dva deteta</u>.	Ona ima <u>dvoje dece</u>.
Moji prijatelji imaju <u>dva deteta</u>.	Moji prijatelji imaju <u>dvoje dece</u>.

tri deteta	troje dece
četiri deteta	četvoro dece
dva mala deteta	dvoje male dece
tri mala deteta	troje male dece
četiri mala deteta	četvoro male dece

Single (unpaired) drill: e.g. Moji prijatelji imaju <u>petoro dece</u>

<u>petoro dece</u>	šestoro male dece
šestoro dece	desetoro male dece
desetoro dece	dvanaestoro male dece
dvanaestoro dece	

Čekaju vas napolju <u>dva deteta</u>.	Čeka vas napolju <u>dvoje dece</u>.
U sobi su <u>dva deteta</u>.	U sobi je <u>dvoje dece</u>.
U ovoj kući žive <u>dva deteta</u>.	U ovoj kući živi <u>dvoje dece</u>.
Dolaze <u>dva deteta</u>.	Dolazi <u>dvoje dece</u>.

dva brata	dvoje braće
tri brata	troje braće
četiri brata	četvoro braće
dva gospodina	dvoje gospode
tri gospodina	troje gospode
četiri gospodina	četvoro gospode

Single (unpaired) drill: e.g. Čeka vas <u>petoro dece</u>.

<u>petoro dece</u>	petoro braće	petoro gospode
sedmoro dece	sedmoro braće	sedmoro gospode
osmoro dece	osmoro braće	osmoro gospode
jedanaestoro dece	jedanaestoro braće	jedanaestoro gospode

GD 14.2   Controlled Adaptation Drill
GD 14.2.1 Nouns: /déca/, /bràća/, and /gospóda/

<u>Vaši srodnici</u> čekaju kod kuće.   <u>Vaša deca</u> čekaju kod kuće.

    <u>vaši srodnici</u>   <u>vaša deca</u>

    vaši sinovi   vaša braća

    naši očevi   ta gospoda

    vaše kćeri   Zorina deca

The following sentences are for the above drill:

<u>Vaši srodnici</u> su unutra u sobi.
<u>Vaši srodnici</u> stanuju u Puškinovoj ulici.
<u>Vaši srodnici</u> dolaze danas posle podne u tri i deset.

Ima pismo od <u>mojih sinova</u>.   Ima pismo od <u>moje dece</u>.

    <u>moji sinovi</u>   <u>moja deca</u>

    Jovanove sestre   vaša braća

    moje kćeri   ona gospoda

    vaše sestre   naša deca

The following sentences are for the above drill:

On stanuje blizu <u>mojih sinova</u>.
Oni se sećaju <u>mojih sinova</u>.
Ja dobijem pismo od <u>mojih sinova</u> iz države Mičigan za tri-četiri dana.
Pismo <u>mojih sinova</u> se neki put zadrži pet do sedam dana.
Kuća <u>mojih sinova</u> je preko puta jednog velikog parka.

Dajte ovo pismo <u>mojim sestrama</u>.   Dajte ovo pismo <u>mojoj deci</u>.

    <u>moje sestre</u>   <u>moja deca</u>

    moji srodnici   vaša braća

    vaše kćeri   ta gospoda

The following sentences are for the above drill:

Donesite po kafu <u>mojim sestrama</u>.
<u>Mojim sestrama</u> trebaju hitno dve velike sobe.
<u>Mojim sestrama</u> je žao što ne možete doći.
<u>Mojim sestrama</u> je milo što imate lepu i udobnu kuću.
Javite <u>mojim sestrama</u> da prekosutra dođu u konzulat.

Želim da vidim sutra <u>vaše sestre.</u>   Želim da vidim sutra <u>vašu decu.</u>

<u>vaše sestre</u>	<u>vaša deca</u>
moji srodnici	Jovanova braća
Zorini roditelji	ta gospoda
moji veliki prijatelji	Zorina deca
naši očevi	ta velika gospoda

The following sentences are for the above drill:

Čekam <u>moje sestre.</u>
Zora traži <u>moje sestre.</u>
Treba mi soba za <u>moje sestre.</u>
Oni poznaju dobro <u>moje sestre.</u>
Žao mi je da zadržim <u>vaše sestre</u> od puta.

GD 14.3   Adaptation Drill
GD 14.3.1 Nouns: /deca/, /braća/, and /gospoda/

Traže vas <u>neki ljudi,</u> gospodine Joviću.   vaša deca

                                             Jovanove sestre
                                             vaši prijatelji
                                             vaša braća
                                             vaši srodnici

The following sentences are for the above drill:

Gospodina Smita čekaju <u>neki ljudi.</u>
Unutra su <u>neki ljudi.</u>
U ovu kuću dolaze <u>neki ljudi</u> svako veče.
<u>Neki ljudi</u> dobijaju brzo poštu iz Amerike.

Danas ima pismo za Zoru od <u>njenih kćeri.</u>   njena deca   ti ljudi

                                                     moje sestre   ta gospoda
                                                     njena braća

The following sentences are for the above drill:

Ona stanuje blizu <u>njenih kćeri.</u>
Mi se sećamo dobro <u>njenih kćeri</u> sa letovanja.
Naše mesto u pozorištu je do Zore i <u>njenih kćeri.</u>

Kuća njenih kćeri je u jednom velikom i lepom mestu.

Recite mojim kćerima da mi se jave čim dođu kući.   moja deca
                                                          moje sestre
                                                          vaša braća
                                                          ti ljudi
                                                          ta gospoda

The following sentences are for the same drill:

Dajte ovaj novac mojim kćerima.
Javite mojim kćerima da se vraćam kući iduće nedelje.
Mojim kćerima ne trebaju nikakve sobe.
Mojim kćerima je milo što imate lepu i čistu sobu.
Mojim kćerima je žao što imate malu i prljavu sobu.

Jovan treba da sačeka svoje srodnike na železničkoj stanici.   neka stara gospoda
                                                                naši stari roditelj
                                                                svoja braća
                                                                vaši sinovi

The following sentences are for the above type of drill:

On čeka svoje srodnike na železničkoj stanici.
Oni žele da vide svoje srodnike.
Toma i Jovan traže svoje srodnike u selu.
Oni poznaju svoje srodnike.

Drill with plural transform

Jovana i Zoru čeka jedno dete.   Jovana i Zoru čekaju neka deca.
U sobi je vaš brat.
U ovu kuću dolazi svako veče neki gospodin.
Traži vas Tomino dete, gospodine Joviću.
U ovoj kući stanuje jedan gospodin.

Ima za vas pismo od <u>jednog starog</u>
<u>gospodina</u> iz Jugoslavije.

Mi se sećamo dobro <u>Zorinog brata</u>
s letovanja.

Zorino mesto u pozorištu je do
<u>njenog deteta.</u>

Ovo je kuća <u>tog starog gospodina.</u>

Mi stanujemo blizu <u>vašeg brata.</u>

Oni sutra posle podne odlaze u
posetu kod <u>jednog starog</u>
<u>gospodina.</u>

Ima za vas pismo od <u>neke stare</u>
<u>gospode,</u> iz Jugoslavije.

Kažite <u>tom detetu</u> da mi se javi kući.
Dajte ovo pismo <u>mom bratu.</u>
Javite <u>tom gospodinu</u> da dođe u ambasadu
u deset sati pre podne.
<u>Jovanovom detetu</u> je već dobro.
<u>Zorinom</u> bratu još nije dobro.
<u>Tom starom gospodinu</u> je hladno.

Kažite <u>toj deci</u> da mi se jave kući

Jovan treba da sačeka na železničkoj
stanici <u>neko dete.</u>
Zora želi da vidi danas <u>vašeg brata.</u>
Oni traže sobu za <u>jednog starog gospodina.</u>
Oni poznaju <u>to dete</u> s letovanja.

Jovan treba da sačeka na
železničkoj stanici <u>neku decu.</u>

GD 14.4   Questions and Answers
GD 14.4.1 Informational Answers

Koliko <u>dece</u> imate?

Substitute: brat

Imam jedno <u>dete.</u>
Imam dva <u>deteta.</u>
Imam tri <u>deteta.</u>
Imam četiri <u>deteta.</u>
Imam petoro <u>dece.</u>
Imam sedmoro <u>dece.</u>

Imam jedanaestoro <u>dece</u>.

Imam trinaestoro <u>dece</u>.

Koliko <u>dece</u> ima vaš prijatelj?   Nema nijedno <u>dete</u>.

On nema <u>dece</u>.

Substitute: brat

kći

Gde žive vaša braća?   Oni žive u Americi.   ova gospoda

<u>Moja braća</u> žive u Americi.   Zorina deca

Jovanove kćeri

Koliko <u>male dece</u> ima u ovoj kući?   Ima samo jedno.

Nema nijedno.

Substitute: stara gospoda   Ima samo jedno <u>malo dete</u>

u ovoj kući.

Nema nijedno <u>malo dete</u> u

ovoj kući.

Ima dva mala <u>deteta</u>.

Ima <u>petoro male</u> dece.

Ima mnogo <u>male dece</u>.

U kojoj kući stanuju <u>ova mala deca</u>?   Ona stanuju u trećoj kući od naše.

<u>Ta mala deca</u> stanuju u trećoj kući od

naše.

Jovanova braća   Ne znam gde stanuju <u>ta mala deca</u>.

ta stara gospoda

Zorine kćeri

GD 14.4.2 Yes and No Answers

Da li imate dece, gospođo?   Da, imam.

Imate li dece, gospođo?   Ne, nemam.

Imate dece, gospođo?   Da, imam jedno dete.

Ne, nemam <u>dece</u>.

Da, imam dvoje dece, velikog sina i

malu kćer.

Da, imam troje <u>dece</u>, dva velika sina i

malu kćer.

Da, imam četvoro <u>dece</u>, dva velika sina
i dve male kćeri.

Da, imam petoro dece, dva velika sina
i tri male kćeri.

Repeat this drill with the following questions:

Da li imate dece, gospodine Pavloviću?

Imate dece, gospodine?

Da li Zora ima dece?

Da li Zora i Toma imaju dece?

Da li hoćete da mi promenite <u>pet</u> dolara u dinare?	Ne, ne mogu da vam promenim dolare u dinare.	10 14
Hoćete da mi promenite <u>pet</u> dolara u dinare?	Vi morate da promenite do- lare zvaničnim putem.	17 19 25

Da li hoćete da mi pozajmite <u>dve</u> <u>hiljade</u> dinara do sutra?	Da, hoću vrlo rado.	3.500
	Izvinite, nije da neću da vam pozajmim <u>dve</u> hiljade dinara, ali nemam ni ja dovoljno dinara.	4.200 7.000 10.500 11.000

GD 14.5 Question and Answer Drill with Prompt

Ja imam jedno dete. /Ja imam dva deteta. /Ja imam dvoje dece. /Ja imam petoro dece.	Koliko dece imate? /Da li imate dece?
Jovan ima samo jednog sina.	Koliko sinova ima Jovan? /Da li Jovan ima sinova?
Toma ima jednu kćer.	Koliko kćeri ima Toma? /Da li Toma ima kćeri?
Sin ima pet godina, a kći dve.	Koliko godina imaju vaša deca?
Ja imam petoro braće.	Koliko braće imate? /Da li imate braće?
Od petoro braće samo jedan je oženjen.	Da li su vaša braća oženjena?

Od jedanaestoro dece moj prijatelj   Koliko kćeri ima vaš prijatelj?
  ima samo jednu kćer.

Dajte ovo pismo jednom od moje braće.   Kome da dam ovo pismo?

Recite da jedan od gospode odmah   Šta da kažem toj gospodi?
  dođe u ambasadu.

Deca su verovatno gladna i traže   Šta hoće deca? /Šta traže deca?
  da jedu.

Jovanova deca su dobra.   Kakva su Jovanova deca?

Jovanovoj deci je dobro.   Kako je Jovanovoj deci?
  /Jovanova deca su dobro.   /Kako su Jovanova deca?

Smitovi se sećaju vaše braće.   Koga se sećaju Smitovi?
                                              /Da li se Smitovi sećaju moje braće?

Oni se sigurno ničega ne sećaju.   Čega se oni sećaju? /Da li se oni
                                              sećaju nečaga (/čega)?

GD 14.6 Conversations - Razgovori
GD 14.6.1

                 A   B

Šta želite, gospodine Joviću?   Trebaju mi tri sobe.

Za koga vam trebaju sobe?   Za moju braću.

Zar vaša braća, gospodine Joviću,   Ne, ne žive.
  ne žive ovdje?

Za kad vam trebaju sobe?   Za slijedeću subotu. Moja braća dolaze
                                         ovdje slijedeće subote.

Da li vaša braća imaju djece?   Da, imaju.

Koliko djece imaju?   Jedan ima dvoje djece, jednog sina i
                                         jednu kćer.

A koliko djece ima vaš drugi brat?   On ima petoro djece. Za njega mi
                                         trebaju dvije velike sobe.

Jesu li njegova djeca velika?   Jedna kći je velika, a drugo četvoro
                                         djece je malo.

Jako dobro. Imam tri velike sobe   Koliko koštaju sobe?
  za njih.

Jedna soba košta četiri stotine
   pedeset dinara.

U redu.

Шта желите, господине Јовићу?

Требају ми три собе.

За кога вам требају собе?

За моју браћу.

Зар ваша браћа, господине Јовићу,
   не живе овде?

Не, не живе.

За кад вам требају собе?

За идућу суботу. Моја браћа долазе
   овде идуће суботе.

Да ли ваша браћа имају деце?

Да, имају.

Колико деце имају?

Један има двоје деце, једног сина и
   једну кћер.

А колико деце има ваш други брат?

Он има петоро деце. За њега ми требају
   две велике собе.

Да ли су његова деца велика?

Једна кћи је велика, а друго четворо
   деце је мало.

Врло добро. Имам три велике собе
   за њих.

Колико стају собе?

Једна соба стаје четири стотине
   педесет динара.

У реду.

GD 14.6.2

Da li su djeca doma, Ana?

Samo je vaša kći doma, gospodine.

Gdje je ona?

Ona je u svojoj sobi.

Šta radi?

Mislim da uči.

Gdje su druga djeca?

Druga djeca su u kinu.

Da li je moja žena doma?

Ne, ni gospođa nije doma.

Ona je kod gospođe Jovanović.

Да ли су деца код куће, Ана?

Само је ваша кћи код куће, господине.

Где је она?

Она је у својој соби.

313

Шта ради?   Мислим да учи.

Где су друга деца?   Друга деца су у биоскопу.

Да ли је моја жена код куће? Не, ни госпођа није код куће.

           Она је код госпође Јовановић.

GD 14.6.3

Da li je vaš prijatelj oženjen? Ne, nije.

Da li on ima srodnika?   Da, ima veliku obitelj.

Koga on ima?   Ima roditelje i braću i sestre.

Koliko godina ima vaš prijatelj? On je mojih godina.

Da li poznajete vi njegovu braću i Naravno, poznajem ih jako dobro.
 sestre?

Koliko braće on ima?   Mislim petoro braće.

Koliko djece imaju njegovi roditelji? Šest sinova i mislim dvije ili tri
            kćeri. Moj prijatelj je sedmo'dijete
            svojih roditelja.

Šta radi vaš prijatelj?   On je poslovan čovjek. On i njegov brat
            putuju kroz Evropu.

Kad se vraćaju u Ameriku.   Mislim kroz dvije nedjelje.

  ¹/sedmi, -a, -o/ 'seventh'

Да ли је ваш пријатељ ожењен? Не, није.

Да ли он има сродника?   Да, има велику породицу.

Кога он има?   Има родитеље и браћу и сестре.

Колико година има ваш пријатељ? Он је мојих година.

Да ли познајете негову браћу и сестре? Наравно, познајем их врло добро.

Колико браће он има?   Мислим петоро браће.

Колико деце имају негови родитељи? Шест синова и мислим две или три кћери.

Моj приjатељ je седмо дете своjих родитеља.

Шта ради ваш приjатељ?

Он je послован човек. Он и његов брат путуjу кроз Европу.

Кад се враћаjу у Америку?

Мислим кроз две недеље.

GD 14.7 <u>Homework - Domaći zadatak</u>

GD 14.7.1 Write out each of the following sentences using the appropriate form of the items listed.

Jovan ima _____ deteta.   (/3/)

Moj prijatelj ima samo _____.   (jedna kći)

Ja imam _____ deteta.   (/4/)

U hotelu ima mnogo _____.   (stara gospoda)

U ovoj kući stanuje _____.   (/5/), /malo dete/)

Moj prijatelj ima _____.   (/jedan veliki sin i   jedna mala kći/)

_____ moga prijatelja su velika.   (/brat/ or /braća/)

Deca moga prijatelja su _____.   (mali)

Ja imam petoro _____.   (velika deca)

Jovan ima dve _____.   (mala kći)

GD 14.7.2 Turn the above sentences into questions.

UNIT 15

Basic Sentences – Osnovne rečenice

City and Environs	Grad i okolica	Град и околина

A

on Sunday, Sundays	nédjeljōm	недељом
holiday	blȁgdan pl. blȁgdani	прȁзник, прȁзници
on holiday, holidays	blȁgdanom	прȁзником
What do you do Sundays and holidays?	Štȁ rȁdite nédjeljōm i blȁgdanom?	Шта рȁдите недељом и прȁзником?

B

to be making	prȁviti, prȁvīm	правити, правӣм
excursion, trip, picnic	ízlēt	излēт
surrounding area	okolína	околина
or,	okolíca	околица
We usually make trips in ('to') the surrounding area.	Óbično ídemo na ízlēte po okolíci.	Обично правимо излēте у околину.
(name of a mountain)	Frùškā gòra	Фрушкā гора
We're making a trip to Fruška Gora tomorrow.	Sùtra ídemo na ìzlet za Frùšku gòru.	Сутра правимо излēт на Фрушку гору.

A

| with whom | s kȉm | с кӣм |
| Who are you making the trip with? | S kȉm ídete na ìzlet? | С кӣм правите излēт? |

316

B

| With a friend and his wife. | S jédnim prìjateljem i njégovom žénōm. | С једним пријатељем и његовом женōм. |

A

train	vlȁk pl. vlȁkovi (Cr.)	вȏз, вȍзови
automobile, car or,	áuto, m. automóbīl	ауто аутомобил
plane	avíōn, G. avíōna	авиōн, авиōна
bus	autóbus / áutobus	аутобус / аутобус
How are you going, by train or by car?	Kȁko ìdēte, vlȁkom ȉli áutom?	Како идете, вȏзом или аутом?

B

| By car. | Áutom. | Аутом. |

A

car	kòla (n. pl.)	кола
trackless trolley, trolleybus	trólijbus	тролēјбус
Do you go to the office by car or by trolley-bus?	Dȁ li ìdete u ȕred kòlima ȉli trólijbusom?	Да ли идете у канцеларију колима или тролēјбусом?

B

sometimes	pónekad	понекад
streetcar	trámvāj	трамвāј
more seldom, rarer	rjèđī, -ā, -ē	рēђи, -ā, -ē
By car. Sometimes I go by trolleybus or streetcar, but not as often.	Automobílom. Kátkad, ȁli rjèđe, ìdem	Колима. Понекад идем тролēјбусом или

	trólijbusom íli	трамва̄јем, али ређе̄.
	trámvājem.	
fortune, good luck	srèća	срећа
fortunately	srèćōm	срећо̄м
connection, tie, link	vèza	веза
Fortunately, the connection is good with Dedinje and Topchider Hill.	Srèćōm, vèza je dòbra sa Dédīnjem i Tòpčiderskim bŕdom.	Срећо̄м, веза је добра са Дедињем и Топчидерским брдом.

A

| How ('by which way') do you go to your office? | Kòjīm pútem ídete u úred? | Којӣм путем идете у канцеларију? |

B

| Dedinje Boulevard | Dédīnjskī bulévār | Дедӣнски булева̄р |
| I take Dedinje Boulevard and Miloš Street. | Ídem Dédīnjskīm bulevárom i Míloševom ùlicōm. | Идем Дедињским булеваром и Милошевом улицо̄м. |

A

to serve	slúžiti, slûžīm	слу̏жити, слу̏жӣм
to use (with I or /sa/+ I; 'to serve oneself with something')	slúžiti se, slûžīm se	слу̏жити се, слу̏жӣм се
to use (with A) (with /se/: I or /sa/+ I)	korístiti, kórīstīm / kórīstiti	користити, корӣстӣм / користити
city (adj.)	gràdskī, -ā, -ō	гра̏дскӣ, -а̄, -о̄
pertaining to transport	prévōznī, -ā, -ō	пре̄во̄зни, -а̄, -о̄

or,   sàobraćājnī̇, -ā,   саобраħā̄јни̇, -ā, -ō
                         -ō

means   srédstvo   средство

Why don't you use public   Zàšto ne kòristite   Зашто се не служите чешħе
 ('city') transportation   češće grȁdska   градским превозним
 (means) more often?   prȅvozna srédstva?   средствима?

                              B

on account of, be-   zbòg   због
 cause of (with G)

because of that   zbog tògā   због тога

because (plus verb)   zbog tògā što̍   због тога што
     or,   zàto što̍   зато што

by means of him it   njȉm, njȉme   њим

by means of them   njȉma   њима

Because I have a car and   Zbog tògā što ȉmam   Зато што имам кола и
 use that.   àuto i slùžim se   служим се (са) њима.
                            njȉme.

                              A

to organize, put in   uréditi, da   уре́дити, да уре́дим
 order   úrēdīm

organized, put in order úrēđen, -a, -o   уре́ħен, -a, -o

traffic   sàobraćā̄j   саобраħā̄ј
     or,   prȍmet   про́мет

How is public ('city')   Kàko je úređen grȁdski Како је уре́ħен градски
 transportation organized? prȍmet?   саобраħā̄ј?

                              B

to grow, to be growing   rásti, rástēm   ра́сти, ра́стēм

319

The cities are growing very rapidly here.	Grádovi ȏvdje rástū jáko bŕzo.	Грáдови ȏвде рȁстȳ врло бȑзо.
certain	ìzvestan, ìzvesna, -o	извéстан, извéсна, -о
difficulty	poteškóća	тéшкоħа
So we have certain difficulties with public transportation.	Záto ȉma nèkih poteškóćā sa grádskim prȍmetom.	Зáто ȉма извéсних тéшкōħā са грáдским саобрáħājем.

A

understandable	razúmljiv-, -a, -o	разýмљив, -а, -о
That's understandable.	Tȏ je razúmljivo.	Тȏ је разýмљиво.

B

of course		дабóме
Of course. (/'it's understood')	Razúmijē se.	Пȁ дабóме.

Days of the Week

Sunday	nédjelja	нéдеља
Monday	ponédjeljak, G. ponédjēljka, pl. ponédjēljci, Gpl. ponédjeljākā	понéдељак, понéдēљка, понéдēљци, понéдељāкā
or		понéдēљник
Tuesday	útorak, G. útōrka, Gpl. útorākā	ýторак, ýтōрка, ýторāкā / ýтōрник, ýтōрници
Wednesday	srijéda	срéда
Thursday	četvŕtak	четвȑтак
Friday	pétak, pl. péci, G. pètākā	пéтак, пȅци, пȅтāкā
Saturday	súbota	сýбота

320

Grammatical Notes

Note 15.1 Noun / Adjective: Instrumental Case

S jednim prijateljem i njegovom ženom.

Šta radite nedeljom i praznikom?

Kako idete, vozom ili autom?

Da li idete u kancelariju kolima ili trolejbusom?

Ponekad idem trolejbusom ili tramvajem.

Srećom, veza je dobra sa Dedinjem i Topčiderskim brdom.

Kojim putem idete u kancelariju.

Idem Dedinjskim bulevarom i Miloševom ulicom.

Zašto se ne služite češće gradskim prevoznim sredstvima?

Zato ima izvesnih teškoća sa gradskim saobraćajem.

These sentences give a large number of examples of the instrumental case.

Masculine and neuter nouns have the ending /-om/ or, after palatals, /-em/ in the singular. The /o/ or /e/ is short. The plural ending is /-ima/. Compare:

Sg.   Non-palatal

           m.   n.

N	praznik	gospodin	trolejbus	voz	bulevar	brdo
I	praznikom	gospodinom	trolejbusom	vozom	bulevarom	brdom

           Palatal

           m.   n.

N	prijatelj	tramvaj	saobraćaj	Dedinje
I	prijateljem	tramvajem	saobraćajem	Dedinjem

Pl.

N	prijatelji	kola	sredstvo
I	prijateljima	kolima	sredstvima

One masculine noun in the sentences above has two different forms for the instrumental, /pútem/ and /pútom/. /pútem/ is used when the instrumental is used independently; /pútom/ is used when it is preceded by a preposition (as /sa pútom/). (See below on usage.)

The adjective ending is the same singular or plural, masculine and neuter: /-īm/ (/-im/ when adjective is not under primary stress).

321

Compare:

Sg.

N	jedan	Topčiderski	Dedinjski	gradski
I	jednim	Topčiderskim	Dedinjskim	gradskim

Pl.

N	naši	gradski	prevozni	
I	našim	gradskim	prevoznim	

Feminine a-nouns have /-ōm/ (~/-om/) in the singular, /-ama/ in the plural. The adjective has /-ōm/ (~/-om/) in the singular, /-īm/ (~/-im/) in the plural.

Sg.

N	žena	nedelja	gospođa	ulica
I	ženom	neделjom	gospođom	ulicom

Pl.

N	žene	nedelje	gospođe	ulica
I	ženama	nedeljama	gospođama	ulicama

Feminine i-nouns are not illustrated. The endings are /-ju/, /-u/ or /-i/ in the singular, /-ima/ in the plural. /-ju/ is the regular ending, as /kćērju/. /u/ may occur after palatals, as /nòću/ and occasionally after /r/. /i/ is also sometimes used: /kćèri/, /stvàri/. When the noun is used adverbially as /nòću/ 'by night', the ending is regularly /-u/. /-t-ju/ becomes /-ću/ as /dužnost/, /dužnošću/ (see below for /s/ > /š/.

The instrumental case endings for adjectives and nouns may be summarized:

	Masculine/Neuter		Feminine /a/		Feminine /i/	
	Adj.	Noun	Adj.	Noun	Adj.	Noun
Sg.	-īm	-om	-ōm	-ōm	-ōm	-ju / -u
		/-em				/-i
Pl.	-īm	-ima	-īm	-ama	-īm	-ima

Note 15.2 Pronoun: Instrumental Case

Zato što imam kola i služim se (sa) njima.   Zbog toga što imam auto i
S kim idete u pozorište?   služim se njime.

The instrumental case forms of the pronouns are recognizably the same as noun of adjective endings (compare /-ima/ and /-īm/ above) but must be listed.

/njìma/ is plural, referring to the neuter plural /kòla/. /njîme/ is singular, referring to the masculine singular /áuto/.

Personal Pronouns

	I	you	he, it	she	we	you	they
N	jà	tI	ȍn, óno	óna	mȉ	vī	óni, óna, óne
I	mnȏm	tòbōm	njȉm, njȉme	njȏm	nàma	vàma	njìma

Demonstrative Pronouns

	Reflexive	the referred to	this	that
N	_____	tȍ	óvō	ónō
I	sòbōm	tȉm	óvIm	ónIm

Interrogative Pronouns

	who	what
N	kȍ	štā / štò
I	kȉm	čȉm / čȉme

Note 15.3   Instrumental Case: Usage

Nouns, noun phrases and pronouns in the instrumental occur a) by themselves b) after certain prepositions.

Used independently (that is, without a preposition) the instrumental may indicate the a) means or instrument by which something is done, b) the manner in which something is done or c) the time when something is regularly done. Examples are: a) /vozom/ 'by train', /putem/ 'by the road', /bulevarom/ 'by way of the boulevard', /gradskim prevoznim sredstvima/ 'by city transportation means' b) /srećom/ 'luckily' c) /nedeljom/ 'on Sunday[s]', /praznikom/ 'on holiday[s]'. (There are several other meanings which the instrumental by itself may express, to be met later.)

The meaning of the instrumental after prepositions is dependent on the preposition used. Only /s/ - /sa/ has been illustrated. /s/ or /sa/ with the instrumental indicates 'with' (of accompaniment or association). (See Note

15.4 below.) Other prepositions which may precede the instrumental are /nad/
'above', /pred/ 'in front of', /pod/ 'underneath', /za/ 'behind', /među/ 'between, among'. Used with the instrumental each of these indicates place where,
not place to which. The accusative is used for place to which. (Compare the
use of dative for place where and accusative for place to which with /u/, /na/,
etc.)

Note 15.4 Preposition /s/, /sa/

Da li je prtljag vašeg prijatelja donet sa železničke stanice?
S kim pravite izlet?

        The preposition /s/ - /sa/ followed by the genitive case indicates 'out
of (a vehicle), down from, off (a horse, plane)'. The basic meaning is direction down from a spot on which one is (off and down from). It is therefore used
of getting off a horse, off a wagon (and so off a plane or out of a car). It
is used of coming down from a place on a hill or off the roof of a house. As
the basic meaning of /stànica/ is the place, rather than the building, it is
something one gets off of.

        Followed by the instrumental /s/ - /sa/ is 'with', usually of accompaniment
or association. Note also /služim se sa njima/.

        The form /sa/ is used before words beginning with /s/, /z/, /š/, /ž/ and
before words beginning with certain groups of two or more consonants, as /sa
mnom/ 'with me'. Otherwise, either /s/ or /sa/ may be used.

        Although not reflected in the spelling, /s/ is usually /š/ before /č ć
nj lj/: /šnjima/ (spelled s njima). /s/ is regularly replaced by /š/ before
these consonants, and when within a word, this change is reflected by the
spelling (e.g. /čèsto/ 'often' but /čèšćē/ 'more often'). /s/ before /dž đ/
is usually /ž/. Before other voiced paired consonants it is /z/.

<u>Grammatical Drills</u>

GD 15.1   Learning Drill
GD 15.1.1   Instrumental without Adjectives

Alternative Drill

Idem u kancelariju <u>autom</u>.	automobilom
Ne idem u kancelariju <u>autom</u>, nego <u>trolejbusom</u>.	autobusom
	vozom
	tramvajem

Substitution Drill

<u>Subotom</u> idemo u pozorište.	nedeljom
<u>Subotom</u> ne idemo u pozorište, nego u bioskop.	ponedeljkom/ponedeljnikom
Na žalost, on radi <u>subotom</u>.	utorkom/utornikom
Srećom, on ne radi <u>subotom</u>.	sredom
	četvrtkom
	petkom

With preposition /sa/ - /s/ meaning 'with'

The following drills are alternative with /sa/

Idem u pozorište s <u>majkom</u>.	braćom	prijateljem
Ne idem u pozorište s <u>majkom</u>,	gospodicom Jović	ocem
već s <u>bratom</u>.	decom	
	Jovanom	kćeri
	gospodinom Jovićem	kćerju
	gospođom Jović	

Jovan je zadovoljan sa <u>čistoćam</u> ovde.	
portirom	
poštom	
društvom	
saobraćajem	

The following drills are not alternative with /s/

Idem u pozorište sa <u>ženom</u>.	srodnikom
Ne idem u pozorište sa ženom, nego sa <u>sestrom</u>.	sinom

Veza sa <u>Zagrebom</u> je dobra.	Skopljem
Veza sa <u>Zagrebom</u> nije dobra.	Sarajevom
	Smederevom
	Srbijom

GD 15.1.2 Instrumental with Adjectives

Alternative Drill

Idem u kancelariju Dedinjskim bulevarom.	Avalskim putem	Miliševom ulicom
	ovim putem	Šekspirovom ulicom
Ne idem u kancelariju Dedinjskim bulevarom, već Avalskim putem.	tim putem	Puškinovom ulicom
		Knez-Mihailovom ulicom
		ovom ulicom
		tom ulicom

Idem u bioskop s jednim prijateljem.	vašim ocem	mojom majkom
	mojim bratom	našom sestrom
Ne idem u bioskop s jednim prijateljem, već s Tominim bratom.	nekim gospodinom	mojom braćom
	Tominim detetom	nekom gospodom
		mojom decom
		mojom kćeri
		našom kćerju

Ja sam zadovoljan sa mojim poslom.

našim društvom	vašom porukom	svojom dužnošću
našim letovanjem	Zorinim pismom	
Jovanovim obaveštenjem		
gradskim saobraćajem		

GD 15.1.3 Instrumental with plural

Substitution Drill

Zadovoljni smo s pozorištima ovde.	bioskopima	kafanama
Nismo zadovoljni s pozorištima ovde.	ljudima	sobama
	putevima	kućama
	hotelima	posteljama
	restoranima	

Idemo u bioskop s našim sestrama.	vašim prijateljima	našim ženama
Ne idem u bioskop s našim sestrama, nego s našim prijateljima.	njegovim srodnicima	našim kćerima
	našim očevima	
	vašim roditeljima	

The following sentences are for the above drill:

Mi govorimo srpskohrvatski s <u>našim sestrama</u>.

Prekosutra idemo na izlet s <u>našim sestrama</u> na Frušku goru.

GD 15.1.4 Instrumental with Personal Pronouns

Substitution with negative transform

Jovan ide u bioskop <u>sa mnom.</u>	s tobom	s nama
On želi da se upozna <u>sa mnom.</u>	s njim	s vama
Zora želi da govori <u>sa mnom.</u>	s njom	s njima
Majka je zadovoljna <u>sa mnom.</u>		

GD 15.2 Adaptation Drill

GD 15.2.1 Instrumental without Adjectives

Obično idem u kancelariju <u>autom.</u>	trolejbus
Retko kad idem u kancelariju <u>autom.</u>	automobil
	voz
	tramvaj
	autobus

<u>Alternative Drill</u>

Uvek putujem u Zagreb <u>vozom.</u>	avion
Nikad ne putujem u Zagreb <u>vozom</u>, već <u>automobilom.</u>	auto
	autobus

Moji prijatelji često idu <u>subotom</u> u pozorište.	nedelja
Moji prijatelji retko idu <u>subotom</u> u pozorište.	ponedeljak/ponedeljnik
Na žalost, ja često radim <u>subotom.</u>	sreda
Srećom, ja ne radim često <u>subotom.</u>	utorak/utornik
	četvrtak
	praznik / blagdan
	petak

Use the preposition /sa/ when required in the following drills:

Alternative Drill

Zora ide u pozorište zajedno s <u>majkom.</u>

Zora ne ide u pozorište zajedno s <u>majkom,</u> već s <u>bratom.</u>

muž	suprug
otac	braća
sestra	Jovan
deca	gospodin Jović
sin	gospođa Jovanović
kći	gospodica Smit
	gospodin i gospođa Jović

Substitution Drill

Železnička veza s <u>Beogradom</u> je vrlo dobra.

Železnička veza s <u>Beogradom</u> nije tako dobra.
   Prilično je rđava.

Zagreb	
Dalmacija	Skoplje
Sarajevo	
Hercegovina	
Kragujevac	
Split	

GD 15.2.2 Instrumental with Adjectives

Obično idem u grad <u>Avalskim putem.</u>
Retko kad idem u grad <u>Avalskim putem.</u>
Često puta idem u grad <u>Avalskim putem.</u>
Ne idem u grad <u>Avalskim putem.</u>
Nikad ne idem u grad <u>Avalskim putem.</u>

Dedinjski bulevar
Miloševa ulica
ovaj put
Puškinova ulica
taj put
ova ulica
ta ulica

U nedelju idem na izlet zajedno sa
   <u>jednim prijateljem.</u>
U nedelju ne idem ni s kim na izlet.

moj brat
moja majka
Tomina braća
moja deca
naša sestra
moj sin
moja kći
Zorin otac
moj srodnik

The adjective for the negative answer is given in parenthesis for each item.

Mi smo potpuno zadovoljni s našim autom.
Mi nismo potpuno zadovoljni s našim autom. Mali je.

naša soba	(mali)	naša ulica	(prljav)
naš hotel	(skup)	gradski saobraćaj	(neuređen)
Zorin sin	(slab)		

Mi se služimo ovim stolom, jer je dobar.
Mi se ne služimo ovim stolom, jer je mali.

taj krevet	(neudoban)	ova stolica	(neispravan)
ovaj put	(rđav / loš)	gradski saobraćaj	(rđavo uređen)
naš auto	(neispravan)	ovo ogledalo	(mali i rđav)
		/zrcalo	/loš

Mi se služimo srpskohrvatskim jezikom, ali ne govorimo dobro.
Mi se ne služimo srpskohrvatskim jezikom, jer ga ne znamo dovoljno.

engleski jezik	nemački jezik	francuski jezik

Alternative Drill

Veza s Novim Sadom je dobra.
Veza s Novim Sadom nije tako dobra, kao sa Sremskom Mitrovicom.

Stara Pazova	Slavonska Požega
Gornji Milanovac	Slavonski Brod
Niška Banja	Bosanski Brod
Generalski Stol	
Vrnjačka Banja	
Gorski Kotar	
Rogaška Slatina	
Zidani Most	

GD 15.2.3 Instrumental with Plural

Zora i Jovan su zadovoljni s pozorištima ovde.   kafana
Zora i Jovan nisu zadovoljni s pozorištima ovde.   restoran
                                                        kuća
                                                        bioskop
                                                        put
                                                        ljudi

                                                           voz / vlak
                                                           autobus
                                                           tramvaj

Večeras izlazimo zajedno s <u>našim prijateljima</u>.   naše sestre
Večeras ne izlazimo zajedno s <u>našim prijateljima</u>.   naši srodnici / rođaci
                                                           Jovanovi sinovi
                                                           Markove kćeri
                                                           naši očevi
                                                           naše majke
                                                           ovi ljudi

The following sentences are for the above drill:

Mi pravime često izlete s <u>našim prijateljima</u> po okolini Beograda.
Često razgovaramo srpskohrvatski s <u>našim prijateljima,</u> jer oni znaju dobro
    jezik.

Plural Transform Drill

Mi se ne služimo <u>ovom stolicom.</u>   Mi se ne služimo ovim stolicama.

Idem večeras u bioskop s <u>mojom sestrom.</u>
Ja govorim srpskohrvatski svakog dana s <u>mojim sinom.</u>
Zora razgovara kod kuće sa <u>svojim detetom</u> francuski.
Treba da svršim jedan posao sa <u>ovim gospodinom.</u>
Mi se ne služimo <u>ovim stolom.</u>   Mali je.
Moj prijatelj se ne služi <u>nijednim stranim jezikom.</u>   /jezicima/
Jovan ide u pozorište s <u>jednom gospođicom.</u>
Treba da razgovarate s <u>tom ženom.</u>
Moj otac želi da se upozna s <u>tim čovekom.</u>

GD 15.2.4 Instrumental with Personal Pronouns

Substitution with negative transform.

Jovan ide često u bioskop sa <u>mnom.</u>   ti
Majka želi da razgovara sa <u>mnom.</u>   on
Roditelji govore srpskohrvatski sa <u>mnom.</u> ona
Oni žele da se upoznaju sa <u>mnom.</u>   mi
Otac je zadovoljan sa <u>mnom.</u>   vi
On stanuje zajedno sa <u>mnom.</u>   oni

330

Oni idu u kancelariju zajedno sa <u>mnom</u>.

In the following sentences the corresponding pronoun should be substituted for the underlined noun. e.g.

Subotom idem u kafanu zajedno
  sa <u>Tomom.</u>

Subotom idem u kafanu zajedno
  s njim.

Retko kad idem u pozorište s <u>Jovanom.</u>
Često razgovaram srpskohrvatski sa <u>Zorom.</u>
Želim da sa upoznam sa <u>Jovićima.</u>
Otac je zadovoljan s <u>decom,</u> a majka nije.
Brat stanuje zajedno s <u>roditeljima</u> i sa mnom.
Mi smo zadovoljni s <u>vama</u> i <u>vašim bratom.</u>

GD 15.3   Question and Answers
GD 15.3.1 Informational Answers

S kim idete u pozorište večeras?

S <u>majkom.</u>
Večeras idem u pozorište s <u>majkom.</u>
Ne idem ni s kim.

brat	deca	kći
otac	prijatelj	gospodin Jović
žena	braća	sestra
gospođica Smit		

S kim pravite izlet ove nedelje,
  gospođo Smit?

S <u>našim prijateljima Jovićima.</u>
Ove nedelje pravimo izlet s <u>našim
  prijateljima Jovićima.</u>
Ove nedelje ne idemo na izlet.
Ove nedelje ne idemo ni s kim na izlet.

jedan prijatelj	gospodin i gospođa Jović	moj otac
naša deca	moja kći	sestra moga muža
moja sestra	neki prijatelji	neka gospoda

The following questions may be drilled in the same manner:

S kim idete večeras u bioskop?
S kim govorite srpskohrvatski.
S kim treba da razgovorate, gospođo?
S kim želi Toma da se upozna?

331

Kako idete u kancelariju?   <u>Autom.</u>

Idem u kancelariju <u>autom</u>.

kola	tramvaj	trolejbus
automobil	voz / vlak	autobus
gradska prevozna sredstva		
gradska saobraćajna sredstva		

Kako putujete u Zagreb?   <u>Vozom.</u>

Putujem <u>vozom</u>.

auto	autobus	kola
avion	automobil	

Kako idete u kancelariju?   <u>Autobusom.</u>

Idem <u>autobusom</u>.

tramvaj	trolejbus	voz / vlak
kola	auto	automobil

Kojim putem idete u grad?   <u>Dedinjskim bulevarom.</u>

Idem u grad <u>Dedinjskim bulevarom.</u>

Avalski put	Miloševa ulica
Puškinova ulica	Šekspirova ulica

Kakva je veza sa <u>Zagrebom</u> vozom?   Vrlo je dobra.

Nije tako dobra.

Veza sa <u>Zagrebom</u> vozom je vrlo dobra.

Veza sa <u>Zagrebom</u> vozom nije tako dobro.

Niš	Novi Sad	Slavonski Brod	Gornji Milanovac
Kragujevac	Stara Pazova	Bosanska Gradiška	Slavonska Požega
Gorski kotar	Slavonska Gradiška	Generalski Stol	Vrnjačka Banja

Kakva je veza gradskim prevoznim sredstvima sa <u>železničkom stanicom</u>?   Dobra je.

Nije dobra.

Veza sa <u>železničkom stanicom</u> gradskim prevoznim sredstvima je dobra.

Veza sa <u>železničkom stanicom</u> gradskim prevoznim sredstvima nije dobra.

Miloševa ulica   Cvetni trg

Topčidersko brdo   Zeleni venac

Senjak   Dedinje

Jovanova ulica   Zorina ulica

Kako ide sa <u>srpskohrvatskim</u>   Ide prilično dobro. Još ne govorim,

  (jezikom)?   ali već prilično razumem.

                                 Ne ide dobro. Ne govorim i ne

                                 razumem.

engleski   francuski   nemački

Use the instrumental of one or more of the nouns on the right to answer each of the questions on the left.

Kad obično idete na posao?   nedelja

Kad izlazite uveče.   ponedeljak/ponedeljnik

Kojim danima izlazite uveče?   utorak/utornik

Koje dane radite?   sreda

  /Kojim danima radite?   četvrtak

Koje dane ne radite?   petak

  /Kojim danima ne radite?   subota

                                    praznik / blagdan

Use the instrumental plural of the nouns given for substitution.

Kako ste zadovoljni s <u>pozorištima</u> ovde?   Zadovoljan sam mnogo.

                                                 Nisam zadovoljan.

voz   trolejbus   tramvaj

muzej   čovek   put

park   kafana

Use first the instrumental singular, then the plural.

S kim idete u bioskop?   S <u>mojom sestrom.</u>

moja sestra   moja kći   Tomino dete

jedan gospodin   vaš brat   njihov otac

naš prijatelj   moje dete

GD 15.3.2 Yes and No Answers

Da li idete u kancelariju <u>autom</u>?   Da, idem.

                                              Ne, ne idem.

                                              Da, obično idem u kancelariju <u>autom</u>.

                                              Ne, retko kad idem u kancelariju <u>autom</u>.

                                              Ne, nikad ne idem u kancelariju <u>autom</u>.

trolejbus	voz / vlak	tramvaj
gradska saobraćajna sredstva	kola	automobil
autobus	gradska prevozna sredstva	

Alternative Drill

Da li putujete uvek u Zagreb vozom?   Da, putujem.

                                              Ne, ne putujem.

                                              Da, putujem uvek u Zagreb <u>vozom</u>.

                                              Ne, ne putujem uvek vozom.

avion	autobus
kola	automobil

Da li izlazite <u>subotom</u> negde?   Da, izlazim.

                                              Da, obično izlazim <u>subotom</u>.

                                              Da, uvek izlazimo <u>subotom</u>.

nedelja   praznik /blagdan

Da li idete u pozorište ponedeljnikom?   Ne, ne idem.

                                              Ne, ne idem u pozorište <u>ponedeljkom</u>.

                                                 Ja radim <u>ponedeljkom</u>.

                                              Retko kad idem u pozorište <u>ponedeljkom</u>,

                                                 jer je ponedeljak radni dan.

utorak	sreda
četvrtak	petak

Da li vi radite <u>subotom</u>?   Da, na žalost, ja često radim <u>subotom</u>.

                                              Ne, srećom ja nikad ne radim <u>subotom</u>.

nedelja   praznik / blagdan

Da li je železnička veza s <u>Beogradom</u> Da, dobra je.
    dobra?   Ne, nije tako dobra.
                                             Da, železnička veza s <u>Beogradom</u> je
                                                 vrlo dobra.
                                             Ne, železnička veza s <u>Beogradom</u> nije
                                                 dobra. Rđava je.

Zagreb	Sarajevo	Hercegovina
Skoplje	Dalmacija	Kragujevac
Split	Niš	

Da li idete u grad <u>Avalskim putem?</u>   Da, obično idem u grad <u>Avalskim putem.</u>
                                             Ne, retko kad idem u grad <u>Avalskim</u>
                                                 <u>putem.</u>
                                             Da, često puta idem u grad <u>Avalskim</u>
                                                 <u>putem.</u>
                                             Ne, ne idem u grad <u>Avalskim putem.</u>
                                             Ne, nikad ne idem u grad <u>Avalskim</u>
                                                 <u>putem.</u>

Dedinjski bulevar	taj put
Puškinova ulica	Miloševa ulica
ta ulica	

The adjective for the negative answer is given in parentheses for each
item.

Da li je Jovan zadovoljan sa <u>svojim</u>   Jeste.
    <u>kupatilom?</u>   Nije.
                                             Da, on je zadovoljan sa <u>svojim kupatilom.</u>
                                             Ne, on nije zadovoljan sa <u>svojim</u>
                                                 <u>kupatilom.</u> Neispravno je.

njegova soba (prljava)	gradski saobraćaj (neuređen)
svoj (/njegov) hotel (skup)	njegov novi auto (nije u redu)

Da li se vi služite <u>ovim stolom?</u>   Da, služimo se.
                                             Ne, ne služimo se, jer je vrlo dobar.
                                             Da, služimo se <u>tim stolom.</u>
                                             Ne, ne služimo se <u>tim stolom,</u> jer je
                                                 mali.

taj krevet (neudoban)   vaš auto (neispravan)

ova stolica (neispravna)   gradska prevozna sredstva (neureden)

Da li se služite srpskohrvatskim   Da, služim se.

   jezikom?   Ne, ne služim se.

                                         Da, služim se srpskohrvatskim jezikom,

                                            ali ne govorim dobro.

                                         Ne, ne služim se srpskohrvatskim

                                            jezikom. Na žalost, ja ne znam

                                            srpskohrvatski.

engleski jezik   francuski jezik

neki stran jezik   nemački jezik

Da li je veza vozom s Novim Sadom   Jeste, dobra je.

   dobra?   Ne, nije dobra.

                                         Jeste, veza s Novim Sadom je dobra.

                                         Ne, veza s Novim Sadom nije dobra.

                                            Prilično je rdava.

Stara Pazova   Niška Banja   Slavonska Požega   Vrnjačka Banja

Slavonski Brod   Generalski Stol   Bosanski Brod   Gorski kotar

Rogaška Slatina   Sremska Mitrovica

   Use the instrumental plural of the nouns listed:

Da li su vaši prijatelji zadovoljni   Jesu, zadovoljni su.

   s pozorištima ovde?   Ne, nisu zadovoljni.

                                         Da, moji prijatelji su zadovoljni

                                            mnogo sa pozorištima ovde.

                                         Ne, moji prijatelji nisu zadovoljni

                                            sa pozorištima ovde.

kafana   kuća   put

čovek   autobus   restoran

bioskop   hotel   voz / vlak

trolejbus   gradsko prevozno sredstvo   tramvaj

GD 15.4 Question and Answer Drill with Prompt

U kancelariju idem autom.	Kako idete u kancelariju?
U pozorište i bioskop idemo četvrtkom i subotom.	Kad idete u pozorište i bioskop?
U pozorište idemo s našim prijateljima gospodinom i gospođom Jović.	S kim idete u pozorište? /Da li idete u pozorište u društvu s nekim?
Srećom, ja subotom ne radim.	Da li vi radite subotom?
U kancelariju idem Dedinjskim bulevarom i Miloševom ulicom.	Kojim putem idete u kancelariju? /Kuda idete u kancelariju?
Ja se retko služim gradskim saobraćajnim sredstvima.	Da li se služite gradskim saobraćajnim sredstvima?
Veza s Topčiderskim brdom je prilično dobra.	Kakva je veza s Topčiderskim brdom?
Jovan putuje često u Zagreb.	Da li Jovan putuje često u Zagreb?
Jovan nikad ne putuje u Zagreb vozom, već kolima ili avionom.	Zar Jovan nikad ne putuje u Zagreb.
On putuje češće kolima nego avionom.	Da li on putuje češće kolima ili avionom?
Jovan putuje sutra u Zagreb s jednim gospodinom. /Jovan ne putuje sutra u Zagreb ni s kim. On putuje sam.	S kim Jovan putuje u Zagreb?
Vi treba da se upoznate s Jovićima.	S kim treba da se upoznamo?
Mi se služimo srpskohrvatskim jezikom, ali ne govorimo.	Da li se služite srpskohrvatskim jezikom? /Da li se služite nekim stranim jezikom?
Zora govori srpskohrvatski svakog dana sa mnom.	Da li govorite s nekim srpskohrvatski.
Jovan je zadovoljan sa čistoćam u hotelu.	Da li je Jovan zadovoljan sa čistoćam u hotelu?
Ja sam zadovoljam sa svojom novom dužnošću.	Da li ste zadovoljni sa svojom novom dužnošću?

GD 15.5   Conversations - Razgovori
GD 15.5.1

A

Da li poznajete gospodina i gospođu Jović?

Oni su jako dobri i prijatni ljudi.

Mi idemo često kod njih i oni dolaze kod nas.

To je lako. Oni dolaze u četvrtak uveče kod nas na kavu. Ako želite da se upoznate s njima, dođite i vi kod nas poslije osam.

Šta je s tim, i ja radim. Mi ne ostajemo dugo.[1]

Onda, znate šta? Jeste li slobodni u subotu?

Mi idemo s Jovićima na izlet u subotu. Ako hoćete, možete i vi ići s nama.

Ne, i mi i naši prijatelji volimo društvo.

Idemo na Frušku goru.

Nije. To je u okolici Novog Sada, ako znate gdje je Novi Sad.

Ne, ovaj put idemo preko Srijemske Mitrovice.

B

Ne, ne poznajem ih.

Da, znam. Svi naši prijatelji to kažu.

To je jako lijepo. Meri i ja želimo da se upoznamo s njima.

Hvala, ali ne mogu da dođem. Ja petkom radim.

Žao mi je, ali ne mogu ostati uveče kad sutradan radim.

Jesam.

Vrlo rado, Meri i ja inače još ne poznajemo okolicu Beograda. Samo ne želimo smetati vas i vaše prijatelje.

Ako je tako, onda u redu. Gdje idete na izlet?

Da li je Fruška gora daleko odavde?

Da, znam. Da li idete putem u pravcu Novog Sada?

Vrlo dobro.

Да ли познајете господина и госпођу Јовић?

Они су врло добри и пријатни људи.

Не, не познајем их.

Да, знам. Сви наши пријатељи то кажу.

---

[1] /óstati/ 'to stay', /óstajati, óstajēm/ 'to be staying'

Ми одлазимо често код њих и они долазе код нас.

То је лако. Они долазе у четвртак увече код нас на кафу. Ако желите да се упознате с њима, дођите и ви код нас после осам.

Шта је с тим, и ја радим. Ми не седимо дуго.

Онда, знате шта? Јесте слободни у суботу?

Ми идемо с Јовићима на излет у суботу. Ако хоћете, можете и ви ићи с нама.

Не, и ми и наши пријатељи волимо друштво.

Идемо на Фрушку гору.

Није. То је у околини Новог Сада, ако знате где је Нови Сад.

Не, овај пут идемо преко Сремске Митровице.

То је врло лепо. Мери и ја желимо да се упознамо с њима.

Хвала, али не могу да дођем. Ја петком радим.

Жао ми је, али не могу да седим увече кад сутрадан радим.

Јесам.

Врло радо, Мери и ја иначе још не познајемо околину Београда. Само не желимо да узнемиравамо вас и ваше пријатеље.

Ако је тако, онда у реду. Где идете на излет?

Да ли је Фрушка гора далеко одавде?

Да, знам. Да ли идете путем у правцу Новог Сада?

Врло добро.

GD 15.5.2

Čujem da putujete u Zagreb.

Kad putujete?

Kako idete, autom ili vlakom?

S kim putujete?

Kakav je saobraćaj sa Zagrebom? Ima li dovoljno vlakova?

Da, putujem.

Prekosutra.

Idem vlakom.

Putujem sa ženom i djecom.

Saobraćaj je vrlo dobar. Ima mnogo vlakova.

Da li je udobno putovati vlakom?   Da, jest.

Da li su vlakovi ovdje skupi?   Nisu.

Kakve su ovdje ceste?   Nisu loše.

Putujete li često?   Da, putujem.

Da li se služite autom kad putujete?   Da, mnogo više autom nego vlakom.

Hoćete li negdje putovati?   Da, treba putovati za Niš, a ne znam
                                               kakva je cesta.

Cesta do Niša je dobra. Možete   Jako dobro. Hvala vam na obavještenju.
  putovati autom.

Nema na čemu.

Чујем да путујете у Загреб.   Да, путујем.

Кад путујете?   Прекосутра.

Како идете, колима или возом?   Идем возом.

С ким путујете?   Путујем са женом и децом.

Каква је веза са Загребом?   Веза је врло добра. Има много возова.
Да ли има довољно возова?

Да ли је удобно путовати возом?   Да, јесте.

Да ли су возови овде скупи?   Нису.

Какви су овде путеви?   Нису рђави.

Да ли ви путујете често?   Да, путујем.

Да ли се служите колима кад путујете?   Да, много више колима него возом.

Да ли хоћете негде да путујете?   Да, треба да путујем у Ниш, а не знам
                                               какав је пут.

Пут до Ниша је добар.   Врло добро. Хвала вам на обавештењу.
Можете путовати колима.

Нема на чему.

GD 15.5.3

Gdje stanujete?	Stanujem na Dedinju.
Kako idete u ured?	Idem autom.
Kojim putem idete?	Idem Dedinjskim bulevarom.
Zašto ne idete Avalskim putem?	Idem neki put i Avalskim putem.
	Idem jednim ili drugim putem.
	Vi stanujete na Topčiderskom brdu, zar ne?
Jest.	Kako vi idete u ured?
Idem obično trolejbusom.	Je li veza trolejbusom sa Topčiderskim brdom dobra?
Jest. Da li vi idete nekad trolejbusom u ured.	Ne idem nikad.
Zašto se nikad ne koristite trolejbusom?	Nije dobra veza sa uredom.

Где станујете?	Станујем на Дедињу.
Како идете у канцеларију?	Идем колима.
Којим путем идете?	Идем Дедињским булеваром.
Зашто не идете Авалским путем?	Идем неки пут и Авалским путем.
	Идем једним или другим путем.
	Ви станујете на Топчидерском брду, је л'те?
Јесте.	Како ви идете у канцеларију?
Идем обично тролејбусом.	Да ли је веза тролејбусом са Топчидерским брдом добра?
Јесте. Да ли ви идете некад тролејбусом у канцеларију?	Не идем никад.
Зашто се никад не служите тролејбусом?	Није ми добра веза са канцеларијом.

GD 15.6   Homework - Domaći zadatak

GD 15.6.1   Make questions to which the following sentences will be the appropriate <u>informational answers.</u>

Obično idem u grad Avalskim putem.

U nedelju idem na izlet s jednim prijateljem.

Veza vozom s Novim Sadom je vrlo dobra.

Mi razgovaramo srpskohrvatski sa Zorom.

Roditelji stanuju zajedno sa bratom.

Treba da svršim jedan hitan posao sa savetnikom Smitom.

Mi se služimo francuskim jezikom.

Jedna žena želi da razgovara sa gospodinom savetnikom.

Treba da razgovaram s ovim čovekom.

Mi želimo da se upoznamo s Jovićima.

GD 15.6.2   Write out another set of questions with /da li/ and give negative long answers.

UNIT 16

Basic Sentences - Osnovne rečenice

Travelling by Train	Putovanje vlakom	Путовање возом

A

Why are you going by train and not by car gentlemen)?	Zašto putujete vlȁkom, a ne áutom gȍspodo?	Зашто путујете во̏зом, а не кȍлима госпоѣо?#
automobile highway	áuto-put / autoput	áуто-пӯт / аутопӯт
ready, finished	gótov, -a, -o	готов, -а, -о
The autoput to Skopje is finished.	Àutoput do Skȍplja je gótov.	Аутпӯт до Ско̏пља је | готов.

B

because, for	jȅr	јер
safer	sigúrnije	сигу́рније
winter, cold	zȋma	зи̏ма
Because I think it is safer to go by train than by car. It's still winter.	Jȅr mȉslȋm, da je sigúrnije putovati vlȁkom nȅgo áutom. Jȍš je zȋma.	Јȅр мислȋм, да је сигурније путовати во̏зом | него кȍлима. Још је | зи̏ма.

A

international express or,	ékspres međunárodnȋ bȑzȋ vlȁk	експрес међуна̑роднӣ бр̏зи во̑з
Yugoslav express	bȑzȋ vlȁk	бр̏зи во̑з
What train are you going by, the international, or the Yugoslav express?	Kȍjim vlȁkom pútujēte, eksprésom ili bȑzȋm?	Којим во̏зом путу́јете, експресом‖ или бр̏зим во̑зом?#

343

(We're going) by the Yugoslav express.	Pútujēmo br̀zīm.	Пу́ту̀је̄мо ̀бр̀зӣм.
to take, get	úzēti, da ùzmēm	у́зе̄ти, да у̀зме̄м
taxi	tàksi (m.)	такси
We must take a taxi to the station, Tom.	Tȍmo, mȍramo úzeti tàksi do kȍlodvora.	Тȍмо#, мȍрамо у́зети та̀кси до ста́нице.
to be afraid of (with G)	bȍjati se, bȍjīm se	бȍјати се, бȍјӣм се
to be late	zakásniti, da zákasnīm	за́каснити, да за́каснӣм
or,	zadȍcniti, da zádocnīm	задȍцнити, да за́доцнӣм
lest we be late, that we not be late or,	da ne zákasnīmo da ne zádocnīmo	да не за́каснӣмо да не за́доцнӣмо
I'm afraid we might be late.	Bȍjīm se da ne zákasnīmo.	Бȍјим се да не за́доцнӣмо.

<u>At the Railroad Station</u>   Na Kȍlodvoru   <u>На жȅлезничко̄ј ста̀ници</u>

A

card, ticket	kȁrta	ка̄́рта
class	rázred	кла́са
Two first-class tickets, express, to Skopje, please.	Mȍlim dvȉje kȁrte prvog rázreda br̀zīm, do Skȍplja.	Мо̀лӣм две̄ ка̀рте прве̄ кла̀се, бр̀зӣм, до Скȍпља.

C

Here you are, three thousand eight hundred dinars.	Izvólte, trȉ tȉsuće ȍsam stȍtina dȉnārā.	Изво́лте#, трȉ хȉљаде ̀осам стȍтина дина́ра̄.
(He gives [him] 5000 dinars.)	(Dȁje 5.000 [pȅt tȉsuća] dȉnārā.)	(Дȁје 5.000 /пȅт хȉљада/ дина́ра̄.)

344

With the Porter	Sa nosáčem	Са но̀са́чем (носа̀ч)

A

to carry in	únijeti da unésēm	уне́ти, да унесе́м
carry in!	unésite	унесите
suitcase	kóvčeg pl. kóvčezi (Cr.) Gpl. kòvčegā	ку̀фер

Please take these two suitcases to the express train for Skopje.	Mòlīm, unésite òva dvȃ kòvčega u bȓzī vlȃk za Skòplje.	Мо̀лӣм унѐсите о̀ва два́ ку̀фера у бр̏зи во̑з за Ско̀пље.

to occupy, take	zaúzeti, da záuzmēm	зау̀зе̄ти, да зау̀зме̄м
take	zaúzmite	зау̀змите
compartment	kúpē m.	купе̄
possible	mógūće	мо̀гӯће
beside, next	pòkraj	по̀ред
window	prózor	про̑зор

Take two seats in a first-class compartment next to the window, if it is possible.	Zaúzmite dvȃ mjèsta u kupéu pȑvog rázreda, ako je mogūće, pòkraj prózora.	Зау̀змите два́ ме̏ста у купе́у пр̏ве̄ кла̏се, ако је мо̀гӯће, по̀ред про̑зора.

D

Yes, sir.	Mòlīm, gospòdine.	Мо̀лӣм, госпо̀дине.

In the First-Class Waiting Room	U čekaóni pȑvog rázreda (čekaóna)	У чѐкао̀ници пр̏ве̄ кла̏се (чѐкао̀ница)

A

to be starting, leaving	pólaziti, pólazīm	по̀лазити, по̀лазӣм
When does the express train for Skopje leave?	Kȁd pólazi bȓzī vlȃk za Skòplje?	Ка̏д по̀лази бр̏зи во̑з за Ско̀пље?

345

E

hour	sȁt G pl. sátɪ	сȁт, са́ти
or,	úra (Cr.)	
or,	čȁs pl. čȁsovɪ	чȁс, чȁсови
It leaves at 6:20 P.M.	Pȯlazi u 18 sátɪ i 20 minútā.	Пȯлази у 18 часо̄ва̄ и 20 минӯта̄.

A

to arrive, to be arriving	stȉzati, stȉžēm	стȉзати, стȉже̄м
And when does it arrive in Skopje?	A kȧd stȉžē u Skȍplje?	А кȧд стȉже̄ у Скȍпље?

E

exact, correct	tȍčan, tȍčna, -o	тȁчан, тȁчна, -о
exactly, correctly	tȍčno	тȁчно
drive, driving, riding	vȍžnja	вȍжња
time-table	rȅd vȍžnjē	ред вȍжње̄
ticket window	blágājna	шȁлтер
I don't know exactly; look at the time-table or ask at the window.	Nè znām tȍčno, vȉdite u rȅdu vȍžnjē ili pȉtajte na blágājni.	Не знам тȁчно, видите у реду вȍжње̄ или пȉтајте на шȁлтеру.

A

to buy	kúpiti, da kȕpīm	ку́пити, да кȕпӣм
departure	pȯlazak, pȯlaska, pl. pȯlasci	пȯлазак, пȯласка, пȯласци
Do I have time to buy a time-table before the train leaves?	Dȁ li ȉmam vrȅmena da kȕpīm rȅd vȍžnje prȉje pȯlaska vláka?	Дȁ ли ȉмам времена да купим ред вȍжње̄ пре поласка вȍза?

E

full, plenty	pȕn, púna, púno	пӯн, пȕна, пȕно
You have plenty of time.	ȉmate mnȍgo vrȅmena.	Имате пӯно времена.

to drink up	pópiti, da pòpijēm	попити, да попијем
to start, leave	póći, da pòđem	поћи, да пођем
before it leaves	prȉje što pòđē	пре него што пође
You can not only get a time-table but also drink something before the train leaves.	Mòžete ne sȃmo ùzeti rȇd vòžnjē vèć i pòpiti nèšto prȉje pólaska.	Можете не само узети ред вожње, већ и попити нешто пре него што пође воз.

A

Thank you kindly.	Hvála lȋjepa.	Хвала лепо.

E

Don't mention it.	Mòlīm lȋjepo.	Нема на чему.

Note: The spelling Skopje is based on the Macedonian pronunciation of the word. The Serbo-Croatian is /Skòplje/. For the alternation of /p/ with /plj/ in Serbo-Croatian see Note 25.2.

Grammatical Notes

Note 16.1 Noun: Vocative

Dobar dan, gospodine Joviću.

Milo mi je gospodo da se upoznamo.

Da li je Toma kod kuće gospođo?

Kelner, donesite mi molim još jednu kafu.

Ana, dajte tu kafu mojoj majci.

Most masculine and feminine nouns have in the singular a special ending when used as terms of address. The most frequent masculine ending is /-e/: /gospódine/ 'sir!'. After palatals, and (unpredictably) with certain other nouns, the ending is /-u/: /Jóviću/. Most feminine a-nouns have /o/: /gòspodo/, /gospođo/. Those in /-ica/ regularly have /-e/: /gòspođice/. There is no vocative for neuter nouns, the nominative form being used. A number of /a/ nouns, and some masculine nouns, use the nominative form: /Ana/, /kèlner/. With some /a/ nouns either the nominative or the vocative may be used: /mȁjka/ 'mother' /mȁjka/ or /mȁjko/ 'mother!', /deda/ 'grandfather' (m. noun) /dèda/ or /dèdo/ 'grandfather!', though the use of the nominative here is considered colloquial.

347

There is also very frequently a shift or change of stress, a short fall on the
first syllable being very common in the vocative (/gòspodo/ but /gósoda/).
There is no adjective vocative ending. The nominative is used when an adjective
accompanies a noun in the vocative: /dragi moj prijatelju/ 'my dear friend!',
/draga moja sestro/ 'my dear sister!'. A few plurals have a vocative in /ˇ/
where the nominative has /ˊ/: Np /séstre/ Vp /sèstre/. Otherwise there is no
vocative plural form. (/dèco/ 'children!') is regular in form. Np /žéne/ V /žène/
would be a slightly shorter example.

Note 16.2 Noun and Adjective: Review

   Following are examples of nouns and adjectives, illustrating the forms
which have been discussed. The vocative is omitted where not likely to be used.
The forms given for the indefinite adjective are not the traditional ones for
GDI but the definite with a short vowel, reflecting usage rather than school
grammars. In literary style the genitive and dative indefinite masculine singular endings of the adjectives are the same as for the noun: /-a/ and /-u/, so
1.1.1 below G /lépa krèveta/ D /lépu krèvetu/, 1.1.2 G /dóbra kèlnera/ D /dóbru
kèlneru/, etc. These forms may be met in reading.

1   Masculine
1.1   Non-palatal stems, adjective and noun
1.1.1   Inanimate

	Indefinite		Definite	
N	lèp krèvet	lépi krèveti	lèpī krèvet	lèpī krèveti
A	lèp krèvet	lépe krèvete	lèpī krèvet	lèpē krèvete
G	lépog krèveta	lépīh krèvētā	lèpōg krèveta	lèpīh krèvētā
D	lépom krèvetu	lépīm krèvetima	lèpōm krèvetu	lèpīm krèvetima
I	lépim krèvetom	lépīm krèvetima	lèpīm krèvetom	lèpīm krèvetima

Noun with /k/ to /c/ before /-i/, /-ima/.

N	prȁznīk	prȁznicī
A	prȁznīk	práznīke
G	prȁznīka	prȁznīkā
D	prȁznīku	prȁznīcima
I	prȁznìkom	prȁznīcima

1.1.2 Animate

	Indefinite		Definite	
N	dóbar čóvek	dóbri ljȕdi	dòbrῑ čóvek	dòbrῑ ljȕdi
A	dóbrog(a) čovéka	dóbre ljȕde	dòbrōg(a) čovéka	dòbre ljȕde
G	dóbrog(a) čovéka	dóbrῑh ljúdῑ	dòbrog(a) čovéka	dòbrῑh ljúdῑ
D	dóbrom(e) čovéku	dóbrῑm(a) ljȕdima	dòbrōm(e) čovéku	dòbrῑm(a) ljȕdima
I	dóbrῑm čovékom	dóbrῑm(a) ljȕdima	dòbrῑm čovékom	dòbrῑm(a) ljȕdima
			dòbrῑ čòveče	dòbrῑ ljȕdi

1.1.3 Non-palatal stem, noun, extended

N	grȁd	grȁdovi
A	grȁd	grȁdove
G	grȁda	gradóvā
D	grȁdu / grȃdu	gradóvima
I	grȁdom	gradóvima

1.2 Palatal stems

1.2.1 Palatal stem, adjective (with inanimate noun)

	Indefinite		Definite	
N	vrȕć dȁn	vrȗći dȁni	vrȗći dȁn	vrȕćῑ dȁni
A	vrȕć dȁn	vrȗće dȁne	vrȕćῑ dȁn	vrȗćē dȁne
G	vrȗćeg dȁna	vrȗćῑh dȃnā	vrȕćēg dȁna	vrȗćῑh dȃnā
D	vrȗćem dȃnu /dȁnu	vrȗćῑm dȁnima	vrȕćēm dȁnu /dȁnu	vrȗćῑm dȁnima
I	vrȗćῑm dȁnom	vrȗćῑm dȁnima	vrȕćῑm dȁnom	vrȗćῑm dȁnima

1.2.2 Palatal stem, noun (animate), with non-palatal adjective

Definite

N	dòbrῑ prȉjatelj	dòbrῑ prȉjatelji
A	dòbrōg prȉjatelja	dòbrē prȉjatelje
G	dòbrōg prȉjatelja	dòbrῑh prȉjatēljā
D	dòbrōm prȉjatelju	dòbrῑm prȉjateljima
I	dòbrῑm prȉjateljem	dòbrῑm prȉjateljima
V	dòbrῑ prȉjatelju	dòbrῑ prȉjatelji

349

1.2.3 Palatal stem, noun, extended

with moveable /a/

N	mȕž	mùževi	ótac	óčevi
A	mȕža	mùževe	óca	óčeve
G	mȕža	mužévā	óca	óčēvā
D	mȕžu	mužévima	ócu	óčevima
I	mȕžem	mužévima	ócem	óčevima
V	mȕžu	mùževi	òče	óčevi

1.3 Nouns with replacement of stem in the plural

N	gospódin	gospóda	bràt	bràća	čóvek	ljȕdi
A	gospódina	gospódu	bràta	bràću	čovéka	ljȕde
G	gospódina	gospódē	bràta	bràćē	čovéka	ljúdī
D	gospódinu	gospódi	bràtu	bràći	čovéku	ljúdima
I	gospódinom	gospódōm	bràtom	bràćōm	čovékom	ljúdima
V	gospódine	gòspodo	bràte	bràćo	čovèče	ljȕdi

2 Neuter

2.1 Non-palatal stems, adjective and noun

N	lȇpo sélo	lȇpa sèla	lȇpŏ sélo	lȅpā sèla
A	lȇpo sélo	lȇpa sèla	lȇpŏ sélo	lȅpā sèla
G	lȇpog séla	lȇpīh sèlā	lȇpŏg séla	lȅpīh sèlā
D	lȇpom sélu	lȇpīm sèlima	lȇpŏm sélu	lȅpīm sèlima
I	lȇpim sélom	lȇpīm sèlima	lȇpīm sélom	lȅpīm sèlima

2.2 Palatal stems, adjective and noun

N	nàše pòlje	nàša pólja
A	nàše pòlje	nàša pólja
G	nàšeg pòlja	nàšīh póljā
D	nàšem pòlju	nàšīm póljima
I	nàšīm pòljem	nàšīm póljima

2.3 Shortened stem in Nominative/Accusative. Replacement stem in plural

N	dȇte	déca
A	dȇte	décu
G	déteta	décē
D	détetu	dèci
I	détetom	décōm
V	dète	dèco

350

3 Feminine

3.1 Feminine Nouns in /a/

3.1.1

	Indefinite			Definite	
N	lépa žéna	lépe žéne	lèpā žéna	lèpē žéne
A	lépu žénu	lépe žéne	lèpū žénu	lèpē žéne
G	lépē žénē	lépīh žénā	lèpē žénē	lèpīh žénā
D	lépōj žéni	lépīm žénama	lèpōj žéni	lèpīm žénama
I	lépōm žénōm	lépīm zénama	lèpōm žénōm	lèpīm žénama
			lèpā žèno	lèpē žène

3.1.2 Feminine /a/ noun with moveable /a/

N	séstra	séstre
A	séstru	séstre
G	séstrē	sestárā
D	séstri	séstrama
I	séstrōm	séstrama
V	sèstro	sèstre

3.1.3 Feminine /a/ noun with G pl. in /-ī/. Note also /k/ to /c/ before /-ī/.

N	mȁjka	mȁjke
A	mȁjku	mȁjke
G	mȁjkē	mȁjkī
D	mȁjci	mȁjkama
I	mȁjkōm	mȁjkama
V	mȁjko	mȁjke

3.2 Feminine /i/ nouns

	Regular		Unpredictable in Nom.	
N	nȍć	nòći	kćī	kćèri
A	nȍć	nòći	kćèr	kćèri
G	nòći	nóćī	kćèri	kćérī
D	nóći	nóćima	kćèri	kćérima
I	nòću	nóćima	kćèri/kćèrju	kćérima
V	nòći	nòći	kćèri	kćèri

Note 16.3 Pronoun and Pronominal Adjectives: Review

Following is a general review of the pronouns and pronominal adjectives.

Personal Pronouns

			m. n.	f.
N	jȁ	ti	ȍn, óno	óna
A	ménē me	tébe te	njéga ga	njȕ je/ju
G	ménē me	tébe te	njéga ga	njè je
D	méni mi	tébi ti	njému mu	njȏj joj
I	mnȍm	tòbōm	njȋm	njȏm

351

			m.	n.	f.
N	mȉ	vȉ	óni,	óna,	óne
A	nȁs nas	vȁs vas	njȉh ih		
G	nȁs nas	vȁs vas	njȉh ih		
D	nàma nam	vàma vam	njȉma im		
I	nàma	vàma	njȉma		

Reflexive Pronoun		Demonstrative Pronouns			
N	——	NA	tȍ	óvȍ	ónȍ
A	sébe se	G	tòga	óvoga	ónoga
G	sébe	D	tòme	óvome	ónome
D	sébi	I	tȉm	óvȉm	ónȉm
I	sòbȍm				

Interrogative Pronouns

kò	štà
kóga kòg	štà
kóga kòg	čéga
kóme kòm	čému
kȉme kȉm	čȉm

/kómu/ may also be heard for /kóme/.

The derivative /nȉšta/ 'nothing' is declined like /štà/, /nȉko/ like /kò/.

Pronominal Adjectives

	m.		n.	f.	m.	n.	f.
N	tȁj		tȍ	tȁ	tȉ	tȁ	tȅ
A	tȁj	tòga	tȍ	tȕ	tȅ	tȁ	tȅ
G	tòga			tȅ	tȉh		
D	tȍm			tȍj	tȉm		
I	tȉm			tȍm	tȉm		

/óvaj/ and /ónȃj/ are declined the same way.

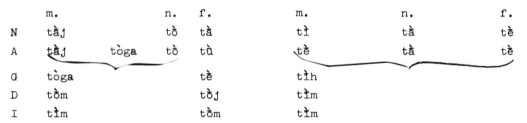

	m.		n.	f.	m.	n.	f.
N	kójȋ		kójē	kójā	kójȋ	kójā	kójē
A	kójȋ kòga / kójega		kójē	kójū	kójē	kójā	kójē
G	kòga / kójega			kójē		kójȋh	
D	kòm / kójem			kójȏj		kójȋm	
I	kójȋm			kójȏm		kójȋm / kójȋma	

/nèkĭ/ 'some' is similarly declined N /nèki/ G /nèkog, nèkoga/ D /nèkom/
I /nèkim/ etc. /mòj/ 'my' and /svòj/ 'one's own' have the same type of shortened
forms as /kójĭ/: N /svòj/ G /svòga/ or /svójega/, etc.

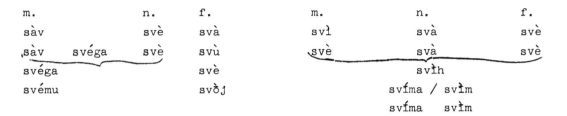

m.		n.	f.	m.	n.	f.
sàv		svè	svà	svĭ	svà	svè
sàv	svéga	svè	svù	svè	svà	svè
svéga			svè		svĭh	
svému			svòj		svíma / svĭm	
					svíma svĭm	

Grammatical Drill

GD 16.1   Review of the Nouns and Pronouns - Case Drill

GD 16.1.1 Nominative

    1. Make the substitutions indicated with plural transform.

    2. Repeat the same drill with pronoun transform.

<u>Moj sin</u> putuje avionom u Jugoslaviju.

moja kći	naša majka	Zorina sestra	ovaj stari gospodin
naš otac	moj brat	Tomin prijatelj	ovo dete

The following sentences are for the above drill:

<u>Moj sin</u> mora uzeti taksi da ne zadocni za voz.
<u>Moj sin</u> se boji da ne zadocni za voz.
Moj sin je zadovoljan svojim putem u Evropu.

Substitution Drill with /ima/ 'there is'

Ima <u>jedna lepa velika soba.</u>
Nema <u>nijedna lepa velika soba.</u>

jedno lepo pozorište	jedan mali, ali dobar **res**toran	jedna lepa zgrada
jedan dobar bioskop	jedno ispravno kupatilo	jedan udoban krevet
jedno malo ogledalo	jedna poruka	

GD 16.1.2 Genitive

Substitution drill with plural transform.

Kuća <u>moga prijatelja</u> je vrlo lepa.
Kuća <u>moga prijatelja</u> nije tako lepa.

moj brat   Jovanova sestra   njegovo dete
Tomin sin   vaša kći   vaš srodnik

The following sentences are for the above drill:

Pismo moga prijatelja je vrlo lepo.
Restoran moga prijatelja je vrlo dobar, iako je jeftin.
Soba moga prijatelja je velika i udobna.
Hotel moga prijatelja je dobar, ali skup.
Posao moga prijatelja je težak.

Substitution Drill

Moram uzeti taksi do železničke stanice, jer ne želim da zadocnim.

kancelarija   hotel   Topčidersko brdo
Dedinje   kuća moga prijatelja   Zeleni venac
ambasada   Narodno pozorište   bioskop

The following sentences are for the above drill:

Moji roditelji stanuju blizu železničke stanice.
Brat dolazi sa železničke stanice kroz pola sata. (Use preposition /sa/ or /iz/
   as required. With item /kuća moga prijatelja/ use preposition /od/ only.)
Deca moraju uzeti taksi od železničke stanice do kuće, jer je već noć.

Substitution drill with negative transform

Ima crnog vina.

hladna voda   hladno pivo   teleće meso   hladno meso
vruć čaj   crni hleb   vruća supa   hladan čaj

U gradu ima dobrih bioskopa.

lep park   lepa zgrada   udobna kuća
dobra kafana   lep spomenik   dobro pozorište

The following sentences are for the above drill:

Jovan kaže da u gradu ima nekoliko dobrih bioskopa.
Jovan kaže da u gradu nema mnogo dobrih bioskopa.
Jovan ne zna da li u gradu ima dobrih bioskopa.

Moj prijatelj ide <u>svakog dana</u> na Topčidersko brdo.

svaka subota	ova subota	taj dan
svaki ponedeljak	to veče	svaki četvrtak
ova sreda	ovaj petak	ovaj utorak

Make each 1 substitution with original sentence, then with each 2 substitutions. Use /dve/ as appropriate.

               2   1

U ovoj kući stanuju <u>dva stara čoveka</u>.

1	2
mala porodica	tri
naš prijatelj	četiri
Zorin srodnik	
stari gospodin	
stara gospođa	
malo dete s majkom	

         2   1

U gradu ima <u>pet velikih hotela</u>.

1	2
dobar bioskop	sedam
mala kafana	mnogo
lepa ulica	osam
lep spomenik	malo
dobro pozorište	nekoliko
	jedanaest

         2   1

U ovoj kući stanuje <u>petoro male dece</u>.

1	2
stara gospoda	dvoje
moja braća	mnogo
	šestoro
	nekoliko
	desetoro

Substitution Drill

Dobro se sećam <u>vašeg brata</u>.

Ne sećam se dobro <u>vašeg brata</u>.

Tomin otac	naš izlet na Frušku goru
Jovanova majka	naš put u Dalmaciju

Jovan se boji <u>rđavog vremena.</u>
Jovan se ne boji <u>rđavog vremena.</u>

neispravna kola	neuređen saobraćaj	teškoće na putu
rđav put	veliki saobraćaj	hladno vreme

Substitution drill with pronoun transform.

Jovići stanuju blizu <u>Tome.</u>   Jovići stanuju blizu njega.

Zora	vi i vaš brat	moja sestra
moja žena i ja	Jovan i Zora	moj brat

The following sentences are for the above drill:

Oni dolaze sutra u posetu kod <u>Tome.</u>
On stiže u Beograd pre <u>Tome.</u>

Substitution Drill with negative transform.

On <u>me</u> se seća.	ti
Oni <u>me</u> se boje.	on
	ona
	mi
	vi
	oni

GD 16.1.3 Dative

1. Make the indicated substitutions with plural transform.
2. Repeat the same drill with pronoun transform, using the emphatic
     forms of the pronouns only for the items in the beginning of the
     sentence.

Dajte ovo pismo <u>mojoj kćeri.</u>   Dajte ovo pismo <u>mojim kćerima.</u>
                                       Dajte <u>joj</u> ovo pismo.

moj sin	vaš prijatelj	ta žena	njihov otac
moja sestra	moj brat	taj gospodin	njihova majka

The following sentences are for the above drill:

Recite <u>mojoj kćeri</u> da odmah dođe u ambasadu.
Javite <u>mojoj kćeri</u> da sam u kancelariji i dan imam posla.

Mojoj kćeri treba za sutra soba sa kupatilom.

Mojoj kćeri je milo, gospođo, što ste zadovoljni.

Mojoj kćeri je žao, gospođice, što ne možete doći.

Dajte mi taj novac.

    on   mi

    ona   oni

The following sentences are for the above drill:

Kažite mi kad dolazi.

Milo mi je što ste dobro.

Žao mi je što niste dobro.

Treba mi hiljadu dinara.

In the sentences on the left side a pronominal adjective with a noun is used. In the sentences on the right side the dative of the corresponding personal pronoun is substituted for the adjective. The meaning of the sentence is the same. The sentences on the right side being only more colloquial.

Moja kći je vrlo dobra.	Kći mi je vrlo dobra.
Tvoja kći je vrlo dobra.	Kći ti je vrlo dobra.
Njegova kći je vrlo dobra.	Kći mu je vrlo dobra.
Njena kći je vrlo dobra.	Kći joj je vrlo dobra.
Naša kći je vrlo dobra.	Kći nam je vrlo dobra.
Vaša kći je vrlo dobra.	Kći vam je vrlo dobra.
Njihova kći je vrlo dobra.	Kći im je vrlo dobra.

The following sentences are for the above drill:

Moja soba je lepa i čista.

Moj restoran je lep i čist, iako je jeftin.

Moj posao je vrlo dobar, ali težak.

Moja dužnost je laka.

Moja kafa je potpuno hladna i ne mogu da je pijem.

Moje pivo je vruće i ne mogu da ga pijem.

Moj auto je nov.

Moja kola su nova.

Moja deca nisu ovde.

In the following drill use the preposition /na/ instead of /u/ when required.

Jovan je u <u>svojoj sobi</u>.

narodno pozorište   svoj hotel   pošta
zološki vrt   američka ambasada   put

Moji prijatelji stanuju u <u>Jovanovoj ulici br. 10</u>.

lep kraj grada   Cvetni trg br. 6
Topčidersko brdo   Knez-Mihailova ulica br. 34

GD 16.1.4 Accusative

    1. Make the substitutions as indicated with plural transform.
    2. Repeat the same drill with pronoun transform. Use enclitic forms,
        since they are more commonly used in this type of sentences.

Želim da vidim <u>Jovanovu sestru</u>.

vaš brat   Zorina kći   taj čovek   ta žena
taj gospodin   vaš otac

The following sentences are for the above drill:

Otac i najka čekaju <u>Jovanovu sestru</u>.
Neko traži <u>Jovanovu sestru</u>.
Jovići poznaju <u>Jovanovu sestru</u>.
Oni žele da upoznaju <u>Jovanovu sestru</u>.
Majka zove <u>Jovanovu sestru</u>.

Substitution drill with plural transform.

Grad ima <u>dobar hotel</u>.

dobro pozorište   velika i lepa ulica   veliki trg
čista kafana   lep i veliki spomenik   dobar restoran

Substitution Drill

Možete popiti <u>kafu</u> pre nego što pođe voz.

čaj   jedno pivo   jedno vino

Voz stiže u Skoplje u 10 časova.

| Ljubljana | Sežana | Sarajevo |
| Zagreb | Zidani most | Rogaška Slatina |

Oni žele da je vide.

| ja | on | vi |
| ti | mi | oni |

Sentences for further drill:

Traže je neki ljudi.
Oni je dobro poznaju.
Treba mi soba za nju.
Ima pismo od nje.

GD 16.1.5 Instrumental

Moj prijatelj ima izvesnih teškoća s njegovim kolima.

| svoja deca | jedan gospodin | neka gospoda | svoj brat |
| jedno dete | posao | Jovanova braća | |

Jovan ide večeras u bioskop sa mnom.

| ti | ona | vi |
| on | mi | oni |

GD 16.2 Review of the Nouns and Pronouns - Pronoun Transform Drill

In the sentences on the left side an adjective-noun phrase in one or another case is used. On the right side a pronoun (in one sentence a pronominal adjective) substitutes for the noun phrase. This drill may be used as a transform drill or as question and answer with prompt. As a transform drill, the student responds with the sentence on the right, substituting the pronoun form for the noun phrase. As a prompt drill, the sentences on the left are given and an appropriate question made on the basis of it. The pronoun transform or a similar sentence will be the answer.

Moj brat putuje avionom u Zagreb.   On putuje avionom u Zagreb.

Kuća moga brata je lepa i velika.   Njegova kuća je lepa i velika.

Ima pismo od moga brata.   Ima pismo od njega.

Mi stanujemo blizu moga brata.   Mi stanujemo blizu njega.

Gospodin Jović se ne seća moga brata.   Gospodin Jović ga se ne seća.

Oni se ne boje moga brata.   Oni ga se ne boje.

Dajte ovaj novac mom bratu.   Dajte mu ovaj novac.

Dajte ovaj novac mom bratu, a ne Tomi.   Dajte ovaj novac njemu, a ne Tomi.

Recite mom bratu da dođe u ambasadu.   Recite mu da dođe u ambasadu.

Mom bratu treba soba sa kupatilom.   Njemu treba soba sa kupatilom.

Mom bratu je milo što imate lepu sobu.   Njemu je milo što imate lepu sobu.

Mom bratu je žao što nemate lepu sobu.   Njemu je žao što nemate lepu sobu.

Ovaj gospodin želi da vidi moga brata.   Ovaj gospodin želi da ga vidi.

Ovaj gospodin želi da vidi moga brata,   Ovaj gospodin želi da vidi njega,
   a ne vas.   a ne vas.

Ova gospoda čekaju moga brata.   Ova gospoda ga čekaju.

Jovan traži moga brata.   Jovan ga traži.

G. Jović ne poznaje moga brata.   G. Jović ga ne poznaje.

Jovići žele da upoznaju moga brata.   Jovići žele da ga upoznaju.

Jedan gospodin želi da govori s   Jedan gospodin želi da govori s njim.
   mojim bratom.

G. i g-đa Smit razgovaraju srpsko-   G. i g-đa Smit razgovaraju srpskohrvatski s mojim bratom.   hrvatski s njim.

Jovići idu večeras u pozorište s   Jovići idu večeras u pozorište s njim.
   mojim bratom.

    moja sestra   Zorina deca   vaša kći
    ti ljudi   Tomini sinovi   Zorina majka

GD 16.3 Review of the Nouns and Pronouns - Question Drill

a) On the left side a set of affirmative sentences with an adjective-noun phrase in various cases is given. On the left side of each sentence an appropriate question is made to which that sentence is a common answer.

b) Make the substitutions indicated and give an affirmative answer. The negative answers may be only of the type /Niko ne putuje u Zagreb/ etc. The phrases for substitution are underlined.

Moj brat putuje u Zagreb.   Ko putuje u Zagreb?

Ima pismo od moga brata.   Od koga ima pismo?
Moj brat se boji rđavog vremena.   Čega se boji vaš brat?
Oni se boje moga brata.   Koga se oni boje?
To je kuća moga brata.   Čija je ovo kuća?
Oni se sećaju moga brata.   Koga se oni sećaju?
Moj brat se seća izleta na Frušku goru.   Čega se seća vaš brat?

Dajte ovaj novac mom bratu.   Kome da dam ovaj novac? /Šta da dam
                                                 vašem bratu?

Mom bratu treba soba za nedelju i   Kome treba soba? /Šta treba vašem bratu?
   ponedeljak.
Recite mom bratu da danas posle podne   Šta da kažem vašem bratu?
   dođe u ambasadu.
Ova gospoda čekaju moga brata.   Koga čekaju ova gospoda?
Moj brat čeka voz.   Šta čeka vaš brat.
Ta žena traži moga brata.   Koga traži ova žena?
Moj brat traži odavno kuću na Dedinju.   Šta traži vaš brat?

Moj brat putuje vozom u Zagreb.   Kako putuje vaš brat u Zagreb?
Moj brat želi da se upozna sa Jovićima.   S kim želi da se upozna vaš brat?
Moj brat razgovara svakog dana sa   S kim vaš brat razgovara svakog dana
   Zorom srpskohrvatski.   srpskohrvatski?

Moj brat putuje u Zagreb.   Gde putuje vaš brat? /Kuda putuje vaš
                                                 brat?

Moj brat stanuje na Dedinju.   Gde stanuje vaš brat?
Moj brat ide u kafanu svake subote.   Gde ide vaš brat svake subote? /Kuda ide
                                                 vaš brat svake subote?

361

<u>Moj brat</u> je večeras u kafani.   Gde je vaš brat?

    Tomina sestra   Zorin otac

    moji roditelji   Jovanov prijatelj

    Repeat this drill using the questions with /da li/ and give affirmative
and negative answers first short, and then long. e.g.

Da li <u>vaš brat</u> putuje u Zagreb?   Da, putuje.

                                 Ne, ne putuje.

                                 Da, <u>on</u> putuje u Zagreb.

                                 Ne, <u>on</u> ne putuje u Zagreb.

                                 Izvinite, ali ne znam da li <u>on</u> putuje

                                    u Zagreb.

GD   16.4   Conversations - Razgovori

GD   16.4.1

              A   B

Čujem da često putujete u Skoplje.   Jest, ja često putujem poslom u Skoplje.

  Da li je to točno?

Kako putujete, vlakom ili autom?   Obično putujem vlakom.

Zašto putujete vlakom kad imate auto? Zbog lošeg vremena. Još je zima.

Kojim vlakom putujete?   Brzim vlakom.

Da li ima međunarodnih vlakova do   Da, ima, ali ja rijetko kad putujem

  Skoplja?   ekspresom.

Zašto?   Ne dobijam ništa u vremenu, a ekspres je

                                       vrlo skup za mene.

Da li su jugoslovenski brzi vlakovi   Jesu. Vožnja prvim razredom je jako

  udobni.   prijatna i udobna.

Koliko razreda ima na vašim vlakovima? Imaju dva razreda, prvi i drugi.

Koliko stoji karta drugog razreda?   Ne znam točno jer ne putujem drugim

                                       razredom.

Da li je točno da karta prvog razreda Mislim da je otprilike tako.

  stoji dvaput više od druge.

Чујем да често путујете у Скопље.
   Да ли је то тачно?

Јесте, ја често путујем послом у
   Скопље.

Како путујете, возом или аутом?

Обично путујем возом.

Зашто путујете возом кад имате ауто?

Због рђавог времена. Још је зима.

Којим возом путујете?

Брзим возом.

Да ли има међународних возова до
   Скопља?

Да, има, али ја ретко кад путујем
   експресом.

Зашто?

Не добијам ништа у времену, а експрес
   је врло скуп за мене.

Да ли су југословенски брзи возови
   удобни?

Јесу. Вожња првом класом је врло
   пријатна и удобна.

Колико класа има на вашим возовима?

Имају две класе, прва и друга.

Колико кошта карта друге класе?

Не знам тачно, јер не путујем другом
   класом.

Да ли је тачно да карта прве класе
   кошта двапут више од друге.

Мислим да је отприлике тако.

GD 16.4.2

Da li vaši jugoslavenski prijatelji
   govore engleski?

Ne, ne govore.

To je jako dobro za vas. Vi sigurno
   govorite s njima srpskohrvatski,
   zar ne?

Da, govorimo, ali ne uvijek. Ima tu
   jedna poteškoća.

Kakva poteškoća?

Kao što znate mi učimo srpskohrvatski
   i želimo da govorimo srpskohrvatski
   kad god možemo.

To znam, ali ne razumijem kakva tu
   ima poteskoća. To je jako jedno-
   stavno.[1]

Čekajte malo, da čujete. Nije tako
   jednostavno, kao što vi mislite.

---

[1] /jédnostāvan, jédnostāvna, -o/ 'simple'

Ne razumijem zašto. Recite u čemu je stvar!

Stvar je u tome što oni uče engleski.

Pa tako kažite. Sad razumijem.

Mi želimo da govorimo s njima srpskohrvatski, a oni s nama engleski.

Pa što radite?

Pa mi govorimo s njima malo srpskohrvatski, a oni s nama engleski i zaista nije loše.[1]

Šta mislite kad kažete nije loše?

Pa naše poteškoće na srpskohrvatskom su njihove poteškoće na engleskom i ide jako dobro.

To je lijepo.

Da, tako je. Treba samo da nas čujete kad razgovaramo.

Да ли ваши југословенски пријатељи говоре енглески?

Не, не говоре.

То је врло добро за вас. Ви сигурно говорите с њима српскохрватски, зар не?

Да, говоримо, али не увек. Има ту једна тешкоћа.

Каква тешкоћа?

Као што знате ми учимо српскохрватски и желимо да говоримо српскохрватски кад год можемо.

То знам, али не разумем каква ту има тешкоћа. То је врло просто.

Чекајте мало, да чујете. Није тако просто, као што ви мислите.

Не разумем зашто. Реците у чему је ствар.

Ствар је у томе што они уче енглески.

Па тако кажите. Сад разумем.

Ми желимо да говоримо с њима српско-хрватски, а они с нама енглески.

Па шта радите?

Па ми говоримо с њима мало српско-хрватски, а они с нама енглески и да видите није рђаво.

Шта мислите кад кажете није рђаво.

Па наше тешкоће на српскохрватском су њихове тешкоће на енглеском и иде врло добро.

---

[1] /záista/ 'indeed'

To je lepo.

Да, тако је. Треба само да нас чујете кад разговарамо.

GD 16.4.3

Jedan gospodin traži gospodina Jovića.

Zašto mu ne kažete da moj muž nije kod kuće?

On ipak želi da razgovara s vama.

Dobro, pustite ga unutra.

Dobar dan, gospođo.

Dobar dan, gospodine.

Ja sam Đordević, prijatelj vašeg muža.

Milo mi je gospodine Đordeviću, da se upoznam s vama. Žao mi je što Toma nije kod kuće.

Mi treba da svršimo zajedno jedan posao. Kad on dolazi kući?

On je još na putu.

Zar je on još na putu?

Jest.

Kad se vraća s puta?

Vraća se sutra.

Molim vas, recite mu da dođe u četvrtak kod mene kući, poslije ureda.

Jako rado. Da li on zna gdje stanujete?

Da, zna.

Hvala lijepo i do viđenja, gospođo?

Do viđenja, gospodine.

Један господин тражи господина Јовића.

Зашто му не кажете да мој муж није код куће?

Он ипак жели да разговара с вама.

Добро, пустите га унутра.

Добар дан, госпођо.

Добар дан, господине.

Ја сам Ђорђевић, пријатељ вашег мужа.

Мило ми је господине Ђорђевићу, да се упознам с вама. Жао ми је што Тома није код куће.

Ми треба да свршимо заједно један посао. Кад он долази кући?

Он је још на путу.

365

Зар је он још на путу?   Јесте.

Кад се враћа с пута?   Враћа се сутра.
                                          Имате неки поруку за Тому?

Молим вас, реците му да дође у   Врло радо. Да ли он зна где станујете?
   червртак код мене кући, после
   канцеларије.

Да, зна.

Хвала лепо и довиђења, госпођо.   До виђења, господине.

GD   16.5   Homework - Domaći zadatak

GD   16.5.1 Substitute in the following sentences a corresponding pronoun for
each underlined phrase.

Moj prijatelj je vrlo dobar čovek.
On stanuje blizu mene i moje žene.
Moja žena i ja mnogo volimo našeg prijatelja i njegovu ženu.
Moj prijatelj i ja često izlazimo zajedno.
Mom prijatelju gospodinu Smitu je žao što ne govori srpskohrvatski.
Mojoj ženi i meni treba kuća sa pet soba i kupatilom.
Javite mojoj ženi i kćeri da se vraćam u Beograd u četvrtak, a ne u sredu.
Moj prijatelj želi da vidi svoga brata, a ne svoju sestru.
Jedan čovek traži gospodina Jovića.
Večeras moja žena i ja idemo u pozorište sa gospodinom i gospođom Jović.

GD   16.5.2 Make questions to which the above sentences will be the appropriate
answers. Use /da li/ or /li/ when no question word is involved.

UNIT 17

Basic Sentences - Osnovne rečenice

In Belgrade	U Beogradu	У Београду

A

you came	dòšli ste (dóći, da dòđem)	дòшли сте (дóћи, да дòђем)
or,	vî ste dòšli	вû сте дòшли
When did you arrive in Belgrade?	Kàd ste dòšli u Beógrad?	Кад сте дòшли у Беòград?#

B

I came (man speaking)	dòšao sam	дòшао сам
or,	jà sam dòšao	jû сам дòшао
past, last	pròšlī, -ā, -ō	пròшлū, -ā, -ō
alone, -self	sàm, sáma, sámo	сàм, сáма, сáмо
I arrived last week, by myself ('but alone'.)	Dòšao sam pròšle nèdjelje, ali sàm.	Дòшао сам пròшле недеље, али сàм.
hasn't come (f.)	níje dòšla	нûjе дòшла
My wife and children haven't arrived yet.	Žèna sa djécōm jòš níje dòšla.	Жèна са дèцōм jòш нûjе дòшла.

A

were you, have you been	jèste li bíli	jèсте ли бûли
early	ràno	ràно
earlier	ránije	ránиjе
Have you been in Belgrade before?	Jèste (li) bíli ránije u Beógradu?	Jèсте (ли) бûли ránиjе у Беòграду?#

B

it was	bílo je	бûло jе
a long time ago	dávno	дáвно

| Yes, but it was a long time ago. | Jésam, ali tô je bílo dávno. | Јėсам, али то је било дȃвно. |

| civil servant, official, officer | činóvnīk pl. činóvnīci | чинȍвнӣк чинȍвнӣци |

| I was in Belgrade as a young officer fifteen years ago. | Bȋo sam u Beógradu, kao mlȃd činóvnīk prȋje pétnaest gòdīnā. | Био сам у Београду, као млȃд чинȍвнӣк прȇ петнаест гȍдӣнȃ. |

A

| I heard (man speaking) | čuo sam (čùti, da čùjēm) | чуо сам (чȳти, да чȳјȇм) |

| or, | jȃ sam čuo | jȃ сам чуо |

| then, at that time | táda | тȃда |

| they were not | nȋsu bȋli | нӣсу били |

| I heard that the hotels were not good at that time. | Čuo sam da hotėli táda nȋsu bȋli dóbri. | Чуо сам да хȍтели тȃда нӣсу били добри. |

B

| Well, they weren't that bad. | Pa nȋsu bȋli tȁko lòši. | Па нӣсу били тȁко рђави. |

| at least | bàrem / bàr | бȁр / бȁрем |

| to regret; (with /se/) to complain | žȁlīm (se) | жȁлити (се), жȁлӣм (се) |

| At least, I can't complain. | Bȁrem jȃ ne mȍgu da se žȁlīm. | Бȁр jȃ не могу да се жȁлӣм. |

A

| you dwelled, lived | stanóvali ste (stanóvati, stánujēm) | стȁновȃли сте (станȍвати, стȁнујȇм) |

| or, | vȋ ste stanóvali | вӣ сте станȍвȃли |

| Where did you live? | Gdjė ste stanóvali? | Где сте стȁновȃли?# |

B

| At first I lived downtown. | Prvo sam stanóvao u grádu. | Прво сам становао у грȁду. |

368

I had (man speaking)	ímao sam / jȁ sam ímao	ѝмао сам / jȁ сам ѝмао
living quarters, apartment	stȁn pl. stȁnovi	стȁн, стȁнови
I had a small apartment.	Ímao sam mȁli stȁn.	Ѝмао сам мȁли стȁн.
late	kȁsno	кȁсно
later	kásnije	кácниjе
I got (man speaking)	dȍbio sam (dóbiti, da dȍbijem)	дȍбио сам (дóбити, да дȍбиjем)
or,	jȁ sam dȍbio	jȁ сам дȍбио
Later, I got a house in Dedinje.	Kásnije sam dȍbio kȕću na Dȅdinju.	Кácниjе сам дȍбио кȕћу на Дȅдињу.
did you live	dȁ li ste žívjeli	дȁ ли сте жѝвели
or,	jȅste li žívjeli	jȅсте ли жѝвели
Have you lived in Yugoslavia before?	Dȁ li ste živjeli ránije u Jugosláviji?	Дȁ ли сте жѝвели раниjе у Jугослȁвиjи?#
I never lived (man speaking)	nísam nȉkad žívio	нѝсам нȉкад жѝвео
I've never lived in Yugoslavia before.	Nísam nȉkad ránije žívio u Jugosláviji.	Нѝсам нȉкад раниjе жѝвео у Jугослȁвиjи.
recently, almost	skóro	скóро
My wife has been in Dalmatia recently.	Mȍja žȅna je bȉla skóro u Dȁlmāciji.	Мȍjа жȅна je бȉла скóро у Дȁлмȁциjи.
we were going, we went	mȉ smo ȉšli	мѝ смо ѝшли
or,	ȉšli smo	ѝшли смо
We also went to Dalmatia several times.	I mȉ smo ȉšli nȅkoliko púta u Dȁlmāciju.	И мѝ смо ѝшли нȅколико пȗта у Дȁлмȁциjу.

Grammatical Notes

Note 17.1   Verb: Past
Note 17.1.1   Past: Form

a) Došao sam prošle nedelje.

Bîo sam u Beogradu.

Čuo sam da hoteli nisu bili dobri.

Prvo sam stanovao u gradu.

Imao sam mali stan.

Kasnije sam dobio kuću na Dedinju.

Nisam nikad ranije živeo u
    Jugoslaviji.

b) Žena sa decom još nije došla.

Naša soba je bila dobra.

Moja žena je bila skoro u Dalmaciji.

c) To je bilo davno.

d) Jeste li bili ranije u Beogradu?

Pa nisu bili tako rđavi.

Gde ste stanovali.

Da li ste živeli ranije u
    Jugoslaviji?

I mi smo išli nekoliko puta u
    Dalmaciju.

The past of the verb is normally a compound tense in Serbo-Croatian, as illustrated above. The present of the verb 'to be' is used with a past participle in /-o/ or /-l-/. The participle agrees with the subject (but see below). All of the examples in a) are spoken by a man. The participles are masculine singular in form, ending in /-o/. If these were said by a woman, the ending would be /-a/, as in b). They would then be:

Došla sam prošle nedelje.   Imala sam mali stan.

Bila sam u Beogradu.   Kasnije sam dobila kuću na Dedinju.

Čula sam da hoteli nisu bili dobri.   Nisam nikad ranije živela u

Prvo sam stanovala u gradu.   Jugoslaviji.

In other words, the real verb in these constructions is the verb /sam/. The /došao/ - /došla/ etc. are participles or verbal adjectives.

The examples in c) are neuter singular and those in d) plural (common plural, masculine plural, or polite singular with 'you'). There are also (exclusively) feminine plural forms in /-l-e/, as /sve sobe su bile dobre/ and neuter plural forms in /-l-a/, as /sva ogledala su bila čista/.

The /-o/ of the masculine singular is the same as the /-l-/ of the other forms; /l/ at the end of a syllable is usually replaced by /o/ in Serbo-Croatian. (Compare /Beógrad/ for /bel-/ 'white' plus /grad/ 'citadel'.) The /-o/~/-l-/

370

is the participle formative. The endings are the adjective endings (-zero for masculine singular, /-a/ for feminine singular, etc.)

In most, but by no means all, cases verbs have the same stem in the /1/ participle as in the infinitive. This is seen from the following list of the /1/ participle forms of the verbs found in the above examples. The infinitive is given first. The first person present forms are added in parentheses after the others for comparison and contrast. (See Note 17.2 for more examples.)

		ímati	stanóvati	žíveti
Sg.	m.	ímao	stànovao	žíveo
	f.	ímala	stànovāla	žívela
	n.	ímalo	stànovālo	žívelo
Pl.	m.	ímali	stànovāli	žíveli
	f.	ímale	stànovāle	žívele
	n.	ímala	stànovāla	žívela
		(ìmām)	(stánujēm)	(zìvīm)

		íći	dóći	dóbiti	čùti	bìti
Sg.	m.	ìšao	dòšao	dòbio	čùo	bìo
	f.	íšla	dòšla	dòbīla	čùla	bíla
	n.	íšlo	dóšlo	dòbilo	čùlo	bílo
Pl.	m.	íšli	dóšli	dòbili	čùli	bíli
	f.	íšle	dóšle	dòbile	čùle	bíle
	n.	íšla	dóšla	dòbila	čùla	bíla
		(ídēm)	(dóđēm)	(dòbijēm)	(čùjēm)	(sam)

The stem (or stems) of the infinitive and /1/ participles are:

Infinitive	íma-	stanóva	zíve-
/1/ participle		stànova-	
(where different)		stànovā-	

Infinitive	i-	dó-	dóbi-	čù-	bì-
/1/ participle	ìša-	dòša-	dòbi-		bì-
(where different)	ìš	dòš-			bí-

/ìšao/ and /dòšao/ both have movable /a/. The verb 'go' and a typical derivative from it are illustrated by these two verbs. The forms of these verbs are
irregular.

Note 17.1.2   Past: Use

The past tenses of all the above verbs may be made by using the present of
the verb 'to be'. The unstressed forms occur after the /l/ participle if the
latter is the first stressed form of the clause. In the negative the forms
/nîsam/, etc. always come before (earlier in the sentence of clause than) the
/l/ participle, as they are always stressed.

ímao sam	'I had	nîsam ímao	'I didn't have'
ímala sam		nîsam ímala	
ímao si	you had	nîsi ímao	'you didn't have'
ímala si		nîsi ímala	
ímao je	he had	níje ímao	'he didn't have'
ímala je	she had	níje ímala	'she didn't have'
ímalo je	it had	níje ímalo	'it didn't have'
ímali smo	we had	nîsmo ímali	'we didn't have'
ímale smo		nîsmo ímale	
ímali ste	you had	nîste ímali	'you didn't have'
ímale ste		nîste ímale	
ímali su	they had	nîsu ímali	'they didn't have'
ímale su		nîsu ímale	
ímala su		nîsu ímala	

The plural in /i/ is by far the most frequent, as the purely feminine may only
be used when feminine forms alone are involved. The polite /vi/ is used for all
genders:

        kad ste vi došli   (to man, woman, men   mixed group)

For 'we' and 'they' the subject must be exclusively feminine for the
participle to be feminine.

372

mi smo došli	(men, mixed group)
mi smo došle	(exclusively women)
oni su došli	(men, mixed group)
one su došle	(exclusively women)
ona su došla	(neuter plural reference)

(See Note 18.1 for more detail on agreement of the /l/ participle with various subjects. Compare also Note 7.2.)

The example /šta vam se najviše dopalo usput?/ shows that the participle and /se/ are used, without /je/, in the third person singular affirmative past of reflexive verbs. The singular of this verb is /dopao sam se, dopala sam se, dopao si se, dopala si se, dopao se, dopala se, dopalo se/. It is also possible to use /je/: /dopao se je/, but this is less frequent.

Two constructions with /li/ are common:

1. Stressed /jèsam, jèsi/ etc. + li + /l/ participle

            jeste   li   bili....

2. Da li + enclitic /sam, si/, etc. + /l/ participle

   Da li   ste   živeli...

/li/ is frequently omitted in colloquial speech in the first construction, though not after /je/. Other enclitics are used after /li/ or /ste/ as required. The enclitics and their order, given in Note 12.4, should be noted in connection with the past. The short form /ju/ 'her', listed in Note 12.2 is used when followed by /je/ 'is', as in /on ju je video/ 'he saw her'. Many speakers avoid the use of /ju/, preferring to use a construction with /njù/, except in writing.

The short answer a (yes-no) question using the past is usually the long form of the verb 'to be':

Jeste li imali...?	Da, jesam.
Da li ste imali...?	/Jesam.
	Ne, nisam.
	/Nisam.

Compare the English use of 'have':

Have you had your breakfast?	Yes, I have.
	No, I haven't.

In both English and Serbo-Croatian the real verb form (usually called the 'auxiliary' verb) is that which is used in the answer, not the participle.

Note 17.1.3 Past: Aspect

Most past tense forms are from perfective verbs, as the past tense is most frequently used of completed actions. However, most of the past tenses used in this unit are imperfective. Verbs such as 'live', 'dwell', etc. may often be used in the past to refer to a continuing state of affairs. Compare the perfective and imperfective forms found in the Basic Sentences:

Perfective		Imperfective	
došao	having come	stanovali	having dwelled
čuo	having heard	imao	having had
dobio	having received	živeo	having lived
		išao	having gone
		putovali	having travelled

A rough idea of the pattern of usage may be seen from the two verbs /dàti/ and /dávati/:

dájēm	I'm giving	(želim da) dām	I (want to) give
dávao sam	I was giving	dào sam	I gave

The English simple past will usually correspond to a perfective verb in Serbo-Croatian. Exceptions are generally verbs indicating states, as above, or activity which is normally described as in process (/služio sam/ - the verb refers to the activity, not to its termination).

/išao sam/ is somewhat specialized in meaning. The sentence /I mi smo išli nekoliko puta u Dalmaciju./ 'We also went several times to Dalmatia.' does refer to the going, the movement involved, not the completion of it. The most normal English equivalent is 'We were also in Dalmatia several times.' This may also be /I mi smo bili nekoliko puta u Dalmaciji./ Here there is reference only to the 'being', not to the going, but the two sentences are situationally equivalent.

Note 17.2 Verb: Review

Following is a list of verbs which have occurred, giving the infinitive, the present and the /l/ participles. The perfective verbs are listed first then the imperfectives. Masculine and feminine forms of the /l/ participles are given, to show moveable /a/ when it occurs, /a̅/ before /-la/ or other variables.

Infinitive	Present	/l/ participle		meaning

Perfective Verbs

čùti	da čùjēm	čùo	čùla	to hear
dàti	da dȁm (dȃmo 1p)	dào	dȃla	to give
dòbiti	da dòbijēm	dòbio	dòbīla	to receive
dṍći	da dȍđēm	dòšao	dòšla	to come
dònēti /donijéti	da donésēm	dòneo /dònio	dònēla /dònijela	to bring
dozvóliti	da dózvolīm	dozvólio	dozvólila	to allow, permit
izvíniti	da ízvīnīm	izvínio	izvínila	to excuse
izvóleti	da ízvolīm	izvóleo	izvólela	to permit
jáviti se	da se jȁvī	jávio se	jávila se	to report oneself
kázati	da kȁžēm	kázao	kázala	to say
kúpiti	da kúpīm	kúpio	kúpila	to buy
opròstiti	do óprostīm	opróstio	opróstila	to pardon
otíći	da òdēm	otišao	ótišla	to go, leave
oženiti se	da se óženīm	oženio se	_____	to get married (of man)
plátiti	da plȁtīm	plátio	plátila	to pay
pṍći	da pȍđēm	pòšao	pòšla	to start off
pógledati	da pógledām	pógledao	pógledala	to look
pópiti	da pòpijēm	pópio	pópila	to drink
pozájmiti	da pózajmīm	pozájmio	pozájmila	to loan
prṍći	da pròđēm	próšao	próšla	to pass by
proméniti /promijéniti	da prómenīm /da prómijenīm	proménio /promijénio	proménila /promijénila	to change
pùstiti	da pùstīm	pùstio	pùstila	to let
réći	da rèčēm	rékao	rékla	to say
sáčekati	da sáčekām	sáčekao	sáčekala	to wait for
sèsti /sjèsti	da sèdnēm /da sjèdnēm	sèo /sjèo /sȉo	sèla /sjèla	to sit down
svŕšiti	da svŕšīm	svŕšio	svŕšila	to finish

údati se	da se údām		ùdāla se	to get married (of woman)
únēti /unijéti	da unésēm	úneo /únio	únela /únijela	to carry in
upóznati	da upóznām	úpoznao	úpoznāla	to introduce
urédīti	da úrēdīm	urédio	urédila	to put in order
úzēti	da ùzmēm	ùzeo	ùzēla	to take
zadócniti	da zádocnīm	zadócnio	zadócnila	to be late
zadŕžati se	da se zadŕžīm	zádržao se	zádržala se	to be delayed
zaúzēti	da zaúzmēm	zàuzeo	zàuzēla	to take

Imprefective Verbs

bìti	(jé)sam	bìo	bíla	to be
bójati se	bójīm se	bójao se	bójala se	to be afraid
brìnuti se	brìnēm se	brìnuo se	brìnula se	to worry
čèkati	čèkām	čèkao	čèkala	to (be) wait(ing)
dávati	dàjēm	dávao	dávala	to be giving
dešávati se	dèšávā se	dešávao se	dešávala se	to be happening
dobíjati	dóbījām	dobíjao	dobíjala	to be receiving
dólaziti	dólazī	dólazio	dólazila	to be coming
dópadati se	dópadā se	dópadao	dópadala	to please
govóriti	góvorīm	govório	govórila	to speak
htèti / htjèti	(hó)ću (hò)će 3	htèo / htìo	htèla / htjèla	to will, want
íći	ídēm	íšao	íšla	to go
ímati	ímām	ímao	ímala	to have
ízlaziti	ízlazīm	ízlazio	ízlazila	to be going out
jèsti	jèdēm	jèo	jèla	to eat
kóštati	kòštā	kóštao	kóštala	to cost
mìsliti	mìslīm	mìslio	mìslila	to think
mócí	mógu mòže 3	mògao	mógla	to be able
mólīti	mòlīm	mólio	mólila	to pray, beg
mórati	mòrām	mórao	mórala	to have to
ódlaziti	ódlazīm	ódlazio	ódlazila	to be leaving
pítati	pìtām	pítao	pítala	to ask
pìti	pìjēm	pìo	píla	to drink
póčinjati	póčinjēm	póčinjao	póčinjala	to be beginning
pólaziti	pólazīm	pólazio	pólazila	to be starting off

poznávati	póznajēm	poznávao	poznávala	to know
pràviti	pràvīm	pràvio	pràvila	to be making
prósiti	pròsīm	prósio	prósila	to beg
provóditi	próvodīm	provódio	provódila	to spend time
putóvati	pútujēm	pùtovao	pùtovāla	to travel
ráditi	rȁdīm	rádio	rádila	to work, do
rásti	rástēm	rástao	rásla	to grow
razgovárati	razgóvarām	razgovárao	razgovárala	to be conversing
razúmeti /razúmjeti	razúmēm /razúmijēm	razúmeo /razúmio	razúmela /razúmjela	to understand
sècati se /sjècati se	sècām se /sjècām se	sècao se /sjècao se	sècala se /sjècala se	to remember
sédeti /sjéditi	sédīm /sjédīm	sédeo se /sjédio	sédila /sjédila	to be sitting
slúžiti	slùžīm	slúžio	slúžila	to serve
stàjati	stàjē 3	stàjao	stàjāla	to cost
stanóvati	stánujēm	stànovao	stànovāla	to dwell
stìzati	stìžēm	stìzao	stìzala	to be arriving
svídati se	svȋđa se	svíđao	svíđala	to please
trážiti	trážīm	trážio	trážila	to look for
trèbati	trèbā 3	trèbalo (n.)		to be necessary
účiti	účīm	účio	účila	to learn, teach
uznemirávati	uznemíravēm	uznemirávao	uznemirávala	to (be) disturb(ing)
vìdeti /vìdjeti	vìdīm	vìdeo /vìdio	vìdela /vìdjela	to see
vóleti /vóljeti	vólīm	vóleo /vólio	vólela /vóljela	to like
vràćati se	vràćām se	vràćao	vràćala	to be returning
znàti	znȁm	znào	znȁla	to know
zváti	zóvēm	zvào	zvála	to call
žàliti	žȁlīm	žȁlio	žȁlila	to regret
žéleti /žéljeti	žélīm	žéleo /žélio	žélela /žéljela	to wish, want
žíveti /žívjeti	žìvīm	žíveo /žívio	žìvela /žìvjela	to live

Note that the stress of the /l/ participle is generally the same as that of the infinitive.

Note 17.3 Verb: Classification

The list of verbs in Note 17.2 gives sufficient examples to illustrate most of the major types of verbs. Verbs are classified according to the shape of the stem immediately before the endings. For this purpose 'endings' mean the infinitive suffix /-ti/, the present tense suffixes /-m -š - mo/ etc.,

377

the /l/ of the /l/ particle and others which have not yet been discussed. For
example, the following verbs have different stems before the endings:

A	govor-i-ti	govor-ī-m	govor-i-o	govor-i-la
B	vol-e-ti	vol-ī-m	vol-e-o	vol-e-la
C	pit-a-ti	pit-ā-m	pit-a-o	pit-a-la
D	stanov-a-ti	stanu-jē-m	stanov-a-o	stanov-ā-la
E	kaz-a-ti	kaž-ē-m	kaz-a-o	kaz-a-la

These are examples of A. i-verbs, B. e-verbs, C. a-verbs, D. a/jē-verbs,
E. a/Jē verbs. Type E. is similar to D. but shows a change of the final consonant of the stem (/z/ to /ž/). This change and other like changes are given the
symbol /J/. Verbs from the list in Note 17.2 belonging to these types are:

i-verbs

dozvóliti	P	blagodáriti	I	prósiti	I
izvíniti	P	dólaziti	I	provóditi	I
jáviti se	P	govóriti	I	ráditi	I
opròstiti	P	ízlaziti	I	slúžiti	I
pozájmiti	P	mìsliti	I	trážiti	I
proméniti	P	móliti	I	účiti	I
pústiti	P	ódlaziti	I	žàliti	I
svřšiti	P				

e-verbs

izvóleti	P	sédeti	I	žéleti	I
vóleti	I	vìdeti	I	žíveti	I

a-verbs

pógledati	P	čèkati	I	svíđati se	I
sáčekati	P	desávati	I	trèbati	I
		dobìjati	I	uznemirávati	I
		dópadati se	I	vràćati se	I
		ímati	I	kóštati	I
		mórati	I	pítati	I
		razgovárati	I	sèćati se	I

Most a-verbs are imperfective.

378

a/jē-verbs and a/jē

Verbs having /a/ in the infinitive and /ē/ in the present are of two types, according to the /l/ participle. One type has short /a/ before /o/ and long /ā/ before other forms of the /l/ participle:

| stanóvati stánujēm | - | stánovao | stánovāla | stánovālo | stánovāli, etc |

| putóvati pútujēm | - | pútovao | pútovāla | pútovālo | pútovāli, etc. |

The other type has short /a/ in all forms of the /l/ participle:

| dávati dàjēm | - | dávao | dávala | dávalo | dávali, etc. |

| poznávati póznājēm | - | poznávao | poznávala | poznávalo | poznávali, etc. |

All of these verbs have stem extensions: /ov/, /v/. In the present tense of the first type the extension is /u/ (/stan-u-jē-m/): in the present tense of second type it is lost (/da-jē-m/).

To the first type belong verbs such as /zvati/:

| zvàti zòvēm | - | zvào | zvála | zvâlo | zváli, etc. |

To the second type belong verbs such as the following:

| póčinjati póčinjēm | - | póčinjao | póčinjala | póčinjalo | póčinjali, etc. |

| stàjati stàjēm | - | stàjao | stàjala | stàjalo | stàjali, etc. |

| kázati kàžēm | | kázao | kázala | kázalo | kázali, etc. |

| stìzati stìžēm | | stìzao | stìzala | stìzalo | stìzali, etc. |

(None of these examples has the /ov/ ∼ /v/ extension.)

Verbs with short /a/ in the /l/ participle will be labelled a/ǰē verbs. The
/ǰ/ may-

> change the preceding consonant: kázati   kàžem
> be /ǰ/ after a vowel: dávati   dáǰem
> drop after /ǰ/:   póčinjati   póčinjēm

Verbs with long /ā/ before /-l-/ are either

> a/ē verbs: zvàti   zóvēm   zvào   zvála
> a/ǰē verbs: stanóvati   stánujēm   stànovao   stànovāla

These groupings have left a large number of verbs in the list unclassified.
Examination shows that none of these fit precisely into these classifications.
Without going into details, the following groupings may be made:

Consonant stems - verbs having no stem vowel between the root and the
endings. To show this, the root is given to the left for each verb. In most
cases, considerable change occurs in the shape of the root from form to form.

jed-	jèsti	jèdēm	jèo	jèla
rek-	réći	rèčēm	rékao	rékla
mog-	móći	mógu, mòže	mògao	mògla
rast-	rásti	rástem	rástao	rásla
sed-	sèsti	sèdnēm	sèo	sèla

The last verb shows an /n/ extension in the present. More will be said of this
extension later.

The root 'to go' forms a special class of consonant stems:

| id- | íći | ídēm | íšao | íšla |
| | dóći | dòdēm | dòšao | dòšla |

Certain consistencies of treatment are seen here. Except for /íći/, a root in
/d/ replaces /d/ with /s/ before /-ti/ (/jesti/), but loses the /d/ before /o/ -
/l/ (/jeo/, /jela/). Roots in /k/ or /g/ replace /kti/, /gti/, with /ći/ and
have moveable /a/ before /o/, there may be change of /k/ to /č/, /g/ to /ž/ in
the present (/ǰ/ changes, see above). /rast-/ has /ras-/ before /-ti/ and /-l/
but /rast-/ before a vowel (/rastem/, /rastao/). Combinations such as /-tt-/
and /-stl-/ do not occur in Serbo-Croatian. Double consonants are replaced by
single ones and /t/ between consonants is generally lost.

Vowel verbs - verbs having a root ending in a vowel and no suffix between this vowel and the infinitive ending. Some verbs with an extension after the root are also vowel verbs. Examples are:

pi-	pi-ti	pi-je-m	pi-o	pi-ˉ-la
ume-	razume-ti	razume-ˉ-m	razume-o	razume-la
		razume-jū 3 pl.		
zna-	zna-ti	zna-ˉ-m 3 pl.	zna-o	zna-ˉ-la

Some verbs have roots which end in a vowel before certain endings, in a consonant before others. For example:

nē-/nes-	dónē-ti	donés-ē-m	dòne-o donē-la

Two vowel verbs must be considered unique: /bìti/ ¹to be¹ /htèti/ ¹to will, want¹. A more complete verb classification is given in Note 43.2.

Grammatical Drill

GD 17.1   Past Tense - Prošlo vreme. - Substitution-Learning Drill
GD 17.1.1 First Person - Prvo lice

Singular - Jednina	Plural - Množina

Masculine Subjects

Došao sam juče[1] u Beograd.	Došli smo juče u Beograd.
Ja sam došao juče u Beograd.	Mi smo došli juče u Beograd.
Nisam došao juče u Beograd.	Nismo došli juče u Beograd.
Ja nisam došao juče u Beograd.	Mi nismo došli juče u Beograd.

Substitutions for mi, masculine and mixed genders:

otac i ja	ja i sin	majka i ja
brat i ja	ja i dete	kći i ja

Feminine Subjects

Došla sam juče u Beograd.	Došle smo juče u Beograd.
Ja sam došla juče u Beograd.	Mi smo došle juče u Beograd.
Nisam došla juče u Beograd.	Nismo došle juče u Beograd.
Ja nisam došla juče u Beograd.	Mi nismo došle juče u Beograd.

---

[1] /juče/ ¹yesterday¹

Substitutions for <u>mi</u>, feminine subjects only:

majka i ja	gospođa Jović i ja
sestra i ja	kći i ja

Sentences for the above drill:

Služio sam u Beogradu pre petnaest godina.	Kasnije sam dobio kuću na Dedinju.
Prvo sam stanovao u gradu.	Čuo sam da vozovi polaze i dolaze na vreme.
Živeo sam ranije u Beogradu.	Bio sam nekoliko puta u Dalmaciji.
Imao sam mali stan u gradu.	Bio sam zadovoljan sa svojim stanom.

GD   17.1.2   Second Person - Drugo lice

       Singular - Jednina   Plural - Množina

Masculine Subjects

Došao si juče u Beograd.	Došli ste juče u Beograd.
Ti si došao juče u Beograd.	<u>Vi</u> ste došli juče u Beograd.
Nisi došao juče u Beograd.	Niste došli juče u Beograd.
Ti nisi došao juče u Beograd.	<u>Vi</u> niste došli juče u Beograd.

Substitutions for <u>vi</u>, masculine and mixed genders:

vaš otac i vi	vaša majka i vi
Jovan i vi	vaša žena i vi
Tomin prijatelj i vi	Jovanova sestra i vi

Feminine Subjects

Došla si juče u Beograd.	Došle ste juče u Beograd.
Ti si došla juče u Beograd.	<u>Vi</u> ste došle juče u Beograd.
Nisi došla juče u Beograd.	Niste došle juče u Beograd.
Ti nisi došla juče u Beograd.	<u>Vi</u> niste došle juče u Beograd

Substitutions for <u>vi</u>, feminine gender only:

      vaša majka i vi   vaša sestra i vi   vaša kći i vi

Sentences for the above drill:

Služio si odavno u Beogradu, zar ne?
Prvo si stanovao u gradu.

Imao si mesto u vozu pored prozora.

Živeo si ranije u Beogradu.

Kasnije si dobio mesto u prvoj klasi.

Čuo si da je autoput do Skoplja gotov.

Bio si nekoliko puta u Dalmaciji.

Bio si zadovoljan sa vožnjom.

The second person drills may be made into questions to give more natural sentences. They are here affirmative to present a uniform set of illustrative sentences.

GD 17.1.3 Third Person - Treće lice

| Singular - Jednina | Plural - Množina |

Masculine Subjects

Došao je juče u Beograd.	Došli su juče u Beograd.
On je došao juče u Beograd.	Oni su došli juče u Beograd.
Nije došao juče u Beograd.	Nisu došli juče u Beograd.
On nije došao juče u Beograd.	Oni nisu došli juče u Beograd.

Substitutions for on:

Jovan	Toma	otac
brat	njegov sin	ovaj čovek

Substitutions for oni, masculine and mixed genders:

Jovan i Toma	otac i brat	sin i kći
žena i dete	sestra i brat	g. i gđa Jović
Jovići	moji roditelji	ti ljudi

Feminine Subjects

Došla je juče u Beograd.	Došle su juče u Beograd.
Ona je došla juče u Beograd.	One su došle juče u Beograd.
Nije došla juče u Beograd.	Nisu došle juče u Beograd.
Ona nije došla juče u Beograd.	One nisu došle juče u Beograd.

Substitution for ona:

Zora	sestra	gospođa Smit
majka	Meri	moja kći

Substitutions for one, feminine subjects only:

sestre	naše majke	vaše žene
žena i kći	gospođa i gospodica Jović	

Sentences for the above drill:

Služio je u Beogradu dve godine.   Kasnije je dobio kuću na Dedinju.

Prvo je stanovao u gradu.   Čuo je da vozovi tada nisu bili
                                              dobro uređeni.

Živeo je ranije u Beogradu.   Bio je nekoliko puta u Dalmaciji.

Imao je kartu prve klase.   Bio je zadovoljan sa hotelom.

Neuter Subjects   (and plurals of feminine singular form)

Došlo je juče u Beograd.   Došla su juče u Beograd.

Ono je došlo juče u Beograd.   Ona su došla juče u Beograd.

Nije došlo juče u Beograd.   Nisu došla juče u Beograd.

Ono nije došlo juče u Beograd.   Ona nisu došla juče u Beograd.

Substitutions for ono: Substitutions for ona:

1. dete   1. Neuter plural for the first
                                              sentence only:
2. for the first sentence only: pismo

                                                  kola   pisma

                                          2. Feminine singular forms:

                                                  deca   braća

                                                  ta gospoda   moja deca

Sentences for drill with feminine singular participle and plural verb:

Deca su prvo stanovala u gradu.   Deca su bila nekoliko puta u Dalmaciji.

Deca su živela ranije u Beogradu.   Deca su bila u prvoj klasi brzog
                                              voza.

Deca su imala red vožnje.   Deca su kasnije dobila mesta pored
                                              prozora.

GD 17.1.4 Third Person with Count Nouns - Treće lice sa stvarnim imenicama

Onda je taj put bio dobar.   Onda su ti putevi bili dobri.

Onda taj put nije bio dobar.   Onda ti putevi nisu bili dobri.

      kufer   kupe   voz   sto
      krevet / postelja   tramvaj

Onda je ta soba bila dobra.   Onda su sobe bile dobre.

Onda ta soba nije bila dobra.   Onda sobe nisu bile dobre.

kafana   stolica   kuća
ulica   veza   stanica

Leto je bilo hladno.   Leta su bila hladna.
Leto nije bilo hladno.   Leta nisu bila hladna.

    jutro

To be drilled with singular only:

    vino   pivo   meso

GD 17.2 Past Tense - Substitution-Correlation Drill

In this drill the student should use and drill only the gender forms appropriate to himself or herself.

Make the substitutions indicated and give the negative transforms.

Bio sam juče na železničkoj stanici.
Bila sam juče na železničkoj stanici.

ja	on	ona	mi (masc. genders)	mi (f. gender)
(ti)	Jovan	moja žena	otac i ja	majka i ja
ti	otac	kći	sinovi i ja	sestra i ja
	g. Jović	g-đa Jović	deca i ja	kći i ja
			sestra i ja	

mi (mixed gend.)	oni	one
majka i ja	g. i g-đa Jović	naše sestre
žena i ja	Jovići	Tomine kćeri
otac i ja	naši roditelji	gospođe

Sentences for the above drill:

Stanovao sam na Topčiderskom brdu deset godina.
Imao sam mali stan u jednoj velikoj kući.
Živeo sam dugo vremena u Jugoslaviji.
Dobio sam sobu u hotel Metropolu.

GD 17.3   Present Tense - Past Tense Drill

Imam dobar stan ovde.

Imao sam dobar stan, kad sam bio u Beogradu.

Imaš dobar stan ovde.

Imao si dobar stan, kad si bio u Beogradu.

On ima ovde dobar stan.

On je imao dobar stan kad je bio u Beogradu.

Moj prijatelj ima ovde dobar stan.

Moj prijatelj je imao dobar stan, kad je bio ovde.

Ona ima dobar stan ovde.

Ona je imala dobar stan, kad je bila u Beogradu.

Zora ima ovde dobar stan.

Zora je imala dobar stan kad je bila u Beogradu.

Mi imamo ovde dobar stan.

Mi smo imali dobar stan, kad smo bili u Beogradu.

Moja porodica i ja imamo ovde dobar stan.

Moja porodica i ja smo imali dobar stan, kad smo bili u Beogradu.

Vi imate ovde dobar stan gospodine, zar ne?

Vi ste imali dobar stan, kad ste bili u Beogradu gospodine, zar ne?

Vi imate ovde dobre stanove gospodo, zar ne.

Vi ste imali dobre stanove kad ste bili u Beogradu gospodo zar ne?

Oni imaju ovde dobar stan.

Oni su imali dobar stan, kad su bili u Beogradu.

G. i g-đa Smit imaju ovde dobar stan.

G. i g-đa Smit su imali dobar stan, kad su bili u Beogradu.

One imaju ovde dobar stan.

One su imale dobar stan, kad su bili u Beogradu.

Moje sestre imaju ovde dobar stan.

Moje sestre su imale dobar stan, kad su bile u Beogradu.

Sentences for the above drill:

Zadovoljan sam sa vožnjom u Skoplje.
Služim ovde od pre godinu dana.
Idem na železničku stanicu da donesem prtljag.

Bio sam zadovoljan sa vožnjom u Skoplje.
Služio sam u Beogradu pre godinu dana.
Išao sam juče na železničku stanicu da donesem prtljag.
Bio sam juče na železničkoj stanici da donesem prtljag.

Stanujem u jednoj maloj kući u
  Puškinovoj ulici 10.
Živim i radim dugo u Beogradu.
Dolazim kući u 7:00.
Treba da dobijem kuću na Dedinju.
Čujem da brzi voz stiže na vreme u
  Skoplje.

Stanovao sam u jednoj maloj kući u
  Puškinovoj ulici 10.
Živeo sam i radio dugo u Beogradu.
Došao sam kući u 7:00 sati.
Dobio sam kuću na Dedinju.
Čuo sam da brzi voz stiže na vreme u
  Skoplje.

GD 17.4   Questions and Answers
GD 17.4.1   Informational Answers
GD 17.4.1.1 Substitution-Learning Drill

Kakav je bio <u>vaš stan</u>?

(/Kakav <u>vam</u> je bio <u>stan?</u>)

Bio je dobar.
Nije bio dobar.
Moj stan je bio dobar. (/Stan mi je bio dobar.)
Moj stan nije bio dobar. (/Stan mi nije bio
               dobar.)

vaš hotel	njegov čaj	put (road)	saobraćaj u Beogradu
izlet	vaš krevet	put vozom (trip)	

Kakva je bila <u>vaša soba</u>?

(/Kakva <u>vam</u> je bila <u>soba?</u>)

Bila je dobra.
Nije bila dobra.
Moja soba je bila dobra. (/Soba mi je bila
               dobra.)
Moja soba nije bila dobra. (/Soba mi nije
               bila dobra.)

vaša kafa	njihova kuća	vožnja avionom
voda	veza sa Zagrebom	

Kakvo je bilo <u>vaše kupatilo</u>?

(/Kakvo <u>vam</u> je bilo <u>kupatilo?</u>)

Bilo je dobro.
Nije bilo dobro.
Moje kupatilo je bilo dobro. (/Kupatilo mi je
               bilo dobro.)
Moje kupatilo nije bilo dobro. (/Kupatilo mi
               nije bilo
               dobro.)

Tomino pivo	vaše vino	meso	njeno mesto u vozu
vaše pivo	vaše mesto u vozu		

Kakvi su bili ranije <u>stanovi</u>?	Bili su dobri.	hoteli
	Nisu bili dobri.	bioskopi
	<u>Stanovi</u> su bili ranije dobri.	putevi (roads)
	<u>Stanovi</u> ranije nisu bili dobri.	gradovi
		međunarodni
		vozovi /vlakovi
Kakve su bile ranije <u>sobe</u>?	Bile su dobre.	kafane
	Nisu bile dobre.	kuće
	<u>Sobe</u> su bile ranije dobre.	ulice
	<u>Sobe</u> nisu bile ranije dobre.	
Kakva su bila ranije <u>pozorišta</u>? /kazališta	Bila su dobra.	prevozna sredstva
	Nisu bila dobra.	gradska saobraćajna sredstva
	<u>Pozorišta</u> su bila ranije dobra.	sela (use /mali/ for /dobar/)
	<u>Pozorišta</u> nisu bila ranije dobra.	

Other questions for above type of drill:

Koliki je bio vaš stan?

Kolika je bila vaša soba.

Koliko je bilo vaše kupatilo?

The use of vi-form - Upotreba vi-oblika

Kad <u>ste</u> došli u Beograd, gospodine?	Pre dve nedelje.	
	Došao sam pre dve nedelje.	
Kad <u>ste</u> došli u Beograd, gospođo?	Pre nekoliko dana.	
	Došla sam pre nekoliko dana.	
Kad ste <u>vi i vaš otac</u> došli u Beograd, gospodine?	Pre nekoliko dana.	vi i vaš sin
	Došli smo pre nekoliko dana.	vi i deca
Kad ste <u>vi i vaš otac</u> došli u Beograd, gospođo?		vi i Toma
Kad ste <u>vi i vaša kći</u> došle u Beograd, gospođo?	Pre tri dana.	vi i vaša majka
	Došle smo pre tri dana.	vi i gospođa Jović
		vi i gospođica Smit

Following is a set of questions with suggested answers. Go through all questions on this pattern. The long answers are suggested by the answers given below:

Kad <u>ste</u> živeli u Jugoslaviji, gospodine?   Pre deset godina.

Kad <u>ste</u> dobili stan, gospodine?   Pre tri dana.

Kad <u>ste</u> bili u Dalmaciji, gospodine?/   Pre četiri nedelje.

Kad <u>ste</u> išli u Dalmaciju, gospodine?

Gde <u>ste</u> stanovali, gospodine?   Na Dedinju.

Gde <u>ste</u> bili danas, gospodine?/   Na Železničkoj stanici.

Gde <u>ste</u> išli danas, gospodine?   Na Železničku stanicu.

Zašto <u>ste</u> išli u ambasadu, gospodine?   Imao sam posla.

Od koga <u>ste</u> dobili pismo, gospodine?   Od oca.

Koliko soba <u>ste</u> imali u kući, gospodine?   Pet soba.

GD 17.4.1.2 Substitution-Correlation Drill

Kad je <u>Jovan</u> došao u Beograd?	<u>Pre</u> <u>godinu dana.</u>	Zora
	<u>On</u> je došao u Beograd	vaša majka
	pre godinu dana.	vas sin
	<u>Jovan</u> je došao u Beograd	Zorina kći
	pre godinu dana.	vi (polite form)
		vi (plural)
		vaši roditelj
		Tomine sestre
		g. i g-đa Smit
		vaše kćeri

Following is a set of questions with suggested answers. Go through all substitutions with each question. The long answers are suggested by the answers below:

Kad je <u>Jovan</u> bio u Skoplju?   Pre tri dana.

Kad je <u>Jovan</u> služio u Jugoslaviji?   Odavno.

Kad je <u>Jovan</u> išao na Železničku stanicu?   Juče posle podne.

Kad je <u>Jovan</u> dobio stan na Dedinju?   Pre godinu dana.

Zašto je <u>Jovan</u> išao u ambasadu?   Imao je posla.

GD 17.4.2 Yes and No Answers

    The feminine forms are for the use of women in the class.

389

a. Da li ste (vi) došli juče u Beograd?   Jesam.
                    or,   Nisam.

b. Jeste li (vi) došli juče u Beograd?   Da, došao sam juče u Beograd./
                                                Da, došla sam juče u Beograd.
                                                Ne, nisam došao juče u Beograd./
                                                Ne, nisam došla juče u Beograd.

Jovan   ona   vaš otac
on   Zora   Tomina kći   plural masculine and mixed subjects:

                                          vi i žena   vi i deca   vi i kći
                                          vaši roditelji   Toma i Zora   g. i g-đa
                                                                             Jović

                                          feminine plural subjects:

                                          vi i kći   vaše sestre
                                          vi i kći   Tomine kćeri
                                          vi i g-đa Jović   g-đa i g-ca Jović

Following questions and answers are to be drilled with the same substitutions:

c. Zar ste vi došli juče u Beograd?   Da, jesam. [Došao sam iznenada.]/ (1)
                                            Da, jesam. [Došla sam iznenada].

                                            Ne, ne, nisam došao juče./
                                            Ne, ne, nisam došla juče.

d. Zar vi niste došli juče u Beograd?   Ne, nisam. [Došao sam danas iznenada]./
                                            Ne, nisam. [Došla sam danas iznenada].

                                            Pa došao sam juče. Zašto pitate?/
                                            Pa došla sam juče. Zašto pitate?

e. Da vi niste došli juče u Beograd?   Ne, nisam.
                                            Pa, jesam.
                                            Ne, nisam došao juče u Beograd./
                                            Ne, nisam došla juče u Beograd.
                                            Pa došao sam juče./ Pa došla sam juče.

---

(1) /iznenada/ 'suddenly, unexpectedly' added as appropriate. The parts of the
     answers in brackets must be adapted for each sentence.

Following is a set of questions to be drilled on the pattern given above. Go
through all substitutions and all type of questions. Give short and long affirmative and negative answers.

Da li ste dobili stan na Dedinju?   Da li ste stanovali prvo u gradu?

Da li ste bili na železničkoj stanici? Da li ste išli juče u ambasadu?

GD 17.5 Question and Answer Drill with Prompt

Moj prijatelj je došao juče u Beograd. Kad je vaš prijatelj došao u Beograd?

Moj prijatelj još nije došao u Beograd. Da li je vaš prijatelj već došao u
                                            Beograd?

 /Moj prijatelj je već došao u   /Kad vaš prijatelj dolazi u Beograd?
    Beograd.

Moj prijatelj je živeo ranije u   Da li je vaš prijatelj živeo ranije u
    Beogradu.   Beogradu?

On je služio u Beogradu pre petnaest   Da li je on služio u Beogradu?
    godina.

 /On nije nikad služio u Beogradu.

Oni su putovali po Jugoslaviji.   Da li su oni putovali po Jugoslaviji?

Oni su bili nekoliko puta u Dalma-   Da li su oni bili u Dalmaciji?
    ciji.

 /Oni nisu nikad bili u Dalmaciji.

Bio sam zadovoljan sa čistoćom.   Da li ste bili zadovoljni sa čistoćom?

Nisam bio zadovoljan sa čistoćom.   Zar niste bili zadovoljni sa čistoćom?

Imao sam sobu sa dva kreveta i   Kakvu sobu ste imali? /Kakvu ste sobu...
    kupatilom.

Mi smo bili vrlo dugo u hotelu.   Koliko ste bili u hotelu?

Stanovali smo u gradu.   Da li ste stanovali u gradu?

Imali smo mali stan blizu parka.   Kakav ste stan imali?

Naš stan je bio u Njegoševoj ulici   U kojoj ulici je bio vaš stan.
    br. 10.

U tom stanu smo bili godinu dana.   Koliko ste bili u tom stanu?

Posle smo dobili kuću na Dedinju.   Gde ste posle dobili stan?

To je bila lepa i udobna kuća.   Kakvu kuću ste dobili?

391

Mi smo bili vrlo zadovoljni s našom   Da li ste bili zadovoljni s vašom
   kućom.   kućom.

Kuća nije bila daleko od grada.   Da li je vaša kuća bila daleko od grada?

Juče sam bio na železničkoj stanici.   Gde ste bili juče?

Išao sam na stanicu da donesem naš   Zašto ste išli na stanicu?
   prtljag.

Srećom prtljag je već bio na stanici.   Da li je prtljag bio na stanici?

Doneo sam ga kući.   Da li ste doneli prtljag kući?

Ja dolazim kuću u 7 sati.   Kad dolazite kući?

Došao sam kući u 7 sati.   Kad ste došli kući?

Ranije sam dolazio kući u 6.   Kad ste dolazili kući ranije?
                                            /Zar vi ne dolazite kući u 6 sati?

Imao sam teškoća s kolima i zato   Zašto niste došli na vreme?
   nisam došao na vreme.

GD 17.6 Conversations - Razgovori
GD 17.6.1   A   B

Kad ste došli u Beograd?   Došao sam prije nekoliko dana.

Je li i vaša obitelj došla s vama?   Jest. Došli smo zajedno.

Kako ste došli?   Došli smo avionom do Njemačke.

                                          Iz Njemačke smo došli autom do
                                             Beograda.

Koliko dana ste putovali od Njemačke   Putovali smo dva dana.
   do Beograda?

Jeste li dobili stan?   Ne, još smo u hotelu. Sada tražimo
                                             stan.

Da li ste bili ranije u Jugoslaviji?   Jesam, nekoliko puta.

Gdje ste bili?   Bio sam dvaput u Beogradu i jedanput u
                                             Zagrebu.

Da li vam se sviđa Zagreb?   Da, jako mi se sviđa.

Jeste li živjeli ranije u Jugoslaviji?   Ne, nisam nikad.

Кад сте дошли у Београд?   Дошао сам пре неколико дана.

Је ли и ваша породица дошла с вама?   Јесте. Дошли смо заједно.

Како сте дошли?   Дошли смо авионом до Немачке.

Из Немачке смо дошли колима до Београда.

Колико дана сте путовали од Немачке до Београда?   Путовали смо два дана.

Јесте ли добили стан?   Не, још смо у хотелу. Сада тражимо стан.

Да ли сте били раније у Југославији?   Јесам, неколико пута.

Где сте били?   Био сам двапут у Београду и један пут у Загребу.

Да ли вам се свиђа Загреб?   Да, свиђа ми се много.

Да ли сте живели раније у Југославији?   Не, нисам никад.

GD 17.6.2

Kako je ovdje sa stanovima?   Prilično je teško.

Gdje vi stanujete?   Sada stanujem u lijepom dijelu grada.

U kom dijelu grada stanujete?   Stanujem na Dedinju.

Gdje ste stanovali ranije?   Stanovao sam u gradu.

Kako je stanovati u gradu?   Nije loše.

Kakav stan ste imali?   Imao sam mali, ali lijep stan sa kupaonom.

Koliko soba ste imali?   Imao sam dvije velike i jednu malu sobu.

U kojoj ulici ste stanovali?   U ulici Prvog maja.

Je li to daleko od ambasade?   Ne, jako je blizu ambasade.

Je li to lijep kraj?   Jest. Vrlo je lijep.

Što ste dobili na Dedinju, stan ili   Kuću. Nema stanova na Dedinju.
    kuću?

Како је овде са становима?   Прилично је тешко.

Где ви станујете?   Сада станујем у лепом крају града.

У ком крају станујете?   Станујем на Дедињу.

Где сте становали раније?   Становао сам у граду.

Како је становати у граду?   Није рђаво.

Какав стан сте имали?   Имао сам мали, али леп стан са
                                                купатилом.

Колико соба сте имали?   Имао сам две велике и једну малу собу.

У којој улици сте становали?   У улици Првог маја.

Је ли то далеко од амбасаде?   Не, врло је близу амбасаде.

Је ли то леп крај?   Јесте. Врло је леп.

Шта сте добили на Дедињу, стан или   Кућу. Нема станова на Дедињу.
    кућу?

GD 17.6.3

Da li ste bili ranije u Beogradu?   Jesam, ali to je bilo davno.

Kad ste bili?   Bio sam prije četrnaest godina.

Kako je bilo onda u Jugoslaviji?   Nije bilo kao sada.

Kakvi su bili hoteli?   Nisu bili loši. Bili su čisti.

Kakvu ste sobu imali?   Imao sam prilično lijepu i veliku sobu
                                                sa dvije postelje.

Jeste (li) imali sobu sa kupaonom.   Da, imao sam.

Kakva je bila vaša kupaona.   Bila je u redu, iako je bila stara.

Да ли сте били раније у Београду?   Јесам, али то је било давно.

Кад сте били?   Био сам пре четрнаест година.

Како је било онда у Југославији?   Није било као сада.

Какви су били хотели?

Нису били рђаво. Били су чисти.

Какву сте собу имали?

Имао сам прилично лепу и велику собу са два кревета.

Јесте (ли) имали собу са купатилом?

Да, имао сам.

Какво је било ваше купатило?

Било је исправно, иако је било старо.

GD 17.7 Homework - Domaći zadatak

GD 17.7.1 Write out each of the following sentences in the past tense. The verbs for the sentences 3 and 9 are given, because they are different than those employed in the sentences.

1. Moja žena je zadovoljna sa hotelom.   (moji roditelji)

2. Moji prijatelji služe u Beogradu godinu dana.   (moja braća)

3. Toma dolazi u Jugoslaviju. (doći)   (moja sestra)

4. Jovan i Toma su kod kuće.   (gospoda)

5. Mi idemo na železničku stanicu po naše stvari.   (Toma)

6. Moji roditelji stanuju u gradu.   (moja kći)

7. Jovan i Zora žive u Dalmaciji.   (g. i g-đa Jović)

8. Čujem da putujete u Zagreb.   (otac)

9. Imam pismo od majke. (dobiti)   (brat)

10. Poruka je hitna.   (pismo)

GD 17.7.2 Write out each of the above sentences in the past tense using the subjects on the right side in parentheses.

UNIT 18

Basic Sentences - Osnovne rečenice

A Trip to Skopje	Put u Skoplje	Пут у Скопље

A

a few days ago	nèkī dàn	нèкӣ дàн
You were in Skopje, a few days ago [weren't you], John?	Vī ste bīli nèkī dàn u Skòplju, Jòvane?	Вӣ сте бӣли неки дàн у Скòпљу, Jòване?
to interest; (with /se/:) to be interested (in: /za/)	interesírati interésīrā (me)	интересовати, интересyjē ме
to entertain, take an interest; (with /se/:) be engaged in (with I)	zanímati, zánīmā	занимати, занимā
to spend time; (with /se/:) to have a nice time, enjoy	provésti, da provédēm, próveo	провèсти, да провéдēм прòвео
to amuse, entertain; (with /se/:) amuse oneself, have a nice time	zábavljati, zábavljām	забáвљати, забáвљам
I'm interested [to know] how you enjoyed your trip.	Zánīmā me, kàko ste se zabávljali na pútu.	Интересyje ме, кàко сте се прòвели на пyту.

B

although, but, though	màda	màда
crowded	prètrpān	прètрпāн
The trip was ('I travelled') very nice and comfortable, but the train was rather crowded.	Putòvao sam jàko dobro i údōbno, màda je vlȁk bio prìlično prètrpān.	Путовао сам врло добро и yдōбно, мада je вȍз био прилично прètрпāн.
interesting	interesántan, interesántna, -o	интересáнтан, интересáнтна, -о

or,	zanímljiv, -a, -o	занимљив, -а, -о
The trip itself was also very very interesting. ('interesting and interesting')	Sȃm je pȗt bȉo takȍđer jȁko interesántan i zanímljiv.	Сȁм пȗт је бȉо такȍђе врло интересȁнтан и занимљив.

A

the highest	nȁjvišī, -ā, -ē	нȁјвишӣ, -ā, -ō
the most	nȁjvíše	нȁјвише
to please	dópasti se, da se dópadnē, dópao	дȍпасти се, да се дȍпаднē, дȍпао се
or,	svȉdjeti se, da se svȉdī, svȉdio, svȉdjela	свȉдети се, да се свȉдӣ, свȉдео, свȉдела
along, up (with Acc)	ȕz	ȕз
on the way	ȕz pūt / ùspūt	ȕз пȗт / ȕспȗт
What did you like best on the trip?	Štȍ vam se nȁjvíše svȉdjelo ùspūt?	Штȁ вам се нȁјвише дȍпало успут?

B

pertaining to Morava	móravskī, -ā, -ō	мȍравскӣ, -ā, -ō
to be passing by, passing away	prólaziti, prólazīm, prólazio	прȍлазити, прȍлазим прȍлазио
valley	dolína	долина
wonderful	krȁsan, krȁsna, -o	дȉван, дȉвна, -о
hilly	brdóvit, -a, -o	брдȍвит, -а, -о
region, area, country-side, landscape	prédjel m G. prédjela pl. prédjeli	прȅдео прȅдела, прȅдели

Up to the Morava valley the train went through beautiful, mountainous areas.	Do Moravske dolíne vlâk je prȍlazio krâsnim, brdȍvitim prȅdjelima.	До Моравске долине воз је пролазио кроз дивне, брдовите пределе.
to go in, enter	úći, da ȕđem, úšao	ући, да уђем, ушао
along (with G)	dûž	дуж
river	rijéka	река
When we went into the Morava valley, the train went along the river.	Kȁd smo ȕšli u Moravsku dolínu, vlâk je pȕtovao dûž sâmē rijéke.	Кад смо ушли у Моравску долину, воз је ишао дуж саме реке.
to line up (with /se/: intransitive)	rȅđati (se), rȅđā (se) rȅđao (se)	ређати (се), ређа (се), ређао (се)
or,	nízati (se), nȉžē (se) nízao (se)	низати (се), ниже (се) низао (се)
after, behind (with I)	za	за
in front of, before	ȉspred	испред
The villages and towns appeared ('lined up in front of us') one after another, like a movie.	Sȅla i grȁdovi su se nízali jȅdni za drȕgim ȉspred nâs, kȁo na fȉlmu.	Села и градови су се ређали једни за другим испред нас, као на филму.

A

impression	dȏjam G dȏjma pl. dȏjmovi Cr.	утисак, утиска, утисци
to make	nápraviti, da nápravīm, nápravio	направити, да направим направио
to do	učíniti, da účinīm, účinio	учинити, да учиним, учинио

What kind of impression did our villages and towns make on you?	Kàkav su dòjam nà vas učínila nàša sèla i gràdovi?	Ка̏кав су у̏тисак на̀ вас на̏прави̍ла на̑ша сѐла и гра̀дови?

B

to look, appear, look like	izglédati, ízglēdā, izglédao	изгле̑дати, и̍згле̑да̑, изгле̑дао
better	bòljī, -ā, -ē	бо̀љӣ, -а̑, -е̑
better (adv.)	bòlje	бо̀ље
The villages look better than the towns.	Sèla izglédaju bòlje nègo gràdovi.	Сѐла изгле̑да̑ју бо̀ље него̀ гра̀дови.
towards, according to (with D)	prèma	прѐма
I would not say	ne bih rèkao (rèći)	не би̏х рѐкао (рѐћи)
land, country	zémlja	зе̑мља
poor	siròmašan, siròmašna, -o	сиро̀машан, сиро̀машна, -о
Based on what I've seen, I wouldn't say that your country is poor.	Prèma ònome što sam vìdio. nè bih rèkao da je vàša zémlja siròmašna.	Прѐма о̀номе што сам ви̏део, не би̏х рѐкао да је ва̏ша зе̑мља сиро̀машна.

A

part, section	dìo, G. dìjela pl. dijélovi	дѐо, дѐла, де̑лови
rich	bógat, bogáta, bogáto	бо̏гат, бога́та, бога́то
fertile, fruitful, productive, copious, prolific	plòdan, plòdna, -o	пло̀дан, пло̀дна, -о
Unfortunately, all parts of the country aren't as rich and fertile as the Morava valley.	Nàžalōst, svì dijélovi zémljē nìsu tàko bógāti, kào Mòravska dolína.	На̏жало̑ст, сви̏ де̑лови зе̑мље ни̏су та̀ко бо̏гати, ка̏о Мо̏равска доли̍на.

399

opinion	mnìjēnje	мѝшљēње
about (with D)	o	o
railroad	žéljeznica	жѐлезница
What do you think about our railroads?	Kȁkvo je vȁše mnìjēnje o nȁšim žéljeznicama?	Каѐкво је ваше мѝшљēње о нашим жѐлезницама?

B

straight, just	prȁvo	прȁво
to turn	óbraćati, óbraćām, óbraćao	ȍбраћати, ȍбраћāм, ȍбраћао
attention	pȁžnja	пȁжња
To tell you the truth, I paid more attention to the countryside ('areas') than to the train itself.	Prȁvo da vam kȁžēm, jȁ sam óbraćao pȁžnju vȉše na prédjele nȅgo na sȁm vlȁk.	Прȁво да вам кажем, jȁ сам ȍбраћао пажњу више на прѐделе него на сам вȍз.

indeed	zbȉlja	збȉља
or,	záista	заѝста
Your country is indeed beautiful, and I like it very much.	Vȁša zémlja je záista lijépa i mnȍgo mi se dȍpadā.	Ваша је земља збиља лѐпа и много ми се дȍпадā.

A

| kind | ljúbazan, ljúbazna, -o | љубазан, љубазна, -о |
| Thank you, John, you're very kind. | Hvála, Džóne, vȉ ste jȁko ljúbazni. | Хвȁла, Џȍне, вȉ сте врло љубазни. |

Notes   .

Note 18.1 Verb: Past Tense

Note 18.1.1 Verb: Subject Agreement in Past Tense

   Sela i gradovi su se redali jedni za drugim ispred nas.

   Kakav su utisak na vas napravila naša sela i gradovi?

   The above examples are of subjects consisting of mixed genders. /sela i gradovi/ is neuter plural plus masculine plural. The /l/ participle is in /-i/. In the second example the same nouns are the subject, but the participle is in /-a/. The agreement of the /l/ participle is the same as that of an adjective (see Note 7.2). Since subjects of mixed genders are likely to occur with great frequency, the matter of agreement is taken up here in some detail with regard to the past tense.

   Whenever two nouns of mixed gender precede the /l/ participle, the participle has the /-i/ ending. When the participle comes first, it usually agrees in form with the nearer of the two nouns, here /sela/. If the order were /gradovi i sela/, the first sentence would still have /redali/, the second would be /kakav su utisak na vas napravili naši gradovi i sela?/. Note that /naš/, like the participle, agrees with the nearer of the two nouns. It is also possible for the participle to be in /-i/ before any mixed subject. The second sentence may also be /Kakav su utisak na vas napravili naša sela i gradovi?/. The pattern followed in these units is that of the examples from the Basic Sentences. If the participle follows a subject with mixed genders, it is in /-i/, if it precedes a subject with mixed genders, it agrees with the nearer (or nearest) noun of the subject.

   The following examples by no means exhaust the possible combinations of subject and verb in the past tense. They do illustrate the above remarks as well as review the forms of Note 17.1.

Agreement of Participle with Subject

Pronouns:

jȁ	(speaker masculine)	ja	sam	bio
jȁ	(speaker feminine)	ja	sam	bila
tȉ	(person addressed masculine)	ti	si	bio
tȉ	(person addressed feminine)	ti	si	bila
ȍn		on	je	bio
óna	(feminine singular)	ona	je	bila

óno		ono	je	bilo
mî	(reference to men only)	mi	smo	bili
mî	(reference to men and women)	mi	smo	bili
mî	(reference to women only)	mi	smo	bile
vî	(plural, exclusively feminine)	vi	ste	bile
vî	(all other references, 'you' singular and plural)	vi	ste	bili
óni		oni	su	bili
óne		one	su	bile
óna	(neuter plural)	ona	su	bila

Nouns:

    One noun only

Masculine singular	voz	voz je bio
Feminine singular	soba	soba je bila
	kći	kći je bila
Neuter singular	dete	dete je bilo
Masculine plural	vozovi	vozovi su bili
Feminine plural	sobe	sobe su bile
Neuter plural	ogledala	ogledala su bila
Feminine singular form, plural meaning (m. [f. sg.] pl.)	braća	braća su bila

Noun + Pronoun

N + ja	otac i ja smo bili
	majka i ja smo bili
	dete i ja smo bili
N + vi	otac i vi ste bili
	majka i vi ste bili
	dete i vi ste bili
N + on	otac i on su bili
	majka i on su bili
	dete i on su bili
N + ona	otac i ona su bili
	majka i ona su bile
	dete i ona su bili

Noun + Noun

    Nouns of same gender.

m. + m.	otac i brat su bili
f. + f.	majka i kći su bile
n. + n.	pismo i ogledalo su bili

Nouns of different gender before /l/ participle - all have participle in /-i/

m. + f.	otac i majka su bili
f. + m.	majka i brat su bili
m. + n.	otac i dete su bili
n. + m.	selo i grad su bili
f. + n.	žena i dete su bili
m. pl. + f. sg.	sinovi i kći su bili
f. pl. + m. sg.	sestre i brat su bili
m. pl. + f. pl.	sinovi i kćeri su bili
f. sg. + m. [f. sg.] pl.	žena i deca su bili
f. pl. + m. [f. sg.] pl.	sestre i braća su bili

Nouns of different genders after /l/ participle. It is possible to say:

m. + f.	Gde je bio otac i majka?
f. + m.	Gde je bila majka i sin?
m. + n.	Gde je bio otac i dete?
n. + m.	Gde je bilo vino i hleb?
f. + n.	Gde je bila žena i dete?
n. + f.	Gde je bilo meso i supa?
m. pl. + f. sg.	Gde su bili sinovi i kći?
f. sg. + m. pl.	Gde je bila žena i sinovi?
f. pl. + m. sg.	Gde su bile sestre i brat?
m. sg. + f. pl.	Gde je bio brat i sestre?

All above sentences may be /Gde su bili.../. The use of /su bili/ is considered standard and is more common in most of the above constructions.

Note 18.1.2 Verb: Word order in Past Tense

    The word order of the examples from the Basic Sentences may also be noted:

Subject	Verb	Adjective to Subject	Prepositional Phrase
Sela i gradovi	su se ređali	jedni za drugim	ispred nas.

Object (+Verb)	Prep. Phrase	Verb	Subject
Kakav su utisak	na vas	napravila	naša sela i gradovi.

The order of the second sentence is determined by the fact that the question word is a modifier of the object. Question words (other than /li/) come at the beginning of the sentence or clause.

Sentences with /da li / (Note 17.1) may have the subject before or after the /l/ participle if the latter is not followed by other predicate forms:

Da li su vaši otac i majka došli?
Da li su došli vaši otac i majka?

If there are other predicate forms associated with the participle, the subject usually comes before it:

Da li su vaši otac i majka došli juče u Beograd?

Note 18.2 Verbs: New Verbs

Beginning with this unit new verbs will be listed in a special note, giving the infinitive, the present, and the meaning. The l-participle, as well as other forms, will be given when it is felt to be necessary (that is, when they are unpredictable). The verb type will also be indicated, as well as the aspect. Where a verb occurs in an aspect pair, both members of the pair will be given, the simpler or more basic form being listed first. Verbs not normally occurring in aspect pairs will be given first, as in the list below.

Verb Type	Aspect	Infinitive	Present	(l-participle)	Meaning
a	I	izglédati	ízglēdā		to look
a	I	interesírati	interésīrā		to interest
c	P	réći	da rèčēm	rèkao, rékla	to say
a	I	zanímati	zánīmā		to take an interest

i	I	čìnīti	čìnīm		to do
i	P	učìniti	da ùčinīm		
C/n	P	dòpasti se	da se dòpadnē	dòpao se, dòpala se	to please
a	I	dòpadati se	dòpadā se		
a/Jē	I	ìnteresovati (se)	ìnteresujē (se)		to interest; refl.
a/Jē	P	zàinteresovati (se)	da (se) zaintéresujē		to be interested in
a/Jē	I	nízati	nìžēm		to line up
a/Jē	P	nanízati	da nánīžēm		
i	P	obrátiti	da óbrātīm		to turn, refl.
a	I	óbraćati	óbraćām		to turn to
i	I	pràviti	pràvīm		to make
i	P	nápraviti	da nápravīm		
C	P	próći	da pròđēm	próšao, próšla	to pass by
i	I	prólaziti	prólazīm		
C	P	provésti	da provédēm	próveo provéla	to spend time; refl. to enjoy
i	I	provóditi	próvodīm		
a	I	rèđati (se)	rèđām (se)		to line up
a	P	izrèđati (se)	da (se) ízrēđām		
e/i	P	svìdeti se /svìdjeti se	da se svìdī da se svìdī,	svìdeo svìdio, svìdjela	to please
a	I	svíđati se	svìđā se		
C	P	úći	da ùđēm	úšao, úšla	to enter, go in
i	I	úlaziti	úlazīm		
i	P	zábaviti (se)	da se zábavīm		to amuse
a	I	zábavljati (se)	zábavljām (se)		

405

Grammatical Drill

GD 18.1   Substitution-Learning Drill

GD 18.1.1 Past Tense with Plural Subjects - Statements

Masculine Gender

With subjects in singular with negative transform.

Jovan i njegov sin su zadocnili za voz, jer nisu uzeli taksi.

otac i brat   moj i Zorin otac
moj prijatelj i njegov sin   g. Jović i g. Popović

With subjects in plural:

Moji prijatelji su zadocnili za voz, jer su se zadržali dugo u gradu.

Tomin roditelji   oni
Zorini sinovi   ovi ljudi
naši srodnici   Jovići

Feminine Gender

With subjects in singular:

Majka i sestra su zadocnile za voz mada su otišle rano na stanicu.

moja žena i kći   g-đa Jović i moja žena
Jovanova i moja sestra   g-ca Jović i moja kći

With subjects in plural:

Naše sestre su zadocnile za voz mada su kupile karte ranije.

moje kćeri   gospođe   one
naše majke   Tomine sestre i kćeri

Neuter Gender

With subjects in singular

Pivo i vino su bili dobri i jeftini.
Pismo i ogledalo su bili na stolu.

meso i crno vino   hladno pivo i teleće meso

Leto i proleće su bili lepi.

Jutro i veče

With subjects in plural:

Leta su bila topla.
Ova pisma su došla jutros, gospodo.
Pisma i ogledala su bila na stolu.
Sela u dolini su bila velika i lepa.

Mixed Genders:

Gospodin i gospođa Jović su putovali vozom, jer nisu imali kola.

Masculine + f. or n.	Feminine + m. or n.	Neuter + m. or f.
otac i majka	moja žena i sin	jedno dete i jedna žena
sin i kći	žena i deca	moja deca i braća
on i dete	gospođe i gospoda	moja braća i sestra
sinovi i kćeri	sestre i braća	ove gospođe i gospoda

I čaj i kafa su bili topli.

m. + f. or n.	f. + m. or n.	n. + m. or f.
dan i noć	bela kafa i čaj	jutro i dan
dan i veče	supa i meso	veče i noć

GD 18.1.2 Past Tense with pronouns referring to persons /kò/, /nèko/, /nìko/
and /svàko/.

Ko je došao?
Neko je već došao.
Niko još nije došao.
(Svako je došao na vreme.)

The last sentence is put in parentheses, as it is not used in all situations.
The sentence /Svi su došli na vreme./ may be used in all situations.

The following sentences are for the above drill:

Ko je dobio pismo od Jovana?
Ko je ušao unutra?
Ko je zadocnio za voz?

Ko je popio kafu?

Ko je razumeo šta ovaj čovek govori?

Ko je govorio sa Zorom?

Ko se sećao Jovana posle toliko godina?

Ko se žalio na čistoću u hotelu?

GD 18.1.3 Past Tense with pronouns referring to things /štà/, /nèšto/, /nìšta/
           and /svàšta/.

Šta se (je) čulo?

Nešto se čulo.

Ništa se nije čulo.

(Svašta se čulo.)

The sentences on the left side are to be drilled without the last sentence, and
the sentence on the right with all sentences:

Šta se tražilo?   Šta se govorilo?

Šta se dobilo?

Šta se svršilo?

Šta se učilo?

Šta je trebalo reći?

GD 18.1.4 Past Tense with Numbers - Prošlo vreme sa brojevima
Present-Past Tense Drill

Jedan čovek traži g. Smita.   Jedan čovek je tražio g. Smita.

Dva čoveka traže g. Smita.   Dva čoveka su tražila g. Smita.

Pet ljudi traži g. Smita.   Pet ljudi je tražilo g. Smita.

Pet ljudi traže g. Smita.   Pet ljudi su tražili g. Smita.

The following sentences are for the above drill:

Jedan čovek pita da li je g. Smit kod   Jedan čovek je pitao da li je. g.
  kuće?   Smit kod kuće?

Jedan čovek putuje sa mnom u Zagreb.   Jedan čovek je putovao sa mnom u
                                             Zagreb.

Jedan čovek hoće da razgovara s vama,   Jedan čovek je hteo da razgovara s
  gospodine.   vama, gospodine.

408

Past Tense Drill with feminine counterpart

Jedan čovek je tražio g. Smita.	Jedna žena je tražila g. Smita.
Dva čoveka su tražila g. Smita.	Dve žene su tražile g. Smita.
Pet ljudi je tražilo g. Smita.	Pet žena je tražilo g. Smita.
Pet ljudi su tražili g. Smita.	Pet žena su tražile g. Smita.

The following sentences are for the above drill:

Jedan čovek je sedeo u sobi i čekao gospodina Smita.	Jedna žena je sedela u sobi i čekala gospodina Smita.
U ovoj kući je stanovao jedan čovek.	U ovoj kući je stanovala jedna žena.

GD 18.1.5 Past Tense with words of quantity and the numbers /pet/ (and above) on Substitution drill with feminine counterpart

Mnogo ljudi je putovalo vozom.	Mnogo žena je putovalo vozom.
Mnogo ljudi nije putovalo vozom.	Mnogo žena nije putovalo vozom.

    malo   šest   nekoliko

Sentences for the above drill:

U sobi je bilo mnogo ljudi.
Mnogo ljudi je išlo tramvajem u grad.
Mnogo ljudi je govorilo srpskohrvatski.
Mnogo ljudi je zadocnilo za voz.
Bilo je mnogo ljudi u redu ispred mene.
Mnogo ljudi se žalilo na čistoću.

GD 18.2 Substitution-Correlation Drill

Moj brat je putovao pre nekoliko dana brzim vozom u Zagreb.

(ja)	dva naša prijatelja	moje kćeri
Zora	moja žena i deca	

Sentences for the above drill:

Moj brat je već bio u Narodnom muzeju, ali još nije bio u Narodnom pozorištu.
Moj brat je obraćao pažnju više na predele nego na voz.
Moj brat je morao da ide na železničku stanicu za svoje stvari.
Moj brat je zauzeo sobu za sebe u hotelu Metropol.

Moj brat je kupio red vožnje na stanici.

Moj brat je juče tražio stan.

Moj brat je upoznao Joviće u Beogradu.

Moj brat se upoznao sa jednim činovnikom vaše ambasade.

Moj brat je uneo svoje kufere u voz.

Razumeo sam sve što je Zora rekla.

     majka   moji prijatelji   moj otac   g. i g-đa Smit

Sentences for the above drill:

Danas sam govorio srpskohrvatski s mojim prijateljima.

Malo pre sam razgovarao sa Zorom.

Sedeo sam kod njih do 9 sati uveče.

Kazao sam vašem srodniku da dobro govori srpskohrvatski.

Popio sam kafu pre polaska voza.

Upoznao sam Jugoslaviju dobro.

Rekao sam Zori da idemo večeras na put.

Video sam vrlo lep deo zemlje.

Zvao sam ih često puta da dođu kod nas.

Past Tense of reflexive verbs in third person singular.

Jovan se (je) već upoznao sa Zorom.

Jovan se još nije upoznao sa Zorom.

     moj brat   gospodica Smit   gospođa Smit

Sentences for the above drill:

Jovan se sećao svojih prijatelja, mada ih dugo nije video.

Jovan se bojao da ne zadocni za voz, ako ne uzme taksi.

Jovan se već video sa Tomom.

Jovan se proveo vrlo dobro na putu.

Jovan se već razgovarao sa svojim prijateljima.

Jovan se mnogo interesovao za stare grčke spomenike.

Jovanu se dopala Dalmacija.

Jovan se dopao mojim roditeljima.

GD 18.3   Questions and Answers
GD 18.3.1   Informational Answers
GD 18.3.1.1 Past Tense with plural subjects of different genders

<u>Subjects in Singular after the past participle:</u>

Gde su bili <u>vaš otac i majka</u>?   Bili su kod kuće.

<u>Moj otac i majka</u> su bili kod kuće.

<u>Moji otac i majka</u> su bili kod kuće.

I <u>otac i majka</u> su bili kod kuće.

vaš sin i kći   gospođa i gospodin Jović   brat i sestra

Tomina žena i dete   vaša sestra i brat   Tomino dete i žena

Gde je bio vaš <u>otac i majka</u>?   I <u>otac i majka</u> su bili kod kuće.

Bili su kod kuće.

<u>Moj otac</u> i majka su bili kod kuće.

Otac je bio u kancelariji, a <u>majka</u> kod kuće.

vaš sin i kći   g. Jović i njegova žena

Gde je bila <u>vaša žena i sin</u>?   <u>Žena</u> je bila kod kuće, a <u>sin</u> ne znam gde je
bio.

Oboje su bili kod kuće.

Bili su kod kuće.

Moja žena i sin su bili kod kuće.

vaša majka i otac   vaša sestra i brat

<u>Subjects in singular before the past participle:</u>

Gde su <u>vaš otac i majka</u> bili?   Bili su kod kuće.
Gde su <u>vaši otac i majka</u> bili?   <u>Moj otac i majka</u> su bili kod kuće.

<u>Moji otac i majka</u> su bili kod kuće.

Tomina žena i sin   Tomino dete i sestra

The following sentences are for the above drill:

Kad su <u>vaš otac i majka</u> došli u Beograd?
Gde su <u>vaš otac i majka</u> proveli praznike?
Gde su <u>vaš otac i majka</u> putovali?

Subjects in plural after the past participle:

With masculine first

Kakvi su bili hoteli i kafane?   Bili su dobri i čisti.

                                                   Nisu bili dobri i čisti.

                                                   Hoteli i kafane su bili čisti.

                                                   Hoteli i kafane nisu bili čisti.

       stanovi i kuće   trgovi i ulice
       bioskopi i pozorišta   gradovi i sela

With feminine first

Kakve su bile kuće i stanovi?   I kuće i stanovi su bili lepi i čisti.

                                                    Kuće su bile lepe, a stanovi nisu.

                                                   Bili su lepi i čisti.

                                                   Ni kuće, ni stanovi nisu bili lepi i čisti.

                                                   Kuće su bile bolje nego stanovi.

       kafane i restorani   ulice i trgovi
       sobe i kupatila   stolice i stolovi

With neuter first

Kakva su bila pozorišta i bioskopi?   I pozorišta i bioskopi su bili dobri.

                                                   Pozorišta su bila dobra, a bioskopi nisu.

                                                 Bili su dobri.

                                                 Ni pozorišta ni bioskopi nisu bili dobri.

                                                 Pozorišta su bila bolja nego bioskopi.

sela i gradovi   pozorišta i kafane   kupatila i sobe

GD 18.3.1.2 Verb Drill

Kako ste putovali do Skoplja?   Putovao sam brzim vozom.

                                                   Putovala sam brzim vozom.

Jovan   vaši roditelji   Putovao sam vrlo udobno.
Zora   g. i g-đa Jović   Putovala sam vrlo udobno.

The following questions and answers are for the above substitution drill:

Gde ste kupili karte?	Karte sam kupio na šalteru.
Gde ste zauzeli sobu za mene?	Zauzeo sam sobu za vas u hotelu Metropol.
Šta ste videli usput?	Video sam divne i interesantne predele.
Šta ste rekli gospodinu Joviću?	Rekao sam mu da dođe kod nas.
Kako ste se proveli na putu?	Proveo sam se vrlo prijatno.

Kuda je prolazio voz?	Voz je prolazio Moravskom dolinom kroz
put autobus	divne i bogate predele.

Šta vas je najviše interesovalo na putu?	Najviše me je interesovala Moravska dolina.
Šta je Zoru najviše interesovalo na putu?	Najviše ju je interesovala Moravska dolina.

Jovan	vaša sestra	vaši prijatelji Amerikanci
vaš prijatelj	g. i g-đa Smit	oni
on		

Drill the following questions and answers with the same substitutions:

Kakav su utisak na vas napravila naša sela i gradovi?	I sela i gradovi su napravili na mene vrlo lep utisak.
Šta vam se najviše dopalo usput?	Najviše su mi se dopali divni predeli i sela.
Šta se Jovanu najviše dopalo usput?	Najviše mu se dopala Moravska dolina kroz koju je voz prolazio.

Zora	vaš prijatelj Jugosloven	on	g. i g-đa Smit
ona	vaša žena	vaš brat	oni

Drill the following questions and answers with the same substitutions:

Šta vam je kazao g. Jovanović?	Kazao mi je da mu je žao što ne može ići s nama u pozorište.
Zar vi niste uzeli taksi?	Nisam.
	Nisam mogao da dobijem taksi. Bilo je rđavo vreme i nije bilo taksija.

on   ona   vaša žena   oni   vaši roditelji

Questions and answers to be used with the above substitutions:

Zar <u>vi</u> niste zauzeli sobu za nas?   Nisam. Mislio sam da možete uvek dobiti
                                                sobu.

Zar ste <u>vi</u> zadocnili za voz?   Pa jesam. Šta da radim. Nisam mogao da
                                                dobijem taksi.

Zašto n<u>iste</u> ušli u čekaonicu?   Nisam još kupio karte.

GD 18.3.2   Yes and No Answers
GD 18.3.2.1 Past Tense with plural subjects of different genders

<u>Subjects in Singular before the past participle:</u>

Da li su <u>vaš otac i majka</u> bili u   Da, bili su.
   Jugoslaviji?   Ne, nisu bili.
Da li su <u>vaši otac i majka</u> bili u   Da, <u>moj otac i majka</u> su bili u **J**ugoslaviji.
   Jugoslaviji?   Ne, <u>moj otac i majka</u> nisu bili u Jugo-
                                                slaviji.

Tomina <u>žena i dete</u>   vaša majka i braća   vaša žena i deca   vaša braća i sestre

Da li su <u>vaš hotel i soba</u> bili   Da, bili su dobri.
   dobri?   Ne, nisu bili dobri.
Da li su <u>vaši hotel i soba</u> bili   Da, <u>moj hotel i soba</u> su bili dobri.
   dobri?   Ne, moj hotel i soba nisu bili dobri.

vaša soba i kupatilo   vaše vino i pivo   vaša supa i meso

<u>Subjects in Plural before the past participle:</u>

<u>With masculine or other genders first:</u>

Da li su <u>hoteli i kafane</u> bili čisti.   Da, bili su čisti.
                                                Ne, nisu bili čisti.
                                                Da, i <u>hoteli i kafane</u> su bili čisti.
                                                Ne, ni <u>hoteli ni kafane</u> nisu bili čisti.
                                                Da, <u>hoteli i kafane</u> su bili čisti.
                                                Ne, <u>hoteli i kafane</u> nisu bili čisti.

sobe i kreveti   ulice i trgovi   pozorišta i bioskopi   sela i gradovi

Subjects in Plural after the past participle:

With masculine first:

Da li su bili čisti hoteli i kafane?   Da, i hoteli i kafane su bili čisti.

                                 Ne, ni hoteli ni kafane nisu bili čisti.

                                 Da, bili su.

                                 Ne, nisu bili.

gradovi i sela   bioskopi i pozorišta   ljudi i žene   vozovi i stanice

With feminine first:

Da li su bile čiste sobe i kreveti?   Da, i sobe i kreveti su bili čisti.

                                 Ne, ni sobe ni kreveti nisu bili čisti.

                                 Da, bili su.

                                 Ne, nisu bili.

kafane i restorani   ulice i trgovi

With neuter first:

Da li su bila čista kupatila i sobe?   Da, i kupatila i sobe su bili čisti.

                                 Ne, ni kupatila ni sobe nisu bili čisti.

                                 Da, bili su.

                                 Ne, nisu bili.

sela i gradovi   pozorišta i bioskopi   gradska prevozna sredstva

GD 18.3.3 Verb Drill

Da li ste pili kafu?   Da, pio sam.

                                 Ne, nisam pio.

                                 Da, pio sam kafu.

                                 Ne, još nisam pio kafu.

Nada   vaš brat   Jovan i Toma

Jovan   vaša majka   vaši prijatelji

Questions for the above drill:

Da li ste govorili sa Nadom?

Da li ste razumeli šta ovaj čovek hoće?

Da li ste zauzeli sobu za mene?

Da li ste uzeli karte za put?

Da li ste kupili sve što vam treba?

Da li su vam se dopala naša sela i gradovi?

Da li ste čuli kako je gospodin Jović?   Jesam.   On je dobro.

                                             Ne, nisam. Šta je s njim?

                                             Da, čuo sam. Bolje mu je.

                                             Ne, nisam čuo. Ne znam kako mu je.

gospođa Jović   g. i g-đa Jović   Tomina žena i deca

vaši prijatelji Jovići   Zora i njena majka

Da niste zadocnili za voz?   Na žalost, jesam.

                                          Hvala Bogu, nisam.

                                          Na žalost, zadocnio sam. Nisam uzeo
                                             taksi.

                                          Hvala Bogu nisam zadocnio. Uzeo sam
                                             taksi.

vaš otac   vaši roditelji   gospodin i gospođa Jović

vaša majka   Tomina deca   Jovići

Questions for the above drill:

Treba mi Jovan, da ga niste videli? Ne nisam.   etc.

Da niste putovali u Zagreb vozom? Kako je putovati vozom?

GD 18.4 Question and Answer Drill with Prompt

Jovan je zadocnio za voz, jer nije   Da li je Jovan zadocnio za voz?
  uzeo taksi.

Jovan nije zadocnio za voz, jer je
  uzeo taksi.

On se bojao da ne zadocni za voz i   Zašto je on uzeo taksi?
  uzeo je taksi.

Ja se bojim da ne zadocnim.   Čega se vi bojite?

Jovan je svršio posao (/posla) i   Da li je Jovan svršio posla?
  sutra se vraća kući.

Ja sam prolazio nekoliko puta kroz
  Moravsku dolinu.

Da li ste prolazili kroz Moravsku
  dolinu?

Ja sam prošao samo jedanput kroz
  Moravsku dolinu.

Nisam prošao (/polazio) nijedanput
  kroz Moravsku dolinu.

Zar niste prosli (/prolazili) nijedanput kroz Moravsku dolinu?

Brzi voz za Skoplje polazi na vreme.

Da li brzi voz za Skoplje polazi na
  vreme?

Vozovi ovde polaze i dolaze na vreme.

Da li ovde vozovi polaze i dolaze na
  vreme?

Voz za Skoplje nije pošao na vreme.

Da li je voz za Skoplje pošao na vreme?

Proveo sam na putu tri dana.

Koliko (vremena) ste proveli na putu?

Proveo sam se na putu vrlo dobro.

Kako ste se proveli na putu?

Nisam se proveo dobro na putu.

Vaši vozovi su pretrpani.

Šta mislite o našim vozovima?

Od Beograda do Velike Plane nisam
  imao mesto.

Da li ste imali mesto u vozu?

Dopali su mi se vaši predeli.

Šta vam se dopalo usput? /Da li su vam
  se dopali naši predeli?

Jovan je ušao u sobu.

Da li je Jovan ušao u sobu? /Gde je
  Jovan?

Jovana interesuju muzeji.

Da li Jovana interesuju muzeji?

Jovana ne interesuju muzeji.

Vaša zemlja je vrlo lepa i bogata.

Kakav je utisak na vas napravila naša
  zemlja?

Mene su najviše interesovali predeli.
  /Ja sam se najviše interesovao
    za predele.

Šta vas je najviše interesovalo na putu?

GD 18.5   Conversations - Razgovori

GD 18.5.1   A   B

Čujem da ste putovali u Skoplje.   Da, točno je. Putovao sam u Skoplje.
    Da li je to točno.

Kojim vlakom ste putovali?   Putovao sam brzim vlakom.

Kakvi su ovdje brzi vlakovi?   Nisu loši. Ne znam šta vas interesira.

Interesira me da li su čisti?   Moj kupe je bio čist.

Kojim razredom ste putovali?   Putovao sam prvim razredom.

Da li je točno da su vlakovi   Da, točno je. Vlakovi su pretrpani.
    pretrpani?

Zašto su vlakovi pretrpani? Zbog   Vlakovi su ovdje glavno prevozno
    čega?   sredstvo. Zato su pretrpani.

Da li ste imali mjesto za sjedenje?   Da, imao sam mjesto za sjedenje.

Da li je bilo dovoljno mjesta (za   Da, bilo je dovoljno mjesta. (Ne, nije
    sjedenje) u prvom razredu?   bilo dovoljno mjesta.)

Da li ste imali društva usput?   Da, razgovarao sam sa nekoliko
                                              Jugoslavena.

Чујем да сте путовали у Скопље.   Да, тачно је. Путовао сам у Скопље.
    Да ли је то тачно?

Којим возом сте путовали?   Путовао сам брзим возом.

Какви су брзи возови овде?   Нису рђави. Не знам шта вас интересује.

Интересује ме да ли су чисти?   Мој купе је био чист.

Којом класом сте путовали?   Путовао сам првом класом.

Да ли је тачно да су возови   Да, тачно је. Возови су претрпани.
    претрпани?

Зашто су возови претрпани?   Возови су овде главно превозно средство.
    Од чега то долази?   Зато су претрпани.

Да ли сте имали место за седење?   Да, имао сам место за седење.

Да ли је било довољно места (за   Да, било је довољно места. (Не, није
    седење) у првој класи?   било довољно места

Да ли сте имали друштва успут?   Да, разговарао сам са неколико
                                              Југословена.

GD 18.5.2

Kako ste se vi i vaš prijatelj proveli na putu u Skoplje?	Proveli smo se jako lijepo. Ali, u malo nismo zakasnili.
Kako to, zar niste uzeli taksi?	Jesmo, ali ja nisam bio gotov na vrijeme. Taksi je morao čekati.
Pa šta je bilo?	Srećom, imali smo toliko vremena da kupimo karte i uđemo u vlak.
Ipak ste bili sretni.	Naravno. Vlak je pošao čim smo mi ušli. Kao da je čekao na nas, pa da pođe.
Jeste imali dobra mjesta?	Jesmo. Sjedeli smo pokraj prozora.
Kako vam se sviđa naša zemlja?	Vlak je prvo prolazio kroz krasne, brdovite predjele, koje ja mnogo volim.
To je još bila okolica Beograda, zar ne?	Jest. Tako je bilo sve do jedne stanice, ne znam kako se zove. Od te stanice vlak je stalno prolazio dolinom rijeke Morave.
To je sigurno Velika Plana ili Lapovo.	Velika Plana. Tu je vlak ušao u Moravsku dolinu.
Jeste li ranije prolazili Moravskom dolinom?	Nisam. Zato me je taj dio puta najviše zanimao.
Pa kako vam se dopala Moravska dolina?	Od prijatelja sam čuo da je vrlo lijepa, ali nisam znao da je tako plodna i bogata.
Da li je brzi vlak stajao[1] često usput?	Nije.
Da li ste izlazili iz vlaka na nekoj stanici?	Da, izlazio sam samo u Nišu.

---

[1] /stàjati/ 'to cost, [Unit 13] to stop, be stopping'

Како сте ви и ваш пријатељ провели на путу у Скопље?	Провели смо се врло лепо. Али, у мало нисмо задоцнили.
Како то, зар нисте узели такси?	Јесмо, али ја нисам био готов на време. Такси је морао да чека.
Па шта је било?	Срећом, имали смо толико времена да купимо карте и уђемо у воз.
Ипак сте били срећни.	Наравно. Воз је пошао чим смо ми ушли. Као да је чекао на нас, па да пође.
Јесте имали добра места?	Јесмо. Седели смо поред прозора.
Како вам се допала наша земља?	Воз је прво пролазио кроз дивне, брдовите пределе, које ја много волим.
То је још била околина Београда, је л'те?	Јесте. Тако је било све до једне станице, не знам како се зове. Од те станице воз је стално пролазио долином реке Мораве.
То је сигурно Велика Плана или Лапово.	Велика Плана. Ту је воз ушао у Моравску долину.
Јесте ли раније пролазили Моравском долином?	Нисам. Зато ме је тај део пута највише интересовао.
Па како вам се допала Моравска долина?	Од пријатеља сам чуо да је врло лепа, али нисам знао да је тако плодна и богата.
Да ли је брзи воз стајао често успут?	Није.
Да ли сте излазили из воза на некој станици?	Да, излазио сам само у Нишу.

GD 18.5.3

Da li je vlak došao na vrijeme u Skoplje?	Pravo da vam kažem nisam obraćao naročito pažnju na to. Ali, mislim da jest.

U koje doba dana ste došli u Skoplje?

Bilo je pred večer, ali još se lijepo vidjelo.

Što vam se dopalo u Skoplju?

Kao što znate, Skoplje ima stari i novi dio grada.

Mi smo bili i u jednom i u drugom dijelu.

Kako vam se svidio stari dio grada.

Meni su se svidjele neke zgrade u starom i novom dijelu grada.

Koje zgrade su vam se svidjele?

Svidio mi se kolodvor, koji je vrlo lijep, iako je nov.

To ste lijepo kazali. Sve nove zgrade zbilja nisu lijepe, ali to nije točno za kolodvor u Skoplju. Zanima me, koje su vam se druge zgrade svidjele?

U Skoplju sam vidio nekoliko lijepih starih zgrada. Naročito mi se svidjela zgrada u kojoj je muzej.

To je sigurno Kuršumli Han.

Jest, tako se zove. Vi mora biti da volite Skoplje, kad se tako dobro sjećate svega.

Da, volim. I milo mi je što se i vama sviđa Skoplje.

Vaša zemlja je zaista jako lijepa i interesantna.

Да ли је воз дошао на време у Скопље?

Право да вам кажем нисам обраћао нарочито пажњу на то. Али, мислим да јесте.

У које доба дана сте дошли у Скопље?

Било је пред вече, али још се лепо видело.

Шта вам се допало у Скопљу?

Као што знате, Скопље има стари и нови део града.

Ми смо били и у једном и у другом делу.

Како вам се допао стари део града?

Мени су се допале неке зграде и у старом и у новом делу града.

Које зграде су вам се допале?

Допала ми се железничка станица, која је врло лепа, иако је нова.

То сте лепо казали. Све нове зграде збиља нису лепе, али то није тачно за станицу у Скопљу. Интересује ме, које су вам се друге зграде допале?

У Скопљу сам видео неколико лепих старих зграда. Нарочито ми се допала зграда у којој је музеј.

То је сигурно Куршумли Хан.

Јесте, тако се зове. Ви мора бити
да волите Скопље, кад се тако добро
сећате свега.

Да, волим. И мило ми је што се и
вама допада Скопље.

Ваша земља је збиља врло лепа и
интересантна.

GD 18.6   <u>Homework - Domaći zadatak</u>

GD 18.6.1 Fill the blank with the proper form of the verb given to the right
            of each sentence.

1.	Moj sin i kći su _____ jutros u Zagreb.	otići	(Gde)
2.	Ovi ljudi i žene su _____ juče iz Beograda.	doći	(Ko)
3.	Moja majka i sestra su _____ taksi od stanice do kuće.	uzeti	(Da li)
4.	Ove gospođe i deca su _____ polazak voza.	čekati	(Šta)
5.	Moj brat i sin su _____ u sobi.	sedeti	(Gde)
6.	Dve gospođe su _____ da razgovaraju s vama.	hteti	(Šta)
7.	Pet ljudi je _____ vozom.	doći	(Koliko)
8.	Pivo i vino su _____ hladni.	biti	(Kakav)
9.	U čekaonici je _____ mnogo ljudi.	čekati	(Da li)
10.	Otac i majka su _____ praznike kod kuće.	provesti	(Gde)
11.	I kuće i stanovi su _____ lepi i čisti.	biti	(Kakav)
12.	Pivo je _____ hladno i dobro, ali vino nije.	biti	(Kakav)

GD 18.6.2 Make questions to which the above sentences will be appropriate
            answers. The question words to be used are given in parentheses.

UNIT 19

Basic Sentences - Osnovne rečenice

Meeting a Friend	Sastanak sa prijateljem	Састанак са пријатељем
	A	
will you go	hóćete li íći	хóħете ли и̏ħи
Are you going to go to the National Museum today?	Hóćete li íći dánas u Národni múzēj?	Хо̏ħете ли и̏ħи да̀нас у На̏родни му̑зēј? #
	B	
I'll go	íći ću	и̏ħи ħу
this afternoon	dánas pòslije pódne	да̏нас по̏сле по̑дне
Yes, I'm going this afternoon.	Dà, íći ću dánas pòslije pódne.	Да, и̏ħи ħу да̀нас после по̑дне.
to eat lunch, noon meal	rúčati, rȕčām	ру̏чати, ру̀ча̑м
I'll eat lunch	rúčaću / rúčat ću (Cr)	ру̏чаħу
cafeteria	ékspres-restórān	ékспрес-ресто́рāн
I'll eat lunch in a cafeteria.	Rúčat ću u jednom ékspres-restoránu.	Ру̏чаħу у је̏дном éкспрес-ресто́рāну.
lunch, noon meal	rúčak, G. rȕčka	ру̏чак, ру̏чка
And immediately after lunch I'm going to the museum.	I òdmah pòslije rȕčka ídem u múzēj.	И о̀дма̑х после ру̏чка идем у му̑зēј.
	A	
to remain, stay	óstati, da óstanēm	о́стати, да о̏станēм
you'll stay	vȋ ćete óstati	ви̑ ħете о̏стати
How long are you going to be ('stay') in the museum?	Kòliko ćete óstati u muzéju?	Колѝко ħете о̏стати у музе́ју?
	B	
I'll stay	óstaću / óstat ću (Cr)	о̀стаħу
while	dòk	до̏к

until	dok nè	док нè
to look over	rázgledati, da rázgledām	рàзгледати, да рàзгледāм
I'll stay until I see everything that interests me.	Óstat ću dok ne rázgledam svè što me zánīmā.	Остàħу док не рàзгледāм свè што ме ѝнтересује.
whole	cìjel (/cìo), cijéla, -o	цèо, цéла, цéло
That'll certainly be all afternoon.	Tȏ će bìti sìgurno cijélo póslije pódne.	Тȏ ħе бити сигурно цéло после пȍдне.
perhaps, maybe	váljda	вàљда
or,	móžda	мȍжда
to forget (with /na/)	zabóraviti, da zabóravīm	забȍравити, да забȍравӣм
meeting, appointment	sástanak G sástānka pl. sástānci	сáстанак сáстāнка сáстāнци
You haven't forgotten our meeting by any chance?	Nìste móžda zabóravili na nȁš sástanak?	Нисте вàљда забȍравили на наш сáстэнак?#
I wouldn't like	nè bih žélio	не бих жéлео
again	ópēt	ȍпēт
to happen	dèsiti se, da se dèsī	дèсити се, да се дèсӣ
or	dogóditi se, da se dógodī	догодити се, да се дȍгодӣ
No, I haven't. I wouldn't want that to happen again.	Nè, nìsam. Nè bih žélio da se to ópet dógodī.	Нè, нисам. Не бих жéлео да се тȏ опет дèсӣ.

A

to return, refl. to get back	vrátiti se, da se vrátīm	врáтити се, да се врáтӣм
you'll return	vȋ ćete se vrátiti	ви ħете се врáтити
Will you get back home by seven?	Dà li ćete se vrátiti dòma do sèdam?	Дà ли ħете се врáтити куħи до сèдам?#

B

to depend (on: /od/)	závisiti, závisī	зависити зависӣ
I'll be kept	jȁ ću se zadržati	јȁ ћу се задржати
That depends on how long I spend ('I'll be kept') in the museum.	Tȏ závisi od tȍga kȍliko ću se zadržati u muzéju.	Тȏ зависи од тȍга колико ћу се задржати у музéју.
to close	zatvárati, zátvārām	затвáрати, зȃтвāрāм
is closed	zátvārā se	зȃтвāрā се
When does the museum close?	Kȁd se zátvara múzēj?	Кад се затвара музеј?

A

since, as; after	pòšto	пòшто
to open	otvóriti, da ótvorīm	отвóрити, да óтворӣм
open; openhearted	ótvoren, -a, -o	óтворен, -а -о
Since today's Friday, the museum is open till 7:00.	Pȍšto je dȁnas pȇtak, múzej je ótvoren do 19:00 sátī.	Пȍшто је дȁнас пȇтак, музеј је отворен до 19:00 часōвā.

B

I won't be able	nȅću mȏći	нȅћу мȏћи
Then I won't be able to get home by seven.	Ȍnda se nȅću mȏći vrátiti dòma do sèdam.	Ȍнда се нȅћу мȏћи врȁтити кȕћи до сȅдам.
to, toward (with D) dinner, evening meal	k, ka vèčera	к, ка вèчера
But do you know what, come over to my place for dinner after seven-thirty.	Znȃte štȁ, dȏđite vȋ k mèni pòslije pȍla ȍsam na vèčeru.	Него знȃте штȁ, дóђите вȋ код мене после пола ȍсам на вèчеру.

A

| All right. | U rȇdu. | У рȇду. |

B

up to certain point of time or space	dòtlē	дòтлē
to arrive	stȉći, da stȉgnēm, stȉgao	стȉћи, да стȉгнēм, стȉгао
I'll arrive	jā̀ ću stȉći	jā̀ ћу стȉћи
I'll probably be home by then.	Dòtle ću mòžda stȉći kùći.	Дòтле ћу ва̀ьда стȉћи кȕћи.
we'll eat supper	mȋ ćemo vèčerati	мȋ ћемо вèчерати
during (with G)	za vrijéme	за врȇме
peace	mȉr G mȋra	мȉр, мȋра
quietly, undisturbed	na mȋru	на мȋру
Then we'll have dinner together and talk about everything at leisure, during dinner.	Ònda ćemo zȁjedno vèčerati i za vrijéme vèčere u mȋru razgovárati o svèmu.	Ònда ћемо за̏jедно вèчерати и за врȇме вèчере на мȋру разговárати о свèму.

A

convenient	zgòdan, zgòdna, -o	згòдан, згòдна, -о
the most convenient	nȁjzgódnijī, -ā, -ē	на̏jзгóднијī, -ā, -ē
Fine, that's perhaps the most convenient.	Dòbro, tȁko je mòžda nȁjzgódnijē.	Дòбро, тȁко je мòжда на̏jзгóднијē.

NOTES

Note 19.1 Verb: Future

a) Koliko ćete ostati u muzeju?

b) Ostaću dok ne razgledam sve što me interesuje.

c) Hoćete li ići danas u Narodni muzej?

d) Onda se neću moći vratiti kući do sedam.

There are two basic types of future constructions. Both involve the present forms of the verb /htèti/ (see Note 13.4 and the examples of /htèti/). This verb, like /bìti/, has short, long and negative forms:

Short		Long		Negative	
ću	ćemo	hóću	hóćemo	nèću	nèćemo
ćeš	ćete	hòćeš	hóćete	nèćeš	nèćete
će	ćē	hòće	hóćē	nèće	nèćē

One future construction, illustrated in b) above, suffixes the short present tense forms of /htèti/ to the stem of the verb. The form of the stem is usually the same as in the infinitive. (see Note 20.1 for variants).

rȕčati	rȕča-ću
ósta-ti	ósta-ću
véčera-ti	véčera-ćemo
vráti-ti	vráti-će
dóbi-ti	dóbi-ću

This kind of construction occurs only in the affirmative. A variant spelling (with no difference in pronunciation) is used in Croatia: /ostat ću/, /večerat ćemo/, /vratit će/, /dobit ću/.

If the infinitive ends in /-ći/, two forms are possible. The whole infinitive may be followed by /ću/, /ćeš/, etc. (this is considered standard) or the stem which occurs before /-ći/ may have /ću/, /ćeš/, etc. suffixed:

íći	íći ću	or	íću
dóći	dóći ću	or	dóću
stȉći	stȉći ću	or	stȉću

The shorter forms are often used but are not considered standard.

This first type of construction - stem plus /-ću/. etc. - is used when there is no emphasis on the subject and the verb comes first in the clause.

The second type of future formation has the present of /hteti/ followed by the infinitive. This is illustrated by a), c), d). The short form /ćete/ occurs in a), the long form /hoćete/ in c) and the negative /neću/ in d). In this construction the emphasis is upon some factor other than the action indicated by the infinitive. Question words, such as /koliko/, and constructions such as /da li/ normally come first in the clause, as in a). In future questions the auxiliary verb frequently comes first, as in c). The emphasis may also be on other words, such as /onda/ in d). Compare:

To će biti sigurno celo posle podne.	Emphasis on referent /to/
Da li ćeti se vratiti kući do sedam?	Emphasis on question
To zavisi od toga koliko ću se zadržati u muzeju.	Emphasis on /koliko/
Dotle ću valjda stići kući.	Emphasis on /dotle/
Onda ćemo zajedno večerati.	Emphasis on /onda/

This second type of future construction is, of course, regularly used when the subject is expressed either by a preceding noun or pronoun: /moja majka će ići/, /ja ću ići/. It is regularly used after 'clause introducers', such as the question words /koliko/, /kàd/, etc. (see above), as well as others such as /štò/, /da/, etc. For example: /Mislim da ću ostati u muzeju celo posle podne./ In summary, the future forms using /ići/ as the example, are:

Type 1

Stem +				Infinitive +	
óstaću	óstaćemo	íću	ićemo	íći ću	íći ćemo
óstaćeš	óstaćete	íćeš	ićete	íći ćeš	íći ćete
óstaće	óstaće	íće	íće	íći će	íći će

Type 2

Affirmative   Negative

Unemphatic				Interrogative		

-ću	íći	da li ću íći	hòću li íći	nèću íći
-ćeš	íći	da li ćeš íći	hòćeš li íći	nèćeš íći
-će	íći	da li će íći	hòće li íći	nèće íći
-ćemo	íći	da li ćemo íći	hòćemo li íći	nèćemo íći
-ćete	íći	da li ćete íći	hòćete li íći	nèćete íći
-će	íći	da li će íći	hòće li íći	nèćē íći

Note: Questions without /li/ also occur. For example, /hoćete li íći/ may be replaced by /hoćete íći/ with question intonation.

Both perfective and imperfective verbs occur in the future. Verbs used in the Basic Sentences of this unit as futures are:

Perfective	Imperfective
óstati	íći
rázgledati	móći
zabóraviti	rúčati
vrátiti se	véčerati
stìći	

It is more common for most verbs to occur in the perfective, as the future generally refers to the anticipated completion of the act. 'We'll return', 'we'll forget' are more frequently used than 'we'll be returning', 'we'll be forgetting'. On the other hand, imperfective verbs like 'be able', 'dine' are frequent in future use.

Compare the English and Serbo-Croatian for past, present and future of 'give':

	Imperfective			Perfective	
Present	dájēmo	we're giving	Present	dòk ne dāmo	until we give
Past	dávali smo	we were giving	Past	dáli smo	we gave
Future	dávaćemo	we'll be giving	Future	dàćemo	we'll give

The most frequently used forms are the imperfective present 'we're giving', the perfective past and future 'we gave', 'we'll give'.

It should be noted that negative future questions are uncommon. An example is /Nećete li ići danas u Narodni muzej?/.

It should also be mentioned that the future of /želeti/ and /hteti/ (see GD 19.2.2) are used only in the second and third persons.

Note 19.2 Verb: Review of Aspect

The following charts contrast the use of familiar English constructions with the use of different aspects in Serbo-Croatian.

	Action in Process	Repetitive/Habitual Action	Completed Action
Present:	I'm drinking coffee now	I drink coffee every day.	
Past:	I was drinking coffee, when John came.	I drank coffee every day or I used to drink coffee every day.	I drank the coffee and went away.
Future:	I'll be drinking coffee when John comes.	I'll drink coffee every day.	I'll drink the coffee and go away.

	Action in Process	Repetitive/Habitual Action	Completed Action
Present:	Ja pijem kafu sada.	Ja pijem kafu svaki dan.	
Past:	Ja sam pio kafu, kad je Jovan došao.	Ja sam pio kafu svaki dan.	Ja sam popio kafu i otišao.
Future:	Ja ću piti kafu, kad Jovan dođe.	Ja ću piti kafu svaki dan.	Ja ću popiti kafu i otići.

Note 19.3   New Verbs

a	I	rúčati	rùčām		to eat lunch
a	I	véčerati	véčerām		to eat dinner
i	I	závisiti	závisī		to depend
i	P	dèsiti se	da se dèsī		to happen
a	I	dešávati se	déšāvā se		
i	P	dogóditi se	da se dógodī		to happen
a	I	dogáđati se	dógađā se		
V/n	P	óstati	da óstanēm		to stay, remain
a/Jē	I	óstajati	óstajēm		
i	P	otvóriti	da ótvorīm		to open
a	I	otvárati	ótvārām		
a	P	rázgledati	da rázgledām		to look over
a	I	razglédati	rázglēdām		
		/razglédāvati	/razglédāvām		
C/n	P	stíći	da stìgnēm	stìgao	to arrive
		/stìgnuti			
a/Jē	I	stìzati	stìžēm		
i	P	vrátiti (se)	da (se) vràtīm		to return
a	I	vràćati (se)	vràćām (se)		
i	P	zatvóriti	da zátvorīm		to close, shut
a	I	zatvárati	zátvārām		

Grammatical Drill

19.1   Learning Drill - Vežba za učenje

19.1.1 Future Tense - Substitution Drill - Buduće vreme - Vežba sa zamenom

Verbs: /vratiti se/ and /ići/

First Person - Prvo lice

Singular - Jednina	Plural - Množina
Vratiću se kući do sedam.	Vratićemo se kući do sedam.
Ja ću se vratiti kući do sedam.	Mi ćemo se vratiti kući do sedam.
Neću se vratiti kući do sedam.	Nećemo se vratiti kući do sedam.

431

Ja se neću vratiti kući do sedam.   <u>Mi</u> se nećemo vratiti kući do sedam.

Ići ću danas posle podne u Narodni   Ići ćemo danas posle podne u Narodni
    muzej.   muzej.

Ja ću ići danas posle podne u Narodni   <u>Mi</u> ćemo ići danas posle podne u
    muzej.   Narodni muzej.

Neću ići danas posle podne u Narodni   Nećemo ići danas posle podne u
    muzej.   Narodni muzej.

Ja neću ići danas posle podne u   <u>Mi</u> nećemo ići danas posle podne u
    Narodni muzej.   Narodni muzej.

       Substitutions for /mi/:

           otac i ja   majka i ja   kći i ja   žena i ja

Second Person - Drugo lice

Čekaćeš me na večeru do sedam.   Čekaćete me na večeru do sedam.

Ti ćeš me čekati na večeru do sedam.   <u>Vi</u> ćete me čekati na večeru do sedam.

Nećeš me čekati na večeru do sedam.   Nećete me čekati na večeru do sedam.

Ti me nećeš čekati na večeru do sedam. <u>Vi</u> me nećete čekati na večeru do sedam.

Ući ćeš u voz odmah čim dozvole.   Ući ćete u voz odmah čim dozvole.

Ti ćeš ući u voz odmah čim dozvole.   <u>Vi</u> ćete ući u voz odmah čim dozvole.

Nećeš ući u voz odmah čim dozvole.   Nećete ući u voz odmah čim dozvole.

Ti nećeš ući u voz odmah čim dozvole.   <u>Vi</u> nećete ući u voz odmah čim dozvole.

       Substitutions for /vi/:

otac i vi   vi i vaša kći   gospođa i vi   vi i Tomin sin

vaš muž   vi i dete

Third Person - Treće lice

Ručaće u ekspres-restoranu.   Ručaće u ekspres-restoranu.

<u>On</u> će ručati u ekspres-restoranu.   <u>Oni</u> će ručati u ekspres-restoranu.

Neće ručati u ekspres-restoranu.   Neće ručati u ekspres-restoranu.

<u>On</u> neće ručati u ekspres-restoranu.   <u>Oni</u> neće ručati u ekspres-restoranu.

Stići će na vreme za voz.   Stići će na vreme za voz.

<u>On</u> će stići na vreme za voz.   <u>Oni</u> će stići na vreme za voz.

Neće stići na vreme za voz.   Neće stići na vreme za voz.

<u>On</u> neće stići na vreme za voz.   <u>Oni</u> neće stići na vreme za voz.

Substitutions for /on/:

Jovan	ona	vaše dete
vaš sin	vaša žena	Tomin prijatelj
Tomina kći		

Substitutions for /oni/:

Jovan i Toma	one
vaši roditelji	vaše sestre
g. i g-đa Jović	g-đa i g-ca Jović

GD 19.1.2   Present Tense with Future Transform

Present Tense

Verb /vraćati se/

Vraćam se u Beograd iduće nedelje.

ti	Ti se vraćaš u Beograd iduće nedelje.
on	On se vraća u Beograd iduće nedelje.
Toma	Toma se vraća u Beograd iduće nedelje.
Ona	Ona se vraća u Beograd iduće nedelje.
moja žena	Moja žena se vraća u Beograd iduće nedelje.
mi	Mi se vraćamo u Beograd iduće nedelje.
žena i ja	Žena i ja se vraćamo u Beograd iduće nedelje.
vi	Vi se vraćate u Beograd iduće nedelje.
oni	Oni se vraćaju u Beograd iduće nedelje.
žena i deca	Žena i deca se vraćaju u Beograd iduće nedelje.

Future Tense

Verb /vratiti se/

Vratiću se u Beograd iduće nedelje.

Ti ćeš se vratiti u Beograd iduće nedelje.

On će se vratiti u Beograd iduće nedelje.

Toma će se vratiti u Beograd iduće nedelje.

Ona će se vratiti u Beograd iduće nedelje.

Moja žena će se vratiti u Beograd iduće nedelje.

Mi ćemo se vratiti u Beograd iduće nedelje.

Žena i ja ćemo se vratiti u Beograd iduće nedelje.

Vi ćete se vratiti u Beograd iduće nedelje.

Oni će se vratiti u Beograd iduće nedelje.

Žena i deca će se vratiti u Beograd iduće nedelje.

The following sentences are for the same type of drill:

stizati, stižem - stići, da stignem

Stižem u Beograd u petak.   Stići ću u Beograd u petak.

ići, idem

Idem opet u muzej danas posle podne.   Ići ću opet u muzej danas posle podne.

dolaziti, dolazim - doći, da dođem

Dolazim kući (uvek) u sedam sati.   Doći ću (danas) kući u sedam sati.

večerati, večeram

Subotom večeram u restoranu.   U subotu ću večerati u restoranu.

Repeat the above drill with negative transform e.g.

Ne vraćam se u Sarajevo iduće nedelje.   Neću se vratiti u Sarajevo iduće nedelje.

GD   19.1.3   Future Tense with Past Tense transform

	Vratiću se u Sarajevo u subotu.	Vratio sam se u Sarajevo u subotu.
on	On će se vratiti u Sarajevo u subotu.	On se vratio u Sarajevo u subotu.
Jovan	Jovan će se vratiti u Sarajevo u subotu.	Jovan se vratio u Sarajevo u subotu.
Zora	Zora će se vratiti u Sarajevo u subotu.	Zora se vratila u Sarajevo u subotu.
mi	Mi ćemo se vratiti u Sarajevo u subotu.	Mi smo se vrati i u Sarajevo u subotu.
vi	Vi ćete se vratiti u Sarajevo u subotu, je l'te?	Vi ste se vratili u Sarajevo, u subotu, je l'te?
oni	Oni će se vratiti u Sarajevo u subotu.	Oni su se vratili u Sarajevo u subotu.
vaši prijatelji	Vaši prijatelji će se vratiti u Sarajevo u subotu, je l'te?	Vaši prijatelji su se vratili u Sarajevo u subotu, je l'te?
vaše sestre	Vaše sestre će se vratiti u Sarajevo u subotu, je l'te?	Vaše sestre su se vratile u Sarajevo u subotu, je l'te?

The following sentences are for the same type of drill:

Ostaću u kancelariji do sedam sati.	Ostao sam u kancelariji do sedam sati.
Biću u muzeju celo posle podne.	Bio sam u muzeju celo posle podne.
Stići ću na vreme za brzi voz.	Stigao sam na vreme za brzi voz.
Doći ću u 8 sati.	Došao sam u 8 sati.
Večeraću kod kuće.	Večerao sam kod kuće.
Uzeću red vožne na stanici.	Uzeo sam red vožnje na stanici.
Uneću stvari u brzi voz.	Uneo sam stvari u brzi voz.

Repeat the above drills in the negative:

Neću se vratiti u Beograd u subotu.	Nisam se vratio u Beograd u subotu, etc.

Include in the negative drill the following sentences:

Neću moći da dođem kod vas u subotu.	Nisam mogao da dođem kod vas u subotu.

GD 19.2   Substitution-Correlation Drill

GD 19.2.1   Future Tense

Ostaću u muzeju dok ne razgledam sve što me interesuje.

Toma	oni	moji roditelji
Zora	žena i kći	g. i g-đa Jović

The following sentences are for the above type of drill:

To zavisi od toga koliko ću se zadržati u muzeju.
Vratiću se iz muzeja čim razgledam sve što me interesuje.
Onda ću popiti kafu pre nego što pođe voz.
Dotle ću valjda stići kući.
Ne znam da li ću doći kući na vreme.

Present Tense with Future transform:

Toma se vraća danas iz Zagreba.	Toma će se vratiti danas iz Zagreba.

Zora	mi	naši prijatelji	Toma i Jovan

The following sentences are for the same type of drill:

Toma stiže danas kući.	Toma će stići danas kući.
Toma ide danas u kancelariju iako je subota.	Toma će ići danas u kancelariju, iako je subota.

Toma dolazi vozom iz Zagreba.   Toma će doći vozom iz Zagreba.

Toma večera subotom u restoranu.   Toma će večerati u subotu u restoranu.

Toma ruča danas u ekspres-restoranu.   Toma će ručati danas u ekspres-
                                         restoranu.

Future Tense with Past Tense transform:

Doći ćemo sa stanice taksijem.   Došli smo sa stanice taksijem.

moja žena i deca   moja sestra   Toma i Jovan   oni   mi

The following sentences are for the same type of drill:

Žena i ja ćemo večerati kod Metropola.   Žena i ja smo večerali kod Metropola.

Ostaćemo u Dalmaciji dve nedelje.   Ostali smo u Dalmaciji dve nedelje.

Bićemo kod kuće za vreme praznika.   Bili smo kod kuće za vreme praznika.

Zadržaćemo se u gradu malo duže.   Zadržali smo se u gradu malo duže.

Stići ćemo kući dockan u noć.   Stigli smo kući dockan u noć.

Razgovaraćemo o svemu na miru za   Razgovarali smo o svemu na miru za
  vreme večere.   vreme večere.

GD 19.2.2 Verb /želeti/ varying with /hteti/

Želim da idem danas u Narodni muzej.   Hoću da idem danas u Narodni muzej.

Ne želim da idem danas u Narodni muzej. Neću da idem danas u Narodni muzej.

Želeo sam da idem danas u Narodni   Hteo sam da idem danas u Narodni muzej,
  muzej, ali ne mogu ići, zbog posla.   ali ne mogu ići, zbog posla.

Jovan   moja kći   naši srodnici

On će sigurno želeti da ide u Narodni   On će sigurno hteti da ide u Narodni
  muzej.   muzej.

deca   gospoda   naši jugoslovenski prijatelji

moj sin   g. i g-đa Jović   vaši američki prijatelji

GD 19.3   Questions and Answers
GD 19.3.1   Informational Answers
GD 19.3.1.1 Substitution Drill

436

Use of vi-form - Upotreba vi-oblika

Kad ćete ići, gospodine, na železničku
  stanicu?

Danas posle podne.

Kad ćete ići, gospođo, na železničku
  stanicu?

Ići cu danas posle podne na železničku
  stanicu.

Još ne znam.

Još ne znam kad ću ići na železničku
  stanicu.

Kad ćete ići, <u>gospodo,</u> na železničku
  stanicu?

Danas posle podne.

Ići ćemo danas posle podne na
  železničku stanicu.

Još ne znamo.

Još ne znamo kad ćemo ići na
  železničku stanicu.

Substitutes for /vi/:

vi i vaša porodica

vi i vaša majka

vi i vaš muž

vi i brat

Use of Third Person - Upotreba trećeg lica

Singular - Jednina

Kad će <u>Jovan</u> ići na put.

Sutra posle podne.

On će ići   na put sutra posle podne.

Ne znam.

Ne znam kad će <u>Jovan</u> ići na put.

Substitutions for /Jovan/:

on	vaš otac	ona
vaša majka	njen sin	Zorin sin

Plural - Množina

Kad će <u>oni</u> ići na izlet?

Sutra posle podne.

<u>Oni</u> će ići na izlet sutra posle podne.

Ništa ne znam o tome.

Ne znam kad će <u>oni</u> ići na izlet.

Substitutions for /oni/:

njihovi srodnici	vaši majka i sestra	deca
Zorini prijatelji	one	vaša braća
vaši roditelji	vaše sestre	ta gospoda

GD 19.3.1.2 Substitution-Correlation Drill

Koliko ćete se zadržati na sastanku?   Najviše sat-dva.

Zadržaću se najviše jedan do dva sata.

Ne znam tačno.

Ne znam tačno koliko ću se zadržati na sastanku.

vi (pl)   vaša majka   vaši prijatelji   g. i g-đa Smit

The following questions with short answers are for the above type of drill:

Koliko ćete ostati u Skoplju?	Samo dva dana.
Gde ćete biti danas posle podne?	Kod kuće.
Gde ćete sutra večerati?	Kod Metropola.
Kad ćete razgovariti sa g. Jovićem?	Sutra posle podne.
Kad ćete stići u Jugoslaviju?	Iduće nedelje.
Kakav ćete stan imati u Beogradu?	Imaću mali stan.
Koliku ćete kuću imati u Zagrebu?	Imaću malu kuću.
Kad ćete ići na letovanje?	Ove subote.
Gde ćete danas ručati?	Ručaću u ekspres-resotranu.

GD 19.3.2 Yes and No Answers

Hoćete (li) ići danas na poštu?   Da, hoću. /Da, ići ću.

Ne, neću. /Ne, neću ići.

Da li ćete ići danas na poštu.   Da, ići ću danas na poštu.

Ne, neću ići danas na poštu.

Zar ćete ići danas na poštu?   Da, hoću.

Da, ići ću danas na poštu.

Zar nećete ići danas na poštu.   Na žalost neću.

Na žalost neću ići danas na poštu.

Nemam vremena.

Pa možda ću ipak ići, ali nije sigurno
Zavisi od posla.

Da nećete ići danas na poštu?

Verovatno da ću ići. Pre da hoću nego
da neću.

Nije sigurno, možda neću.

(vi [pl])	Zora	g. i g-đa Jović
Toma	vaša majka	vaši jugoslovenski prijatelji

The following questions are for the above type of drill:

Hoćete (li) ići ove godine na letovanje?

Hoćete (li) biti večeras kod kuće?

Hoćete (li) se zadržati dugo u Zagrebu?

Hoćete (li) stići na vreme za voz?

Hoćete (li) doći na sastanak sa Jovanom?

Hoćete (li) se vratiti kući do pola osam?

GD 19.4 Question and Answers Drill with Prompt

Još nisam išao u Narodni muzej.

Da li ste išli u Narodni muzej?

Danas posle podne ću ići u Narodni
muzej.

Hoćete (li) ići danas u Narodni muzej?

Još nisam ručao.

Da li ste ručali?

Ručaću u jednom ekspres-resotranu.

Gde ćete ručati?

Biću u muzeju celo posle podne.

Da li ćete biti u muzeju celo posle
podne?

Ostaću u muzeju dok ne razgledam sve
što me interesuje.

Koliko ćete ostati u muzuje?

Neću se vratiti kući do sedam.

Da li ćete se vratiti kući do sedam?

Zadržaću se u muzeju do pola osam.

Dokle ćete se zadržati u muzeju?

Dotle ću (do osam) valjda stići kući.

Da li ćete doći kući do osam?

Još nisam večerao.

Da li ste večerali?

Toma i ja ćemo zajedno večerati.

S kim ćete večerati?

Nisam zaboravio na naš sastanak.

Da li ste zaboravili na naš sastanak?

Još nisam razgovarao s Tomom o vašoj
stvari.

Da li ste razgovarali s Tomom o mojoj
stvari?

Za vreme večere ćemo na miru razgovarati o tome.

Kad ćete razgovarati s njim o tome?

Moji otac i majka još nisu došli u
Beograd.

Da li su vaši otac i majka došli u
Beograd?

439

Oni će doći kroz tri dana.   Kad će oni doći?

Oni će stići u subotu uveče.   Kad će oni stići u Beograd?

Majka i žena još nisu došle kući.   Da li su vaša gospođa majka i žena
                                             došle kući?

One će se zadržati u gradu malo duže.   Koliko će se one zadržati u gradu?

Vratiće se kući oko osam.   Kad će se vratiti kući?

Želim (/Želeo bih) da vidim Narodni   Šta želite da vidite?
  muzej.

Hoću (/Hteo bih) da vidim Narodni
  muzej.

Moji prijatelji će sigurno želeti da   Da li vaši prijatelji žele da vide
  vide Narodni muzej.   Narodni muzej?

Moji prijatelji će sigurno hteti da
  vide Narodni muzej.

GD 19.5   Conversations - Razgovori

GD 19.5.1   A   B

Je li vaš prijatelj došao u Beograd?   Ne, još nije.

Da li znate kad će doći?   Da, on dolazi u subotu, ako vrijeme
                                             dozvoli.

Čega zajedničkog ima vrijeme s tim?   To je jako prosto. On dolazi avionom.

Naravno.   A u ovo doba godine vrijeme je obično
                                             loše.

Da, to je razumljivo. Da li će on   Ne, on dolazi preko Pariza. Javio je da
  doći pravo iz Amerike.   će se zadržati nekoliko dana u Parizu.

Onda nije sigurno da će on doći i u   Može biti, u Parizu čovjek obično
  subotu, ako ne mora.   ostane duže nego što misli.

Da, to se često događa.   Ja sam jedanput ostao u Parizu, dvije
                                             nedjelje, iako sam mislio da ostanem
                                             samo tri dana.

Da, samo ako imate sredstava.   Točno je tako. Ostao sam dok imao
                                             novaca.

Да ли је ваш пријатељ дошао у Београд?

Не, још није.

Да ли знате кад ће доћи?

Да, он долази у суботу, ако време дозволи.

Какве везе има време с тим?

То је врло просто. Он долази авионом.

Наравно.

А у ово доба године време је обично рђаво.

Да, то је разумљиво. Да ли ће он доћи право из Америке?

Не, он долази преко Париза. Јавио је да ће се задржати неколико дана у Паризу.

Онда није сигурно да ће доћи и у суботу, ако не мора.

Може бити, у Паризу човек обично остане дуже него што мисли.

Да, то се често дешава.

Ја сам једанпут остао у Паризу две недеље, иако сам мислио да останем само три дана.

Да, само ако имате средстава.

Тачно је тако. Остао сам док сам имао новаца.

GD 19.5.2

Da li ćete večeras biti kod kuće?

Ne, nećemo.

Gdje idete?

Idemo u Narodno kazalište.

U koliko sati počinje kazalište?

Kazalište počinje točno u pola osam.

Jeste li večerali?

Nismo.

Pa kad ćete večerati. Sada je već sedam.

Večeraćemo posle kazališta.

Gdje ćete večerati? Da nije kasno?

Večeraćemo kod Metropola.

Zar se može večerati tako kasno kod Metropola?

Da, može tako reći[1] u svako doba.

To je jako dobro.

Da, mi smo već nekoliko puta večerali kod Metropola poslije kina ili kazališta.

To je jako zgodno.

Da, jest.

---

[1] /tako reći/ 'almost'

Да ли ћете вечерас бити код куће?

Не, нећемо.

Где идете?

Идемо у Народно позориште.

У колико сати почиње позориште?

Позориште почиње тачно у пола осам.

Јесте вечерали?

Нисмо.

Па кад ћете вечерати. Сада је
   већ седам.

Вечераћемо после позоришта.

Где ћете вечерати? Да није доцкан?

Вечераћемо код Метропола.

Зар се може вечерати тако доцкан код
   Метропола?

Да, може тако рећи у свако доба.

То је врло добро.

Да, ми смо већ неколико пута вечерали
   код Метропола после биоскопа или
   позоришта.

То је врло згодно.

Да, јесте.

GD 19.5.3

Koliko ćete ostati u Zagrebu?

Ostaću još sutra.

Zar nećete ostati duže?

Neću. Prekosutra moram biti u
   Beogradu.

Mi smo mislili da ćete ostati bar
   četiri-pet dana.

I ja sam želio ostati duže, ali na
   žalost ne mogu.

Da li ćete dolaziti skoro opet?

Ne znam točno, ali kad dođemo drugi
   put, ostaćemo bar tri-četiri dana.

To je najmanje[1], ako želite upoznati
   grad i okolicu.

Da, ja bih želio upoznati Zagreb.
   Mnogo mi se dopadaju i grad i okolica.

Gdje ćete danas ići?

Nećemo ići nigdje.

Ovde ima vrlo lijepih muzeja. Ja
   sam mislio da ćete razgledati
   neki muzej.

Ne, danas ćemo razgledavati sam grad.
   Moja žena želi vidjeti ulice, trgove
   i parkove.

To je jako dobro.

Za muzeje treba više vremena nego što
   mi imamo.

Da, to je točno.

Vrijeme je lijepo i bar ćemo vidjeti
   kako izgleda grad.

---

[1] /najmanje/ 'least, the minimum'

Колико ћете остати у Загребу?

Зар нећете остати дуже?

Ми смо мислили да ћете остати бар
четири-пет дана.

Да ли ћете долазити скоро опет?

То је најмање, ако желите да упознате
град и околину.

Где ћете данас ићи?

Овде има врло лепих музеја. Ја сам
мислео да ћете ићи да разгледате
неки музеј.

То је врло добро.

Да, то је тачно.

Остаћу још сутра.

Нећу. Прекосутра морам бити у Београду.

И ја сам желео да останем дуже, али
на жалост не могу.

Не знам тачно, али кад дођемо други пут,
остаћемо бар три-четири дана.

Да, ја бих желео да упознам Загреб.
Много ми се допадају и град и околина.

Нећемо ићи нигде нарочито.

Не, данас ћемо разгледати сам град.
Моја жена жели да види улице, тргове
и паркове.

За музеје треба више времена него што
ми имамо.

Време је лепо и бар ћемо видети како
изгледа град.

GD 19.6   Homework - Domaći zadatak

GD 19.6.1 Complete sentences 1-6 using the future of the verb given to the right, in the person indicated either by the sentence or by the pronoun in brackets. The pronoun is not to be used. Change sentences 7-10 to the future, changing the aspect of the verb if appropriate.

1. _____ u muzeju celo posle podne.   ([ja] - ostati)
2. _____ kući iz kancelarije do pola osam. ([mi] - vratiti se)
3. Jovan i Zora _____ večeras kod kuće.   (biti)
4. Moj muž _____ u kancelariji duže nego obično. (zadržati se)
5. _____ o tome na miru za vreme večere.   ([mi] - razgovarati)
6. _____ posle pozorišta kod Metropola.   ([oni] - večerati)
7. Jovići dolaze večeras kod nas.
8. Ja se vraćam u subotu iz Zagreba.
9. Brzi voz iz Zagreba stiže na vreme.
10. Ja razgovaram srpskohrvatski s mojim jugoslovenskim prijateljima.

GD 19.6.2 Make questions to which the above sentences are appropriate answers.

UNIT 20

Basic Sentences - Osnovne rečenice

Seeing the Sights	Znamenitosti grada	Знаменитости града
	A	
to put up, stay (for a short time)	ódsjesti, da ódsjednēm, ódsjeo	óдсести, да óдседнēм, óдсео
What hotel are you in ('in which hotel did you put up?')?	U kŏm hotelu ste ódsjeli?	у кŏм хотелу сте óдсели? #
	B	
We're in the Metropol.	Ódsjeli smo u hotelu Metrópol.	óдсели смо у хòтелу Метрóпол.
	A	
to find	nā́ći, da nàđēm, nàšao	нā́ћи, да нàђēм, нàшао
Have you found a place to live?	Dà li ste nàšli stȁn?	Дà ли сте нашли стȁн? #
	B	
only, for the first time	tèk	тèк
to begin, start	póčeti, da pòčnēm	póчети, да пòчнēм
same	ìstī, -ā, -ō	ùстū, -ā, -ō
to be looking over	razgledávati, razglédāvām	разглéдати, рáзглēдāм
No, we've just begun to look for a place and we're looking over the city at the same time.	Nè, tèk smo pòčeli trȁžiti stȁn i u ìsto vrijeme razgledavamo grȁd.	Не, # тèк смо почели да трȁжимо стȁн i у исто време рáзглēдāмо грȁд.
	A	
to show; (se) to prove to be	pokázati, da pókažēm	показати, да пóкāжēм

444

sightseeing	znàmenitōst f.	знаменитост
Who is going to show you the sights (of the city)?	Kò će vam pokázati znàmenitosti gràda? #	Kò ће вам показати знаменитости грàда? #

B

to be worth(y)	vrijédíti, vrijédī	вре́дети, вре́дū
Our friends will show us everything that is worth seeing.	Nàši prìjateljì će nam pokázati svè što vrijédi vìdjeti.	Наши пријатељи ће нам показати све што вреди видети.

A

besides (with G) or,	sèm òsim	сèм òсим
pertaining to council or cathedral	sábornī, -ā, -ō	саборнū, -ā, -ō
church	cȑkva	црква
the Belgrade citadel or,	Beògradski grȁd Beògradska tvȓđava	Београдски грȁд Београдска твȓђава
zoological	zóološkī, -ā, -ō [zoóološkī]	зоо́лошкū, -ā, -ō [зоо́лошкū]
garden	vȑt or vȑt pl. vȑtovi	вȑт, вȑт вртови
In addition to the Orthodox cathedral and Topchider park, you must see the (Belgrade) citadel and the zoo.	Òsim Sáborne cȑkve i Topčiderskog pàrka, trèba vìdjeti Beògradsku tvȓđavu i zóološki vȑt.	Сèм Саборне цркве и Топчидерског пàрка, треба да видите Београдски грȁд и зоолошки вȑт.
to be finding; (se) to be located	nálaziti, nálazīm	налазити, налазūм
(a section of Belgrade)	Kalemégdān/ Kalimégdān	Калемегдāн / Калимегдāн

445

They are located on Kalemegdan.	Òni se nálaze na Kalemegdánu.	Они се налазе на Калемегдáну.
favorite, beloved	ómiljen, -a, -o	óмиљен, -а, -о
promenade	šétalīšte	шéталūште
Belgrader (man)	Beógrađanin pl. Beógrađāni	Бео́грађанин Бео́грађани
That's a favorite place for the people of Belgrade to go walking.	Tò je ómiljeno šétalīšte Beógrađānā.	Тò је óмиљено шéталūште Бео́грађāнā.

B

unknown	néznan, -a, o	нéзнан, -а, -о
hero	júnak G junáka pl. junáci	jýнак, jунáка jунáци
(name of a mountain near Belgrade)	Àvala	Àвала
assembly	skùpština	скỳпштина
main, chief	glávnī, -ā, -ō	главнū, -ā, -ō
You have already seen the Tomb of the Unknown Soldier on Avala, the National Assembly, and the Main Post Office.	Spòmenik Néznanog junáka na Àvali, Národnu Skùpštinu i Glávnu pòštu, véć ste vìdjeli.	Спòменик Нéзнаног jунáка на Àвали, Нáродну Скỳпштину и Глáвну пòшту, већ сте вùдели.
to lead	vóditi, vòdīm	вòдити, вòдūм
market place	tržnica (Cr)	пùjaцa
Tomorrow they're going to take us to one of Belgrade's market places.	Sùtra će nas vóditi na jèdnu od beógradskih tržnīcā.	Сỳтра ће нас вòдити на jèдну од београдских пùjāцā.

A

busy	zàuzēt, -ā, -ō	зàузēт, -ā, -ō
pertaining to goods	ròbnī, -ā, -ō	ро̀бни, -ā, -ō
department store	ròbna kùća	ро̀бна кỳћа
or,	magázīn pl. magazíni	магáзūн, магазūни

store; work, action	rádnja Gpl. rádnjī	ра̏дња ра̏дњӣ
self-service	samoposluživanje	самопо̏слуга
supermarket	rádnja sa samo-posluživanjēm	ра̏дња за самопо̏слугом
If you're not busy, I can show you a department store and supermarket the day after tomorrow.	Ȁko nȉste zàuzēti, jȃ vam mȍgu pokázati prèkosutra jèdnu rȍbnu kȕću i rádnju sa samoposluživanjēm.	А̏ко нисте за̀узети, jа̏ вам могу показати прѐкосутра jедну ро̏бну ку̏ћу и ра̏дњу за самопо̏слугом.

B

pleasure	zadovóljstvo	задово̏љство
to be selling, to sell	prodávati, pródājēm	прода̏вати, про̏да̄jе̄м
is sold	pródājē se	про̏да̄jе̄ се
price	cijéna	це̏на
We're not; we'll enjoy seeing ('it will be a pleasure for us to see') what they sell there and what the prices are.	Nȋsmo, bȉce nam zadovóljstvo da vȉdimo štȁ se tȁmo pródājē i kolȉke su cijéne.	Нисмо, би̏ће нам задово̏љство да видимо шта се тамо про̏да̄jе̄ и колике су це̏не?

A

shop, store	dúćān G dućána	ду̏ћа̄н, ду̏ћана
to supply	opskŕbiti, da ópskr̄bīm (Cr.)	сна̏бдети, да сна̏бде̄м
supplied	ópskr̄bljen, -a	снабде̏вен, снабдеве̏на, -о
goods	ròba	ро̏ба
You'll see that the stores are rather well supplied with goods.	Vȉdjećete da su dućáni prȉlično dȍbro ópskr̄bljeni rȍbōm.	Виде̏ћете да су ра̏дње прилично добро снабдевене ро̏бо̄м.

447

to drop in, stop off	svrátiti, da svrátīm	сврáтити, да сврȁтӣм
Come back to our place after dinner.	Svrátite kod nȃs pȍslije vèčerē.	Сврáтите код нас после вȅчерē.

B

to look	glèdati, glèdām	глȅдати, глȅдāм
Thank you, we'll see about coming.	Hvála, glèdaćemo da svrȁtīmo.	Хвáла, глȅдаħемо да сврȁтӣмо.
if we should be	ako bùdēmo	ако бȕдēмо
too much	sùvišē	сȕвишē
or,	prèviše	прȅвише
tired	ùmōran, ùmōrna, -o	ȕмōран, ȕмōрна, -о
telephone	teléfōn	телéфōн
But, if we're too tired, we'll phone you ('let you know by phone') so that you don't wait for us.	Àli àko bùdemo prèvišе ùmōrni, jávićemo vam telefónom da nas ne čèkāte.	Àли, ако бȕдемо сȕвишē ȕморни, jàвиħемо вам телефóном да нас не чȅкāте.

Grammatical Notes

Note 20.1 Verb: Future; Special Forms

It is not necessary to list the future forms of most verbs, as they are predictable. Either the infinitive is used, or the suffixes are added to the stem (infinitive form without /-ti/ (or /-ći/). There is a regular change which occurs in certain verbs, which makes it preferable to list them. For example, from /čuti/, /voleti/, /stanovati/, the future forms /ćuću/, /voleću/ and /stanovaću/ are predictable, but compare:

Infinitive	Stem	Future with Suffix
dópasti se	dopas-	dópašće se
rȃsti	ras-	rȃšću
sèsti	ses-	sèšću

These examples show the regular replacement of /s/ by /š/ before /ć/ (compare Notes 25.2, 26.1.2).

Note 20.2 Enclitics: Order of Enclitics - Summary

    Da li ćete se vratiti kući do sedam?

    The short forms /ću/ etc. fall into the same slot as /sam/, etc. The enclitics introduced so far, and their order, are:

1	2	3	4	5
li	sam	mi	me	se
	si	ti	te	je (is)
	smo	mu	ga	
	ste	joj	je (f.)/ju	
	su	nam	nas	
		vam	vas	
	ću	im	ih	
	ćeš			
	će			
	ćemo			
	ćete			
	će			

As previously noted, /je/ 'is' does not normally occur after /se/: /vratio se/ or /on se vratio/ 'he returned'. If both /se/ and /je/ do occur, /se/ precedes /je/: /vratio se je/. Except for /ju/ (rarely used), the forms in column 4 are both accusative and genitive. Use of the genitive enclitics is common with some verbs (/on ga se setio/).

Note 20.3 Verb: /htèti/

    The verb /htèti/ 'to will, to want' has been mentioned in Notes 13.4 and 19.1. The present tense forms, both short and long, are used in forming the future. /htèti/ is also used as a regular verb 'to want' wish'. It is usually replaceable by /želeti/ in such cases:

hoću da idem	želim da idem
on će hteti da ide	on će želeti da ide
hteo sam da idem	želio sam da idem

/hteti/ is stronger 'I want to go'. It is generally more polite to use /želeti/, which is more like 'I'd like to go'.

The future of these two verbs is rare and usually used in connection with /možda/ 'perhaps', /sigurno/ 'surely' or the like. They are not used in the first person in the future.

Note 20.4   Clause Introducer: /štò/

> Prema onome što sam video, ne bih rekao da je vaša zemlija siromašna.

> Ostaću dok ne razgledam sve što me interesuje.

Serbo-Croatian always has a clause introducer for a subordinate clause, that is, a subordinate clause with a verb form showing person and number. In the above sentences the clauses beginning with /što/ are in apposition to the preceding word in each case: 'according to that (which I saw)', 'everything (which interests me)'.

This is seen even more clearly when a preposition is used. For example /došao je pre nego što je otišao voz/ 'he came before the train left'. Here the whole clause is treated the same as a noun after the preposition. The preposition cannot be followed by a verb, but only by a nominalized verb clause.

The combination /dok ne/ corresponds to English 'until'. The literal translation of the example from the Basic Sentences is something like 'I shall stay as long as the situation is such that I don't see all that interests me'. However, /dok/ is occasionally used without /ne/ in the sense of 'until'.

Note 20.5   /Beogradski grad/

> Treba da vidite Beogradski grad.

The word /grȁd/ here means 'citadel, fortress'. It apparently originally referred to a 'walled area', hence a 'fortress' which in turn became identified with the 'city'.

> /grȁd Beógrad/ is 'the city of Belgrade'.

Note 20.6   New Verbs

e	I	vrédeti /vrijéditi	vrédī /vrijédī		to be worth
			---.---		
a	I	glèdati	glèdām		to look
a	P	pógledati	da pógledām		
C	P	náći	da nàđēm	nàšao, nášla	to find
i	I	nálaziti	nálazīm		
C	P	ódsesti	da ódsednēm	ódseo, ódsela	to put up
a	I	ódsedati	ódsedām		
i	P	opskŕbiti	da ópskŕbīm		to supply
e	P	pòčeti	da pòčnēm	pòčeo, pòčēla	to begin
a/Jē	I	pòčinjati	pòčinjēm		
a/Jē	P	pokázati	da pókāžēm		to show
a/Jē	I	pokazívati	pokázujēm		
a	P	pródati	da pródām	pròdao, pròdāla	to sell
a/Jē	I	prodávati	pródājēm		

(for /razglédati/, /razgledávati/ see Note 19.3)

V	P	snábdeti /snábdjeti	da snábdēm /da snábdīm		to supply
e					
a	I	snabdévati /snabdijévati	snábdēvām /snábdijevām		
i	P	svrátiti	da svràtīm		to drop in
a	I	svràćati	svràćām		
i	I	vòditi	vòdīm		to lead, take
C	P	odvésti	da odvédēm	ódveo, odvéla	to take away
i	I	odvóditi	ódvodīm		
V	P	zaúzeti	da záuzmēm	zàuzeo, zàuzēla	to occupy
a	I	zaúzimati	zaúzimām		

Grammatical Drills

GD 20.1 Substitution-Correlation Drill

<u>Naši prijatelji</u> će nam pokazati sutra <u>Sabornu crkvu.</u>
  1   2

	1		2
on	g-đa Jović	Beogradski grad	Glavna pošta
Jovan	Toma i Jovan	Narodna skupština	Spomenik Neznanog junaka na Avali
		Zološki vrt	Jedna beogradska pijaca
		Jedna robna kuća	

The following sentence is for the above drill:

<u>Naši prijatelji</u> će nas voditi u petak da vidimo <u>Sabornu crkvu.</u>

Substitution-Correlation Drill. Use the preposition /na/ or /u/ when required.

Dobiću stan na <u>Topčiderskom brdu.</u>
  1   2

	1		2
(mi)	ona	Miloševa ulica	Dedinjski bulevar
moj prijatelj	on	Dedinje	Knez-Mihailova ulica
Smitovi	oni	Zorina ulica	Avalski put

The following sentences are for the above drill:

Stanovaću na <u>Topčiderskom brdu.</u>
Svratiću u jednu kafanu na <u>Topčiderskom brdu.</u>
Večeraću u jednom malom restoranu na <u>Topčiderskom brdu.</u>
Onda ću otići kod jednog srodnika koji stanuje na <u>Topčiderskom brdu.</u>
Pogledaću prvo jedan stan na <u>Topčiderskom brdu.</u>
Tražiću stan ili kuću na <u>Topčiderskom brdu.</u>
Znam da ću teško naći stan na <u>Topčiderskom brdu.</u>

Substitution-Correlation Drill with pronoun transform.

Prove<u>šćemo</u> celo letovanje u Dalmaciji.   <u>Mi</u> ćemo provesti celo letovanje u
                  Dalmaciji.

   Jovan   moja žena i kći
   Zora   moji roditelji

The following sentences are for the above drill:

Provešćemo se lepo u Dalmaciji.	(provesti)
Putovaćemo za vreme praznika kroz celu zemlju.	(putovati)
Izlazićemo svakog dana dok ne vidimo sve što vredi videti.	(izlaziti)
Popićemo po kafu u ovoj maloj kafani.	(popiti)
Sešćemo pored prozora da bolje vidimo predele.	(sesti)
Odsešćemo y hotelu Metropol.	(odsesti)
Ostaćemo u hotelu dok ne nađemo stan.	(ostati)
Sedećemo u čekaonici dok nas ne puste u voz.	(sedeti)
Proći ćemo kroz Ljubljanu i Zagreb na putu za Beograd.	(proći)
Svratićemo usput u Ljubljanu i Zagreb.	(svratiti)
Pitaćemo portira da li je donet naš prtljag.	(pitati)
Sačekaćemo vas na železničkoj stanici.	(sačekati)
Sećaćemo se uvek puta kroz Dalmaciju i Crnu Goru.	(sećati se)

Present Tense drill with Future transform.

provoditi-provesti

Provodim mnogo vremena na putu.   Provešću mnogo vremena na putu.

on   ja   njihovi prijatelji

moj otac   moji roditelji   mi

The following sentences are for the above type of drill:

odlaziti-otići

Sutra odlazim odavde.   Sutra ću otići odavde.

davati-dati

Dajem rado svoja kola za izlet na   Daću rado svoja kola za izlet na Frušku
Frušku goru.   goru.

čekati-sačekati

Čekam Jovana i Zoru.   Sačekaću Jovana i Zoru.

dobijati-dobiti

Dobijam mnogo u vremenu, ako putujem   Dobiću mnogo u vremenu, ako putujem
avionom.   avionom.

praviti-napraviti

U nedelju pravim izlet na Avalu.   U nedelju ću napraviti izlet na Avalu.
Želim da vidim spomenik Neznanog   Želim da vidim spomenik Neznanog
Junaka.   Junaka.

interesovati

Jovana interesuju znamenitosti grada.   Jovana će sigurno interesovati znameni-
                                        tosti grada.

Njega interesuju znamenitosti grada.   Njega će sigurno interesovati znameni-
                                        tosti grada.

Interesuju ga znamenitosti grada.   Sigurno će ga interesovati znamenitosti
                                        grada.

        Zora   ova deca
        moji prijatelji   ova gospoda

dopadati se-dopasti se

Jovanu se dopadaju Saborna crkva   Jovanu će se sigurno dopasti Saborna
    i Beogradski grad.   crkva i Beogradski grad.
Njemu se dopadaju Saborna crkva i   Njemu će se sigurno dopasti Saborna
    Beogradski grad.   crkva i Beogradski grad.
Dopadaju mu se Saborna crkva i   Dopašće mu se sigurno Saborna crkva i
    Beogradski grad.   Beogradski grad.

        gospođica Smit   moji prijatelji   moja majka i žena
        Smitovi   ta gospoda

Give the future transform of each of the following sentences, as illustrated by
the first.

Brzi voz polazi u 5:00 sati.   Brzi voz će poći u 5:00 sati.
Brzi voz polazi na vreme.
Žao mi je, ali ekspres ne polazi na vreme.
Brzi voz dolazi u 6:15.
Pošta ne dolazi pre 9:00 časova.
Ekspres dolazi na vreme.
Brzi voz iz Zagreba stiže kroz pola sata.   /stići/
Vaš prtljag stiže sutra.
Vaši kuferi dolaze drugim vozom.

Future Tense with Past Tense transform.

Ješćemo danas u restoranu.   Jeli smo danas u restoranu.

    (ja)   sestra i majka   oni   Zora

    Jovan   moji roditelji   deca   moja kći

The following sentences are for the above drill:

Pićemo kafu u kafani.	Pili smo kafu u kafani.
Danas ćemo doneti naš prtljag sa železničke stanice.	Danas smo doneli naš prtljag sa železničke stanice.
Kazaćemo Marku da ga čekate.	Kazali smo Marku da ga čekate.
Reći ćemo Marku da ga čekate.	Rekli smo Marku da ga čekate.
Javićemo Tomi čim Marko dođe.	Javili smo Tomi čim je Marko došao.
Poći ćemo na izlet rano ujutru.	Pošli smo na izlet rano ujutru.
Kupićemo karte za voz na železničkoj stanici.	Kupili smo karte za voz na železničkoj stanici.
Zadocnićemo za voz, ako ne uzmemo taksi.	Zadocnili smo za voz, jer nismo uzeli taksi.
Uzećemo karte za voz na železničkoj stanici.	Uzeli smo karte za voz na železničkoj stanici.
Pokazaćemo vam sve što vredi videti u gradu.	Pokazali smo vam sve što vredi videti u gradu.
Zauzećemo vam sobu kod Metropola.	Zauzeli smo vam sobu kod Metropola.
Ići ćemo danas u jednu radnju sa samoposlugom.	Išli smo danas u jednu radnju sa samoposlugom.
Vodićemo g. Smita u petak na jednu od beogradskih pijaca.	Vodili smo g. Smita u petak na jednu od beogradskih pijaca.
Bićemo zauzeti ceo dan.	Bili smo zauzeti ceo dan.

GD 20.2   Questions and Answers
GD 20.2.1 Informational Answers

Kad će vam vaši prijatelji pokazati   U petak.
    znamenitosti grada?   Oni će mi pokazati znamenitosti grada u
                     petak.
                     Ne znam. Još nismo razgovarali o tome.

Zora   g. Jović   g-đa i g-ca Jović   ta gospoda

455

Ko će dati kola za put u Ljubljanu?   <u>Ja</u> ću dati.

                                      <u>Ja</u> ću dati kola za taj put.

                                      Ne znam.

                                      Ne znam ko će dati kola.

moj prijatelj Amerikanac   Smitovi   Jovan   Zora

The following questions are for the above type of drill:

Ko će sačekati g. i g-đu Jović na železničkoj stanici?
Ko će kazati Marku da ga čekam?
Ko će reći Marku da sam došao?
Ko će javiti Tomi da je Marko došao?
Ko će svratiti kod Tome da vidi kako mu je?
Ko će mi pokazati znamenitosti grada?
Ko će me voditi na Avalu da vidim spomenik Neznanog junaka?

     Change the pronominal adjective in the answer according to the change of subject in the question.

S kim ćete ići na izlet u okolinu   S <u>mojim</u> prijateljima Jugoslovenima.
   Beograda?   Ići ću na izlet s <u>mojim primateljima</u>
                                           Jugoslovenima.

vi (pl)   Jovan   vi i Džon   g-ca Smit   ta gospoda   ti ljudi

GD 20.2.2   Yes and No Answers

Da li ćete dobiti kuću na Dedinju?   Da, hoću. /Da, dobiću.
Hoćete li dobiti kuću na Dedinju?   Ne, neću. /Ne, neću dobiti.
Vi ćete dobiti kuću na Dedinju,   Ne, na žalost neću dobiti tu kuću.
   je l'te?

Zar ćete dobiti kuću na Dedinju?   Da, hoću.
                                     Da, izgleda da ću dobiti.
                                     Još nije sigurno, možda neću.

Zar nećete dobiti kuću na Dedinju?   Na žalost neću.
                                     Izgleda da neću dobiti tu kuću.
                                     Pre da neću nego da hoću.

The following questions with short answers are for the same type of drill:

Kad će vas <u>vaši prijatelji</u> voditi, na jednu od beogradskih pijaca?	Jednog dana ove nedelje.
Kad će <u>vaši prijatelji</u> opet doći u Beograd?	Idućeg leta.
Kad će <u>vaši prijatelji</u> doneti njihov prtljag sa železničke stanice?	Danas posle podne.
Kad će <u>vaši prijatelji</u> proći kroz Beograd?	Ovog četvrtka.
Kad će vaši prijatelji početi da uče srpskohrvatski?	Već su počeli.

Gde ćete dobiti stan?	Na Dedinju.
	Dobiću stan na Dedinju.
	Još ne znam gde ću dobiti stan.

vaš prijatelj Amerikanac	vaši srodnici	oni
Smitovi	Zora	vi (pl.)

The following questions with short answers are for the same substitution drill:

Gde ćete stanovati?	U Miloševoj ulici broj 54.
Gde ćete provesti praznike?	U Dalmaciji.
Gde ćete večerati u subotu?	Kod Metropola.
Gde ćete odsesti?	U Metropolu.
Koliko cete ostati u hotelu?	Dok ne nađem stan.
Gde ćete danas ručati?	Ručaću u ekspres-restoranu.
Odakle ćete javiti Tomi da ste došli?	Odavde.
Kako ćete se javiti Tomi?	Telefonom.
Od čega zavisi <u>vaš</u> dolazak.	Od toga da li ću imati vremena.

Čijim kolima ćete ići na izlet?	Mojim kolima.
	Ići ćemo mojim kolima na izlet.
	Ne znam. Još nismo o tome govorili.

on	(mi)	vi i vaši prijatelji Jugosloveni
oni	vi i Jovići	vi i vaši prijatelji Amerikanci

457

The substitutions for /vi/:

vi (pl)	Toma	vaš prijatelj	g. i g-đa Jović	Smitovi

The following questions are for the above type of drill:

Da li ćete doći na sastanak na vreme?

Da li ćete moći svratiti kod nas večeras?

Da li ćete naći stan na Dedinju?

Da li ćete provesti praznike u Beogradu?

Da li ćete čekati dok ne dođe voz?

Da li ćete gledati jugoslovenski film?

Da li ćete praviti negde izlet u nedelju?

Da li ćete izlaziti negde večeras?

Da li ćete odsesti u hotel Metropolu?

Da li ćete svršiti posao na vreme?

Da li ćete se žaliti zbog prljave sobe?

Hoće li brzi voz stići na vreme?
                        Da, hoće.

                                     Ne, neće.

                                     Da, brzi voz će kao i uvek stići na

                                           vreme.

                                     Ne, brzi voz će zadocniti najmanje pola

                                           sata.

Jovan	Zora	g. i g-đa Jović

Da ne<u>će</u>te zadocniti za voz?
            Mislim da neću. Uzeću taksi.

                                     Neće biti dobro ako zadocnim.

                                     Moram danas da budem u Zagrebu.

                                     Imam hitna posla.

vaš prijatelj	g. Jović	ta gospoda	Toma i Jovan

Hoćete li da vidite <u>jednu veliku</u>
            Da, hoću.

  <u>robnu kuću?</u>
                              Da, hoću vrlo rado da vidim jednu robnu

                                     kuću.

znamenitosti grada	Saborna crkva	spomenik Neznanog junaka
Glavna pošta	Jedna radnja sa samoposlugom	Narodna skupština
Jedan nov magazin		Jedan dobro snabdeven dućan
zološki vrt	Topčiderski park	Jedna stara crkva

Substitute /želeti/ for /hteti/.

GD 20.3 Question and Answer Drill with Prompt

Odsešću u hotelu Metropol.	Gde ćete odsesti? /U kom hotelu ćete odsesti?
Hvala, sešću na krevet.	Izvolte sedite na krevet ili na stolicu?
Još nismo počeli da tražimo stan.	Da li ste počeli da tražite stan?
Sutra ćemo početi da tražimo stan.	Kad ćete početi da tražite stan?
Teško ćete naći stan na Topčiderskom brdu.	Da li možemo naći stan na Topčiderskom brdu?
Još nismo razgledali grad.	Da li ste razgledali grad?
Razgledaćemo grad ove nedelje.	Kad ćete razgledati grad?
Vredi videti Sabornu crkvu, Topčiderski park, Beogradski grad, zološki vrt i drugo.	Šta vredi videti ovde?
Naši jugoslovenski prijatelji će nam pokazati znamenitosti grada.	Ko će vam pokazati znamenitosti grada?
Beogradski grad i zološki vrt nalaze se na Kalemegdanu.	Gde se nalaze Beogradski grad i zološki vrt?
Kalemegdan je omiljeni park i šetalište Beograđana.	Šta je Kalemegdan?
Još nismo išli na Avalu.	Da li ste išli na Avalu?
Sutra ćemo ići na Avalu da vidimo spomenik Neznanog junaka.	Kad ćete ići na Avalu?
Još nismo bili ni na jednoj pijaci.	Da li ste bili na nekoj pijaci?
Jovan će nas voditi u četvrtak na jednu pijacu.	Ko će vas voditi na pijacu? /Hoćete li ići sami na pijacu?
Izaći ću večeras kod Metropola.	Hoćete izlaziti negde večeras?
Jovan i ja ćemo ići zajedno.	Da li ćete ići sami?
Ne prolazimo kroz vašu ulicu, ali prolazimo blizu nje.	Da li prolazite kroz moju ulicu?
Vrlo rado ću svratiti po vas ('for you').	Hoćete li da svratiti po mene?
Prvo ću otići po Jovana, onda ću doći po vas.	Hoćete li prvo ići po Jovana?
Mi ćemo lako naći vašu kaću.	Da li ćete moći naći moju kuću?
Mi ćemo poći od kuće u pola devet.	U koliko sati ćete poći od vaše kuće?

GD   20.4   Conversations - Razgovori

GD   20.4.1   A   B

Što vrijedi vidjeti u Beogradu?   Vrijedi vidjeti Beogradski grad.   Tako
                                             mi zovemo staru tvrđavu.

Gdje je tvrđava?   Ona je na Kalemegdanu.

Što još vrijedi vidjeti osim tvrđave?   Na Kalemegdanu se nalazi i stara
                                             gradska crkva, koju Beograđani mnogo
                                             vole.

Kalemegdan mora biti jako veliki, zar   I jest.   To je na prvom njestu omiljeni
ne?   park svih Beograđana, i starih i mladih.

Djeca žele da ih vodimo u zološki vrt.   Jest, i zološki vrt je na Kalemegdanu i
Je li vrt u istom dijelu grada?   to u samoj tvrđavi.

Onda moramo ići na Kelemegdan još   Ako hoćete, moja žena i ja vam možemo
ove nedjelje.   pokazati Kalemegdan.

Vrlo rado.   Biće nam milo.   Kad ćete imati vremena?   Treba vam
                                             najmanje cijelo poslije podne.

Sutra poslije podne, ako je vama   Jest.   Gdje ćemo se naći?
zgodno.

Možemo se naći u ambasadi u 2 sata.   U redu.   Do viđenja do sutra.
Do viđenja.

Шта вреди видети у Београду?   Вреди видети Београдски град.   Тако ми
                                             зовемо стару тврђаву.

Где је град?   Он је на Калемегдану.

Шта још вреди видети сем града?   На Калемегдану се налази и стара градска
                                             црква, коју Београђани много воле.

Калемегдан мора бити врло велики,   И јесте.   То је на првом месту омиљени
јел'те?   парк свих Београђана, и старих и младих.

Деца желе да их водимо у золошки врт.   Јесте, и золошки врт је на Калемегдану
Је ли врт у истом делу града?   и то у самој тврђави.

Онда морамо ићи на Калемегдан још   Ако хоћете, моја жена и ја вам можемо
ове недеље.   показати Калемегдан.

Врло радо.   Биће нам мило.   Кад ћете имати времена?   Треба вам
                                             најмање цело после подне.

Сутра после подне, ако је вама
    згодно.

Јесте. Где ћемо се наћи?

Можемо се наћи у амбасади у 2 сата.

У реду. До виђења до сутра.

До виђења.

GD 20.4.2

Hoćete (li) biti kod kuće poslije
    večere?

Da, hoćemo.

Možemo li doći kod vas oko osam?

Biće nam jako milo, ako dođete.
Jeste (li) našli stan?
Kad mislite da ćete naći stan?

Još nismo, ali tražimo i u isto
    vrijeme razgledavamo grad.

Ne znam točno. To je teško reći.

Gdje želite stanovati?

Na Topčiderskom brdu ili Dedinju,
    ako nađemo tamo stan.

Tamo je teško naći stan.

Gdje ste bili juče?

Bili smo na tržnici.

Na kojoj ste bili?

Na tržnici 'Zeleni venac'.

To je lijepa i velika tržnica.

Da, dobro je opskrbljena i uređena. Mojoj
    ženi se jako dopala.

Хоћете (ли) бити код куће после
    вечере?

Да, хоћемо.

Можемо ли доћи код вас око осам?

Биће нам врло мило, ако дођете.
Јесте (ли) нашли стан?

Још нисмо, али тражимо и у исто
    време разгледамо град.

Кад мислите да ћете наћи стан?

Не знам тачно. То је тешко рећи.

Где желите да станујете?

На Топчидерском брду или Дедињу,
    ако нађемо тамо стан.

Тамо је тешко наћи стан.

Где сте били јуче?

Били смо на пијаци.

На којој пијаци сте били.

На пијаци 'Зелени венац.'

То је лепа и велика пијаца.

Да, добро је снабдевена и уређена.
    Мојој жени се јако допала.

GD 20.4.3

U kom hotelu su odsjeli vaši prijatelji?	Odsjeli su u Metropolu.
Koliko će oni ostati u hotelu.	Oni će ostati u hotelu vjerojatno još tri nedjelje.
Zašto tako dugo? Zar oni još nisu našli stan?	Oni imaju stan, ali njihov stan neće biti slobodan ranije.
Koji stan su dobili?	Oni su dobili stan u kome stanuje g. Smit sa obitelji.
Kad g. i g-đa Smit odlaze odavde?	Oni ostaju ovde još tri nedjelje.
Da li se vašim prijateljima dopada kuća u kojoj stanuju Smitovi?	Da, dopada im se. To je velika i lijepa kuća.
Je li ta kuća u samom gradu.	Ta kuća se nalazi na Dedinju.
To je sigurno lijepa kuća.	Pa jest.

У ком хотелу су одсели ваши пријатељи?	Одсели су у Метрополу.
Колико ће они остати у хотелу?	Они ће остати у хотелу вероватно још три недеље.
Зашто тако дуго? Зар они још нису нашли стан?	Они имају стан, али њихов стан неће бити слободан раније.
Који стан су добили?	Они су добили стан и коме станује г. Смит са породицом.
Кад г. и г-ђа Смит одлазе одавде?	Они остају овде бар још три недеље.
Да ли се вашим пријатељима свиђа кућа и којој станују Смитови.	Да, свиђа им се. То је велика и лепа кућа.
Је ли та кућа у самом граду?	Та кућа се налази на Дедињу.
То је сигурно лепа кућа.	Па јесте.

GD 20.5 Homework - Domaći zadatak.

GD 20.5.1 Write sentences 1-5 with the proper verb of those listed to the right of each sentence or with both verbs where appropriate. In 6-10 fill the blanks with the proper form of the item listed to the right of each sentence. The pronouns are not to be used with the verbs.

1. Mi ćemo _____ u hotelu dok ne nađemo stan.   (odsesti, ostati)

2. Mi ćemo _____ na vreme.   (doći, stići)

3. Hoću _____ Sabornu crkvu.   (videti, da vidim)

4. Brzi voz će _____ pola sata.   (zadocniti, biti dockan)

5.   Moj prijatelj će sigurno _____.   (doći dockan,
                                                          zadocniti)

6.   _____ će sigurno interesovati Kalemegdan.   (on)

7.   On hoće _____ red vožnje.   (uzeti)

8.   _____ u Metropolu.   (ja - odsesti)

9.   _____ kroz Moravsku dolinu.   (mi - proći)

10. Želim _____ na vreme.   (stići)

GD 20.5.2 Make questions to which the above sentences are appropriate
answers.

UNIT 21

Basic Sentences - Osnovne rečenice

Weekend	Vikend	Викенд

A

	hájdemo	хајде́мо / ајде́мо
let's go		
Let's go to the coffeehouse. I'd like to drink a glass of beer.	Hájdemo u kaváni. Htȉo bih pópiti čȁšu pȉva.	Хајде́мо у кафа́ну. Хо̀ћу да попијем чашу пи̏ва.

B

I could	mògao bih	мо̀гао бих
to eat up, finish eating	pójesti, da pójedēm, pójeo	по́јести, да по́једе̄м, по́јео
crescent shaped roll	kífla Gpl. kíflī /róščić (Cr)	ки̏фла, ки̏флӣ
roll	žémička (Cr)	зе́мичка
pastry, cake	kólač pl. kolȃči	ко́лач кола́чи
All right, I'm not thirsty, but I could eat a roll or a cake.	U rédu, jȁ nȉsam žédan, ȁli bih mogao ȕzeti jȅdnu žémičku ȉli kólač.	У ре́ду, ја̏ ни̏сам жȅдан, а̏ли бих могао да поједем једну кифлу или ко̏ла̄ч.

A

weekend	vȉkend	ви̏кенд
Where are you going to spend the weekend?	Gdjȅ ćete próvesti vȉkend?	Где̏ ћете прове́сти ви̏кенд?

B

right, straight, just	prȁv, -a, -o	пра̏в, -а, -о
to intend, plan	namjerávati, namjérāvām	наме́ра̄вати, наме́ра̄ва̄м

To tell the truth I'm tired, and I'm thinking of staying at home.	Prȁvo da vam kȁžem, ùmōran sam i namjérāvām ȍstati kod kȕćē.	Прȁво да вам кȁжем, ỳмōран сам и намéрāвāм да останем кȏд кỳће.

A

don't	némōjte	нéмōjте
best, the best	nȁjboljī, -ā, -ē	нȁjбољī, -ā, -ē
If you are tired, (then) don't go anywhere. That's the best [thing to do].	Ȁko ste ùmōrni ȍnda némojte nȉkuda ȉći. Tȏ je nȁjboljē.	Ȁко сте ỳмōрни ȍнда нéмоjте нигде ȉћи. То je нȁjбољē.

B

to do, work	urádīti, da úrādīm	урáдити, да ýрāдūм
to answer	odgovóriti, da odgóvorīm	одговóрити, да одгȍворūм
Of course, that's that I'm going to do. Anyway, I have to answer some letters.	Pa dȁ, tȁko ću i urádīti. Ȉnače mȍram odgovóriti na nȅkoliko pȉsāmā.	Па дȁ, тȁко ћу и урáдити. Инȃче имам да одговорūм на неколико пȉсāмā.

A

What do you plan [to do]?	Štȍ namjérāvāte?	Штȁ вū намéравате?
by all means, surely	svákāko	свȁкāко
outside (with G) or,	vàn ìzvan	вȁн ùзван
outside the city, in the country	van grȁda	вȁн грȃда
We'll surely go somewhere in the country.	Mȋ ćemo svàkāko ȉći nȅgdje ȉzvan grȁda.	Мȋ ћемо свȁкако ȉћи нȅгде вȁн грȃда.
unwillingly	nèrado	нȅрадо
to be staying, to stay	ȍstajati, ȍstajēm	ȍстаjати, ȍстаjēм

I don't like staying at home on ('during') week-end.	Jȃ nèrado òstajem kod kúće za vrijéme vìkenda.	Jȃ нѐрадо òстаjем кòд куħē за врȇме вѝкенда.

B

to be buying, to buy	kupóvati, kúpujēm	купòвати, кȳпyjēм
pertaining to writing	písāći, -a, -e	пиcāħи, -a, -e
pertaining to office	kancelárijskī, -ā, -ō	канцелȃриjскȳ, -ā, -ō
material	materíjāl	материjȃл
set, kit, outfit	príbor	прȗбор
stationery	písāći príbor/ kancelárijski príbor	пиcāħи материjȃл / канцелȃриjcки материjȃл
Where do you buy stationery?	Gdjȅ kúpujete písāći príbor?	Гдѐ кȳпyjете пиcāħи материjȃл?
pencil	ólōvkā Gpl. ólōvkȳ /ólovākā	óлōвка, óлōвкȳ
envelope	ómot (Cr.)	кóверат, кóверта
paper	hártija	хȃртиjа
or,	pápīr G. papíra	пȃпȳр, папȗра
I have to buy a couple of pencils and some envelopes and paper.	Trȅbam kúpiti nȅkoliko ólovākā i ómōtā i papíra.	Трȇба да кȳпим нȅколико óлōвкȳ и коверата и хȃртиjе.

A

stationery store	pápīrnica	пȃпирница
bookstore	knjížara	кнȗжара
Stationery is sold in stationery stores and bookstores.	Písāći príbor se pródaje u papír-nicama i knjížarama.	Пиcāħи материjал се прóдājē у папирницама и кнȗжарама.

B

| to be writing, to write | písati, pȉšēm | пи̏сати, пи̏ше̄м |

| to write | napísati, da nápīšēm | написати, да на́пӣше̄м |

| Although I don't like to write [letters], I have to write a couple of them ('letters') this weekend. | Mȁda ne vȍlim písati, mȍram ȍvog vȉkenda napísati nȅkoliko pȉsāmā. | Ма̏да не волим да пи̏ше̄м, мо̏рам овог викенда да напи̏ше̄м неколико пӣса̄ма̄. |

A

| How do you spend evening here? | Kȁko ȏvdje prȍvodite vèčeri? | Ка̏ко проводите вѐчери овде? |

B

| We usually eat dinner as soon as I come home. | Mȉ ȍbično vèčerāmo čȉm ja dȍđem kúći. | Ми̏ обично вѐчера̄мо чи̏м ја̏ до̏ђем ку̀ћи. |

| to be reading, to read | čítati, čȉtām | чи̏тати, чи̏та̄м |

| newspaper | nòvine f. pl. | но̀вине |

| to be resting, relaxing | odmárati se, ódmārām se | одма́рати се о̏дма̄ра̄м се |

| Sometimes I read newspapers and relax until dinner is ready. | Pȍnekad čȉtam nòvine i ódmārām se dȍk vèčera ne bȕde gȍtova. | Понекад чи̏там но̀вине и о̏дма̄ра̄м се до̏к вечера не бу̏де го́това. |

A

| city | vároš f. | ва́рош |

| When do you come home from the city? | Kȁd dȍlazite iz grȃda kúći? | Ка̏д долазите ку̀ћи из ва́роши? |

B

| to be getting up, to get up | ústajati, ústajēm | у́стајати, у́стаје̄м |

467

| A while back I used to come home later, because I used to get up later. | Prȉje sam dòlazio kȕći kȁsnije, jȅr sam ùstajao kȁsnije. | Ра̀није сам до̏лазио ку̏ћи ка̀сније, јер сам у̏стајао ка̀сније. |

A

to get up	ùstati, da ùstanēm	у̀стати, да у̀станēм
to read	pročítati, da pročítām	прочи́тати, да прочи́та̄м
departure, leaving	ȍdlazak G. ȍdlaska pl ȍdlasci	о̏длазак о̏дласка о̏дласци

| Now I have to get up early, and read the Yugoslav newspapers before leaving for the office. | Sȁda mȍram ùstati rȁno i pročítati jugoslávenske nóvine prȉje ȍdlaska u ȕred. | Са̏да мо̏рам да у̀станем ра̏но и да прочитам југо-словенске новине пре̏ о̏дласка у канцеларију. |
| Do you know Serbo-Croatian that well? | Zȁr tȁko znȁte dȍbro srpskohŕvātski? | За̏р та̏ко до̏бро зна̏те српскохр̏ва̄тски? |

B

| Yes, I do. | Dȁ, znȁm. | Да̏, зна̏м. |

A

| Good for you. | Blȁgo váma! | Бла̀го вама! |

Grammatical Notes

Note 21.1   Verb: Aspect

Note 21.1.1   Perfective and Imperfective Pairs

> Hoću da popijem čašu piva.
>
> Mogao bih da pojedem jednu kiflu.
>
> Nameravam se da ostanem kod kuće.
>
> Ja nerado ostajem kod kuće za vreme vikenda.
>
> Treba da kupim nekoliko olovki.
>
> Gde kupujete pisaći materijal?
>
> Mada ne volim da pišem, moram ovog vikenda da napišem nekoliko pisama.
>
> Ponekad čitam novine.

468

Sada moram da pročitam Jugoslovenske novine.

Gde ćete provesti vikend?

Kako provodite večeri ovde?

Mi obično večeramo čim ja dođem kući.

Ranije sam dolazio kući kasnije.

These examples from the Basic Sentences illustrate the way in which perfective and imperfective verbs pair. The verbs used are:

pìti	to (be) drink(ing)	I	pópiti	to (finish) drink(ing)	P
jèsti	to (be) eat(ing)	I	pójesti	to (finish) eat(ing)	P
óstati	to stay	P	óstajati	to (be) stay(ing)	I
kúpiti	to (finish) buy(ing)	P	kupóvati	to (be) buy(ing)	I
písati	to (be) writ(ing)	I	napísati	to (finish) writ(ing)	P
čítati	to (be) read(ing)	I	próčitati	to (finish) read(ing)	P
provésti	to (finish) spend(ing)	P	provóditi	to (be) spend(ing)	I
dóći	to (finish) com(ing)	P	dólaziti	to (be) com(ing)	I

What may be considered the 'simpler' verb form of each pair is on the left. The forms on the right are augmented in some way. The augumented form

may have a prefix: <u>póp</u>iti   compare: pìti

may have added a suffix: ósta<u>j</u>ati   compare: óstati

may have changed a suffix: kup<u>óv</u>ati   compare: kúp<u>i</u>ti

These forms illustrate the most fundamental features of the correspondences between perfective-imperfective pairs of verbs. These features are:

1. The simple, most basic, form of the verb may be either perfective or imperfective. For example, /kúpiti/ is perfective, /písati/ is imperfective. Most simple verbs having no prefix are imperfective.

2. A prefix added to a simple form makes it perfective: /písati/ is imperfective, /napísati/ is perfective, /čítati/ is imperfective, /próčitati/ is perfective.

3. Suffixes different from those of the corresponding perfective verb may be added to make the verb imperfective:

Perfective	Imperfective
kúp - i - ti	kup - óv - a - ti
ósta- -ti	ósta - j - a - ti

4. There may be differences in the form of the root itself between perfective and imperfective.

Perfective	Imperfective
pro-vés-ti	pro-vód-iti
pro-véd-ēm	pró-vod-īm

Here the difference is primarily that of the vowel (/-e-/ in the perfective
/-o-/ in the imperfective). (The form in /-s-/ before /-ti/ is predictable.)
Another verb set is:

Perfective	Imperfective
dóći	dólaziti
dòđēm	dólazīm
dóšao	dólazio

In this case the correspondence between perfective and imperfective is completely
unpredictable (like present go and past went in English). This situation is
comparatively rare, but it occurs. (See below for other verbs from completely
different roots which form aspect pairs.)

It is easier to see the relationship between aspect pairs if verbs are
broken up into their component parts.

(Prefix) or (Prefixes)	ROOT	(Extension) or (Extensions)	Stem Formative Suffix	Ending or Endings
	pi-			-ti
po-	pi-			-ti
	kup-		-i-	-ti
	kup-	-ov-	-a-	-ti
	kup-	-u-	-jē-	-m
po-	kaz-	-iv-	-a-	-ti

This analysis will be useful for the following discussion.

As has been seen, nearly all verbs occur in pairs, one being imperfective,
the other perfective. In ordinary speech some verbs are used only in the imperfective form, the perfective counterpart not occurring. This restriction is
more a matter of meaning than of form. These verbs either refer to actions

which in themselves are of a durative nature or to states of being. In other
words, the meanings are in the nature of things imperfective. While it is possible
to consider a perfective aspect of one of these 'enduring' states, it is not
usual to do so. Examples of such imperfective verbs are:

govóriti	to speak	razúmeti	to understand
htèti	to want, will	stanóvati	to dwell
ímati	to have	vrédeti	to be worth
kóštati	to cost	znàti	to know
mìsliti	to think	žíveti	to live
móći	to be able		
mõrati	to be obliged to		

There are only a few basic patterns into which nearly all the aspect
relations of verbs fall. The most frequent pattern is:

Simple Form (I)
Prefix plus Simple Form (P) (as perfective counterpart to simple form, where
such occurs)

Other prefixes plus Simple Form (P)   Other prefixes plus Expanded Form (I)

E.g.   písati   (I)   to be writing
       napísati   (P)   to write
       potpísati (P)   to sign   potpisívati (I) to be signing

/napísati/ is the normal perfective counterpart of /písati/: /pìšem písmo/ 'I'm
writing a letter', /napísao sam písmo/ 'I wrote a letter'. The prefix /pod-/
(here /pot-/ before the voiceless consonant /p/) adds the idea of 'under', 'to
write under' - 'to sign'. There are many other prefixes possible on the same
root. (A survey of verb prefixes is given in Note 39.1.) Each of these other
prefixes plus the simple form is a perfective verb (as /potpisati/) and each of
these verbs has an expanded form as imperfective counterpart (as /potpisivati/).

A second pattern, common but less frequent is:

Simple Form (P)   Expanded Form (I)
Prefix plus Simple Form (P)   Prefix plus Expanded Form (I)
E.g. kázati (P) to say   kazívati (I) to be saying
      pokázati (P) to show   pokazívati (I) to be showing

(Note also the considerable shift of meaning here.) The simple form and expanded
form without prefix form a perfective-imperfective pair. A variation on this

471

pattern is one in which the simple form does not occur:

vóditi (I) to lead

    provésti (P) to spend time   provoditi (I) to be spending time

These two patterns may be summarized:

1a	I		1b	I			2a	P	I		2b		I
	P			P	I	and		P	I			P	I
	P	I											

1b is for those verbs which do not have a perfective counterpart to the simple imperfective form. Not all verbs pattern so neatly, but the vast majority do. A few variations may be mentioned. Occasionally what appears to be a perfective-imperfective pair consists of two completely different verbs, as I /govóriti/ 'to speak' P /réći/ 'to say', P /čȕti/ 'to hear' I /slȕšati/ 'to listen to'. In some cases one verb may serve as a member of more than one pair:

    I   íći   to go
    P   otíći   to go (perfective of /íći/)
                 to leave   I ódlaziti   to be leaving

    There are also verb groups which have no simple verb, such as /izvíniti/. This verb with its related forms belongs to pattern 1.

    There are in addition to the more common imperfective forms some with more specialized meaning. For example:

       I vȉdeti   to see   I víđati   to see (repeatedly, over
                                               and over)

/víđati/ has iterative meaning, indicating something which occurs over and over. In most cases the ordinary imperfective verb is used in reference to such action. Another example of specialized meaning is:

sèsti   to sit down   sèdati   to be in the   sédeti   to be seated
                                act of
                                sitting down

/izvolte sesti/ is 'please sit down'. /sedite/ 'be seated' is also used.

    The following list gives some of the verbs which have occurred so far, according to the above patterns:

bi-	P	dóbiti	to receive	I	dobíjati	to be receiving
bri-	P	brínuti se	to worry			
	P	zabrínuti se	to come to worry about			
ček	I	čèkati	to wait			
	P	sáčekati	to wait up to the point of arrival	I	sačekívati	
čit-	I	čítati	to read			
	P	pročítati	to read (through), finish reading			
drž-	P	zadržati se	to be detained	I	zadržávati se	to be detained
gled-	I	glèdati	to look at			
	P	pógledati	to look at			
	P	rázgledati	to look over	I	razglédati /razgledávati	to be looking over
id-	I	íći	to go			
	P	dóći	to come	I	dólaziti	to be coming
	P	izáći /izíći	to go out	I	ízlaziti	to be going out
	P	náći	to find	I	nálaziti	to be finding
	P	otíći	to go			
			to leave	I	ódlaziti	to be leaving
	P	próći	to pass by	I	prólaziti	to be passing by
	P	úći	to enter	I	úlaziti	to be entering
jed-	I	jèsti	to eat			
	P	pójesti	to eat up, finish eating			
mol-	I	móliti	to ask politely, beg, pray			
	P	zamóliti	to ask politely			
mor-	P	odmóriti se	to rest	I	odmárati se	to be resting
pad-	P	dópasti se	to please	I	dópadati se	to be pleasing
pi-	I	pìti	to drink			
	P	pópiti	to drink up, finish drinking			

pis-	I	písati	to be writing		
	P	napísati	to write		
prav-	I	pràviti	to be making		
	P	nápraviti	to make		
pros-	I	prósiti	to beg, to propose (marriage)		
	P	ísprositi	to beg, propose		
put-	I	putóvati	to travel	(This expanded form with	
	P	ótputovati	to set off travelling	/-ov-/ patterns as a simple one)	
rad-	I	rắditi	to work		
	P	urắditi	to finish work(ing), to do		
	P	sèsti	to sit down	I sèdati	to be in act of sitting down
sed-	P	ódsesti	to put up	I ódsedati /odsẽdati	to be putting up
slug-	I	slúžiti	to serve		
	P	poslúžiti	to serve, do a service	poslužívati	to be serving
sta-	P	óstati	to stay	I óstajati	to be staying
	P	ústati	to get up	I ústajati	to be getting up
vol-	I	vóleti	to like, prefer		
	P	zavóleti	to come to like, fall in love		
	P	izvóleti	to please	I izvolévati	
zajm-	P	pozájmiti	to loan	I pozajmljívati	to be loaning
žel-	I	želeti	to wish, want		
	P	požéleti	to wish, want		
žen	I	ženiti se	to be getting married (of man)		
	P	oženiti se	to get married		

The following verbs also fit in pattern 1, but are listed separately because of the special features involved:

I	pítati	to be asking
P	upítati	to ask
P	zapítati	

I	trážiti	to look for, demand, ask for
P	potrážiti	to demand, ask for
P	zatrážiti	

I	trebati	to be necessary
P	ústrebati	to happen to be necessary
P	zátrebati	

Pattern 2a

P	dàti	to give	I	dávati	to be giving
P	pródati	to sell	I	prodávati	to be selling
P	údati se	to get mattied	I	udávati se	to be getting married
P	kázati	to say	I	kazívati	to be saying
P	pokázati	to show	I	pokazívati	to be showing
P	kúpiti	to buy	I	kupóvati	to be buying
P	plátiti	to pay	I	plácati	to be paying
P	prímiti	to receive	I	prímati	to be receiving
P	réšiti	to decide	I	rešávati	to be deciding
P	vrátiti se	to return	I	vràćati se	to be returning
P	svrátiti	to drop in	I	svràćati	to be dropping in

Pattern 2b

men-	P	prométiti	to exchange	I	ménjati	to change
nos-				I	nósiti	to carry

	P	dónēti		I	donósiti	to be bringing
prost-				I	prȁštati	to be pardoning
	P	oprόstiti	to pardon	I	oprȁštati	
vod-				I	vόditi	to lead
	P	provésti	to spend time	I	provόditi	to be spending time

Note 21.1.2 Verb: Perfective and Imperfective /bìti/

> Ako budemo suvȉše umorni, javićemo vam telefonom.

/budemo/ is an example of the perfective present of /bìti/. There are two sets of present forms for this verb, one imperfective and the other perfective. The perfective forms are used in subordinate clauses, like the above, referring to a future possibility ('if it should be that we be too tired'). The forms are:

	Imperfective					Perfective	
sam	smo	jésam	jésmo	nísam	nísmo	bùdem	bùdēmo
si	ste	jési	jéste	nísi	níste	bùdēš	bùdēte
je	su	jèst, jè	jésu	nìje	nísu	bùdē	bùdū

Note 21.1.3 Aspect usage

While Note 21.1.1 was primarily directed toward the form, a great deal was said or implied concerning the usage of the forms. Following is a summary treatment of the usage.

Imperfective verbs refer to the action or state as in process. The action may be one which takes very little time, as /sèdati/ 'to be in the act of sitting down'. It may refer to a general situation, as /stanόvati/ 'to dwell, live'. It may refer to a state of mind, as /znàti/ 'to know', /razúmeti/ 'to understand'. The same verb may refer to action which is in process or which is repetitive: /putuje u Zagreb/ 'he's travelling to Zagreb' (referring to what he's now doing), /putuje u Zagreb dvaput neděljno/ 'he travels to Zagreb twice a week'.

The perfective, on the other hand, refers to completion of action. It may be a single act, as /sèsti/ 'to sit down'. It may be the beginning of the action. That is, the action of starting is completed, as /otputόvati/ 'to set off travelling'. Compare /zábrinuti se/ 'to come to worry about'. More commonly the perfective refers to the completion of the action indicated by the verb, as /pójesti/ 'to finish eating'.

In Note 19.1 the correspondence of the English simple verb with the Serbo-Croatian perfective and the verb phrases in -ing with the imperfective was pointed out:

ako prodam	if I sell	prodajem	I'm selling
prodao sam	I sold	prodavao sam	I was selling, I used to sell
prodaću	I'll sell	prodavaću	I'll be selling

This is more useful as a guide to the meaning of the forms than as a guide as to any actual correspondence in usage between the two languages. There is a very important exception to this general pattern:

I sell clothes   Prodajem robu

In a general statement English normally uses the simple form of the verb, but Serbo-Croatian normally uses the imperfective. There are, however, certain usages in Serbo-Croatian where the perfective occurs in an independent clause.

As has been pointed out earlier, the perfective frequently occurs after clause introducers such as /da/ 'that', /ako/ 'if', etc. The imperfective may also occur but is less frequent. Some common clause introducers which have occurred are:

                                                        Examples

/da/	'that'		treba da dođem	I should come
			želim da dođem	I want to come
/kad/	'when'		kad dođem	when I come
/ako/	'if'		ako dođem	if I come
/čim/	'as soon as'		čim dođem	as soon as I come
/dok/	'while'	with I	dok dolazim	while I am coming
	'at the time that' with P		dok dođem	when I come
/dok ne/	'until'	with P	dok ne dođem	until I come

Note 21.2 Verb: /ímati/

Imam da odgovorim na nekoliko pisama.

The above sentence may mean either 'I have some letters to answer? or (as in English) 'I have to (that is, must) answer some letters'.

Note 21.3 New Verbs

a	I	namerávati /namjerávati	namérāvām namjérāvām		to intend
a	I	čítati	čítām		to read
a	P	pročítati	da pročítām		
C	I	jèsti	jèdēm	jèo, jèla	to eat
C	P	pójesti	da pójedēm	pójeo, pójela	
i	P	kúpiti	da kùpīm		to buy
a/Jē	I	kupóvati	kúpujēm		
i	P	odgovóriti	da odgóvorīm		to answer
a	I	odgovárati	odgóvārām		
i	P	odmóriti se	da se ódmorīm		to rest
a	I	odmárati se	ódmārām se		

(For /óstati - óstajati/ see Note 19.3)

a/Jē	I	písati	pìšēm		to write
a/Jē	P	napísati	da nápīšēm		
i	I	ráditi	ràdīm		to work, do
i	P	uráditi	da úrādīm		
V/n	P	ústati	da ústanēm		to get up
a/Jē	I	ústajati	ústajēm		

Drill

GD   21.1   Imperfective and Perfective Verbs - Learning Drill
GD   21.1.1   Substitution Drill

Imperfective   ### Perfective

dolaziti - doći

Voz dolazi. /vlak   Voz treba da dođe u 6 sati.
Voz dolazi u 6 sati.   Kad voz dođe onda idemo u hotel.
                                  Čim voz dođe idemo kući da večeramo.
                                  Ako voz dođe na vreme nećemo dugo
                                       čekati.
                                  Čekaćemo dok voz ne dođe.

autobus   otac   g. Jović
avion   majka   naši srodnici /rođaci

piti - popiti

Toma pije kafu.   Toma želi da popije jednu kafu.
         1   2
Toma pije kafu uveče.   Kad popijem kafu idem kući. /doma
         1   1
                                  Čim popijem kafu idem kući.
                                              1
                                  Dok ne popijem kafu neću ići kući.
                                                1

  1   2
čaj   čašu piva
pivo   čašu vode
vino   čašu vina
             čašu mleka

jesti - pojesti

Deca jedu supu.   Toma i Jovan žele da pojedu po jednu
                                       supu.
Deca jedu supu za večeru.   Kad deca pojedu supu dajte im meso.
                                  Čim deca pojedu supu dajte im meso.
                                  Dok deca ne pojedu supu nemojte im
                                       davati meso.

Substitutions for Alternative Drill:

meso	jaje 'egg'
kifla	kolač

ići - otići

Toma ide u Ambasadu u 8 sati.

Toma je išao u Ambasadu u 8 sati.

Toma danas mora da ode u Ambasadu
    ranije nego obično.

Kad Toma ode na stanicu, vi idite kući.

Čim Toma ode na stanicu, vi možete ići
    u Ambasadu.

Dok Toma ne ode na stanicu, nemojte ići
    u varoš.

Toma je otišao u Ambasadu u 8 sati.

Toma će otići u Ambasadu do osam.

(ja)   otac   majka   moja žena

GD 21.2 Transform Drill

This type of drill may be used in several stages.

1) Learning drill (repetition after instructor, books closed). The
instructor should ask for occasional translation to be sure the students understand the difference in usage between the two forms. The first pair is translated to give the general idea.

2) The student gives the transform on hearing the original sentence (books
closed or right column covered).

3) The sentences are used as prompts for question and answer drill.
Examples of some possibilities are:

Jovan čeka roditelje na stanici.   Jovan želi da sačeka roditelje na stanici.
Koga čeka Jovan?   Koga Jovan želi da sačeka?
  /Da li Jovan čeka roditelje?   /Da li Jovan želi da sačeka roditelje?

GD 21.2.1 The following gives sentences using the imperfective present with
transforms using the verb /želeti/ plus the perfective present of the original
verb.

480

Jovan čeka roditelje na stanici.

  John is waiting for his parents
    at the station.

Jovan želi da sačeka roditelje na
  stanici.

  John would like to wait for his
    parents at the station.

Obično izlazim negde subotom uveče.

Toma svršava svoja posla brzo i
  dobro.

Ja unosim sam svoje stvari u voz.

Želim da izađem negde u subotu uveče.

Toma želi da svrši svoja posla brzo
  i dobro.

Ja želim da unesem sam svoje stvari
  u voz.

Oni se vraćaju kući u pet.

Mi svraćamo uvek u Zagreb iz Splita.

Moji roditelji se odmaraju od puta.

Oni žele da se vrate kući u pet.

Mi želimo da svratimo u Zagreb iz Splita.

Moji roditelji žele da se odmore od
  puta.

Zora piše pismo svojoj majci.

Zora želi da napiše pismo svojoj majci.

Repeat the above drill using /treba/ for /želim/.

GD 21.2.2 Following the model given, replace the phrase with /treba/ (as
/treba da kupi/) with the past of the other verb (as /je kupila/).

Zora treba da kupi koverte i hartiju.
  Zora should buy envelopes and
    paper.

Zora je kupila koverte i hartiju.
  Zora bought envelopes and paper.

Treba danas da odgovorim na Jovanovo
  pismo.

Odgovorio sam danas na Jovanovo pismo.

Nosač treba da unese naše kufere u
  voz.

Nosač je uneo naše kufere u voz.

Mi treba da uđemo u voz. Vreme je.

Mi smo ušli u voz čim je bilo vreme.

Treba da uzmemo taksi do železničke
  stanice da ne bi zadocnili.

Uzeli smo taksi do železničke stanice
  da ne bi zadocnili.

Treba da sačekamo Jovana na
  železničkoj stanici.

Sačekali smo Jovana na železničkoj
  stanici.

Jovan treba da zauzme sobu u hotelu
  za nas.

Jovan je zauzeo sobu u hotelu za nas.

Oni treba da dođu kod nas posle
  večere.

Oni su došli kod nas posle večere.

Deca treba da pojedu prvo meso, pa
  onda kolače.

Deca su pojela prvo meso, pa onda
  kolače.

GD 21.2.3 Perfective present to perfective past

Kad napišem pismo majci, onda idem
u bioskop.
> When I finish writing the
> letter to my mother, then
> I'm going to the movies.

Kad sam napisao pismo majci, onda sam
otišao u bioskop.
> When I wrote the letter to my
> mother, then I went to the
> movies.

Čim stignem u Sarajevo otići ću kod
Jovana.

Čim sam stigao u Sarajevo otišao sam
kod Jovana.

Čim kupim koverte i hartiju odgovo-
riću prvo majci.

Čim sam kupio koverte i hartiju
odgovorio sam prvo majci.

Kad Jovan dođe kući javiću vam
telefonom.

Kad je Jovan došao kući javio sam vam
telefonom.

Nećemo ući u voz pre nego što nosač
unese naše kufere u voz.

Nismo ušli u voz pre nego što je nosač
uneo naše kufere u voz.

Dok deca ne popiju mleko neću im
dati kolače.

Dok deca nisu popila mleko nisam im
dala kolače.

Čim puste, mi ćemo ući u voz.

Čim su pustili, mi smo ušli u voz.

Čim pođe voz, ja ću se vratiti kući
sa stanice.

Čim je pošao voz, ja sam se vratio
kući sa stanice.

Kad uzmemo taksi idemo kući.

Kad smo uzeli taksi otišli smo kući.

Kad se odmorim, ići ću kod Jovana.

Kad sam se odmorio, otišao sam kod
Jovana.

Ne mogu da odgovorim na pismo majci,
dok ne kupim koverte i hartiju.

Nisam mogao da odgovorim na pismo
majci, dok nisam kupio koverte i
hartiju.

Oni ne žele da idu u Jugoslaviju,
dok ne nauče srpskohrvatski.

Oni nisu otišli u Jugoslaviju, dok nisu
naučili srpskohrvatski.

GD 21.2.4 Perfective past to perfective future

Toma je danas posle podne napisao
pismo roditeljima.
> Tom wrote a letter to his
> parents this afternoon.

Toma će danas posle podne napisati
pismo roditeljima.
> Tom will write a letter to his
> parents this afternoon.

Mi smo uzeli taksi od železničke
stanice do kuće.

Mi ćemo uzeti taksi od železničke
stanice do kuće.

Toma i Jovan su prvo svršili posla,
pa tek onda otišli u varoš.

Toma i Jovan će prvo svršiti posla, pa
tek onda otići u varoš.

Mi smo došli na stanicu taksijem i
  nismo zadocnili.

Mi ćemo doći na stanicu taksijem i
  nećemo zadocniti.

Nosač je uneo naše stvari u voz.

Nosač će uneti naše stvari u voz.

Toma je ušao u voz i zauzeo mesta,
  dok sam ja kupovao red vožnje.

Toma će ući u voz i zauzeti mesta, dok
  ja kupim red vožnje.

Brzi voz je pošao pet minuta kasnije.

Brzi voz će poći pet minuta kasnije.

Mi smo zauzeli sobu za vas, čim ste
  javili da dolazite.

Mi ćemo zauzeti sobu za vas, čim javite
  da dolazite.

Oni su stigli na vreme u Skoplje.

Oni će stići na vreme u Skoplje.

Jovan je našao stan pre nego što
  je njegova porodica došla.

Jovan će naći stan pre nego što njegova porodica dođe.

GD 21.3 Question Transform Drill

   1) The student is to give the answer to the question (on the left).

   2) The student is to give the transform (on the right) on hearing the
original question, and the next student is to answer this transform.

GD 21.3.1 Imperfective present to Perfective present with /treba/.

Kad Toma (obično) dolazi kući?
  When does Tom usually come home?

Kad Toma treba da dođe kući?
  When is Tom supposed to come home.

Kad idete na železničku stanicu po
  vaš prtljag?

Kad treba da odete na železničku
  stanicu po vaš prtljag?

Kad ustaje vaš otac?

Kad treba da ustane vaš otac?

Kad obično izlazite uveče?

Kad treba da izađete večeras?

U koliko sati deca piju mleko?

U koliko sati deca treba da popiju
  mleko?

Kad stiže brzi voz iz Zagreba?

Kad treba da stigne brzi voz iz
  Zagreba?

Kad polazi brzi voz za Zagreb?

Kad treba da pođe brzi voz za Zagreb?

U koliko sati počinje pozorište?

U koliko sati treba da počne
  pozorište?

GD 21.3.2 Imperfective Past to Perfective Past

Kad su deca leti ulazila u kuću?
  When did the children use to
    go in the house during the summer?

Kad su deca ušla u kuću?
  When did the children go in the
    house?

483

Da li je vaš prijatelj učio srpsko-hrvatski pre odlaska u Jugoslaviju?	Da li je vaš prijatelj naučio srpsko-hrvatski pre odlaska u Jugoslaviju?
U kom hotelu ste obično odsedali?	U kom hotelu ste odseli?
Da li ste uvek ustajali rano?	Da li ste jutros ustali rano?
Zar ste vi uvek dolazili kući posle 10?	Zar ste vi došli kući posle 10?
Kad ste se obično vraćali kući?	Kad ste se vratili kući?
Da li ste vi uvek zadocnjavali za voz?	Da li ste zadocnili za voz?
Da li je Toma pisao pismo roditeljima svake nedelje?	Da li je Toma napisao pismo roditeljima?

GD 21.3.3 Imperfective Present to Perfective Future

Kad (obično) ustajete nedeljom i praznikom?	Kad ćete ustati u nedelju?
When do you usually get up on Sundays and holidays?	When will you get up on Sunday?
Da li uvek ostajete kod kuće za vreme praznika?	Da li ćete ostati kod kuće za vreme praznika?
U koliko sati počinje bioskop?	U koliko sati će početi bioskop?
Kad se otvara radnja sa samoposlugom?	Kad će se otvoriti radnja sa samoposlugom?
Da li se robna kuća zatvara pre sedam?	Da li će se robna kuća zatvoriti pre 7?
Da li polazi međunarodni brzi voz na vreme?	Da li će međunarodni brzi voz poći na vreme?
Da li brzi vozovi ovde zadocnjavaju?	Da li će brzi voz zadocniti?
Da li izlazite negde uveče?	Hoćete izaći negde večeras?
Da li svraćate negde uveče pre nego što odete kući?	Hoćete svratiti negde večeras pre nego što odete kući?
Kad stižemo u Zagreb?	Kad ćemo stići u Zagreb?

GD 21.4 Model Transform with Substitution Correlation Drill

Following is a model showing the transforms to be made for each of the sentences below. The perfective present sentence is given for each, as it varies. Otherwise the sentences are to be transformed according to the model. The order of drill is indicated by the answers with numbers.

Ja obično provodim vikende van grada. Želim da provedem vikend van grada.

Ja sam provodio vikende van grada. ——→ Ja sam proveo vikend van grada.

Ja ću provoditi vikende van grada. ——→ Ja ću provesti vikend van grada.

The subjects of these sentences, beginning with the model, may be drilled in the following order: /ja on ona mi oni/. To this may be added subjects such as /Zora/, /Toma/, /moji prijatelji/, etc.

An alternate method of drill is to use the subject /ja/ in the first sentence only, then /on/, etc. following a fixed order of subjects throughout, so that each sentence has a different subject. Note that the verbs before /da/ (/želim/, /mora/, /treba/) are to be omitted in the past and future transforms.

Sentences for the above drill:

<u>ostajati - ostati</u>

On uvek ostaje kod kuće za vreme vikenda.　　On mora da ostane kod kuće ovog vikenda.

<u>odlaziti - otići</u>

Ona odlazi u kancelariju u pola devet.　　Ona treba da ode danas u kancelariju u pola devet.

<u>dolaziti - doći</u>

Mi dolazimo kući u pola sedam.　　Danas moramo da dođemo kući u pola sedam.

<u>čitati - pročitati</u>

Oni čitaju novine pre odlaska od kuće.　　Oni treba da pročitaju novine pre odlaska od kuće.

<u>ustajati - ustati</u>

Zora ustaje rano svakog jutra.   Zora mora jutros da ustane rano.

<u>kupovati - kupiti</u>

Toma kupuje uvek kartu na železničkoj   Toma treba da kupi kartu na želez-
    stanici.   ničkoj stanici.

<u>učiti - naučiti</u>

Moji prijatelji uče srpskohrvatski   Moji prijatelji treba da nauče
    pre odlaska u Jugoslaviju.   srpskohrvatski pre odlaska u
                                    Jugoslaviju.

<u>odsedati - odsesti</u>

Ja odsedam uvek u Metropolu.   Želim da odsednem u Metropolu.

<u>izlaziti - izaći</u>

On izlazi subotom u kafanu.   On treba da izađe u subotu u kafanu.

<u>zadocnjavati - zadocniti</u>

Ona nikad ne zadocnjava.   Ona ne želi da zadocni.

<u>svršavati - svršiti</u>

Mi svršavamo posla uvek na vreme.   Moramo da svršimo ovo danas.

<u>uzimati - uzeti</u>

Oni uvek uzimaju karte u gradu.   Oni treba da uzmu karte na železničkoj
    Tako im je najzgodnije.   stanici. Dockan je da idu u grad.

<u>voditi - odvesti</u>

Zora vodi nedeljom posle podne decu   Zora treba da odvede decu danas posle
    u bioskop ili pozorište.   podne u bioskop.

GD 21.5 Question and Answer Drill with Prompt on the Basic Sentences

Hoću da popijem čašu mleka.   Šta hoćete da pijete?
                                   /Hoćete (li) nešto da popijete?

Mogao bih da pojedem jednu kiflu ili   Jeste gladni? Hoćete nešto da pojedete?
    kolač.

Moji prijatelji će provesti vikend
na putu.

Gde će vaši prijatelji provesti vikend?

Umoran sam i nameravam da ostanem
kod kuće.

Hoćete (li) vi ići negde za vreme
vikenda?

Nećemo ići nigde dok se ne odmorimo.

Zašto nećete ići nigde?

Ja nerado ostajem kod kuće za vreme
vikenda.

Da li vi ostajete neki put kod kuće
za vreme vikenda?

Imam da odgovorim večeras na nekoliko pisama.

Šta ćete raditi večeras? Da li ste
zauzeti?

Pisaći materijal se prodaje u pa-
pirnicama i knjižarama.

Gde se prodaje pisaći materijal?

Nema nijedna papirnica blizu.

Da li ima blizu neka papirnica?

Ja kupujem pisaći materijal u jednoj
papirnici u Knez-Mihailovoj ulici.

Gde vi kupujete pisaći materijal?

Treba mi nekoliko olovki i koverata
i hartije.

Šta vam treba?

Ja ne volim da pišem pisma. Pišem
samo kad moram.

Da li vi volite da pišete pisma?

Nemam kad (/vremena) da pišem pisma.

Zašto ne volite da pišete pisma?

Juče sam napisao nekoliko pisama.

Šta ste radili juče?

Morao sam da odgovorim nekim
prijateljima.

Zašto ste pisali pisma kad to ne
volite?

Ja se uveče odmaram i čitam novine.

Kako provodite večeri? /Šta radite
uveče?

Mi obično večeramo čim ja dođem
kući.

Kad večerate?

Ja moram da ustanem rano.

Kad ustajete?

Moram da pročitam jugoslovenske
novine pre odlaska u kancelariju.

Zašto morate da ustanete rano?

GD 21.6 Conversations - Razgovori

GD 21.6.1   A   B

Gdje ste proveli vikend, Jovane?

Proveo sam vikend kod kuće.

Zar niste išli negdje izvan grada?

Nisam išao nigdje. Ostao sam kod kuće.

Kako to, da ste ostali kod kuće?

Pravo da vam kažem, bio sam umoran.

Zar se vi možete odmoriti kod kuće?

Zašto da ne. Nisam ništa radio i lijepo
sam se odmorio.

Pa morali ste nešto raditi.

Napisao sam samo nekoliko pisama. To
je sve.

U tome i jest stvar. Ja se ne
  odmaram kad pišem pisma.
  Volite li vi pisati pisma?

Ne, ne volim. Ko voli pisati pisma!

Zašto ste onda pisali pisma kad ste
  bili umorni?

Pisao sam jer sam morao.

Kome ste pisali pisma?

Napisao sam jedno pismo majci.
  Njoj pišem jedno pismo nedjeljno.

To je druga stvar. To razumijem.
  Kome ste još pisali?

Odgovorio sam jednom prijatelju, koji
  dolazi u Beograd na mjesto gospodina
  Smita.

Šta je htio vaš prijatelj?

Tražio je neka obavještenja i morao sam
  mu odgovoriti.

Где сте провели викенд, Јоване?

Провео сам викенд код куће.

Зар нисте ишли негде ван града?

Нисам ишао нигде. Остао сам код куће.

Како то, да останете код куће?!

Право да вам кажем, био сам уморан.

Зар ви можете да се одморите
  код куће?

Зашто да не. Нисам ништа радио и
  лепо сам се одморио.

Па морали сте нешто радити?

Написао сам неколико писама. То је све.

У томе и јесте ствар. Ја се не
  одмарам кад пишем писма.
  Волите ли ви да пишете писма?

Не, не волим. Ко воли да пише писма!

Зашто сте онда писали писма кад сте
  били уморни?

Писао сам зато што сам морао.

Коме сте писали писма?

Написао сам једно писмо мајци.
  Њој пишем једно писмо недељно.

То је друга ствар. То разумем.
  Коме сте још писали?

Одговорио сам једном пријатељу, који
  долази у Београд на место господина
  Смита.

Шта је хтео ваш пријатељ?

Тражио је нека обавештења и морао сам
  да му одговорим.

GD 21.6.2

Kad ste došli u Zagreb?

Došao sam prekjuče.

Gdje ste odsjeli?

Odsjeo sam u hotelu Palas.

Kad se vraćate u Beograd?

Vraćam se prekosutra.

Zar nećete ostati ovdje za vrijeme
vikenda?

Ne, neću.

To je do četvrtka. Ako ostanete i u
petak, onda možete provesti vikend
s nama.
Zar vam se ne dopada Zagreb?

Zagreb mi se mnogo dopada. Ali, moram
se vratiti kući prije vikenda.

Što vam se dopalo u Zagrebu?

Dopao mi se cijeli grad. Nisam znao
da je Zagreb tako lijep.

Koje znamenitosti grada niste vidjeli?

Nisam vidio stari dio grada.

Ako želite mi vam možemo pokazati
taj dio grada.

Naravno. Vi sigurno dobro poznajete
Zagreb.

Vrlo dobro. Gdje ćemo se naći?
Možete li doći kod nas u 2 sata?

Mogu. Do viđenja.

Do viđenja.

Кад сте дошли у Загреб?

Дошао сам прекјуче.

Где сте одсели?

Одсео сам у хотелу Палас.

Кад се враћате у Београд?

Враћам се прекосутра.

Зар нећете остати овде за време
викенда?

Не, нећу.

То је до четвртка. Ако останете и у
петак, онда можете провести викенд
с нама.
Зар вам се не свиђа Загреб?

Загреб ми се много свиђа. Али, морам
да се вратим кући пре викенда.

Шта вам се свидело у Загребу?

Свидео ми се цео град. Нисам знао да је
Загреб тако леп.

Које знаменитости града нисте видели.

Нисам видео стари део града.

Ако желите ми вам можемо показати
тај део града.

Наравно. Ви сигурно добро познајете
Загреб.

Врло добро. Где ћемо се наћи?
Можете ли да дођете код нас у 2 сата?

Могу. До виђена.

До виђена.

GD 21.6.3

Gdje ste bili, Tomo?

Svratio sam u knjižaru.

Zašto ste svratili u knjižaru?

Htio sam kupiti omote i papir.

Pa jeste li kupili omote i papir.

Jesam, ali nisam našao ono što sam
tražio.

U kojoj knjižari ste bili?

Bio sam u onoj knjižari preko puta hotel Mažestika. Ne znam kako se zove.

Ako hoćete ja vam mogu pokazati jednu papirnicu, koja je dobro opskrbljena pisaćim priborom.

Vrlo rado. Ovi omoti, koje sam kupio nisu ni za šta.[1]

Ako hoćete, možemo otići odmah u tu papirnicu.

Hajdemo. Inače, večeras moram napisati nekoliko pisama.

Где сте били, Томо?

Свратио сам у књижару.

Зашто сте свраћали у књижару?

Хтео сам да купим коверте и хартију.

Па јесте ли купили коверте и хартију?

Јесам, али нисам нашао оно што сам тражио.

У којој књижари сте били?

Био сам у оној књижари преко пута хотел Мажестика. Не знам како се зове.

Хоћете ли да вам покажем једну папирницу, која је добро снабдевена писаћим материјалом.

Врло радо. Ови коверти, које сам купио нису ни за шта.

Ако хоћете, можемо отићи одмах у ту папирницу.

Хајдемо. Иначе, вечерас треба да напишем неколико писама.

GD 21.7 Homework - Domaći zadatak

GD 21.7.1 Change the underlined verb forms in the following sentences to 1) the present tense (using the imperfective) and 2) a phrase with /treba/ plus the perfective.

Odseo sam u hotelu Metropol.

Voz je prolazio kroz Moravsku dolinu.

Stigao sam na železničku stanicu pre nego što je pošao voz.

Seo sam na stolicu do Zore.

Proveli smo vidend kod kuće, jer smo bili umorni.

Nosač je doneo prtljag sa stanice.

---

[1] /ni za šta/ ~ /nizašta/ 'aren't [good] for anything'

Pojeli smo kolače, ali nismo pojeli kifle.

Uzeli su karte za voz u varoši.

Pročitao sam jugoslovenske novine pre nego što sam otišao u kancelariju.

GD 21.7.2 Change the above sentences to the future.

UNIT 22

Reading Selection - Štivo za čitanje

Letters from John - The Trip to Belgrade

Jovanova Pisma - Put u Beograd

Драги пријатељу,

Много света прелази југословенско-аустријску границу Коренским прелазом. Тај прелаз је добро везан са аутопутем. Ту се врши преглед пасоша, као и царински преглед. Од границе до Београда има око 630 км., и вожња траје отприлике десет сати са одморима.

До Крања предели су алпски, слични оним у Аустрији и Швајцарској. Али одатле предео се мења. Одмах иза Крања постепено се отвара Љубљанска котлина, чија врата затвара Љубљана. Ово чини положај Љубљане важним. Све до Загреба поред аутопута виде се лепа, живописна села и пут је занимљив. Од Загреба аутопут пролази кроз долину Саве скоро право, избегавајући насељена места.

Аутопутем саобраћају само моторна возила, те се вози брзо и без тешкоћа. На једној бензинској пумпи напунили смо резервоар бензином. На путу се овде-онде виде радници како оправљају покварена возила. Видели смо и један несрећан случај, судар двају кола. То је био једини застој и скретање с пута. Срећом, нама није била потребна никаква помоћ и стигли смо у Београд без икаквих незгода или квара.

Вас и Ваше срдачно поздравља

Ваш пријатељ,
Џон

Dragi prijatelju,

Mnogo svijeta prelazi jugoslavensko-austrijsku granicu Gorenskim prijelazom. Taj prijelaz se dobro spaja sa autoputom. Tu se vrši prijegled pasoša, kao i carinski prijegled. Od grancie do Beograda ima oko 630 km., i vožnja traje otprilike deset sati s odmorima.

Do Kranja predjeli su alpski, slični onima u Austriji i Švicarskoj. Ali odatle predjel se mijenja. Odmah iza Kranja postepeno se otvara Ljubljanska kotlina, čija vrata zatvara Ljubljana. Ovo čini važnim položaj Ljubljane. Sve do Zagreba pokraj autoputa vide se lijepa, slikovita sela i put je zanimljiv. Od Zagreba autoput prolazi kroz dolinu Save skoro pravo, zaobilazeći naseljena mjesta.

Autoputem saobraćaju samo motorna vozila, pa se vozi brzo i bez poteškoća. Na jednoj benzinskoj pumpi napunili smo rezervoar benzinom. Na putu se ovdje ondje vide radnici kako popravljaju oštećena vozila. Vidjeli smo i jedan nesretan slučaj, sudar dvaju automobila. To je bio jedini zastoj i skretanje s puta. Srećom, nama nije bila potrebna nikakva pomoć i stigli smo u Beograd bez ikakvih nezgoda ili kvara.

Vas i Vaše srdačno pozdravlja.

Vaš prijatelj
Džon

Basic Sentences - Osnovne rečenice

world, people	svìjet D svijétu [pl. svjètovi]	свѐт свѐту свѐтови
to be crossing, to cross	prélaziti, prélazīm	прела́зити, прела́зӣм
Yugoslav-Austrian	jugoslávensko-áustrījskī, -ā, -ō	југословенско-а́устрӣјскӣ, -ā, -ō
border, frontier, limit	gránica	гра́ница

crossing, pass	prijélaz	прѐлаз
Korenski Pass	Gorenski prijélaz	Кòренски прѐлаз
A lot of people cross the Yugoslav-Austrian border by the Korenski pass.	Mnȍgo svijeta prelazi jugoslȃvensko-ȁustrijsku grȃnicu Gȍrenskim prijélazom.	Мнȍго свѐта прѐлази jугословенско-ȁустриjску грȃницу Кòренским прѐлазом.
to tie, to connect	vézati, da véžēm	вѐзати, да вѐжēм
to connect, link; (with /se/) be connected	spájati, spȃjām	спȃjати, спȃjām
This pass is well connected with the autoput.	Tȃj se prijélaz dȍbro spȁjā s ȁutoputom.	Тȃj прѐлаз jе дȍбро вѐзан са аутопу̑тем.
to perform, to do, to execute	vŕšiti, vȑšīm	вȑшити, вȑшūм
survey, examination, inspection	prijégled	прѐглед
passport	pȁsoš	па̏сош
pertaining to customs	cȁrinskī, -ā, -ō	цȁринскū, -ā, -ō
There passports are examined, and there is customs inspection.	Tȕ se vȑšī prijégled pȁsošā, kao i cȁrinski prijégled.	Тȕ се врши прѐглед па̏собā, као и царински прѐглед.
kilometre	kílometar	ки́лометар
There are about 630 km. (from the border to Belgrade).	Od grȁnice do Beó-grada ȉma ȍko 630 km (šȅststo trȉdeset kilometárā).	Од грȁнице до Бео́града ȉма ȍко 630 км. (шȅст стȍтина три̏десет кȕло-метā̄ра̄).
to last	trȁjati, trȁjē	тра̏jати, тра̏jē
rest, vacation	ódmor	о́дмор
And the trip takes about ten hours with stops.	A vȍžnja trȁje otprȉlike dȅset sȃtī s ódmorima.	И во̏жња тра̏jе отпри̏лике дȅсет са́ти са о́дморима.

alpine	àlpskī, -ā, -ō	а̏лпскӣ, -а̄, -о̄
similar	slȉčan, -čna, čno	сли̏чан, сли̏чна, -о
Up to Kranj the countryside is Alpine, similar to that in Austria and Switzerland.	Do Krãnja prȅdjeli su àlpskī, slȉčni ónīma u Áustriji i Švícārskōj.	До Кра̑ња пре̏дели су а̏лпскӣ, сли̏чни они̑м у Ау́стриjи и Шва̑jца̑р-ско̑j.
from there	ódātlē	о̏да̄тле̄
to be changing, to change	mijénjati, mȉjenjām	ме́њати, ме́ња̄м
But from there the landscape changes.	Àli ódātlē prȅdjel se mȉjenjā.	Али о̏да̄тле̄ пре̏део се ме́ња̄.
behind	ȉza	иза
gradually	póstepeno	по̏степено
to be opening, to open	otvárati, ótvārām	отва́рати, о́тва̄ра̄м
mountain basin, depression	kótlina	ко́тлина
Immediately after Kranj the Ljubljana basin gradually opens out.	Ȍdmah ȉza Krãnja póstepeno se ótvara Ljúbljanska kótlina.	Одмах и̏за Кра̑ња по̏степено се о́твара Љу́бљанска ко́тлина.
door	vráta (n. pl)	вра́та
Ljubljana closes the gap of this basin.	Vráta ȍve kótlinē zátvara Ljúbljana.	Вра́та о̏ве ко́тлине̄ за́твара Љу́бља̄на.
to do, make; (with /se/:) seem	čȉniti, čȉnīm	чи̏нити, чи̏нӣм
position, location	pòložāj	по̏ложа̄j
important	vážan, vážna, -o	ва́жан, ва́жна, -о
This makes the location of Ljubljana important.	Ȍvo čȉni vážnīm pòložāj Ljúbljanē.	Ово чи̏ни положа̄j Љу́бља̄не ва́жним.
picturesque	slikóvit, -a, -o	живопи̏сан, живо̏писна, -о

495

All the way to Zagreb along the autoput [may] be seen pretty, picturesque villages, and the trip is interesting.	Svȅ do Zȃgreba pȍkraj áutoputa vȉde se lijȇpa slikȍvita sèla i pȕt je zanȋmljiv.	Свȅ до Зȃгреба пȍред ауто- пȳта виде се лȇпа, живо- писна сȅла и пȳт је занȋмљив.
to be avoiding, to avoid	izbjegávati, izbjȇgāvām	избегȃвати, избегȃвȃм
avoiding	izbjegávajūći	избегȃвајȳħи
to bypass	zaobȋlaziti, zaobȋlazīm	заобȋлазити, заобȋлазȋм
bypassing	zaobȋlazēći	заобȋлазȇħи
to settle	naséliti, da náselīm	насȅлити, да нȃселȋм
settled	náseljen, -a, -o	нȃсељен, -a, -o
From Zagreb the autoput goes through valley of the Sava the [in] an almost straight [line], avoiding inhabited places.	Od Zȃgreba ȁutoput prȍlazi kroz dolȉnu Sȃvē, skȍro rȃvno, zaobȋlazēći náseljena mjèsta.	Од Зȃгреба аутопȳт прȍлази кроз долину Сȃве скȍро право, избегавȃјуħи нȃсељена мȅста.
to communicate	saóbraćati, saóbrаćā	саȍбраħати, саȍбраħȃ
pertaining to motor	mòtornī, -ā, -ō	мȍторнȋ, -ȃ, -ȏ
vehicle	vózilo	вȍзило
and	tȅ	тȅ
to drive; refl. to ride	vóziti, vòzīm	вȍзити, вȍзȋм
without	bèz	бȅз
Only motor vehicles go along the autoput, and one drives fast and without difficulty ('difficulties').	Ȁutoputom saȍbraćaju sȁmo mȍtorna vózila, pȁ se vȍzi br̀zo i bez potȅškȏća.	Аутопȳтем саȍбраħају сȃмо мȍторна вȍзила, тȅ се вȍзи бȑзо и бȅз тешкȏħа.

gasoline	bénzīn, īna	бе́нзин, -и́на
pertaining to gasoline	bénzīnskī, -ā, -ō	бе́нзински, -а̄, -о̄
pump	pȕmpa G pl. pȗmpī	пу̏мпа пу̑мпӣ
to fill	nápuniti, da nápunīm	на́пунити, да на́пунӣм
tank	rezérvoār, -ára	резерво́а̄р, -а́ра
We filled our tank with gas at a gasoline station.	Na jédnoj bénzīnskoj pȕmpī nápunili smo rezérvoar bezínom.	На је́дној бе́нзинској пу̏мпи на́пунили смо резерво́а̄р бе́нзӣном.
there	óndje	о̑нде
here and there	óvdje - óndje	о̑вде - о̑нде
worker	rȁdnīk pl. rȁdnīci	ра̏днӣк ра̏днӣци
to be repairing, to repair	ópravljati, ópravljām	о́прављати, о́прављāм
or,	pópravljati, pópravljām	по́прављати, по́прављāм
to spoil, to get put of order	pokváriti, da pókvārīm	поква́рити, да поква́-рӣм
spoiled, out of order, corrupt	pókvāren, -a, -o	по́ква̄рен, -а, -о
damaged	óštećen -a, -o	о́штећен, -а, -о
Here and there on the road workers are to be seen repairing broken-down (L damaged) cars.	Na pȕtu se óvdje-óndje vīde rȁdnīci kȁko pòpravljaju óštećena vózila.	На пу̏ту се о̑вде-о̑нде вӣде ра̏днӣци ка̏ко о́прављājу покварена вȍзила.
case, event	slùčāj D slùčāju pl. slùčajevi/slùčajī	слу̀ча̄ј слу̀ча̄jу слу̀чајеви/слу̀чаjи
accident	nèsretan slùčāj	нѐсретан слу̀ча̄j
collision	sùdār	су̀да̄р

of two	dvájū	два̑jӯ
We also saw an accident, a two car collision.	Vȉdjeli smo i jȅdan nȅsretan slùčaj, sȕdar dváju automobȋla.	Видели смо и jȅдан несрећан случаj, судар два̑jу кола̄.
only	jédīnī, -ā, -ō	jéдӣнӣ, -ā, -ō
stagnation, standstill	zȃstoj	за̑стоj
turning side, deviation	skrètānje	скрета̄ње
That was the only delay and detour.	Tȏ je bȉo jédinī zȃstoj i skrètanje s pȗta.	То̑ je био jéдини за̑стоj и скретање с пу̑та.
necessary	pòtreban, pòtrebna, -o	потребан, потребна, -о
not of any kind	nȉkakov, -a,-o (Cr.)	никакав, никаква, -о
help, aid, assistance	pòmōć f.	помо̑ћ
Fortunately we didn't need their help.	Srèćōm, nȃma nȉje bȉla pòtrebna nȉkakova pòmōć.	Сре̏ћо̄м, на̏ма ни̏jе била потребна никаква помо̑ћ.
any	ȉkakav, ȉkakva, -o	икакав, икаква, -о
mishap, trouble	nézgoda / nèzgoda	не̏згода/не̏згода
break down	kvȁr pl. kvárovi	ква̏р ква̑рови
We arrived in Belgrade without any trouble ('unpleasantnesses or breakdown').	Stȉgli smo u Beógrad bez ȉkakvih nèzgōdā ili kvȁra.	Стигли смо у Београд без икаквих незго̄да̄ или ква̑ра.
cordial	sr̀dačan, sr̀dačna, -o	срдачан, срдачна, -о
to be greeting, to greet	pózdravljati, pózdravljām	поздрављати, поздрављам
[Your friend John] sends hearty greetings (to you and yours).	Vȁs i Vȁše sr̀dačno pózdravljā.	Ва̏с и Ва̏ше срдачно поздрављā.

498

Note 22.1   Verb: Imperative
Note 22.1.1   Verb: Affirmative Imperative

Izvinite!   Pitajte portira.

Oprostite!   Pustite ga unutra!

Idite pravo!   Dođite vi kod mene posle pola osam na večeru.

Dajte mu kafu, molim.   Svratite kod nas posle večere.

Donesite mi drugu, vruću kafu.

These are examples of the imperative of the verb. The imperative ending
itself is /-i/ or /-j/, more rarely nothing at all (no examples above). As a
rule /-i/ occurs after consonants, /-j/ after vowels. The above examples may
be grouped according to verb type:

a-verb	i-verb	Consonant-verb	Vowel-verb
pítajte	izvínite	donésite	dâjte
	opróstite	dô̌dite	
	pùstite	ȉdite	
	svrátite		

An a-verb has the stem formative suffix /-ā/ before the imperative ending. Most
verbs have no stem formative suffix before the imperative /-i/ or /-j/: /izvin-/,
/oprost-/, /dones-/, etc. The precise patterning of the imperative ending with
the other endings is best seen in an overall view of the verb forms (see Note
22.2).

The imperative in /-i/ or /-j/ alone is the second person singular familiar:
/pitaj/, /izvini/, /oprosti/, /donesi/, /idi/, /daj/, etc. This should be
avoided by the learner as impolite to nearly everyone he may meet. The form
with the ending /-te/ is more polite (though an imperative form is not always
the polite way of requesting action).

The first person plural /-mo/ is occasionally used, e.g. /donesimo/ 'let's
carry'. Compare the defective verb /hajdemo/ 'let's go!'. (This verb occurs
only in the imperative, normally /hajde/ or /hajdemo/.)

Traditional grammar compares the third plural of the verb with the imperative. There is no connection between the two forms, and the stress is
often different, but the comparison of the endings may have some mnemonic value.

499

1) When the 3 pl. ends in /-ē/ or /-ū/ after a consonant or /-jū/ after
    a long vowel, the imperative ending is /-i/ (/-ite/)

ídū	they're going	ídi	ídite	go!
góvorē	they're speaking	govóri	govórite	speak!
dájū	they're giving	dáji	dájite	give! (I)

2) When the 3 pl. ends in /-jū/ after a short vowel, the imperative ends
    in a long vowel plus /-j/ (/-jte/).

dàjū	they give (P)	dàj	dàjte	give!
stóje	they're standing	stòj	stòjte	stand!
kúpujū	they're buying	kùpūj	kùpūjte	buy! (I)

(There are some verbs with alternate present forms which will not fit this
pattern.)

Note 22.1.2 Verb: Negative Imperative

The negative imperative, that is, /ne/ plus the imperative, occurs with
all imperfective verbs: /ne kupujte/, /ne dolazite/, /ne govorite/. /ne/ rarely
occurs with perfective verbs, but a few are so used: /ne dajte/.

The negative imperative is not as much used as the negative verb /némōjte/
plus infinitive (see Note 22.1.3).

Note 22.1.3 Verb: /némōjte/

Ako ste umorni, onda nemojte nigde ići.

/némōj/, /némōjte/, is a defective verb, occurring only in the imperative, corresponding to English 'don't!'. It is followed by the infinitive, usually the
imperfective. It may also be followed by perfective infinitives, though not of
all verbs.

Note 22.2 Verb: Stress Patterns

Compare:

kázati	kážēm	kázao
vézati	vèžēm	vézao
vŕšiti	vŕšīm	vŕšio
písati	pìšēm	písao

500

These verbs show a consistent variation in stress. The infinitive and
l-participle have /´/, the present has /˺/. A great many verbs with long root
syllables have this pattern. Compare:

pokázati	pókažēm	pokázao
napísati	nápišēm	napísao

Here the stress moves back to the prefix in the present. If these two types
of stress pattern are outlined, it appears that they are the same. Using V for
a short vowel, VV for a long vowel and /˙/ for stress, the patterns are:

```
- vv̇ - v̇ - v              - V̇V - VV -
- á - a - i               - à - ē - m
k  á z a t i              k  à ž ē - m


- V - vv̇ - v̇ - v          - V̇ - V̇V - VV -
- o - á - a - i           - ó - ā - ē -
p o k  á z a t i          p ó k  ā ž  ē m
```

The pattern for /kázati/ is the same as that for /pokázati/ but lacks the
first V. In other words the /ā/ of /pókažēm/ has the same stress as the /ā/ of
/kàžēm/. Compare:

```
- V - - V - vv̇ - v̇ - v          - V - - V̇ - V̇V - VV -
r a z g o v  á r a t i          r a z g ó v ā  r  ā m
r a z g o v  á r a  o
r a z g o v  á r a j ū
```

a-verbs (of this pattern), which add a syllable (/-ju/) in the third
person plural, have the same stress for this form as they do for the infinitive
and l-participle. The same pattern with only one syllable before the stem formative suffix is:

```
- vv̇ - v̇v- v                - V̇V - VV -
m  ó r a t i                m ò  r  ā m
m  ó r a o
m  ó r a j ū
```

Other variations are possible when the present stem has a short vowel:

$$- V - V - V\overset{\bullet}{V} - \overset{\bullet}{V} - V$$
s a č e k **í** v a t i

s a č e k **í** v a o

$$- V - \overset{\bullet}{V} - \overset{\bullet}{V} - VV -$$
s a č é k u j ē m

Or when both are short vowels:

$$- V - \overset{\bullet}{V} - \overset{\bullet}{V} - V$$
g o v ó r i t i

g o v ó r i o

$$- \overset{\bullet}{V} - \overset{\bullet}{V} - VV -$$
g ó v o r ī m

$$- V - - V - V$$
p ú s t i t i

$$- V - - VV -$$
p ù s t ī m

We have, then, the following pattern, with variant forms:

Infinitive, /l/ part., 3 pl. of a-verbs   Present (less 3 pl. of a-verbs)

1a	-VV̇-V̇	-V	káza(ti)	-V̇V-VV	kằžēm
1b	-V-VV̇-V̇	-V	pokáza(ti)	-V̇-V̇V-VV	pókážēm
1c	-V-VV̇-V̇	-V	(sa)čekíva(ti)	-V̇-V̇ -VV	(sa)čekujēm
1d	-V̇ -V̇	-V	pústi(ti)	-V̇ -VV	pùstīm
1e	-V-V̇ -V̇	-V	govóri(ti)	-V̇-V -VV	góvorīm

A line is drawn after the V for stem formative suffix. This position is the most convenient as a point of reference for the stress shifts. The infinitive ending is in parentheses as not covered by the pattern.

When the imperative is added to the pattern, it is seen that the stress of the imperative falls on the same syllable as in the infinitive for i-, e- and a/jē-verbs but the same syllable as in the present for a-verbs and a/jē-verbs. Examples:

govóriti	govórite	góvorīm
pústiti	pústite	pùstīm
izvóleti	izvól(i)te	ízvolīm
kázati	kážite	kằžēm

but

pítati		pìtām	pìtājte
putóvati		pútujēm	pútujte

502

This is the most frequent stress pattern among verbs. Nearly all verbs with stem extensions in /v/ (/-av-/, /-iv-/, /-ov-/, /ev-/) follow this pattern. Many, if not most, verbs having a single long vowel in the syllable preceding the stem formative suffix (as /jáv-/ in /jáviti/ also follow this pattern. Verbs with short vowels are not predictable.

Some verbs which have occurred and have this pattern are:

1a   -VV̇-V̇ / -V̇V-VV

rádíti	ràdīm	rádite	
plátiti	plàtīm	plátite	
pítati	pìtām		pìtajte
jáviti	jàvīm	jávite	
svŕšiti	svȑšīm	svŕšite	
žíveti	žívīm	žívite	
svíđati	svìđām	_____	
kúpiti	kùpīm	kúpite	
vézati	vèžēm	véžite	

1b   -V-VV̇-V̇ / V̇-V̇V-VV

razgovárati	razgóvārām	razgóvārājte
uznemirávati	uznemírāvām	(ne) uznemírāvājte
		(ne) uznemírūjte
poglédati	póglēdām	póglēdajte ga
poznávati	póznājēm	_____
otvárati	ótvārām	ótvārājte
izbegávati	izbégāvām	izbégāvājte
pokváriti	pókvārīm pokvárite	
namerávati	namérāvām	

1c   -V-VV̇-V̇ / V̇-V̇-VV

sačekívati	sačékujēm	(ne) sačékujte se

1d   -V̇-V̇ / -V̇-VV

pústiti	pùstīm	pústite
vóziti	vòzīm	vózite
vóditi	vòdīm	vódite

le   -V-V̇-V̇ / -V̇-V̇-VV

putóvati	pútujēm	pútujte
provóditi	oróvodīm	próvodite
izvóleti	ízvolīm	izvól(i)te
dozvóliti	dózvolīm	dozvólite
stanóvati	stánujēm	stánujte
zadócniti	zádocnīm	zadócnite
otvóriti	ótvorīm	otvórite

The verb forms involved in discussing this pattern have been the infinitive, the present, the l-participle and the imperative. It is convenient to
restrict the discussion to these forms at the present time.

A large number of verbs have the same stress on all these forms. The
stress varies from verb to verb, but each verb keeps its stress throughout the
forms. With some verbs it is possible to see the consistency of a pattern. For
example:

-V̇ -V-	-V̇-V̇ -V	-V-V̇-V̇ -V
vràćati	óbraćati	saóbraćati
čèkati	sáčekati	
pàsti	dópasti	
pràviti	nápraviti	
	ópravljati	
glèdati	pógledati	
	rázgledati	

A whole series of related verbs may have the same pattern, as:

-V̇-V̇-V			
dólaziti		ódlaziti	prélaziti
nálaziti		pólaziti	prólaziti

Some other verbs having fixed stress in these forms are:

-V̇-V-	-V̇-V̇-V-	-VV̇-V̇-V-	-V-V̇-V̇-
brìnuti se	dópadati se	závisiti	razúmeti
čùti	ódsesti		upóznati
jèsti	óstati		zabóraviti
mìsliti	póčinjati		
sèćati se			

snàbdeti

stàjati   véčerati

stȉći

stȉzati

tràjati   -V-V-V-V-V-

trèbati   ìnteresovati

vȉdeti

žàliti se

For comparison some other verbs having different patterns may be given. In addition to variations among the forms previously mentioned, a number of verbs, have, in some speech, a shift of stress in the present before /-mo/ and /-te/, e.g. /idémo/, /idéte/.

Infinitive	1-Participle		Imperative (where useful)	Present /-mo/	
dàti	dào	dála	dȁjte	da dȃm	dȃmo
dóbiti	dòbio	dòbȉla	dóbite	da dòbijēm	
dȏći	dòšao	dòšla	dȏđite	da dȍđēm	
dóněti /donijéti	dòneo /dònio	dònela /dònijela	donésite	da donésēm	
htèti /htjèti	htèo /htȉo	htèla /htjèla	——	hóću	
íći	ìšao /íšao	ìšla /íšla	ídite	ìdēm /ídēm	(idémo)
ímati	ímao	ímala	ímājte	ímām	(imámo)
otíći /ótići	ótišao	ótišla	otídite	da òdēm /ótidēm	
pȉti	pȉo	pȉla	pȉjte	pȉjēm	
provésti	próveo	provéla	provédite	da provédēm	
rásti /ràsti	ràstao	rásla	rástite	rástēm	
úzēti	ùzeo	ùzēla	úzmite	da ùzmēm	
zaúzēti	zàuzeo	zàuzela	zaúzmite	da záuzmēm	
zadŕžati (se)	zàdržao	zàdržāla	zadŕžite	da zadŕžīm	zadŕžīmo
zváti	zvào	zvála	zóvite	zóvēm	

Note 22.3 New Verbs

a	I	saóbraćati	saóbraćā		to communicate
a/Jē	I	tràjati	tràjē		to last

--- . ---

i	I	číniti	čínīm		to do
i	P	učíniti	da účinīm		
C/n	P	ízbeći	da ízbegnēm	ízbegao	to avoid
		/ízbjeći	/da ízbjegnēm	/ízbjegao	
a	I	izbegávati	izbégāvām		
		/izbjegávati	/izbjégāvām		
a	I	ménjati	mènjām		to change
		/mijénjati	/mìjenjām		
i	P	proméniti	da prómēnīm		
		/promijéniti	/da prómijenīm		
i	P	naséliti	da náselīm		to settle
a	I	naseljávati	naséljāvām		
i	P	ópraviti	da ópravīm		to repair
a	I	ópravljati	ópravljām		

otvóriti - otvárati   see Note 19.3

i	I	pùniti	pùnīm		to fill
i	P	nápuniti	da nápunīm		
i	P	pópraviti	da pópravīm		to correct, repair
a	I	pópravljati	pópravljām		
i	P	pózdraviti	da pózdravīm		to greet
a	I	pózdravljati	pózdravljām		
i	P	spójiti	da spòjīm		to link
a	I	spájati	spàjām		
a/Jē	P	vézati	da vèžēm		to tie, connec
a/Jē	I	vezívati	vézujēm		
i	I	vóziti	vòzīm		to drive
C	P	odvésti	da odvézēm	ódvezao, odvézla	

i	I	vršiti	vršīm		to do, perform
i	P	izvršiti	da izvršīm		to execute
C	P	zaobići	da zaobidēm	zaobišao	to by pass
i	I	zaobilaziti	zaobilazīm		

Grammatical Drill

GD 22.1 Learning Drill - Imperative

<u>piti I - popiti P</u>

Pij kafu samo ujutru.	Popij kafu, pa da idemo.
Pijte kafu samo ujutru.	Popijte kafu, pa da idemo.
Nemojte piti kafu uveče.	Nemojte popiti svu kafu.

<u>jesti I - pojesti P</u>

Jedi meso za večeru.	Pojedi meso za večeru.
Jedite meso za večeru.	Pojedite meso za večeru.
Nemojte jesti meso za večeru.	Nemojte pojesti sve meso za večeru.

<u>ići I - otići P</u>

Idi na železničku stanicu po tvoj prtljag.	Otidi na železničku stanicu po tvoj prtljag.
Idite na železničku stanicu po vaš prtljag.	Otidite na železničku stanicu po vaš prtljag.
Nemojte ići danas na železničku stanicu po vaš prtljag.	_____
Nemojte ići na stanicu dok ja ne dođem kući.	Nemojte otići na stanicu dok ja ne dođem kući.

<u>čitati I - pročitati P</u>

Čitaj novine svakog dana.	Pročitaj danas novine.
Čitajte novine svakog dana.	Pročitajte novine danas.
Nemojte čitati novine danas. Nema ništa u njima.	

<u>učiti I - naučiti P</u>

Uči dobro.	Nauči lekciju dobro.
Učite gospodo dobro.	Naučite gospodo, dobro vašu lekciju.
Nemojte učiti ništa za vreme praznika.	_____

doći P - dolaziti I

Dođite sutra u kancelariju ranije.   Dolazite od sada na vreme.

Nemojte dolaziti sutra pre 8.   _____

provesti P - provoditi I

Provedite sutra vikend kod kuće.   Nemojte provoditi sutra vikend van
   Biće rđavo vreme.   grada. Biće rđavo vreme.

dati P - davati I

Daj Jovanu ovaj pasoš.   Ne daji Jovanu ovaj pasoš.

Ne daj Jovanu ovo pismo.   Nemoj davati Jovanu ovo pismo.

Dajte deci kolače, tek kad pojedu   Ne dajite deci kolače dok ne pojedu
   sve drugo.   sve drugo.

Ne dajte deci kolače dok ne pojedu   Nemojte davati deci kolače dok ne
   sve drugo.   pojedu sve drugo.

Ne dajte Jovanu da izlazi napolje.
   Njemu još nije dobro.

čuti P - slušati I

Čuj me dobro, Jovane.   Slušaj dobro, Jovane, šta govorim.

Čujte šta vam govorim.   Slušajte šta vam govorim.

   _____   Nemojte ga slušati.

kazati P - kazivati I

Kažite Jovanu da mi se javi telefonom.   Ne kazujte ništa Jovanu.

Nemojte kazati ništa Jovanu.   Nemojte kazivati ništa Jovanu.

reći P - govoriti I

Recite Jovanu da mi se javi   Ne govorite ništa Jovanu.
   telefonom.

Nemojte reći ništa Jovanu.   Nemojte govoriti ništa Jovanu.

GD 22.2 Negative Transform Drill with Model

    The perfective - imperfective verb pair involved is given to the right
of each sentence. The student should cover this side during drill, using it
only as necessary.

<u>Donesite</u> danas moj prtljag sa železničke stanice.

    <u>Nemojte donositi</u> danas moj prtljag sa železničke stanice.

Platite, molim vas, moje pivo.	/platiti/ - /plaćati/
Upoznajte se sa Jovićima. Oni su dobro društvo za vas.	/upoznati se / - /upoznavati se/
Javite se Jovanu pre nego što napustite Beograd.	/javiti se/ - /javljati se/
Svršite prvo taj posao.	/svršiti/ - /svršavati/
Promenite odmah novac.	/promeniti/ - /menjati/
Pozajmite Jovanu 10.000 dinara.	/pozajmiti/ - /pozajmljivati/
Vratite se iz varoši pre osam.	/vratiti se/ - /vraćati se/
Vratite Jovanu novac danas.	
Sačekajte me na železničkoj stanici.	/sačekati/ - /čekati/
Kažite Jovanu da je Toma došao iz Zagreba.	/kazati/ - /kazivati/
Prođite kroz moju sobu u kupatilo.	/proći/ - /prolaziti/
Pređite jugoslovensku granicu Korenskim prelazom. On je jedini otvoren.	/preći/ - /prelaziti/
Izvršite pregled prtljaga ove gospode.	/izvršiti/ - /vršiti/
Ostanite u hotelu pet dana.	/ostati/ - /ostajati/
Unesite ove kufere u moju sobu.	/uneti/ - /unositi/
Uzmite taksi, napolju pada kiša.	/uzeti/ - /uzimati/
Otvorite prozor, molim vas.	/otvoriti/ - /otvarati/
Jovane, molim vas, zatvorite vrata.	/zatvoriti/ - /zatvarati/
Deco, ustanite sutra rano ići ćemo na izlet.	/ustati/ - /ustajati/
Kupite danas koverte i hartiju u knjižari.	/kupiti/ - /kupovati/
Provedite odmor u gorskom kotaru. To je najlepši deo zemlje.	/provesti/ - /provoditi/
Odmorite se za vreme vikenda.	/odmariti se/ - /odmarati se/
Pustite decu unutra. Napolju je hladno.	/pustiti/ - /puštati/
Napunite rezervoar benzinom. Nema benzinskih pumpi usput.	/napuniti/ - /puniti/

    The above drill may be repeated using the second person singular (familiar form of the verb and relevant pronouns, e.g.

Platite, molim vas, moje pivo.   Plati, molim te, moje pivo.

GD 22.3   Question and Answer Drill with Prompt

GD 22.3.1 On Imperative

   Each question is to be answered with a sentence using the imperative,
on the basis of the data given in the prompt. Possible answers are given to
the right.

   This drill may be repeated with negative responses. Alternately, every
other answer may be negative.

Želim da popijem čašu mleka.	Šta želite da pijete?	Dajte mi čašu mleka.
Treba mi veliki kufer.	Koji kufer vam treba?	Donesite mi veliki kufer.
Vaši kuferi su doneti sa stanice.	Šta želite da uradimo sa vašim kuferima.	Unesite kufere u moju sobu. Nemojte unositi kufere u moju sobu.
Žao mi je što Toma nije kod kuće.	Šta da kažem Tomi kad dođe kući? Imate neku poruku za njega?	Kažite Tomi da sam ga tražio. Nemojte mu ništa govoriti. Recite mu da dođe kod mene.
Mi treba da pređemo austrij- sko-jugoslovensku granicu.	Gde da pređemo granicu?	Pređite granicu Korenskim prelazom.
Vrata od kuće su otvorena.	Da li treba da zatvorim vrata?	Molim vas, zatvorite vrata.
Treba da otvorimo kufere za carinski pregled.	Da li treba da otvorimo kufere za carinski pregled?	Molim vas, otvorite kufere za pregled. Nemojte još otvarati kufere za pregled.
Ova gospoda čekaju za pregled stvari.	Da li da izvršim pregled stvari ove gospode?	Izvršite odmah pregled stvari ove gospode. Nemojte vršiti pregled njihovih stvari. Oni imaju diplomatski pasoš.

Kola su pokvarena i treba
   da se oprave.

Da li treba da opravim
   kola odmah?

Opravite kola odmah.
   Nemojte opravljati
   kola odmah. Ne morate
   opravljati kola odmah.

Nemamo dovoljno benzina za
   put.

Da li da napunim
   rezervoar benzinom
   u gradu?

Napunite rezervoar
   benzinom u gradu.
   Nemojte puniti rezer-
   voar benzinom u gradu.
   Možete to uraditi na
   autoputu.

Nisam još svršio samo
   jedan posao.

Da li ovaj posao treba
   da svršim danas?

Svršite taj posao danas.
   Hitan je. Nemojte
   svršavati taj posao
   danas. Nije ništa
   hitno.

GD 22.3.2 Questions on the Basic Sentences

Mi smo prešli granicu Korenskim
   prelazom.

Kojim prelazom ste prešli granicu?

Mnogo sveta prelazi granicu tim
   prelazom.

Da li mnogo sveta prelazi granicu tim
   prelazom.

Taj prelaz je dobro vezan sa autoputem.

Da li je taj prelaz dobro vezan sa
   autoputem?

To nije jedini prelaz, koji je
   vezan sa autoputem.

Da li je to jedini prelaz, koji je
   vezan sa autoputem?

Pregled pasoša se vrši na granici.

Gde se vrši pregled pasoša.

Carinski pregled se vrši kad se
   pređe granica.

A gde se vrši carinski pregled?

Pregled naših stvari izvršio je
   jedan vrlo ljubazan carinski
   činovnik.

Ko je izvršio pregled vaših stvari?

On je svršio pregled vrlo brzo.

Koliko je trajao pregled? /Koliko
   traje pregled?

Od granice do Beograda ima oko
   630 km.

Koliko kilometara ima od granice do
   Beograda?

Vožnja je trajala nešto više od
   osam sati sa odmorima.

Koliko je trajala vožnja do Beograda?

Nismo imali nikakvih teškoća usput.

Da li ste imali nekih teškoća usput?

Sa granice smo pošli u 8 sati.

U koliko sati ste pošli sa granice?

U Beograd smo stigli u 4:20 (četiri i dvadeset).

U koliko sati ste stigli u Beograd?

Autoput prolazi do Kranja kroz alpske predele.

Kroz kakve predele prolazi autoput?

Od Kranja autoput ulazi u Ljubljansku kotlinu.

Kakvi su predeli od Kranja?

Autoput prolazi kroz Ljubljanu.

Da li autoput prolazi kroz Ljubljanu?

Mi smo se zadržali u Ljubljani pola sata.

Da li ste se zadržavali u Ljubljani?

/Mi se nismo zadržavali u Ljubljani.

Položaj Ljubljane je i lep i važan.

Kakav je položaj Ljubljane?

Ljubljanska vrata čine Ljubljanu važnom.

Šta čini Ljubljanu važnom?

Dopao nam se Ljubljanski grad.

Šta vam se dopalo u Ljubljani?

Sve do Zagreba put je bio vrlo zanimljiv.

Da li je put bio zanimljiv?

Autoput prolazi kroz Zagreb.

Da li autoput prolazi kroz Zagreb?

Mi smo svratili u Zagreb.

Da li ste svraćali u Zagreb.

/Mi nismo svraćali u Zagreb.

Ručali smo i odmorili se u Slavonskom Brodu. (Tu ima jedan motel i servisna stanica[1] na autoputu.)

Gde ste ručali?

Tu smo kupili i benzin. Nismo kupovali benzin usput.

Gde ste kupili benzin? Da li ste kupovali benzin usput?

Autoput izbegava naseljena mesta.

Da li autoput izbegava naseljena mesta?

Autoputem saobraćaju samo motorna vozila.

Da li autoputem saobraćaju samo motorna vozila?

Videli smo jedan nesrećan slučaj.

Da li ima nesrećnih slučajeva na autoputu?

/Nismo videli nijedan nesrećan slučaj.

---

[1] service plaza

To je bio sudar dvaju kola.

Nama nije bila potrebna nikakva
   pomoć.
   /Nama je bila potrebna pomoć.

Imali smo kvar na kolima.

Jedan radnik nam je opravio kola.
   /Ja sam sam opravio kola.

Kakav je to bio nesrećan slučaj?

Da li vam je bila potrebna neka pomoć
   na autoputu?

Kakva pomoć vam je bila potrebna?
   Šta vam je trebalo?

Ko vam je opravio kola?

GD 22.4 Conversations - Razgovori

GD 22.4.1   A

Da li ste skoro prelazili jugoslo-
   vensko-austrijsku granicu?

Ja moram putovati skoro u Beograd,
   pa me zanima gdje je najzgodnije
   preći granicu.

Koliko prijelaza ima?

Zašto vi prelazite granicu Gorenskim
   prijelazom?

Koliko ima kilometara od granice do
   Beograda?

Za koje vrijeme se prelazi taj put?

Kako je autoput uređen? Može li se
   kupiti benzin na autoputu?

A mogu li se kola opraviti ako se desi
   neki kvar?

To je dobro. Da li ste imali usput
   nekih nezgoda?

Da li put prolazi kroz naseljena
   mjesta?

Gdje ste se odmarali?

                          B

Jesam. Zašto pitate?

Ja prelazim granicu uvijek Gorenskim
   prijelazom.

Ima najmanje četiri-pet.

Zato što je taj prijelaz dobro spojen[1]
   autoputem sa Beogradom.

Nešto više od 630 km.

Put traje oko deset sati sa odmorima.

Autoput je dobro uređen. Ima benzinskih
   pumpi gdje se prodaje benzin.

Mogu.

Nisam, uvijek sam putovao bez ikakvih
   nezgoda.

Ne, put zaobilazi naseljena mjesta
   koliko je moguće.

Odmarao sam se na samom putu.

---

[1] /spojen/ 'connected'

To je dobro. Ja sam mislio da ste
    se odmarali u nekom gradu.

Onda ću i ja ići u Beograd tim putem.

Ne, ja rijetko kad svraćam negdje
    kad putujem. Osim kad moram.

To je najbolje što možete učiniti.

Да ли сте скоро прелазили југословенско-
    аустријску границу?

Ја треба да путујем скоро у Београд,
    па ме интересује где је најзгодније
    прећи границу.

Колико прелаза има?

Зашто ви прелазите границу Коренским
    прелазом?

Колико има километара од границе до
    Београда?

За које време се прелази тај пут?

Како је аутопут уређен? Може ли да
    се купи бензин на аутопуту?

А могу ли кола да се оправе, ако се
    деси неки квар?

То је добро. Да ли сте имали неких
    незгода успут?

Да ли пут пролази кроз насељена места?

Где сте се одмарали?

То је добро. Ја сам мислио да сте
    се одмарали у неком граду.

Онда ћу и ја ићи у Београд тим путем.

Јесам. Зашто питате?

Ја прелазим границу увек Коренским
    прелазом.

Има најмање четири-пет.

Зато што је тај прелаз добро везан
    аутопутем са Београдом.

Нешто више од 630 км.

Пут траје око десет сати са одморима.

Аутопут је добро уређен. Има бензински
    пумпи где се продаје бензин.

Могу.

Нисам, увек сам путовао без икаквих
    сметњи или незгода.

Не, пут избегава насељена места колико
    је могуће.

Одмарао сам се на самом путу.

Не, ја ретко кад свраћам негде кад
    путујем. Сем кад морам.

То је најбоље што можете да урадите.

GD 22.4.2

Kad ćemo stići u Beograd?

Koliko kilometara ima još do
    Beograda.

To je otprilike dva sata vožnje.

Do sada nismo imali nikakvih poteškoća
    ili zastoja usput.

Da, ja sam se htjeo svratiti u
    Ljubljanu.

Mislim da nam treba još oko dva sata.

Ima još 150 km.

Možda nam neće trebati ni toliko.

Nismo, ali smo se često odmarali.

Pa nismo se tako dugo zadržali u
    Ljubljani.

Zadržali smo se prilično dugo.

Da, tvrđava je jako interesantna.
Izgleda vrlo slikovito.

Hoćete valjda da kažete, da je zatvarala
Ljubljansku kotlinu.

Jest, izgleda. To je točno. Ali,
ona je sad samo lijep park i
ništa više.

To je razumljivo.

Vama se dopala Ljubljanska tvrđava?

Ona zatvara Ljubljansku kotlinu.

Pa zar vam ona ne izgleda i sada tako?

Naravno, ona to i jest. Ali, mi
Jugoslaveni je volimo ne samo za
ono što jest, već i za ono što je
bila.

Pa da.

Кад ћемо стићи у Београд?

Колико километара има још до
Београда?

То је отприлике два сата вожње.

До сада нисмо имали никаквих тешкоћа
или застоја успут.

Да, ја сам хтео да свратимо у
Љубљану.

Задржали смо се прилично дуго.

Да, град је врло интересантан.
Изгледа врло живописно.

Хоћете ваљда да кажете, да је затварао
Љубљанску котлину.

Дабоме да изгледа. То је тачно. Али,
он је сад само леп парк и ништа више.

То је разумљиво.

Мислим да нам треба још око два сата.

Има још 150 км.

Можда нам неће требати ни толико.

Нисмо, али смо се често одмарали.

Па нисмо се тако дуго задржали у
Љубљани.

Вама се допао Љубљански град?

Он затвара Љубљанску котлину.

Па зар вам он не изгледа и сада тако?

Наравно, он то и јесте. Али, ми
Југословени га волимо не само за оно
што јесте, већ и за оно што је био.

Дабоме.

GD 22.5 Homework - Domaći zadatak

GD 22.5.1 Change the following imperative sentences from affirmative to
negative.

Pođite na put pre osam sati.

Odvedite decu posle podne u bioskop.

Donesite danas moje stvari sa železničke stanice.

Kupite mi jugoslovenske novine u varoši.

Opravite danas moja kola.

Zatvorite prozor i vrata, molim vas.

Napunite rezervoar benzinom u gradu.

Izvršite odmah pregled pasoša ovoj gospodi.

Pustite ovu gospodu da pređu granicu. Njihovi pasoši su u redu.

Napišite pismo Jovanu.

GD 22.5.2 Change all the following questions using present imperfective forms
of the verbs. Replace clauses with /treba/ plus perfective with the simple
(imperfective) verb.

Gde su vam izvršili pregled pasoša?

Kad treba da odete iz Beograda?

Da li ćemo autoputem izbeći naseljena mesta?

Hoćete li preći granicu Korenskim prelazom?

U koliko sati će se otvoriti prelaz preko granice?

Kad treba da zatvorite radnju?

Gde ste kupili benzin?

Ko vam je opravio kola?

Kad ste stigli u Beograd?

Autoput će se opraviti, zar ne?

Printed in Poland
by Amazon Fulfillment
Poland Sp. z o.o., Wrocław

26413454R00295